A Concise History
of Wales

GERAINT H. JENKINS

CAMBRIDGE
UNIVERSITY PRESS

CAMBRIDGE UNIVERSITY PRESS
Cambridge, New York, Melbourne, Madrid, Cape Town, Singapore, São Paulo, Delhi

Cambridge University Press
The Edinburgh Building, Cambridge CB2 8RU, UK

Published in the United States of America by Cambridge University Press, New York

www.cambridge.org
Information on this title: www.cambridge.org/9780521530712

First published 2007
Reprinted 2008

Printed in the United Kingdom at the University Press, Cambridge

A catalogue record for this publication is available from the British Library

ISBN 978-0-521-82367-8 hardback
ISBN 978-0-521-53071-2 paperback

For my wife
Ann Ffrancon

CONTENTS

ILLUSTRATIONS

PREFACE

Formidable though the task promised to be, for a variety of reasons I was very pleased to accept this commission. I had always believed, and still do, that no self-respecting historian should forego the opportunity of writing the entire history of his or her native land. I also relished the intellectual challenge of preparing a concise and digestible account that would not fall into the trap of squeezing the life out of the past. Moreover, the prospect of completing a work which would meet the needs of an international audience as well as the people of Wales was too tempting to resist. Wales and its history deserves to be much more widely known and appreciated.

I have tried to give due weight to events, movements and ideas in each period, and if the chapters on the modern period are somewhat longer than the others this simply reflects the fact that the material available since the coming of the printed word is much more voluminous and diverse. A book of this kind inevitably owes an irredeemable debt to a great many scholars, both past and present, whose work has stimulated me profoundly. The further reading list at the end of the volume indicates my principal debts, though I have also ventured (gingerly in some periods) into the thickets of original sources, as well as into a mass of articles and Welsh-language publications. I do hope that the reader will sense that the critical synthesis presented here is flavoured with my own ideas, interpretations and the very occasional and pardonable bout of partiality. Most of all, I hope that the book conveys the richness and vitality of the history of Wales.

It's a particular pleasure to thank several colleagues for their assistance. Miranda and Stephen Aldhouse-Green, Robert Johnston, John T. Koch, Huw Pryce, Paul O'Leary, Russell Davies, Neil Evans, Steven Thompson and Chris Williams read drafts of chapters, commented critically upon them and saved me from many errors and infelicities. I gratefully acknowledge their kindness. My greatest debt, however, is to the late Glanmor Williams, whose generosity in improving the work of colleagues and friends was proverbial. He read the best part of the typescript and kept my spirits buoyant by offering constant advice and encouragement. I like to think that he would have enjoyed reading the whole printed version. Needless to say, I alone am responsible for the errors and inadequacies which remain.

My personal assistant, Nia Davies, cheerfully transformed my long-hand scrawl into an immaculate typescript and helped me in all manner of ways to ensure that the work reached the publishers in a fit and proper condition. I thank her most warmly. The staff of the National Library of Wales proved to be unfailingly helpful and courteous. I'm also grateful to John Jenkins, Paul Joyner, Penny Icke and Patricia Moore for their assistance in selecting appropriate illustrations, and to Antony Smith for preparing most of the maps. William Howells kindly prepared the index. Isabelle Dambricourt of Cambridge University Press was a model of patience and efficiency. As always, I owe an enormous debt to my family. My wife Ann knows better than anyone how much this book means to me and how it has robbed us of precious leisure hours and vacations. Since she has lived with this undertaking since its inception, the very least I can do by way of inadequate recompense is to dedicate it to her with my love and admiration.

Geraint H. Jenkins
April 2006

I

The earliest inhabitants

In a dimly lit room in a secluded but sturdy farmhouse in early eighteenth-century Cardiganshire, a gifted young Anglican ordinand, aptly named Theophilus Evans, composed in his native language an epic history of Wales which remained a bestseller until the twilight of the Victorian era. Entitled *Drych y Prif Oesoedd* (A Mirror of the First Ages) (1716), this racy historical narrative of the allegedly glorious origins of the Welsh was Evans's spirited riposte to English satirists who had painted unflattering portraits of Wales as 'a country in the world's backside' and as 'the very rubbish of Noah's flood'. A superb storyteller, he packed his pages with more heroes and gripping incidents than any novel of blood and thunder might have done, and by conjuring up images of luminaries like Gomer, Brutus, Beli, Brân and Arthur (Boudica, styled 'Buddug' by Evans, was the only heroine to elbow her way into this pageant) he caught the imagination of the Welsh reading public and deeply shaped their view of the distant past. This was history, or perhaps mythical writing, on a grand scale, and the vivid tales and heroic victories and defeats in this unashamedly Cambrocentric work were so well tailored to the needs of a people desperately searching for their own national identity that it became a popular classic, especially when editions in the Victorian era began including vivid engraved illustrations. Even the Welsh who emigrated in large numbers to Pennsylvania in the nineteenth century insisted on publishing an English translation at Ebensburg in 1834, so that their American-born offspring could familiarize themselves with key events in the history of the land of their fathers. In an extravagant eulogy to the Welsh edition of 1898, the historian O. M. Edwards claimed that no Welsh history book had ever matched Evans's pantheon of heroes.

An eminent modern Welsh archaeologist, who probably never bothered to read the original version, once described Evans's theatrical pageant as 'a fairly dotty book'. Credulous, uncritical and even dotty it might appear to the modern reader, but it was a formative influence in the development of ideas about the Welsh past. Like most of his contemporaries, the world-view of this unlikely people's remembrancer was dominated by the literal meaning of the most sacred scriptural text. At his side as he wrote, a copy of the Welsh bible – the most authoritative source for every Christian historian – would have provided him not only with irrefutable proof of the manner in which God had created the earth but also an avowedly accurate chronology of the past. Taking his cue from the calculations made by James Ussher, Archbishop of Armagh in the early seventeenth century, he believed that the Creation had occurred in 4004 BC. Had he read John Lightfoot, the Cambridge scholar, he would also have noted the precise time of 18 October 4004 BC, swiftly followed by Adam's creation (at 9 a.m.) five days later. Startling as it may seem to us, Evans took for granted that, following the Creation, humankind derived from Adam and that, after the Flood, the world had been repeopled by Noah's three sons – Shem, Ham and Japhet – and by their descendants, most notably Gomer, founder of the tribe known as the Cimbri, the first colonizers of the land mass which became known as Wales. The most significant part of Evans's tale, therefore, was his proud affirmation that the Welsh had enjoyed a privileged position in the events which unfolded between the Creation and the Flood. In a second edition, he declared: 'here is the blood and race of the old Welsh, as exalted as any earthly lineage could be'. In the context of the time, this was a dramatically reassuring statement.

During the Welsh cultural renaissance of the eighteenth century, interest swiftly developed in the study of ancient Britain and the role of the Celtic peripheries, not least because of the attempts made in Edward Lhuyd's magisterial *Archaeologia Britannica* (The Archaeology of Britain) (1707) to celebrate the honourable ancestry of the Welsh by providing them with seemingly irrefutable proof of the common origin of the Celtic languages. The notion of insular Celts therefore was called into being by this remarkably erudite and far-seeing Welsh polymath. Scholarly and unscholarly thinking about the alleged 'Celticity' of Britain and Ireland thus begins with Lhuyd, and his position as keeper of the Ashmolean Museum at Oxford from 1691 to 1709 lent authority to his writings. As the Welsh themselves began to discover, invent and re-invent literary, historical and musical treasures, they derived comfort from the knowledge that their identity was based on a history considerably older than that of England. Members of the London-based Honourable Society of Cymmrodorion, founded in 1751, claimed to be the descendants of the aboriginal Britons and a flurry of topographical guides and paintings highlighted strikingly attractive prehistoric remains. A wave of Romantic learning, which created the most bizarre and extravagant fantasies about noble ancestors known as Celts, also played a significant role in reviving interest in the history of one of the oldest living literary languages in Europe.

At the end of the eighteenth century Theophilus Evans's patriotic torch was taken up by Edward Williams, who was better known by his bardic pseudonym Iolo Morganwg (Edward of Glamorgan). There has been no greater cultural icon in Wales than this astonishingly erudite and inventive stonemason. Like the Anglican Theophilus Evans, this Unitarian wordsmith from Flemingston in the Vale of Glamorgan believed that the biblical narrative was divinely inspired and that it provided the only convincing explanation of the origins of the universe and the diversity of human and animal life. In a ringing declaration of faith in God's handiwork, he wrote: 'the Almighty audibly proclaimed his existence and instantaneously with that utterance all the creation with a shout of inexpressible joy leapt into existence'. But Iolo Morganwg went much further than Evans. Fuelled by copious supplies of laudanum and a heady mixture of fact, fiction and extravagant fantasies, he became the most successful literary and historical forger in Europe. In the feverish hunt for the Welsh past, Iolo was the leader of the pack and, even to this day, he remains a deeply mysterious and controversial figure. He was fascinated by barrows, earthworks, hillforts and especially stone circles, and his writings were suffused with bardic and druidic lore. His most durable legacy was the Gorsedd of the Bards of the

Iolo Morgannwg
1798

1. The Romantic historian and poet Edward Williams (1747–1826), universally known by his bardic name Iolo Morganwg, exerted an enormous influence on how people interpreted the prehistoric past. This painting, by William Owen Pughe, was made in 1798. (The National Library of Wales)

Island of Britain, a remarkable druidic moot which first met on Primrose Hill, London, in June 1792 and which was subsequently incorporated into the official activities of the National Eisteddfod of Wales. By attracting like-minded Druids, poets, scholars and democrats to this intellectual forcing-house, Iolo hoped not only to popularize the old druidic lore but also to advance the radical cause of Jacobinism and provide a new vision of Welsh nationality. A nation exists and flourishes only in its collective memory, and this first national institution was designed to stiffen the self-confidence and pride of one of the forgotten peoples of Europe. Iolo Morganwg's writings exercised a profound influence on cultural life in nineteenth-century Wales and successfully clouded the judgement of scholars up to the First World War.

The net result was that the story of the Creation, of Noah and the Flood, the dispersal of the nations, the descent of the Cimbri from Japhet, son of Noah, and the role of the Druids as custodians of knowledge and mythic lore became part of the warp and woof of the cultural experience of Welsh people. The increasingly Nonconformist population was thoroughly indoctrinated in the biblical account of the origins of humankind. When, at a Sunday school examination in 1821, Margaret Jones of Ganllwyd, Merioneth, recited aloud with complete accuracy thirty-two chapters of the Old Testament, she articulated the common stock of beliefs which chapel-goers held dear. Even as late as 1890 the young Welsh scholar John Morris-Jones stirred up a hornet's nest when he spoke out against the innocent blind faith of the Welsh in the historicity of Gomer, son of Japhet, son of Noah. Ideas about archaeology, prehistory and history were still rudimentary, and the literal interpretation of Genesis continued to hold sway. The word 'prehistoric' did not enter the vocabulary until 1851, and the lack of an accurate and reliable time frame meant that the long sweep of geological and historical time simply could not be imagined. It is significant that the folk names bestowed on Welsh megalithic tombs – Carreg Samson, Bedd yr Afanc, Barclodiad y Gawres – reflected the scriptural and classical narratives with which the public were so thoroughly familiar.

Although nothing can alter the fact that the dependence on scriptural testimony and mythical lore was inimical to intellectual development, inquiring minds were beginning to turn to new forms of investigation. In the 1830s the geologists Adam Sedgwick and R. I. Murchison began to explore the Lower Palaeozoic rocks of Wales and to develop classification systems such as 'Cambrian',

'Silurian' and 'Ordovician', names which, redolent of the old Celtic tribes, eventually gained international recognition. Few people realize that the co-founder of the theory of the evolution of the species by natural selection was a Welshman. During his travels in Papua New Guinea, Usk-born Alfred Russel Wallace, one of the most progressive scientists in mid-Victorian Wales, had formulated by 1858 (independently of Charles Darwin) the interpretation of life as a catalogue of successful errors within the framework of gradual evolutionary change, and had he been an ambitious self-publicist he might well have eclipsed the great Darwin. Such progressive views, however, were generally mistrusted and often vilified. One prominent Welsh Baptist declared that Darwin and his acolytes were themselves 'more akin to monkeys than their purported progenitor', while John Jones, a monoglot Welsh-speaking Calvinistic Methodist preacher from Tal-y-sarn, reckoned that a concerted attempt was afoot to 'turn the Almighty out of the world which he had created with his own fingers'. But the scriptural framework of prehistory was clearly living on borrowed time, for there were signs that the Welsh were opening their minds to some of the fundamental principles of scientific and archaeological investigation. The expanding web of scientific and philosophical societies, supported by industrialists and professional men, was a striking feature of early Victorian urban communities. The Royal Institution of South Wales, set up in Swansea in 1835, sponsored serious scientific research and saw itself as a university in the making. Growing numbers of amateur historians and gentlemen-scholars were exploring fields, hedgerows and tracks, energetically wielding the spade and coyly recording their discoveries in *Archaeologia Cambrensis*, the house journal of the Cambrian Archaeological Association founded in 1846. Some of their bizarre speculations about artefacts and monuments may still cause us some amusement, but wild guesswork was infinitely preferable to short-sighted dogmatism. When the University of Wales (1893) and the National Museum of Wales (1907) were established, to be swiftly followed by the Royal Commission on the Ancient and Historical Monuments and Constructions in Wales and Monmouthshire (1908), a process began which ultimately transformed the study of archaeology from being a genteel, haphazard antiquarian pursuit into a rigorous academic discipline in which

professional standards of excavation, observation and field recording were set. Recent advances in scientific techniques such as radio-
carbon dating, dendrochronology (the science of tree-ring dating),
the analysis of pollen in soils, peats and lake deposits, as well as aerial
photography of the highest standards, have been of critical importance. Thanks to computer-based modelling, we can now even gaze in
wonder at the likely features of our prehistoric forebears. The fruitful
interplay between archaeologists, geographers, geologists, curators,
artists and even forensic scientists means that the prehistory of Wales
has now become a lively field of inquiry. Yet, to enter prehistoric
Wales is to find oneself in a foreign country. Its chronology is imprecise, textual evidence is almost wholly missing, and archaeological
testimony is patchy and fraught with ambiguities. In a strange way,
too, the closer we examine it, the more mysterious it becomes.

Our story, which is one of migration, settlement, conflict, change
and continuity, begins in the Palaeolithic or Old Stone Age. For
many thousands of years before the Wales we recognize today was
fully formed, the land was covered by ice hundreds of metres thick.
This impenetrable blanket of ice helped to shape the evolution of
the Welsh environment. At that stage, Britain and mainland Europe
were often part of a continuous land mass, and only when less
extreme conditions prevailed did it become possible for hunters to
visit. The best surviving early relics in Wales have been discovered in
the protected conditions of limestone caves. Exciting later twentieth-
century excavation work at Pontnewydd cave in the Elwy valley,
Denbighshire, has revealed that Ice Age hunters were present an
unimaginably long 225,000 years ago. Pontnewydd is thus the
oldest known humanly occupied site in Wales. It also represents
the most north-westerly settlement of its period in Eurasia. Striking
discoveries have been made within the cave of early Neanderthal
remains, extensive fauna, animal bones and artefacts of volcanic
rock rather than flint. Neanderthals were heavily built, probably
pale-skinned people with prominent brows, projecting mid-faces
and huge jaws. They sometimes used well-sheltered caves, living
cheek by jowl with rhinoceros, bears, wolves, red deer and horses,
and they armed themselves with spears and hand axes. Somehow,
against all the odds, these resourceful hunters and scavengers

managed to survive in a forbiddingly cold and sunless environment. Pontnewydd seems to have offered a temporary residence to small groups of Neanderthals, mostly young males, during two separate periods of occupation, around 225,000 and 175,000 years ago. One of the most interesting survivals is the remains of nineteen teeth of five Neanderthals, all of which reveal the characteristic of taurodontism – an enlarged pulp cavity to the teeth and short roots. There is a possibility that hominid remains were deliberately deposited in Pontnewydd cave, and if that proves to be the case Wales will be able to boast of having one of the earliest international examples of the deliberate disposal of human bodies.

Around 30,000 years ago, *homo sapiens neanderthalensis* became extinct and was replaced by our own species, *homo sapiens sapiens*. In January 1823 the Revd William Buckland, Professor in Geology at the University of Oxford, discovered the first Pleistocene human

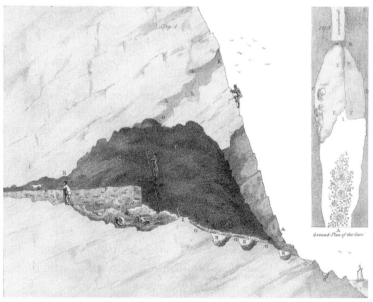

2. Goat's Hole cave, Paviland, on the south Gower coast where the 'Red Lady' was discovered. This illustration appeared in *Reliquiae Diluvianae* (1823) by William Buckland (1784–1856), in which he maintained that the entire globe had been inundated by a great flood. This drawing represents his plan and section of the Paviland cave. (The National Library of Wales)

remains in Wales, at Goat's Hole (Paviland cave), on the Gower peninsula in Glamorgan. An avowed champion of the Deluge hypothesis, Buckland believed that the headless human skeleton he had uncovered had lived and died in Roman times, and might have been an exciseman. He published his findings in *Reliquiae Diluvianae* (Evidence of the Flood) (1823), a work which prompted countless visitors and collectors to examine and pilfer objects at the cave. Since the corpse had been deeply stained with red ochre and decorated with ivory bracelets, word got around that this was a female and, as a result, the 'Red Lady' of Paviland entered the annals of Welsh archaeological folklore. Modern archaeologists, however, have proved beyond doubt that this was a healthy adult male, aged 25–30 and 1.74 m tall, who was interred 26,000 years ago in what may well have been a sacred site for pilgrims. Moreover, the DNA sequence of the mistakenly entitled 'Red Lady' corresponds to the most common extant lineage in Europe. Until – if ever – an earlier burial site is discovered, the extraordinarily elaborate interment of the Paviland male will rank foremost in the story of the coming of fully modern humans to prehistoric Wales. The site's most recent investigator has eloquently shown that the human story of Paviland cave is told 'through its litter of humanly made furniture: stone artefacts of distinctive styles, ornaments of ivory, and even the body of a young man who was accorded a ceremonial burial with rites that lay at, or close to, the head of a European tradition of 5000 years' duration'.

Although aeons of geological time provided the rock formations of Wales, the landforms with which we are familiar have their origins 'at the dripping, thawing, snout of a glacier'. Until large-scale deglaciation – what we would call global warming – occurred, people were in no position to impose their will on the landscape and to establish permanent or semi-permanent settlements. But when the Ice Age ended (around 12,000 BC), sea levels began to rise, the temperature increased, trees (birch, pine and oak) began to etch their silhouette on the skyline, and growing numbers of mobile hunters, armed with multi-purpose stone tools such as pins, needles, harpoons and fish hooks, exploited woodland, constructed rough-and-ready dwellings and lived on deer, oxen, fish and wild plants. Sea levels rose appreciably during the Mesolithic (Middle Stone Age) period, and substantial hectares of land were submerged. Legends of sunken lands associated with Cantre'r Gwaelod and Traeth Lafan remind us that the coastal outline of Wales was rather different from that of our times. The remarkable discovery of the footprints of two adults and a child walking towards the sea on the inter-tidal flats of Uskmouth, near Newport, dating from the seventh millennium BC, bears witness to the effect of climatic changes on the shores of the rising post-glacial sea. By 6000 BC the final land bridge connecting Wales to the continent had been submerged and the contours of the present British Isles had become familiar. By that stage, too, the so-called post-glacial 'climatic optimum' had brought so much warmth that deciduous forests were spreading quickly. Hunter–gatherers, who lived by their wits and were extraordinarily mobile, assembled largely on the coastal plains, their axes glinting in the warm sun as they chopped down trees. At Goldcliff in Monmouthshire, the latest dated site containing a Mesolithic assemblage, they deliberately burnt vegetation in order to accommodate grazing animals, while at the Nab Head, near Marloes in Pembrokeshire, a thriving fishing settlement existed. These early settlers were canny and robust people, ready to do battle with nature and well able to recognize potentially fertile land close to the western seaways. We should not underestimate their skills and perseverance. Indeed, it is hard not to marvel at the bravery and ingenuity of people who, travelling in slender wooden boats through storms, cross-currents and whirlpools, brought with them new and sophisticated ideas and techniques which helped to develop the processes of husbandry and industry. The Welsh historical geographer E. G. Bowen was among the first to highlight the importance of the movement of people during 'the first Golden Age of the western seaways' and the significance of the Atlantic as a binding force. More recently, the archaeologist Barry Cunliffe, keenly aware of the kinship of peoples who lived on, or sailed along, the Atlantic coasts, has argued that the peoples of the long Atlantic facade of Europe developed a set of common beliefs and values over thousands of years, as well as an 'oceanic mentality' which included 'challenge, awe, a heightened awareness of time, and a deep restlessness'.

The western trade routes certainly facilitated brisk trafficking as migrants, sailors and traders linked the European continent with west Britain and Ireland. This meant that Mesolithic peoples were able to draw on, and assimilate, the Neolithic material culture over an extensive period through long-distance exchange networks. The Neolithic period (*c.* 4000–2500 BC) was characterized by a pastoral and agrarian economy based on cattle, sheep, pigs and goats, and some cereal crops. Highly proficient in the use of polished axes, adzes and chisels of polished flint and stone, the Neolithic people set up flourishing axe-making quarries at Y Graig Lwyd, on the seaward slopes of Penmaen-mawr, and on Mynydd Rhiw, in the Llŷn peninsula – both accessible coastal locations. The shift from the world of the hunter–gatherer to that of pastoralism was a critically important stage in the development of human history and, by rearing livestock, cultivating crops and chopping down or slashing and burning forests, highly mobile Neolithic people, living in small social units, made extensive use of open spaces, especially at sites where flint and stone were easily accessible. These pastoralists were by all accounts about 1.6 m tall on average, and were muscular and fleet of foot. Although the availability of foods, as well as tastes, varied from place to place, even at this stage farmers had acquired an intimate knowledge of the land and its resources, and with the passage of time they developed a momentum which brought about change and improvement.

Sir Mortimer Wheeler, the vigorous and far-seeing Director of the National Museum of Wales (1924–6), always used to insist that the remains of people dug up are much more interesting than the artefacts they left behind, and the corpus of skeletal remains in Wales is much more substantial in this period because bones were better preserved in purpose-built tombs. Recent advances in scientific techniques, especially CT scans, have enabled the (renamed) National Museums and Galleries of Wales to produce striking computer images, including one of a handsome Neolithic farmer who lived *c.* 3500 BC and whose skull was discovered in a burial mound at Penywyrlod, Talgarth, in Powys.

Data on early Neolithic house structures, either transient or permanent, are extremely rare, but Wales has a rich array of Neolithic communal tomb buildings whose nature and locations are far more similar to those of Ireland and south-west Scotland than those of southern Britain. These monuments include tombs, enclosures,

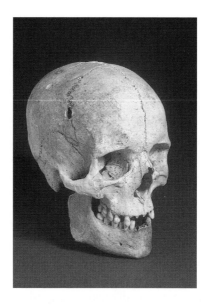

3. The skull and a computer image of the face of a Neolithic farmer who was buried *c.* 3500 BC at Penywyrlod, near Talgarth, Powys. (National Museums and Galleries of Wales)

cursus monuments, henge monuments, stone circles and wooden palisades. Specific parts of the landscape were carefully chosen by the builders of the monuments, and mountains, rivers, the sea and outcrops were attractive sites not only for their visibility but also because of their symbolic associations. Since concepts concerning death and the afterlife loomed large in the lives of these farming communities, considerable investment was made in providing fitting burial places for the deceased. Among the great wonders of the Neolithic period were the impressive megalithic chambered tombs in which groups of men, women and children were buried. Scholars have identified certain regional styles associated with these striking burial places. Portal dolmens clearly prevailed in south-west Wales, reflecting close links with the Irish Sea and the peoples of the Atlantic seaboard. In Anglesey, for instance, the monument known as Barclodiad y Gawres (the Giantess's Apron) can be linked with similar tombs in eastern Ireland. In east Wales, by contrast, a series of substantial long cairns bear witness to the influence of Neolithic traditions in the eastern part of Britain. The impressive tombs at Tinkinswood and St Lythans in Glamorgan share features with those of the Cotswold-Severn group. In the latter part of the Neolithic period, structures known as 'henges' (circular embanked earthworks) appeared, a good example of which is located at Llandygái, near Bangor, where two substantial henge monuments were built. The construction of these grandiose tombs, of which around 150 survive to provide vivid reminders of the ancient past, took hundreds of hours to complete and called for Herculean communal endeavour. We know that 200 people were required to transport and erect the 50-ton capstone which covered the burial mound at Tinkinswood, and geologists have conclusively demonstrated that the spotted dolerite usually called bluestones were dragged by an army of perspiring human ants from the Preselau mountains in Pembrokeshire to the coast, and hence to Stonehenge *c.* 2045 BC. The marvellously impressive burial chamber at Pentre Ifan in Pembrokeshire, which dates from *c.* 3500 BC and which still retains the power to astonish, had such an unusually high capstone that a horseman could pass underneath. These communal burial sites, where people assembled to conduct mysterious ceremonies and to affirm their egalitarianism, are as much memorials to their collective

4. The burial chamber at Pentre Ifan, Pembrokeshire, is one of the finest megalithic sites in Britain. Three of four pointed sidestones support an elegant wedge-shaped capstone. According to Jan Morris, this monument possesses 'an unmistakably soothing and reconciliatory air'. (Crown Copyright: Royal Commission on the Ancient and Historical Monuments of Wales)

strength and ingenuity as they are to their religiosity. How refreshing it is to find modern archaeologists, in seeking to locate these great raised stones within place, myth and history, referring to them as 'stones that float to the sky'.

Farmers during the Bronze Age (*c.* 2500–*c.* 700 BC) were greatly cheered by the balmy summers which made even the rugged uplands more attractive to colonizers. At this juncture, traditional links with Ireland weakened and eastern influences, especially from Yorkshire, the Peak District, and the Severn and Wye valleys, became more apparent. The population was growing – one possibly optimistic estimate places it at between 10,000 and 20,000 at the height of the Bronze Age – and the emergence of metalworking, a technological change of far-reaching significance, enabled people who lived in unenclosed wooden farmsteads or wattle huts to develop specialist crafts as well as produce menacing bronze axes and daggers. Copper, tin and gold became prized commercial assets. Four Bronze Age mines have been identified in Wales, the most sophisticated of which were the Great Orme Mines at Llandudno. The tradition of constructing substantial communal tombs was supplanted by individual burials in barrows and stone circles, a development which coincided with the proliferation of exquisitely decorated pots or beakers associated with groups of people known as the 'Beaker Folk'. The notion that this distinctive bell-shaped pottery was brought to Britain by the 'Beaker Folk' from the Lower Rhine area has been discounted, and it is now reckoned more likely that they were prestige items acquired by exchange or trade with seamen. A range of impressive bronze and gold tools, weapons and ornaments have survived. A priceless gold cape, which was discovered in 1833 in a cairn at Mold, Denbighshire, draped around a male skeleton, bears particularly vivid witness to the sophisticated skills of these Bronze Age craftsmen.

Following the dry and mild climate of the early Bronze Age, the weather took a turn for the worse towards the beginning of the first millennium BC and contributed to socio-economic changes which affected much of Europe. Heavy rain and strong winds impoverished the soil, peat bogs proliferated, deforestation was rife and upland farms were deserted with alarming swiftness. This potentially lethal cocktail of environmental problems caused a general mood of fretfulness and insecurity during the Late Bronze Age and throughout the Iron Age (700 BC–AD 75). An urgent need seems to have arisen for economic and military security, as a result of which Wales became freckled with the most numerous and distinctive relics of prehistoric times, namely the hillforts. These fortified community settlements, around 600 of which have been identified, have always been an attractive field of study for scholars, and aerial surveys as well as painstaking excavation continue to supply valuable information. Such fortifications, both large and small, were erected on hilltops to protect increasingly vulnerable people and animals from predatory warriors and cattle thieves. To the extent that they served as foci for tribal power and authority, they marked the emergence of new social configurations. They were also highly visible symbols of power and prestige. Although these defensive enclosures became an integral part of the military and economic infrastructure of localities, they varied considerably in size and resources. Broadly speaking, the largest and most sophisticated (Llanymynech, Breiddin and Ffridd Faldwyn) were in the north-east Marches, while the smallest, some

5. The multiplicity of hillforts was one of the features of Wales in the Iron Age. This small but superbly located hillfort is Moel Arthur in the Clwydian range of mountains in Flintshire. (Crown Copyright: Royal Commission on the Ancient and Historical Monuments of Wales)

of which measured less than half a hectare, were in the south-west. Considerable manpower was expended in the construction of most of them, and one of the best ways of reliving the sights, smells and sounds of life in the Iron Age is to visit the reconstructed hillfort at Castell Henllys, Pembrokeshire. Some of the most memorable fortifications, located in dramatic settings on top of highly visible hills and overlooking the sea, were territorial units designed to impress as well as deter marauders. One of the most remarkable hillforts is that at Tre'r Ceiri in the Llŷn peninsula, an unusually well-preserved and spectacularly located hillfort where people lived in stone-walled huts enclosed by dry-stone ramparts. Circularity was the order of the day: roundhouse buildings predominated in Wales, with the exception of Goldcliff on the Gwent Levels, where rectangular structures prevailed. Although even the puniest fortifications housed robust warriors, they were also trading units and craft centres within a largely pastoral economy.

This brings us to one of the most controversial areas of research: the applicability of terms like 'Celt', 'Celticism' and 'Celticity' to this particular period. Public interest in the Celts and Celticity has never been greater and it is curious, therefore, that this should coincide with a determined attempt by some scholars, mostly Iron Age archaeologists, to cast deepening doubts on the existence of the Celts as a coherent ethnic group, on the relationship between the Hallstatt and La Tène archaeological cultures and Celticity, and indeed on whether the term 'Celt' itself is valid. The Celticity debate has 'become a battleground' in recent times and it shows no signs of abating. Opposing camps of 'Celtomaniacs' and 'Celtosceptics' regularly strike out right and left against their detractors, and the pages of scholarly works are increasingly spattered with the blood and brains of academic warriors. The details of this controversy, which confirms that archaeologists and philologists carry political as well as intellectual baggage and that the Celts always have and probably always will be reinvented, need not detain us here except insofar as they reflect life in Celtic Wales.

The common-sense view is that by *c.* 500 BC the Celts in Europe were a recognizable people. Although even in their pomp they never managed to establish an empire, the range of their spatial and numerical expansion from the second millennium BC onwards had been quite extraordinary. A people who could summon up the courage and chutzpah to sack both Rome and Delphi were certainly no mean people. The Romans despised (and perhaps secretly feared) these 'barbarians', whose great swathes of territory extended from Ireland in the west to central Turkey in the east, who fought naked on their two-wheeled chariots, brandishing their long swords, yelling bloodcurdling war cries and threatening to decapitate their captives. Tall, fair-skinned, with blue eyes and long hair, they fought like tigers and celebrated their victories on the battlefield with lavish feasts. Notwithstanding their bellicosity and boastfulness, the most remarkable and enduring feature of loosely knit groups of Celts was their extraordinary material culture. In particular, their art has been rightly described as 'one of the glories of the European past'. Their twin cultural heartlands were Hallstatt in the Upper Austrian Salzkammergut and La Tène on the north shore of Lake Neuchâtel in Switzerland, where archaeological finds include craftsmanship of the highest order. La Tène art is especially striking: geometric abstract designs, classical plant decoration and oriental motifs were used to adorn bracelets, brooches, pins, rings, firedogs, tankards, swords and daggers. Its delicacy and subtlety contrasted sharply with the rough and angular style of Hallstatt art. But both cultures reflected the genius of Celtic craftsmanship in metalwork, jewellery, glassware and stone carvings.

How and when did the Celts bring their martial skills, expertise in iron-making and highly sophisticated material culture to Britain? Had this book been written in 1950, the answer would have been: by large-scale invasion after 700 BC. But great events do not necessarily have great causes. Historians have more or less abandoned the migration theory, though without doubting for a moment the key importance of the sea as a major highway of communication. The general trend nowadays is to view the arrival of Celtic-speaking peoples and their rich and diverse material culture as a gradual process which occurred over thousands of years. This culture, in turn, was assimilated, adapted and developed by native societies over a long period of time.

From the Bronze Age onwards, the Celts set aside complex rituals of burial in favour of votive deposits in rivers, lakes, marshes and bogs, which were believed to be sacred locations. Serendipitously, two lakes in Wales have yielded rich evidence of notable votive offerings which had clearly been used to propitiate the gods. During excavations for a reservoir at Llyn Fawr in the Rhondda in 1911, early Hallstatt deposits were recovered embedded in peat, including two sheet-bronze cauldrons, socketed bronze sickles, six socketed bronze axes and three axes dating from *c.* 700–600 BC. Llyn Fawr has also provided the earliest evidence for ironworking in Britain and by smiths more used to Bronze Age technology. Some thirty years later, during the construction of an airfield in Anglesey in 1942, a total of 177 iron and copper alloy artefacts were discovered in peat deposits on the southern margins of Llyn Cerrig Bach near Llanfair-yn-neubwll. At the time, the significance of the metal-work was unrecognized and one of the precious iron gang chains was used by a workman to tow lorries out of the mud. Mercifully, all but four of the finds, which include swords, spears, shield bosses, horse trappings and slave chains, are now safely in the custody of the National Museums and Galleries of Wales. One of the unusual features of these votive deposits is that they were not necessarily pre-Roman: certain elements among the artefacts date from the late first or early second centuries AD, though most of them belong to the period from 300 BC to early Roman times. Other pieces of evidence of La Tène art at its best include the exquisitely decorated Cerrigydrudion (Denbighshire) hanging bowl (though some believe it might be a helmet or a lid), the iron firedog at Capel Garmon

6. This copper alloy decorative plaque, dated *c.* 150–50 BC, depicting human faces, was discovered at Tal-y-llyn, Merioneth. (National Museums and Galleries of Wales)

(Caernarfonshire) and the bronze plaques depicting human faces found at Tal-y-llyn (Merioneth). Prestigious votive offerings of this kind were plunged into watery locations in order to placate the spirits, and such rituals can only be appreciated within the context of people's engagement with the Otherworld. Supernatural powers were believed to be abroad, and both animal and human sacrifices were offered on a substantial scale to the gods.

A handful of bog sites within Wales have yielded human remains of sacrificial victims, and the mysteries surrounding preserved bodies, especially those which were victims of violence, have excited considerable interest. Yet, the most celebrated and convincing archaeological evidence of sacrificial killing in prehistoric times derives from nearby Cheshire. The remains of the semi-naked Lindow Man (probably dating from the mid-first century AD) received worldwide exposure following their discovery in the summer of 1984. There is unequivocal evidence that in this case a plump young male (often referred to by flippant archaeologists as 'Pete Marsh'!) had been beaten around the head and strangled; his throat was then slit and finally he was unceremoniously (or perhaps ceremoniously) dumped face down in a bog-pool. The Druids, a highly venerated class of erudite men, whose wisdom and influence inspired terror and awe in equal measure, often sanctioned these ritual murders and taught their followers that the human soul is immortal and that it enters another body following death. The Druids, however, remain shadowy figures in Wales, especially outside their principal focal points in Anglesey. The literary evidence for them is much stronger in Ireland and from Greek and Roman authors with reference to Gaul, and not until the eighteenth century did the 'druidomania' championed by the likes of Henry Rowlands in Anglesey and Iolo Morganwg in Glamorgan begin to exercise a seductive sway over the imagination of the Welsh.

Attempts to gain insights into the language spoken in Celtic Wales are dogged by the complete lack of written records for the pre-Roman period. No linguistic data in the form of place names or inscribed objects exist. It is certain, however, that prehistoric Wales had its legends, its oral tales about mythical humans, beasts and birds who possessed extraordinary magical powers, and its fund of memorized knowledge of secrets hidden away in dark caves and sacred oak groves. Late medieval prose is replete with fragments of old mythological themes and motifs of which we know little. But even though literacy belonged to the future, some broad generalizations can be made. We know that the Celtic languages descend from a common ancestor. In 1786 the pioneering linguist Sir William Jones, the son of a brilliant Anglesey mathematician, revealed before the Asiatic Society in Calcutta that most European languages and several Asian languages derived from the Indo-European family. Celtic is one of the main branches of that family. Modern scholars draw a distinction between the extinct continental Celtic languages (Gaulish, Celtiberian, Lepontic and Galatian, all of which had perished by the early Middle Ages) and insular Celtic, which comprises two branches: the British, Brittonic or Brythonic branch (P-Celtic), which in a much later period split into Welsh, Breton, Cornish and Cumbrian, and the Goidelic or Gaelic branch (Q-Celtic), which evolved into Irish, Scottish Gaelic and Manx. What can be said with some confidence is that by the twilight of the prehistoric age the Brittonic Celtic language was spoken by P-Celtic tribes throughout most, if not the whole, of the island, and that this was the oral medium through which myths, cults and rites were sustained.

Forty-three years after the birth of Christ, a large and powerful Roman army of 40,000 men led by Aulus Plautius, governor of Panonnia on the river Danube, set foot on British soil. Happily, from the point of view of the invaders, the incursion coincided with warmer and drier conditions and, although the initial objective was to bring southern England to heel, the urge to conquer more distant regions inhabited by those whom the Romans believed to be irremediable barbarians proved irresistible. Scotland resisted successfully and Ireland never experienced the glory and brutality that was Rome, but tribes in Wales soon found themselves in the thick of battle. Cocksure to the point of shameless arrogance, Roman soldiers believed themselves to be invincible. Nothing can be further from the truth than the notion that they were endowed with a Corinthian sense of fair play. Equipped with robust armour and deadly javelins and swords, their well-drilled legions were fearsome killing machines. Four tribal areas lay at their tender mercies in Wales: the Deceangli along the north coast, the Ordovices in the highland zone, the Silures in the south-east and the Demetae in the south-west. Far too much bad blood existed among this rag-bag of warring tribes for them to be able to come together, but it came as something of a shock to the invaders to discover that barbarians in the western parts were ready to mount resistance, however sporadic, and they would surely never have guessed that the conquest would take more than thirty years. In fact, the Roman conquest of Wales proved to be a protracted and painful process which incurred heavy costs. Even as late as AD 78, as many as 30,000 Roman troops were required to be based in Wales. For more than a generation, every effort was made to defy, obstruct and delay the advance of Rome.

When the new governor, Ostorius Scapula, began to make serious inroads in AD 47 into the territory of the Deceangli in north-east Wales, this provoked a fierce backlash, led by the swarthy (according to Tacitus) and mulishly stubborn Silures. Past masters at nip-and-tuck tactics, the Silures marauded like no other guerrillas in the experience of the Romans had done. Their unpredictability played havoc with the morale of Roman troops, who chafed at the inability of their bewildered generals to put a stop to their depredations. Their leader was the intelligent, steely nerved Caratacus, the son of Cunobelinus, an audacious risk-taker who pitted his wits against the invaders with no small success. But even he met his match when he led his fiery but outnumbered warriors into a major battle, close to Caersŵs (Montgomeryshire), in AD 51. It was a disaster for the Silures, who were cut to ribbons by legionaries and auxiliaries whose military prowess and tactical nous far outstripped theirs. Caratacus escaped and fled to the Brigantes, only to be betrayed by Queen Cartimandua, a self-serving opportunist who had become a client ruler of the Romans. Heavily shackled, he was dispatched to Rome, where he maintained his sense of dignity and, in a moving speech, seized the opportunity to rebuke Emperor Claudius publicly for the insatiable greed of his kinsmen:

Had my high birth and rank been accompanied by moderation in my hour of success, I should have entered this city as a friend and not a prisoner. You would not have hesitated to accept me as an ally, a man of splendid ancestry, and bearing rule over many tribes. My present position is degrading to me, but glorious to you. I had horses, warriors and gold; if I was unwilling to lose them, what wonder is that? Does it follow that because you desire universal empire, one must accept universal slavery?

7. The great Celtic warrior Caratacus, or Caradoc, was a thorn in the flesh of the Romans. This sculpture, by J. H. Foley in 1856–9, was based on Caratacus's rousing speech to his soldiers as the Roman army advanced: 'This day must decide the fate of Britain. The era of Liberty or eternal bondage begins from this hour.' (Guildhall Art Gallery, Corporation of London)

The luminosity and courage of Caratacus made such a deep impression that he and his family were pardoned. Both in his time and certainly in subsequent mythology, Caratacus was a warrior hero of epic proportions, and the Welsh version of his name – Caradog – later became a popular name among early Welsh princely families. In the 1790s the Caradogion Society, founded by the London Welsh, proudly displayed a handsome painting of Caratacus railing against Claudius. A splendid statue of him was completed by John Henry Foley by 1859, and in 1898 Edward Elgar composed a cantata in his praise. In many respects, Caratacus can justifiably be considered the first national hero of the Welsh.

Even though they were now bereft of their leader, the obdurate Silures had no intention of submitting meekly to the Roman yoke. Still they tormented the invaders and, on one notable occasion in AD 52, they defeated the Twentieth Legion, an extraordinary military victory which proved such a shock that it sent two troubled governors to an early grave. Under the third governor, Gallus, the Romans regrouped, redoubled their efforts and utilized a chain of newly built auxiliary forts designed to deter both the Silures and Ordovices from penetrating their imperial territory through the major valleys along the Marches. Sensibly, the fifth governor, Suetonius Paulinus, a hardened soldier who was determined to measure up to the task of imposing Roman will, changed the point of attack by mounting a savage assault on the Druid-controlled island of Anglesey in AD 60. Here, deep-seated hatred of the 'uncivilized' Celts led to a bloodbath which lived long in the popular memory. According to the famous account by Tacitus in Book XIV of his *Annals*, the Romans, braving a solid phalanx of fiery warriors, shrieking women dressed in black and spell-casting Druids, massacred them without mercy:

Then, urged by their general's appeals and mutual encouragements not to quail before a troop of frenzied women, they bore the standards onward, smote down all resistance, and wrapped the foe in the flames of his own brands. A force was next set over the conquered, and their groves, devoted to human superstitions, were destroyed. They deemed it, indeed, a religious duty to cover the altars with the blood of captives and to consult their deities by inspecting human entrails.

Had not the Boudican revolt intervened, the whole of north Wales might have become the victim of large-scale genocide. In the event, the conquest (such as it was) remained incomplete until the grimly determined governor Julius Frontinus launched full-scale punitive campaigns during AD 74–78. Faced by this sustained and ruthless onslaught, even the truculent Silures could no longer resist.

Military successes, however incomplete or long delayed, could never have been achieved without a supportive logistical infrastructure. To consolidate their military supremacy, the Romans set up permanent legionary fortresses and temporary auxiliary forts and

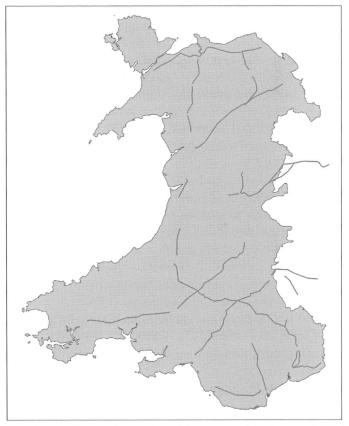

Map 1. Among the most impressive achievements of the Romans in Wales was the construction of a network of strategic roads which linked forts and facilitated the deployment of troops and the supply of resources. (Crown Copyright: Royal Commission on the Ancient and Historical Monuments of Wales)

marching camps. Whereas Celtic craftsmen revelled in sinuous curves, Roman engineers placed their faith in straight lines and geometrical precision. A sophisticated and durable network of all-weather roads was set up, based on a great quadrilateral with two powerful legionary fortresses – Chester (Deva) and Caerleon (Isca) – supported by the auxiliary forts of Caernarfon (Segontium) and Carmarthen (Moridunum Demetarum) located at the respective angles. Forts occupied pivotal positions in the Roman road system and they were chiefly responsible for ensuring that newly conquered territories were effectively policed. By the time of the Flavian conquest (AD 74–77), a comprehensive system of roads, stretching over at least 1025 km, had been laid. By using this remarkable grid of newly paved carriageways, Roman soldiers were able to cover distances at great speed in order to subdue tiresome local tribesmen. However, after AD 75 all forts were not required to maintain a full quota of soldiers, and only in times of crisis were full-scale complements deployed. Troop movements to secure the northern frontier of the province denuded several garrisons, especially when work began on Hadrian's Wall in AD 122.

Caerleon in Monmouthshire stands out as one of the most important Roman military sites in Europe. From AD 75, it became the headquarters of the Second Augustan Legion, a fighting force of 5,500 heavily armed men who were totally committed to the empire. Soldiers of this calibre demanded first-rate facilities, and they were duly billeted in a fortress of 20.5 hectares, which included a barracks, a palace, a hospital, granaries, workshops, public baths (the discovery by archaeologists of jewellery and milk teeth reveals that civilians as well as legionaries sampled the waters) and a stunning amphitheatre, where soldiers were trained and where baying crowds of around 6,000 spectators witnessed bloody gladiatorial contests and barbaric recreations involving bears, wolves and wildcats. On such raucous and bloodthirsty occasions, Caerleon was no place for the squeamish. Much later, the impressive ruins of this major fortification proved to be a source of inspiration for Arthurian authors in south-east Wales.

For the most part, after AD 75 tribes might still be a nuisance, but they were no longer a serious menace. Part of the reason for this was that their leaders were increasingly attracted by opportunities to

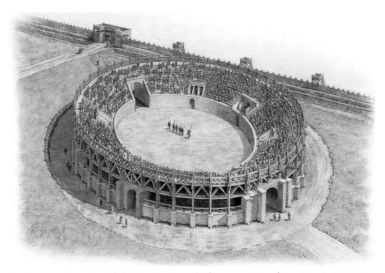

8. A reconstruction of the Roman amphitheatre at Caerleon (Isca). In *Brut y Brenhinedd*, Caerleon was described as 'the second city to Rome in the beauty of her houses, her wealth of gold and silver, and her pride'. (Cadw. Crown Copyright: illustration by John Banbury)

acquire wealth and influence. It is a tribute to the swaggering invaders that they were not only able to subjugate the fiery Silurians but also to coax their warrior aristocracy into coveting the material and cultural benefits of *romanitas*. This was done by ushering in *civitas* administration at the planned provincial capitals of Caerwent (Venta Silurum), the capital of the Silures, and Carmarthen, the capital of the Demetae. This system of local self-government was based on efficient models already tried and tested in Gaul. By treating a whole tribe as if it were a city state, the Romans pandered to the pretensions of the native Britons, who were naturally irresistibly tempted by the prospect of a comfortable life in the towns rather than a precarious existence in the countryside. What Caratacus would have made of those who clambered aboard the gravy train is a moot point, but even the bravest Silurians and Demetae cannot be blamed for considering the personal safety and well-being of their families. They might not have felt any great loyalty to, or affection for, their Roman masters, but they gladly seized on favours of all kinds which improved their lifestyles.

Although it measured only 18 hectares, Caerwent was an exceptionally striking *civitas*. Here, indeed, the imprint of Rome was to be
seen in all its splendour. By the third and fourth centuries, it contained around 3,000 people who experienced at first hand the socio-
cultural advantages of urban, literate Mediterranean civilization.
Caerwent had a forum-basilica (marketplace and civic hall), which
towered above the rest of the public buildings, bath-houses, shops
and taverns, and some of its finest houses possessed painted walls
and ceilings, mosaic floors and hypocaust heating systems installed
by legionary craftsmen or in-migrant stone carvers. Its streets were
laid out on a regular gridiron pattern which created blocks (*insulae*)
of land on which attractive houses and shops were built. An intriguing *graffito* from Caerwent indicates not only growing literacy
among the native stock but also reservations about ethnic inter-
mingling: 'Domitilla [sends love] to her [sweetheart], Victor. For
shame!' Evidently, the path of true love did not always run smoothly
for the Silures and the Romans. Although Carmarthen was a good
deal smaller than Caerwent it, too, had impressive public buildings,
including a large amphitheatre, a Romano-British temple and well-
stocked shops and workshops. In these urban centres, those who
subscribed to *romanitas* enjoyed wealth and comfort to which
poverty-stricken rural dwellers could never aspire. They also spoke
Latin (a high-prestige language) and wielded socio-cultural power.
Conversely, the early Iron Age homesteads, which remained such a
striking feature of much of non-urban Wales, contrasted sharply
with the sophisticated villas of the south-east. In the southern plains,
places like Llantwit Major, Ely and Llandough could boast substantial villa-type farms which bore unmistakable signs of Romanization.
At Llantwit, the grandest courtyard villa of them all had baths,
delicate mosaics and hypocaust heating. Even on the lesser farmsteads
in the Vale of Glamorgan and in parts of Gwent, farmers worked hard
to meet the seemingly insatiable demand from prosperous people for
grain, fresh vegetables and fruit.

But the Romans did not invest exclusively in their two *civitas*
capitals and their hinterland. In more distant parts, but close to
forts, small civilian settlements known as *vici* were set up, where
tradesmen and merchants from other parts of the empire led a quasi-
Romanized way of life. In many areas, new markets were created for

agricultural products (meat, grain, hides and skins) as well as for metal goods, pottery and timber. One of the most successful settlements outside the southern plains was Din Lligwy in north-west Wales. This second-century AD settlement, with its open stock-pens, terraced fields, local crafts and metalworking activities, was a thriving concern. Copper mines flourished on Parys Mountain in Anglesey and at the Great Orme close to Llandudno, and the application of highly sophisticated technology at the gold-mines of Dolaucothi, Carmarthenshire, where remarkable aqueducts were built, brought substantial economic rewards, as indeed did localized mining of iron, coal and silver. The new system of roads was a great incentive to commerce, and the spread of coins in urban communities up to the fourth century indicates that merchants and traders were perfectly at ease with the advanced monetary system of the Romans.

Religion and ritual figured prominently in the Roman culture and, with the single exception of druidism (which the Romans both feared and despised), they allowed a wide array of individual deities which often became fused with Celtic versions. Although they reckoned themselves to be a people of special religiosity and possessed sufficient military might to impose their will, it is to their credit that they neither expected other people to conform to their religion nor abandon the worship of traditional deities. Some developed a taste for oriental mystery cults, and Mithraea at Caerleon and Caernarfon attracted loyal followers. The roots of Christianity, too, were laid in Roman times. Although the initial response to Christian missionaries was hostile – Julius and Aaron were two Christian martyrs who were put to death in Caerleon for disturbing the 'peace of the gods' – a major turning point came in AD 312 when Constantine won a famous battle at the Milvian Bridge, near Rome, and became the first Roman emperor to embrace Christianity. Christianity was now placed on an equal footing with other creeds, and its followers began to exploit the new opportunities opened to them. By the fourth century, small groups of Christians were worshipping regularly in the town of Caerwent and were consciously setting themselves apart from the 'backward' pagans of the countryside. Such groups, too, were the most likely to learn Latin – the imperial language – since it offered a passport to wealth and influence. Latin words clearly entered the vocabulary of the Brythonic tongue, a process which was facilitated by the fact that Brythonic was an inflected language. From Latin came Welsh words like book (*llyfr*), bridge (*pont*) and room (*ystafell*), which continue to this day to testify to the classical heritage which permeates the Welsh language and its literature. Indeed, some of the finest twentieth-century Welsh poems were those in which classical texts and mythology figured prominently.

It would be rash, however, to exaggerate the degree to which the occupying power changed the face of Wales. At no stage over a period of some three and a half centuries was it fully or effectively Romanized. Outside the heavily militarized zones and thriving urban communities, where the Celtic aristocracy embraced Roman citizenship and availed themselves of opportunities to take part in civil government and trade, the imprint of Rome was much less obvious. A mass conversion to Rome would have required far greater resources than the empire could afford. In terms of settlement and lifestyle, therefore, Iron Age society continued much as before in the rugged native heartlands and in many ways it is the continuities rather than the discontinuities which catch the eye. Only a small proportion of the total population wore togas, spoke Latin, could read inscriptions, ate grapes and fresh vegetables, and enjoyed the mellow comforts of hypocaust heating in well-appointed villas. For all their genius for organization and superior lifestyle, the Romans were a minority in Celtic Wales and the departure of the Roman eagle, so inescapably associated with brutality, was not widely lamented by non-elite groups.

The end of Roman rule in Wales was a protracted affair rather than a sudden denouement. By the fourth century, jarring internal unrest was matched by such dangerous external threats from Irish, Frankish and Saxon raiders that maintaining imperial control became increasingly difficult. In the circumstances it was judged prudent to withdraw troops from the island, a trend which was accelerated when it coincided with the continental ambitions of Magnus Maximus, a native of Galicia who was proclaimed emperor by the army in Britain in AD 383. Maximus gambled everything by stripping British garrisons of their finest soldiers in order to further his imperial ambitions in Gaul, where he successfully waged war and maintained himself as emperor until his defeat by Theodosius at Siscia and his subsequent execution at Aquileia in north-west Italy in AD 388. Since Maximus owes his posthumous prestige to myths and legends, it is hard to ascertain wherein lay his reputed charisma. He was clearly a deeply impressive warrior who survives in Welsh mythology as Macsen Wledig, who married Elen Luyddog (Elen of the Hosts), a princess from Segontium (Roman Caernarfon). But although much has been written recently (both by reputable scholars and by more popular cultural movers and shakers) of his role in the making of Wales, the praise lavished on him appears to be misplaced. One influential historian argued that 'in a very real sense, Wales can be said to begin with the British hero Maximus', and on the strength of that bold declaration the rousing popular Welsh song 'Yma o Hyd' (Still Here) claimed that, on his departure in AD 383, Macsen Wledig 'left the nation as one'. Myths, of course, are just as important as realities, but the legends of Maximus and the valuable political function his name fulfilled belonged to the future, and to regard him as the architect of the geographical territory and nation which later became known as Wales is teleological nonsense. Both in the prehistoric age and Roman period, Wales was not and did not become a recognizable physical entity or a distinct political or administrative unit, or even a fiction of the mind. In this chapter, the anachronism 'Wales' has been used simply for the sake of convenience. When, then, does the history of Wales and the Welsh really begin? At this stage, the answer is 'Not yet'.

2

The Heroic Age, 383–1063

From time to time, slipshod historians do the history of Wales a disservice by clinging to outdated or inappropriate labels. Perhaps the most deeply entrenched concept in the interpretation of the period from the withdrawal of Rome to the coming of the Normans is the depiction 'Dark Age Wales'. When this epithet was first used, it was meant to be a commentary on the relative dearth of historical data rather than a pejorative statement. Scholars to this day are painfully aware that this is one of the most obscure and complicated periods in Welsh annals. So much of the historical record, to quote an eleventh-century Welsh commentator, has been lost as a result of 'the constant devourings of moths and the yearly borings of ages through times and seasons' and, in spite of the valiant efforts of scholars, who acquire gainful employment and a sense of worth from subjecting scattered, barely legible and incomplete sources to meticulous scrutiny and analysis, our knowledge of the period remains disturbingly patchy. In the restricted sense that it is a poorly documented period, this was certainly a 'dark age' and it is easy to see why some historians are tempted to quote later evidence to light up the darkness. Even key figures like Cunedda, Arthur and St David are wraiths shrouded in mystery. But the term 'Dark Age' is more often used nowadays to conjure up images of unrelieved war, rape, pillage and squalor, and to give the impression that pre-Norman culture was inferior and the people themselves beneath contempt. Such a view is a serious misrepresentation and oversimplification. In this chapter, a much more generous appraisal of 'the heroic age' is offered. Viewed in this light, the period emerges as one of vigorous politico-religious change, social evolution and cultural development. Four themes stand out: the emergence of multiple political kingdoms, the codification of the native laws, the vigorous missions of the Welsh saints, and the genesis of the Welsh language and the vernacular literature. As the period unfolded, Wales began to emerge as a recognizable territorial and cultural entity.

Even in our modern, economically advanced and culturally sophisticated age, images of brutality, slaughter and destruction retain a compelling, macabre fascination, and it is with this consideration in mind that we should assess the more disagreeable facets of post-Roman Wales. It was, of course, an unimaginably brutal age, ravaged by terror, expulsions, assassinations and hideous cruelties. Poems and sagas 'echo to the croak of ravens glutting themselves on human blood, groan under the graves of heroes and martyrs'. Petty kings had no qualms about wreaking disproportionate vengeance on their enemies: Spanish inquisitors and American gangsters would have smirked approvingly over the ugly deeds – blackmail, extortion, castration, blinding, decapitation and impalement – which characterized these cruel and capricious times. No commentator was more critical of the realpolitik, vanity, greed and immorality of Welsh rulers than the sixth-century reformer Gildas. His celebrated *De excidio Britanniae* (On the ruin of Britain), written in the first half of the sixth century, was an unmitigated tirade against ungodly tyrants who must have winced as the whips and lashes of this puritanical scourge rained down on them. It was Gildas who initiated the legend, later embellished by Nennius, of how in *c.* 400 Vortigern (Gwrtheyrn), founder of the kingdom of Powys, became besotted with Alice Rowena, daughter of the Saxon leader, Hengist, a liaison which led to the slaughter of 300 British warriors by the long knives of Saxons who had been invited to a banquet by Vortigern. The memory of this sorry tale, known as 'The Treachery of the Long Knives', was not allowed to fade. There was no shortage of other examples of hideous cruelty. Nor did matters improve with time. Since the power of Welsh chiefs rested on the spoils of conflict and the bloody elimination of rivals, Welsh annals are shot through with gory tales. Even in the latter half of the period, *Brut y Tywysogyon*

(The Chronicle of the Princes) (late thirteenth century–*c.* 1330) brims with cases of cold-blooded murders, blindings and castrations. Such deeds doubtless grew in the telling. As we shall see, the balance of political power might have shifted in this period, but stomach-churning violence remained a daily fact of life.

That Wales was a cauldron of conflict in this period was a reflection of heavy and persistent internal and external pressures. In the post-Roman period, plurality and diversity were the order of the day. Multiple kingship prevailed and regional identities were very much in flux. Apart from the principal early kingdoms of Gwynedd, Powys, Brycheiniog, Dyfed and Glywysing, a myriad miniscule kingdoms and chiefdoms existed in a bewildering variety of forms, all of which were prone to sudden collapses. The geographical configuration of Wales, the strength of regional loyalties and the proliferation of internecine strife meant that centrifugalism flourished. This loose and unstable confederation of tiny kingdoms was marked by factional conflicts, intrigue, disunity of purpose and shifts of power. As we shall see, those kingdoms with a far-sighted and courageous leader, supported by an elite of crack troops, were best placed to expand and prosper. Paradoxically, too, having to contend with aggressive Anglo-Saxon interlopers from the east and the 'Black Gentiles' (as Scandinavian raiders were dubbed), who launched lightning raids from established winter bases on the Irish coast, aided the emergence of larger and more unified kingdoms. However, it needs to be emphasized that Welsh rulers gave priority to military gains rather than to institutional development. None of their self-serving manoeuvrings was an early exercise in dynamic state-building.

Following the departure of the Romans, new circumstances forced a dramatic transformation in the political configuration of Britain. From *c.* 430 large numbers of Germanic settlers – Angles, Saxons and Jutes – settled in eastern England and began advancing steadily inland, driving the native peoples westwards. Bewildered and helpless in the face of such heavy numbers and firepower, the Britons were little match for the invaders. They either gave ground or submitted. Every dog has his day, however, and at Mount Badon (*Badonicus mons*) – dated 516 in *Annales Cambriae* (The Welsh Annals) (*c.* 450–*c.* 955) – the Anglo-Saxons were routed by the Britons who were led, according to later tradition, by a chieftain

Map 2. Britain in the post-Roman, pre-Viking period, showing Wales in the
Heroic Age and the Brittonic kingdoms of the Old North. (University of
Wales Centre for Advanced Welsh and Celtic Studies)

known as Arthur, whose name has excited the literary and historical
imagination down to our days. It is possible that a historical Arthur
existed, but the evidence is extremely flimsy. Only later, thanks
largely to Geoffrey of Monmouth's largely legendary *Historia
Regum Brittaniae* (The History of the Kings of Britain) (*c.* 1139),

was Arthur elevated to the role of a great national hero and a para-
gon of valour. His life and works became encrusted in legends, and
only in the glow of hindsight did his name come to mean something
to the Welsh. Undeterred by the setback at Mount Badon, however,
the westward expansion of the Saxons continued. At a decisive
battle at Dyrham (Deorham) near Bristol in 577, they not only
opened the way to the subjugation of Cornwall in the tenth century
but also drove an irremovable wedge between the British in Wales
and their cousins in the south-west. Tribal feuds along the respective
frontiers of Northumbria, Mercia and Wessex boded ill for the
surviving Roman-British communities, which were too small and
fragmented to withstand the military onslaughts. During the course
of the seventh century, the British kingdoms of Rheged and
Gododdin were engulfed and only Strathclyde, probably until the
late eleventh century, maintained its independence. The prospect of
land and wealth in the Celtic west whetted the appetites of Mercian
armies, whose incursions between 640 and 800 not only led to large-
scale economic depredations but also to the abandonment of the
royal court at Pengwern, an event marked by the composition of a
genuinely heart-rending sequence of Welsh stanzas (*englynion*) to
the 'Hall of Cynddylan', an elegy to the conquest of Powys. Uttered
by Heledd, Cynddylan's sister, as the court burns, they convey the
brutal reality of defeat, effacement and loss:

> The Hall of Cynddylan is dark tonight,
> Without fire, without bed.
> I weep awhile, then I am silent.
>
> The Hall of Cynddylan is dark tonight,
> Without fire, without candle.
> Save God, who will give me sanity?
>
> The Hall of Cynddylan is dark tonight,
> Without fire, without songs,
> Tears wear away cheeks.
>
> Hall of Cynddylan, each hour I am grieved,
> Deprived of the joyful company
> That I saw on thy hearth.

Unsurprisingly, Celtic kingdoms began to buckle under the extraordinary pressures imposed by Saxon armies. As Roman Britain

disappeared, it was replaced by Anglo-Saxon England and British Wales.

This demarcation became ever more apparent following the construction of a stupendous dyke, the first – as well as the most impressive – public earthwork built by English government. Offa's Dyke (*Clawdd Offa*) runs broadly from the mouth of the Wye in the south to Prestatyn in the north. Although no contemporary records exist to throw light on the date and mode of its construction, it is generally believed that Offa, King of Mercia, was the first post-Roman king with sufficient resources and incentive to build the dyke, probably *c.* 770. Constructed by different groups of impressed gangs of workers (some of the eccentric and abrupt bends suggest this), this extraordinary piece of engineering has been likened by one archaeologist to the building of the Great Pyramid. Offa's Dyke was a defensive earthwork rather than simply a boundary marker. By providing a linear frontier for Mercia it acted as a deterrent to Welsh raiders, whose horses did not relish scaling its 25-foot bank. But this earth embankment, the largest man-made boundary in western Europe, was also an acknowledgement of the otherness of Wales. It provided an agreed frontier between the peoples of the Anglo-Saxon east and the inhabitants of the Celtic west, and although it was often breached by raiders from both sides its very presence helped to shape the extent of Wales and, in the long term, to exercise a profound effect on its people's sense of identity.

Anglo-Saxon pressure along the eastern frontier remained as insistent and irritating as a pecking gull, and the Welsh kings' submission to King Æthelstan and the ensuing border agreement on the river Wye in 927 proved to be a decisive turning point. But for the Welsh, too, there were other pagans to contend with along the western coastline. To the Vikings, Wales was less a focus for settlement than a staging post for hit-and-run raids or a last-minute resting place for its lethal freebooters. From *c.* 800 onwards, but more especially during the second half of the tenth century, Viking forces left their established winter bases on the Irish coast and sped across the Irish Sea in exceptionally mobile raiding fleets in their quest for treasures, slaves and captives. Wielding deadly swords, spears and battleaxes, these intrepid and cruel fighting men terrorized the Welsh coastline. People slept uneasily as they contemplated

9. The extraordinary monument, Offa's Dyke, which stretches for 240 kilometres along the Welsh borders, was probably the work of Offa, King of Mercia (757–96). This dyke helped to identify the extent of, as well as perceptions of, Wales. (Crown Copyright: Royal Commission on the Ancient and Historical Monuments of Wales)

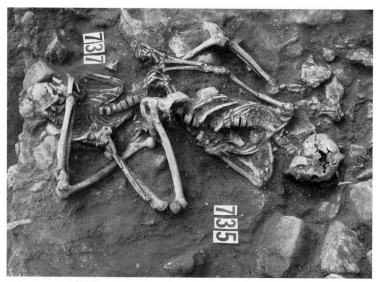

10. Viking marauders, often dubbed the 'Black Gentiles', struck fear into the hearts of the Welsh. Dismembered skeletons discovered at Llanbedr-goch, Anglesey, bear witness to their depredations. (National Museums and Galleries of Wales)

'the fury of the Northmen', and tales of Norse butchery struck terror even into the hearts of seasoned warriors. At Llanbedr-goch in Anglesey, for instance, archaeological excavations have revealed five dismembered skeletons in shallow graves, all of whom had almost certainly come to a grisly demise and been buried at haste by Viking forces during the ninth century. Amid the political uncertainty and turmoil of the times, the Scandinavian raiders were well placed to take advantage. Anglesey, the Llŷn peninsula and Pembrokeshire were sitting targets, and little or no significant opposition was offered. In 987 the Vikings provoked outrage when they made off with 2,000 inhabitants of Anglesey and sold them as slaves. The Church was particularly vulnerable to acts of violence, theft, pillage and devastation. The cathedral of St David's was sacked on four separate occasions in the 980s, and shivers of apprehension were felt by church leaders when (if Gerald of Wales is to be believed) the lax and amoral Morgenau, bishop of St David's, was killed by Viking predators in 999. Yet, we should not exaggerate the extent of Viking depredations in Wales nor their influence on the social, political and cultural life of the people. Coastal communities bore the main brunt of their sporadic seasonal onslaughts, and the bulk of the country was little disturbed by their ravages. No major urban settlements were established by the Northmen, and place-names in north-west and south-west Wales (among them Bardsey Island, Priestholm, Orme's Head, Anglesey, Milford, Fishguard, Ramsey and Skomer) owe significantly less to the influence of the fleeting visits of Viking marauders than to the more long-lasting effects of peaceful maritime activity conducted by traders and merchants up to the end of the eleventh century.

The political history of Wales was deeply conditioned by these external threats, all of which, either from the east or the west, offered fresh challenges and opportunities to Welsh kings who aspired to establishing more powerful dynasties and political ascendancy over much of Wales. Several notable figures rose above run-of-the-mill local feuds by establishing much larger kingdoms and, in some instances, speaking for Wales as a distinctive territorial unit. Gwynedd made the early running. Its first dynasty was established by Cunedda (*fl.* 400 or 450), a chieftain of the Gododdin tribe who, according to the ninth-century *Historia Brittonum* (The History of the Britons), with his eight sons expelled the Irish from north Wales. In the ninth century the torch was taken up by Merfyn Frych (d. 844), a shadowy figure who established a second Gwynedd dynasty, quite possibly from Man, and whose chief claim to fame is that he was the progenitor of a succession of princes who dominated the Welsh kingdoms until the Edwardian conquest. Stepping into the shoes of his father, Rhodri Mawr (Rhodri the Great d. 878) successfully aspired to consolidating princedoms into a greater whole by expanding his overlordship into Powys and Ceredigion. The first Welsh ruler to acquire the appellation 'Great', Rhodri Mawr was an outstandingly able and successful king. He seized the political initiative by welding together the kingdoms of Gwynedd and Powys, and by acquiring through marriage the territories of Seisyllwg (Ceredigion and Ystrad Tywi), which, in effect, meant that over half of Wales lay in his hands. He also pitted his considerable military wits against the Vikings who, infuriated by his temerity, forced him to flee to Ireland. Eventually, in 878 he was cut down in battle by the Anglo-Saxons.

The relative unity established by Rhodri Mawr, and to a lesser degree by his son Anarawd, proved short-lived and the vacuum of authority caused by his demise offered opportunities for Saxons and Vikings to renew their attacks. However, Hywel Dda ap Cadell (d. 950), Rhodri Mawr's grandson, was also cast in the heroic mould. He, more than any other early medieval Welsh ruler, combined political intelligence with physical bravery. The founder of the kingdom of Deheubarth, he came within a whisker of uniting almost the whole of Wales under his overlordship. He inherited Seisyllwg, claimed Dyfed by marrying Elen, daughter of Llywarch ap Hyfaidd, and acquired Gwynedd following the death of Idwal Foel in 942. Only the south-east escaped his clutches, and for a brief eight-year period this far-sighted Welsh Solomon proved to be a man of far greater prestige and sophistication than any of his predecessors. No anglophobe, he recognized the strength of King Æthelstan and was an honoured visitor at the Saxon court. By flattering, cajoling and ingratiating himself with the Wessex dynasty, and at least tacitly accepting English overlordship, he was left in peace to pursue his internal goals. He was not simply or exclusively a warrior-king. Alone among Welsh kings, he was known as 'Hywel the Good' (Hywel Dda), the embodiment of a wise and peaceful ruler. The epithet was almost certainly linked to his far-reaching contribution to the creation of a national code of laws for Wales, a codification which hastened the process by which the Welsh came to think of themselves as a united people. During the twelfth century, a time when enhancing the status of Welsh law as a valid mechanism was a major priority, a tale was concocted that Hywel Dda had summoned six wise luminaries from every commote in the kingdom to Whitland in Carmarthenshire to spend forty days distilling and marshalling the laws of the land. The result of this attractive legend was to create a reputation for Hywel as a peaceful, magnanimous and progressive ruler. He had coins struck for him: a penny, minted at Chester, bore the legend 'Howæl Rex', and therefore presumably ennobled his royal image. By 950, the year of his death, he was at the height of his power. Deeply admired for his magisterial authority, he was hailed in *Brut y Tywysogyon* as 'the Head and Glory of all the Britons'. Ever since, he has had a good press. Portrayed as a sagacious national hero by the artist William Edward Jones in 1876, Hywel Dda became a role model for ardent Welsh patriots, and a late twentieth-century national memorial set up at Whitland (one of the seats of the Kings of Dyfed) celebrates the manner in which this most attractive of rulers provided the first great codification of native law and pointed the way towards the establishment of independent institutions of statehood.

The death of Hywel Dda ushered in a prolonged period of dynastic instability, political squabbling and tribal violence. The union of Gwynedd and Deheubarth, which Hywel had achieved, collapsed, and the Welsh kingdoms were once more turned into war zones. Between 950 and 1063 around thirty-five Welsh rulers perished in grisly fashion, most of them at the hands of their compatriots. Saxon incursions exposed the military weaknesses of the Welsh princes in the border territory, and Viking raiders showed little regard for the already brittle political alignments within the kingdoms of Gwynedd and Deheubarth. Complex internecine warfare meant that kingdoms continued to expand or contract in proportion to the relative military successes of individual rulers. At a time when their English and Irish counterparts would have regarded them as old-fashioned, short of money and certainly less streetwise than themselves, Welsh lords compensated for these deficiencies by showing their colours on the battlefields. In these volatile times, the greatest of the pre-Norman Welsh warleaders was Gruffudd ap Llywelyn, the son of Llywelyn ap Seisyll who had held Gwynedd between 1018 and 1023. Determined never to kneel as a supplicant to Anglo-Saxon kings, as some of his alliance-building predecessors had done, this cynical and utterly ruthless figure burst on the scene in 1039 when he seized Gwynedd and Powys. Shortly afterwards, he repulsed Mercian invaders at the battle of Rhyd-y-groes before, largely by fire and sword, turning his attention to establishing his primacy in Deheubarth and to expelling the local dynasty from Gwent and Morgannwg. Consistent only in the sense that he always improvised, Gruffudd ap Llywelyn made no secret of his ambition to conquer Deheubarth, thereby laying claim to the domination of the whole of Wales, a goal which had eluded all his predecessors. By slaying Gruffudd ap Rhydderch in 1055, he removed the final obstacle to his ambition. In the sense that he proved that the idea of uniting the whole of Wales was achievable, he was the greatest warleader of pre-Norman times. He was certainly the most head-strong and brazen-faced, and he had no qualms about forcibly disposing of rival Welsh princes, royal thegns and even a bishop in order to establish undisputed authority. In 1055 he poked his nose into English politics by reclaiming lands east of Offa's Dyke and by burning and looting Hereford. For a Welsh prince, this was a dangerous game for high stakes. He was also a flamboyant figure: the chronicle *Brenhinedd y Saesson* (The Kings of the English) referred to him as 'the golden-torqued king'. His mantle of state meant a good deal to him, and accounts from a later period suggest that the feasts which he hosted at his palace at Rhuddlan were wondrous affairs.

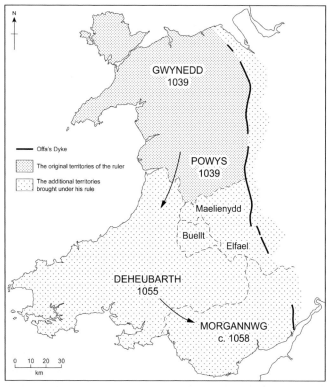

Map 3. For eight years, from 1055 until 1063, Wales found itself in the unprecedented position of having a native prince, Gruffudd ap Llywelyn, whose kingship was recognized by the whole of Wales. This map reveals the extent of his incursions prior to his grisly death in August 1063.

Probably because of his reputation for rapaciousness and brutal physical intimidation, Gruffudd ap Llywelyn has never figured prominently in the pantheon of Welsh patriot-heroes. By liquidating or silencing his rivals, he inevitably made many enemies and his assassination in 1063 was probably the result of internal treachery. His head, chopped off by his own people, was dispatched to his sworn enemy, Harold Godwinesson, as a token of surrender. Not for the first or last time in their history, the Welsh brought dishonour upon themselves. Of his considerable achievements there is no doubt, but the irony is that this powerful man, who had wielded greater power and influence than any of his predecessors, neglected to establish a dynasty. His two sons were too young to follow in his footsteps at the time of his death, and Wales was left feeble, fragmented and vulnerable to the incursions of a Norman army more powerful than anything ever seen before. Gruffudd ap Llywelyn's death at a critical juncture left a gaping political vacuum and a widespread sense of foreboding. In no sense had he been as charismatic a figure as Hywel Dda, but this formidable man stands out as the only native prince to have ruled the whole of Wales. For a brief period – from 1055 to 1063 – he had established a loose confederation in which every kingdom recognized his supremacy and a place in Welsh historical annals as 'the head and shield and defender of the Britons'. To Walter Map, he was the Welsh equivalent of Alexander the Great.

Nineteenth- and twentieth-century nationalist historians often depicted pre-Norman Wales as having already embarked on a pre-ordained march towards a Welsh nation state and viewed several of the aforementioned rulers as proto-nationalist figures. This interpretation is difficult to sustain. Although larger groupings emerged as this period wore on and although the likes of Rhodri Mawr, Hywel Dda and Gruffudd ap Llywelyn strove to bind the Welsh together, Welsh rulers identified first and foremost with their regional base and the prospects of extending it. They had no overarching vision similar to that which prompted the princes of Gwynedd to dream of creating a unified Welsh state in the thirteenth century. Who would wish to portray Gruffudd ap Llywelyn as a progenitor of Welsh statehood? This does not mean, as some have implied, that the Welsh were afflicted by some genetic weakness which rendered them incapable of creating and achieving political nationhood. Geographical impediments and poor communications meant that asserting effective central governance was well-nigh impossible, and institutional development was severely hampered from the ninth century onwards by segmentation – the fragmentation of Welsh families into branches – and by the ambitions of land-hungry Saxons and predatory Viking warlords. Moreover, with the coming of Duke William of Normandy in 1066, there were very real fears that the Welsh would not survive as a distinctive people, let alone become a nation state.

One further point needs to be made. A leading scholar has recently bemoaned the '*absence* of a social history of early medieval Wales'. This palpable defect is partly attributable to the dearth of source material, but it is also closely linked to a preoccupation with early medieval heroes and matters of identity rather than with subjects like settlement patterns, urbanization, commercial exchange and literacy, issues which have exercised European historians of late. Only time will tell whether Welsh historians are capable of rising to this challenge by offering a more multi-faceted understanding of the socio-economic dimensions of power in this turbulent age.

This brings us to our second theme, the Welsh law codes, an extremely complex but revealing body of material which not only throws light on legal custom and practice but also on the socio-economic framework. Since the law was one of the key components of Welsh national identity in the Middle Ages, the significance of its codification can scarcely be overstated. As we have seen, the key figure was the dignified, far-seeing Hywel Dda, who was remembered as having marshalled, restructured and codified existing legal practice and provided lawyers with a corpus of rules and customs which continued to evolve as the Middle Ages unfolded. It is no exaggeration to maintain that the law of Hywel (*cyfraith Hywel*) is one of Wales's most seminal contributions to European civilization. Around eighty Welsh and Latin manuscripts, containing medieval Welsh lawbooks and dating from the mid-thirteenth century, have survived. None of them explain the precise contribution of Hywel Dda to the process of codification, but Dafydd Jenkins, the principal authority on the subject, remains convinced that 'a Hywelian origin' exists for the common core of texts. Although we can be reasonably sure that Hywel took his role seriously and supervised the process of codifying a written text for the laws, the material lived 'in the mouths of lawyers more than in their books' and was continually revised in the light of changing social and economic circumstances. Native Welsh law was thus not so much a set of fixed rules as a fluid and malleable corpus of oral material which was open to a wide variety of interpretations. Over time, the law of Hywel changed, but much of its roots and content lay in the pre-Norman period.

What do the lawbooks tell us about early medieval society? It was unquestionably a society in which people were deeply sensible of the importance of kinship and neighbourhood. In Wales, as in Ireland, kinship was a complex process which involved the subtle interplay of tradition and innovation. It used to be thought that the economy was primarily pastoral and semi-nomadic, and that society was tribally based, but the pendulum has now swung heavily in favour of the notion of a stable, sedentary arable-based sector in which the extended family or clan-group lived in robust farmsteads. In terms of landholding, the general trend was for partible inheritance to nibble away at large estates (*gwelyau*) up until the mid-eleventh century. Apart from the slave, who possessed no rights, there were three important categories: the king (*brenin*), the noble (*breyr*) and the villein (*bilain*), who was tied to both lord and land. Within these groups, claims to status depended on descent, kinship and wealth. A huge socio-economic chain separated the elitist freeman (*breyr*) from the amorphous mass of the unfree (*bilain*). The former could boast a convincing lineage and revel in his legal standing and military prowess, while the latter was ground down by penury and mercilessly exploited for his muscle power in performing onerous labour services. For the unfree, daily life was both a struggle for survival and an exercise in grovelling subordination.

As a compendium of customary law, *cyfraith Hywel* was subject to piecemeal corrections, additions and emendations over a long period of time. These deal for the most part with matters relating to the royal court, land law, suretyship and the status of women. Although there is hardly a page in these valuable manuscripts which does not offer an insight into the mores of early medieval life, only a few of the highlights can be briefly presented here. Under Welsh law, the death penalty was imposed for serious theft rather than for murder. It was believed that those who embarked on wrongdoing by stealth had undermined trust within the community and imperilled the tradition of good neighbourliness. Such a crime thus deserved the harshest punishment. In practice, however, the severity of the punishment was determined by the circumstances of the crime. If a thief was discovered with stolen property 'in hand' he could be punished by death, but if his conviction rested on the evidence of witnesses he was more likely to be banished or sold into slavery. He who stole food to save himself from death by starvation was spared punishment, whilst he who helped himself to goods of modest value was given a relatively lenient fine. In many ways, punishment was reckoned to be less important than compensation (*galanas*) for the victim. *Galanas* was paid according to the status of the victim, and that act of compensation was designed to encourage reconciliation rather than vengeance. Closely associated with *galanas* was the offence known as *sarhaed* (insult), which entitled any victim who could prove that he had suffered harm either to his body or property – wrongdoing which was insulting and contemptible – to claim compensation.

One of the most extraordinary sections in the lawbooks is the treatment afforded to women. In an unashamedly male-dominated world, the law of Hywel tells us a good deal about matrimonial property and sexual norms. The price of a daughter's virginity at the time of her marriage was the *amobr*, which was paid to the lord for protecting the woman's honour until her marriage. Another payment, known as *agweddi* (a form of dower), was payable whenever a marriage ended before seven years had elapsed. This might occur by mutual consent, but could also be justified if the husband was impotent, leprous, a thrice-proven adulterer or plagued by halitosis. The wife who ended a marriage without legal justification forfeited her share of matrimonial property, though she was allowed to retain her *cowyll* (a gift from her husband on the occasion of her marriage or a sum of money calculated according to her social status). Women might not have had a stake in public life in Wales, but they maintained a greater measure of freedom than most of their counterparts in Europe.

The vision of Hywel Dda, the best known law-giver in the history of Wales, outlasted his death in 950 and, by providing the nucleus of legislative practice until the Acts of Union 1536–43, it had a

11. Among several striking illuminations contained in a Welsh lawbook (Peniarth 28) is the portrait of a Welsh king, holding a sceptre, dressed in classical attire and seated on a throne. (The National Library of Wales)

profound effect on Welsh life. The codification, amended and refined over a period of time, accelerated the process by which the Welsh could ponder the merits of political unity and national identity. For instance, *cyfraith Hywel* was pressed into service by the princes of Gwynedd in the thirteenth century to underpin and enhance their efforts to create a Welsh state. In a society in perpetual flux and change, the laws were a symbol of unity, the antithesis of the divisiveness which had bedevilled Wales for so long. Had the diverse systems of law which existed within the tribal society of the time been allowed to haemorrhage away in the tenth century, rather than being deliberately brought together to form a well-regarded legal repertoire, Wales would have been greatly impoverished and its future could conceivably have been very different. At a time when political and administrative unity was at a premium, the Welsh laws symbolized the otherness of Wales and provided a robust,

Welsh-language jurisprudential substructure of government. By any reckoning, the codification of the Welsh laws was a defining moment in the history of Wales.

Of crucial long-term importance to the shaping of Wales, too, was the kindling of the Christian flame, a process which occurred largely as a result of the extraordinary missionary activities of Celtic saints. For the best part of fifteen hundred years, Christianity would stamp its mark on Welsh culture and exercise a profound influence on people's spiritual values. Since our abiding image of this period is dominated by brutality, war and destruction, there is a danger of underestimating the growing importance of highly mobile Celtic saints who strained every sinew in their bid to serve God and the monastic settlements which they established, and the energizing influence this exerted on intellectual life. Before examining religious developments, however, it is as well to dispense immediately with two popular phrases – 'the Celtic Church' and 'Celtic Christianity' – which threaten to contaminate popular and scholarly discourse. Although there was considerable interaction between the Celtic countries of Ireland, Scotland, Wales, Brittany and Cornwall, the notion that a single monolithic 'Celtic Church' existed is untenable, since it presumes a much greater degree of homogeneity and organization than that which in fact existed. It makes far better sense to speak of a Christian church in Celtic-speaking lands and to recognize that practical, institutional and cultural differences prevailed within this context. The term 'Celtic Christianity' is an even more elusive, and potentially insidious, will o' the wisp. The recent upsurge of interest in 'Celtic' spirituality is associated with Druids, pagans and New Age travellers who, for the most part, are far more interested in enriching their own spiritual lives than in fostering a genuine understanding of the past. But respectable scholars, too, have rallied to this banner, and there is something faintly disconcerting about the way in which 'Celtic' theologians are so rashly prepared to leap over unbridgeable chronological chasms in order to reach conclusions based on widely scattered and flimsy evidence. Apologists for, and consumers of, 'Celtic' Christianity continue to multiply, but unless they find more convincing pegs on which to hang their reflections their work is unlikely to inspire confidence.

The unwary reader should also be warned of the perils of taking what medieval hagiographers wrote about their saintly forebears at their own valuation. The *Lives* of the Welsh saints were written five or six centuries after the times of the saints themselves, and their authors were naturally conscious of their duty to reward their chosen subjects not only by depicting them in flattering terms but also by establishing their reputation as men and women who could work wonders. Medieval hagiographers were seasoned spin doctors, propagandists and purveyors of legend, and it would be folly to rely on their testimony in its entirety. It is possible, of course, that some of their tales were based on oral tradition, but for the most part they had a politico-religious agenda to pursue, notably the need from the eleventh century onwards to defend the national character of the Welsh Church and to enhance the metropolitan claims of St David's. We should not lose sight of the fact that virtually all we know about St David, Wales's patron saint, is based on the myths spun by his eleventh-century hagiographer Rhygyfarch (d. 1099), whose aim was to demonstrate that this saintly figure was a herald of truth, a worker of miracles and the archbishop of a Welsh Church which was independent of Canterbury. By no stretch of the imagination were the lives of Welsh saints authentic biographies. A good many of them were written to enhance the importance of the cult which grew around the burial place or relics of a particular saint. It was through them that God worked wondrous miracles. When Samson, the Welsh-born sixth-century saint whose first *Life* was written in Brittany in the seventh or eighth century, was consecrated bishop, it was claimed that fire came forth from his mouth and nostrils; St Cadog enabled a barren woman to conceive; at Llanddewibrefi, St David made the ground rise beneath his feet so that he could address a gathering of priests and followers; and when Winefride was murdered by her spurned lover Caradog, her uncle St Beuno not only brought her back to life but also ensured that a holy spring gushed forth from the place where her head had fallen. This fountain of thaumaturgical water – St Winefride's spring at Holywell – became one of the seven wonders of Wales and remains to this day the best-preserved medieval pilgrimage centre in Britain. To the extent that the *Lives* portray saints as providers of supernatural power through miracles, they are no more than fairy stories. Not for the first or the last time, the creative imagination of the cultural elite in Wales deeply coloured the historical record, and it is difficult not to believe that the achievements of the Welsh saints, however gifted they might have been, were considerably less than the image ghosted for them by their medieval biographers. This material was, and continues to be, an engrossing read, but it serves to remind us that human beings are fallible and credulous creatures.

As might be imagined, it was not without a struggle that the task of bringing Christianity to the attention of social groups outside the elite of Romanized Britons was undertaken. That shrill Jeremiah, Gildas, launched punitive assaults on corrupt churchmen and laymen, claiming that natural disasters like plague and famine, as well as raids by the Picts, the Irish and the Saxons, were God's punishment for their sins. In the remote areas, where Roman influence had been small or ineffectual, pagan customs and beliefs continued to flourish. The Christian faith prospered best in the urban centres of the south-east, where the population was denser and where schools of learning existed. Between the fifth and eighth centuries, however, it was diffused by groups of monks, ascetics and itinerant preachers among a much wider cross section of the hitherto heathen population. Recent scholarship has strongly suggested that British Celts, Bretons, Galicians and others who could boast close kinship with seafaring neighbours developed a cultural and spiritual consciousness which was clearly identifiable as 'Atlantic'. A major work on the economic transition from antiquity to the early medieval period has maintained that Europe was an open rather than an 'inward-looking and economically stagnant place', and shipping routes played a critical role in bringing in new peoples, ideas and goods over relatively long distances. The unifying bond created and sustained by the Atlantic ocean was very much a reality and, as far as Wales was concerned, the sea acted as a major Christianizing superhighway. Wooden boats, filled with missionaries carrying with them the Christian message, travelled the western seaways, linking Wales with Devon, Cornwall, Somerset, Ireland and Brittany. Once on land, these pilgrim saints, travelling on foot, covered hundreds of miles in the heartlands of paganism in a bid to Christianize what was still a dangerous and hostile society.

It is difficult to assemble reliable and attested information about the Celtic saints. One suspects that their lives were much more conventional and humdrum than later hagiographies, suffused as they are with tales of how God worked wondrous miracles through them, would have us believe. But saints were unquestionably 'part of the package of Christianity' and their unusually high moral and devotional standards, as well as their alleged supernatural powers, placed them apart from the rest of society. One of the most influential early saints in south Wales was St Dyfrig (d. *c.* 550), whose fame as a teacher, organizer and bishop spread far beyond his native Erging (Archenfield) and Llandaff, and in the seventh-century *Life of Samson* he is referred to as *papa*. At his feet sat St Illtud (d. early sixth century), an attractive personality who embodied much that was best in early Christian civilization. This learned master of scripture and philosophy turned the monastery of Llantwit Major into a renowned centre of piety and intellectual liveliness. A generous and tender-hearted man, Illtud is reputed to have sailed on corn-ships to Brittany to relieve sufferers from famine. One of his brightest pupils, St Samson, travelled to Brittany in his mature years where he established a monastery and bishopric at Dol. In south-west Wales, the monastic ideals of St Teilo imprinted themselves on the hearts and minds of the people of Llandeilo Fawr in Carmarthenshire. No one doubted the quality of the scholarship displayed by Bishop Sulien (d. 1091) and his four sons, Rhygyfarch, Daniel, Ieuan and Arthen, at the extraordinary cloister of Llanbadarn Fawr, a centre of learning which remained a significant theatre of national identity throughout the Middle Ages. In north Wales, the cult of St Beuno (sixth century) was at Clynnog Fawr, Llŷn, and such was its influence that it survived the Protestant Reformation. Deiniol (mid-sixth century), the founder of the monasteries of Bangor Fawr and Bangor Is-coed, came to be regarded as the first bishop of Bangor. According to Bede, his Brythonic monastery at Bangor Is-coed was the most celebrated monastic house of British Christianity; it numbered over two thousand monks, 1,200 of whom were massacred at the battle of Chester *c.* 615.

The quintessential Welsh saint, however, was David and none was more highly venerated than he. Thanks largely to the influence of Rhygyfarch's *Vita Davidis*, composed in Llanbadarn Fawr *c.* 1095,

David came to be regarded as the patron saint of Wales. In his own lifetime (d. probably in 589), however, he was scarcely a national figure, and his chief sphere of influence was south-west Wales, where he became the acknowledged abbot-bishop of the church at St David's. Some of the earliest references to him are to be found in Irish sources. Ogam inscriptions, place-name and linguistic evidence reveal that the south-west was a Goidelic stronghold, and David himself was an exemplar of the spiritual influence of the early Christian Irish population. It is significant, for instance, that he was the only Welsh saint to figure in the Irish metrical martyrology composed *c.* 830 by Óengus of Tallaght. An early ninth-century Christian monument at Llanddewibrefi bears the Latin inscription: 'Here lies Idnerth son of Iago who has been killed on account of a depredation of St David.' The scholar Asser (d. 909) referred to David in his writings and, according to the vaticinatory poem *Armes Prydein* (The Prophecy of Britain) (*c.* 930), David was a militant warrior-saint whose 'pure banner' would rally his countrymen against the oppressive Saxons. In his depiction of him, Rhygyfarch must have depended on oral anecdotes as well as written scraps of evidence, and as his reputation gathered momentum dozens of churches and wells were dedicated to him, virtually all of them in south Wales. For a variety of reasons, therefore, St David became a genuinely potent symbol of the distinctive identity of the Welsh Church.

As we have already seen, Welsh saints were fêted for their alleged heroic qualities: they were warriors, seers, miracle-workers and healers capable of performing deeds far beyond the reach or ken of ordinary mortals. But a more sober and authentic description of them would be as loosely based groups of people devoted to prayer, learning and good works. The hallmark of their monastic settlements was austerity, simplicity and purity. The most widely used word for a church or Christian ecclesiastical foundation was *llan*, and it was commonly named after the saint or monk who founded or patronized it. Churches and monastic settlements, made of timber or wattle and daub, were Lilliputian by modern standards. Not until the twelfth century did stone churches become common. The church at Ynys Seiriol (Priestholm) was a mere 1.5 metres square, and even when the cathedral church of Llandaff was built of stone in 1120 it was no more than 12.2 metres long. There were also solitary retreats, often perched precariously on storm-tossed islands, where saints, mindful of the fact that the world was a sinful place, could distance themselves from the madding crowd and practise the kind of physical discomfort which would have left lifelong scars – mental and physical – on a more tender individual. When St Samson discovered that monastic life at Caldy Island was too congenial for his fastidious taste, he retreated to a fort or cave near the Severn where spartanism was de rigueur. Until their son, St Cadog, persuaded Gwynllyw and Gwladys that a milder regime would probably improve their spirits, they used to bathe naked all year round in the cold waters of the river Usk. Although celibacy was not expected of either bishop or priest, saints drove home the message that ascetic ideals strengthened people in virtue. St David always practised what he preached: a hard-working, puritanical man of modest means, he walked barefoot, dressed in animal skins and seems to have subsisted on water, bread and vegetables. Even the bare-breasted women, sent by the pagan Boia's wife to set his pulses racing, were firmly rebuffed. Poets and hagiographers referred to him as a waterman (*aquaticus*) and, ironically, many centuries later his career became a leitmotif in the homiletic literature of Welsh temperance reformers in Nonconformist Wales. Over succeeding centuries, too, relics (especially bones) and shrines associated with saints were regularly frequented by pilgrims. Hundreds of holy wells and springs, most of which were believed to have curative properties, had a magnetic appeal to the sick and the curious, and even in the 1990s there was a keen sense of disappointment in Wales when relics which were thought to contain the bones of St David turned out to be of twelfth-century provenance.

There were no dioceses or parishes in the modern sense, and episcopal jurisdiction was extremely loosely organized. In discussing the period up to around the eighth century, scholars refer to Welsh monasteries, but thereafter (even though no evidence exists for this terminology in the pre-Norman period) they use the terms *clas* or mother-church to describe these ecclesiastical communities. The so-called *clas* (better termed *monasterium*) became the linchpin of Christian life, and one of the reasons why clerical celibacy was not frowned upon was because it enabled the *claswr* to bequeath his share of the church and its revenues to his heir. Governed by an abbot, *clasau* were funded by dues paid by the daughter churches which they established and were inhabited by regular monks as well as non-monastic clergy. In piecemeal fashion, therefore, Christianity began to win the affections of growing numbers of people and become an integral part of their lives. As they toiled in harsh and unrewarding territories, their faith in God sustained their mission: 'The world cannot express in song bright and melodious, even though the grass and trees should sing, all thy glories, O true Lord . . . He who made the wonder of the world will save us, has saved us.' Indeed, there are strong grounds for believing that the spread of Christianity helped to develop a distinctive Welsh identity. The Welsh began to see themselves as a largely Christian people who, set apart from the ruffianly Anglo-Saxon pagans, were therefore culturally superior. A cameo of this striking cultural development occurred as early as 603, when the bishops and the learned representatives of the British Church met St Augustine, Pope Gregory's emissary, whose mission was to Romanize his hosts. Not content with seeking the co-operation of the Welsh in converting the godless Anglo-Saxons and their confederates, St Augustine insisted that they recognized him as their pre-eminent spiritual overlord, conformed to the Easter traditions approved by Rome, renounced the Celtic form of administering baptism and confirmation, and abandoned the peculiar tonsure (shaving a semi-circle of hair from the front of their heads) practised by their monks. These matters may appear inconsequential to us, but they touched raw nerves at the time. In particular, Easter – the time of the resurrection of Christ – represented the triumph of light over darkness, and as a result the calculation of the date needed to be both precise and convincing. Infuriated by St Augustine's haughty demeanour and abrasive style, the Welsh refused to renounce their own liturgical customs or suffer public humiliation at his hands. The difference of views was no trifling matter, and it was perfectly understandable that the Welsh should want to defend practices and ideals which they deeply cherished. One suspects that they rather enjoyed dispatching St Augustine with a flea in his ear. They were certainly the last of the Celts to comply with Roman ways: not until 768 did the Welsh opt for their habit of dating Easter. Christianity and the sword were never far apart and, eight centuries later, Richard Davies, bishop of St David's, argued that the Welsh, having doggedly resisted Roman overtures, had succumbed in the end only at the point of the Saxon blade.

Therefore, thanks largely to intensive sea-borne traffic between Ireland, Brittany and Wales, a remarkable new breed of men and women, conspicuous for their tireless devotion to the Christian cause, had embedded a spiritual culture which ran counter to the barbaric turmoils of the secular world. Although the ecclesiastical structures which had been established were arbitrary, loosely defined and hard to pin down, the Christian inheritance was already beginning to exercise a decisive influence in shaping the identity of Wales and its people.

Just as the Christian mission provided a spiritual dynamic, so, too, did cultural influences energize the Welsh. One of the most far-reaching changes was the emergence of the Welsh language on the historical stage and its success in becoming the dominant tongue. We do not know precisely how and when the transition from Brittonic to Welsh occurred, but it seems probable that by the mid-sixth century a vernacular tongue had emerged which was perfectly capable of conveying the heroic poetry of the bards. The famously declamatory Gildas, no lover of homespun poets who pandered to their amoral rulers, described them as a 'rascally crew . . . full of lies and foaming phlegm', but, twelve centuries later, Iolo Morganwg was closer to the truth when, with pardonable exaggeration, he claimed that 'our versification arrived at its full bloom of beauty in ages universally allowed to be dark'. Although the twelve *englynion* in the 'Cambridge Juvencus Manuscript', copied by an Irish scribe called Núada in a Welsh scriptorium in the second half of the ninth century, are the earliest surviving pieces of poetry in Welsh, the tradition of eulogy and elegy began with the heroic poems of Taliesin and Aneirin in the sixth century. It is an ironic fact that these founding fathers of the Welsh poetic tradition were located in the Old North, in the British kingdoms of Gododdin, Strathclyde and Rheged – that territory which is now broadly known as north-ern England and southern Scotland. Taliesin was the court poet of Rheged, a kingdom which included south-west Scotland and Cumberland, while Aneirin sang in the land of the Gododdin, whose capital was Din Eidyn (Edinburgh). The evidence for their existence and their works comes much later in the thirteenth century, but the oral transmission of heroic literature by the *Cynfeirdd* (Early Poets) was clearly immensely popular long before then.

Although we lack a clear sense of his personality, Taliesin (*fl.* late sixth century) achieved such fame as a poet that he was referred to as 'the Chief of Poets'. He delighted in depicting carnage on the battlefield and, of the twelve or thirteen poems reckoned to be authentic works by him, eight bolstered the glory of the warrior-king Urien, lord of Rheged, and his son Owain. Aneirin (*fl.* late sixth century) composed *c.* 570 a dark and intense tour de force known as *Y Gododdin*, a poem which runs to over a thousand lines. It tells the tragic tale of three hundred young warriors, hand-picked and trained by the chieftain Mynyddog Mwynfawr, lord of the Gododdin tribe, who launched a staggeringly foolhardy dawn raid on numerically superior Anglian forces at Catraeth (Catterick), in north Yorkshire. In spite of the courage of these 'golden-torqued' warriors, all but one of them perished on the battlefield: 'Before their hair turned grey', sang Aneirin, 'death came to them.' Tales of their glorious annihilation were sung by poets around campfires for many generations afterwards, and *Y Gododdin* acquired an iconic status in the Welsh heroic tradition as an early parable of the anguish associated with honourable national defeats. When eighteenth-century scholars stumbled across a manuscript copy of the poem, they jubilantly likened the discovery to that of America by Columbus. By the ninth century, however, the Taliesin tradition of panegyric verse seems to have shrivelled, and it may be significant that no eulogies or elegies have survived attesting to the greatness of kings like Merfyn Frych, Rhodri Mawr and Hywel Dda. It was replaced by saga poetry, which was markedly sceptical of the heroic verse which had glorified bloody strife and death. Indeed, the degree of hatred for the terrifying horrors of the past had become visceral. 'The Song of Llywarch Hen' (*Canu Llywarch Hen*) (*c.* 850), possibly composed at the royal and ecclesiastical centre at Llan-gors in Brycheiniog, is a moving lament which focuses on the recollections of an old curmudgeon frustrated by his senile impotence, while 'the Song of Heledd' (*Canu Heledd*) recounts in harrowingly emotional tones the death of her brother Cynddylan, ruler of Powys in the seventh century. The theme of loss and lamentation, as well as the recounting of past glories, was strongly conveyed, though we cannot tell how far this affected the collective identity or morale of the Welsh.

It is a commonplace, of course, that the literary culture was oral, and the dearth of written sources, though regrettable, simply reflects this fact. The oldest extant piece of written syntactical Welsh dates from the early ninth century and may be found in an entry in the Book of St Chad (also known as the Lichfield Gospels). This attractively decorated manuscript, prior to its removal by a circuitous route to the Cathedral library at Lichfield, spent part of its life at Llandeilo Fawr, Carmarthenshire, where it was exchanged for a valuable horse. The entry in Welsh, known as the *Surexit Memorandum*, records, in sixty-four words, the settlement of a dispute between two proprietors over a piece of land known as 'Tir Telych'. In an age of complex intrigues and mixed motives, this passage (even in translation) is a touching testimony of the willingness of ordinary neighbours to seek peaceful means of resolving conflict:

Tudfwlch the son of Llywyd and the son-in-law of Tudri arose to claim 'Tir Telych', which was in the hand of Elgu the son of Gelli and the tribe of Idwared. They disputed long about it; in the end they disjudge Tudri's son-in-law by law. The goodmen said to each other, 'Let us make peace.' Elgu gave afterwards a horse, three cows, three newly-calved cows, only in order that there might not be hatred between them from the ruling afterwards till the Day of Judgement.

More significant in the historical literature of early medieval Wales is *Historia Brittonum*, dated 829/30 and later attributed to Nennius (*fl.* 800), a work which offered a lively portrait of the history of the Britons from the Flood onwards and which exercised a powerful influence on the making of Geoffrey of Monmouth's *Historia Regum Britanniae*, c. 1139. Church scholars, too, their minds uncluttered by worldly concerns, came to occupy an increasingly influential role in conservation within centres of literary and artistic endeavour. By the mid-eleventh century, churches at St David's, Llanbadarn and Llantwit Major boasted the kind of creative milieu which enabled gifted and well-trained scribes to provide intellectual leadership, preserve Latin learning, compose *vitae* of the early saints and jot down in the margins of treatises snatches of Welsh poetry, prose tales and triads. Although their chief aim was

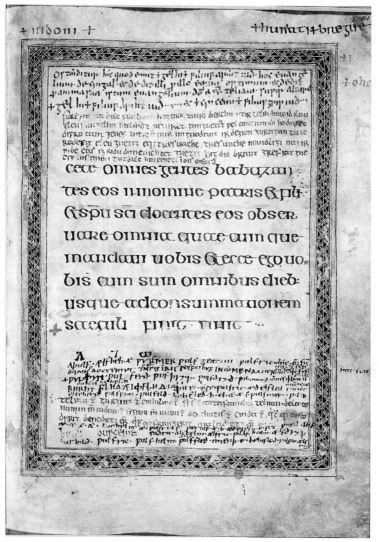

12. The Book of St Chad, otherwise known as the Lichfield Gospels, dates from the early ninth century. Marginalia on this page contains the first known piece of written syntactical Welsh. (The Dean and Chapter of Lichfield Cathedral)

to keep the flame of Christianity burning, there can be little doubt that their writings bore witness to their determination to hold on tightly to an honourable common heritage. This activity provides one of the more heartening aspects of life in this period.

In their own way, too, the inscribed stones which dotted the landscape provide tangible reminders not only of the faith of individuals during the Age of the Saints but also of the processes by which identities were visualized and shaped. Some 535 monuments in Wales have survived successive batterings by Atlantic storms over a period of sixteen hundred years. Those dating from the fifth to the seventh centuries were mostly upright monoliths, bearing inscriptions in Latin or Irish, or Irish inscriptions in the ogam alphabet (a unique form of writing in which strokes and notches marked along the edge of stone monuments represented alphabetic units). As early as the fourth century a colony of Irishmen from the kingdom of the Déisi, co. Waterford, had settled in south-west Wales and remained a sizeable settlement until the tenth century. Its members spoke both Goedelic and Brythonic, and used the ogam alphabet on inscribed stone memorials close to ecclesiastical sites. By contrast, in northwest Wales the monuments served as boundary markers or symbols of landownership by elites alongside Roman roads or near prehistoric and Roman remains. From the seventh to the ninth centuries cross-decorated stones proliferated, functioning for the most part as grave markers within churches or cemeteries, whilst between the ninth and eleventh centuries the imaginative talents of sculptors were reflected in free-standing decorated high crosses, such as those at Nevern and Carew in Pembrokeshire, whose elaborately carved interlaced designs replicated Celtic manuscript sources and called for an extremely high degree of craftsmanship. In this context, too, the importance of the Atlantic seaboard was critical, and current scholarly opinion offers a picture of dynamic and complex interaction and exchanges in the visual culture of the period. Both for their historical significance and artistic merit, these intriguing memorials were robust reminders of the assertion of local, regional and ethnic identities as well as a testament to the Christian inheritance.

When the Normans entered England in 1066, the existence of Wales as a distinctive geographical territory was widely recognized.

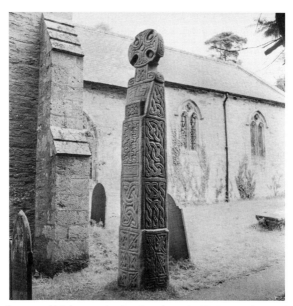

13. The decorated high cross in the churchyard of St Brynach parish church, Nevern, in Pembrokeshire, is one of the most splendid Christian monuments in Wales. (Crown Copyright: Royal Commission on the Ancient and Historical Monuments of Wales)

Thanks to the poets and other transmitters of the historical past, the Britons had retained their historic identity. Cambro-Latin writers spoke of Wales as *Britannia* and the Welsh as *Britones*, and not until the twelfth century were these appellations replaced by the incoming Normans with the terms *Wales* and *Welsh*, which derived from the Old English *Walh* or *Wealh* – derogatory nouns meaning 'foreign land' and 'foreigners'. As early as the seventh century, however, the noun *Cymry* (later changed orthographically to *Cymru*), a word which derives from the Celtic *Cambrogi* (people of the same district or country), had been used in a praise poem to Cadwallon (d. 634), king of Gwynedd, and the early tenth-century poem *Armes Prydein*, the most overtly political verse of its day, referred to the Welsh people as *Cymry*. Among the *Cymry*, a sense of regional consciousness was inevitably stronger than the concept of nationhood, but nevertheless they had their own tongue, their own literature and their own laws. Their admiration for the saints, their endless curiosity about their cults and their readiness to embrace the essentials of the Christian faith which had been bestowed upon their forebears by God were also powerful spurs to greater pride in their identity. The idea of *Cymru* had become a reality. How its rulers and people would react to the arrival of resourceful and heavily armed Norman invaders will be our next theme.

3

The Anglo-Norman conquerors,
c. 1063–1282

In May 1900 Professor John Edward Lloyd of Bangor delivered a lecture, entitled 'Wales and the coming of the Normans', to the Honourable Society of Cymmrodorion in London. Dressed in an immaculate dark grey suit and with his high collar, shirt front and cuffs heavily starched, Lloyd spoke with the austere elegance and luminous clarity of the quintessential Victorian don, and even at this early stage in his career the superior talents of a historian who later became known as 'the lantern-bearer of the lost centuries' were widely appreciated. Although Lloyd was not the most inspiring lecturer – he preferred, for instance, to say 'King Henry dismounted from his steed' rather than 'Henry got off his horse' – he had an unsurpassed knowledge of his field and an unflagging desire to raise intellectual standards. Indeed, Lloyd was the founding father of Welsh medieval studies. His address to the Cymmrodorion provided a foretaste of his magisterial two-volume *A History of Wales from the Earliest Times to the Edwardian Conquest*, published in 1911, a work which stands as a major landmark in the historiography of Wales. Whereas his predecessors had written from their hearts rather than with their heads, Lloyd turned the history of medieval Wales into a serious academic exercise. His work still occupies a hallowed place in Welsh historical writing, and scholars continue to consult his books with profit and pleasure.

Nevertheless, as one would expect, over the past hundred years medieval scholars have revisited the subject from different perspectives, and of late the emphasis on narrative in the grand manner has in general been replaced by greater attention to social analysis and cultural appreciation. Sources much more abundant and diverse than were available in Lloyd's day are nowadays explored, and their availability has enabled scholars to illuminate the lives of inarticulate people and also to provoke ripples of historical controversy. In recent times, two related developments have helped to make the period from the coming of the Normans to the Edwardian conquest much more intelligible and interesting. First, revisionist historians are no longer as prone as their forebears were to lock themselves into the embalmed world of anglocentricity. It has become abundantly clear that during this period Wales was increasingly integrated with, and influenced by, continental Europe. Secondly, no self-respecting medieval historian now believes that the history of Wales, in an era when the Anglo-Normans sought to extend royal authority within the Celtic nations, can be written without due reference to distinctive parallel experiences in Scotland and Ireland. Over the period as a whole, although Wales became a conquered nation, it also became more cosmopolitan, more ethnically and culturally diverse, and more prone to multiple loyalties. These new and refreshing perspectives offer a more convincing interpretative framework for the human drama which accompanied the expansion of the Anglo-Norman realm.

At the outset, we need to emphasize the ideological triggers which ignited the Anglo-Norman incursions into Wales from the latter half of the eleventh century onwards. The Norman conquistadores, who were deeply proud of their reputation as the most brutally proficient fighting stock in Europe and of their achievement in crushing the Anglo-Saxon armies at Hastings and in bringing the Byzantines and Latins in southern Italy, as well as Moslem armies in Sicily, under their heel, were determined to impose their own political, social and cultural norms upon the Celtic peoples. They were motivated by a selective and self-interested pursuit of their own territorial ambitions, and their grotesquely partial view of the native Welsh became a licence for them to brutalize people with impunity. Demeaning stereotypes abounded: the Welsh were depicted as 'a country breeding men of a bestial type', and even Gerald of Wales, who might have been expected to know better, described them as feckless, lazy, promiscuous, and brutal savages. The Welsh were *barbari* (barbarians), an inferior people who stood in urgent need of a sound dose of civilizing values. In their scramble for land and power, the incoming French knights – men of noble blood – had no qualms about shedding the blood of 'rude' and 'immoral' people and denigrating the significance and relevance of native traditions. Their mission was to subjugate and transform. The anonymous compiler of *Brut y Tywysogyon*, writing at Strata Florida abbey, was convinced that the Anglo-Normans were determined 'to annihilate all the Britons so that the name of the Britons should never more be remembered'. Affecting an air of cultural superiority was one of the least attractive traits of the all-conquering incomers, and the 'us' and 'them' mentality which prevailed in Wales and Ireland caused bitter ethnic divisions within their fragmented and vulnerable societies. In contrast, Scotland could boast a stable regal tradition and a robust territorial base which enabled it to resist Anglo-Norman ambitions. It is significant that, by the early twelfth century, Welsh writers of Latin were styling their countrymen *Walenses* (Welsh) and their country *Wallia* (Wales) in the manner of their Anglo-Norman counterparts. This nomenclature reflected English overlordship but also suggested perhaps the glimmer of a desire to convey a more precise definition in Latin of the terms *Cymry* and *Cymru*.

Nothing can disguise the fact that the tactics of the hard-fisted Norman adventurers who spearheaded military incursions were based on brutal intimidation. As horsemen, soldiers and builders, they were tough, resilient and hungry for land and success. They possessed superior weapons and battle dress, and we should not allow the chivalric images of the times to mask the reality of the atrocities which accompanied the battles, skirmishes, sieges, depredations and pillages that occurred as Norman forces rode roughshod over Welsh territories from around 1067 onwards. This was essentially a military enterprise, governed by the power of the sword, and its ultimate aim, certainly by the thirteenth century, was political and cultural uniformity. But although the Welsh could never match the Normans for sheer weapon power, they, too, were geared for war, especially guerrilla warfare based on fleet-footed and skilful hit-and-run raids. The poets who supported their resistance were preoccupied with gallantry, glory and heroic failure, and there was much truth in Gerald of Wales's dictum that the Welsh deemed it a privilege to be cut down in battle but a disgrace to die in bed. They were certainly not trembling innocents: Welsh court poetry is peppered with references to the 'swilling of blood', 'stiff red corpses' and 'bowels on thorns'. Some examples of bloodlust and revenge make the flesh creep: in the kingdom of Arwystli in 1129–30 seven first cousins were blinded, castrated or assassinated by members of their family. In 1130 Maredudd ap Bleddyn of Powys deprived his nephew Llywelyn ab Owain of his eyes and testicles. Even the widely admired Lord Rhys, Prince of Deheubarth (d. 1197), committed incest with his niece. War, bloodshed and turmoil were endemic, and it was with a palpable sigh of relief that a Welsh chronicler noted under the year 1122: 'A year in which there was peace.'

Yet, the task of subjugating Wales was a piecemeal affair, carried out in a protracted, bloody and exhausting manner. William the Conqueror was not much interested in Wales, though he briefly sought to impose his will by leading his army as far as St David's in the summer of 1081. For the most part, the task was entrusted to a trio of überhawks who were licensed to organize and marshal a three-pronged invasion along the principal theatres of war on the Welsh Marches: William Fitz Osbern at Hereford, Roger of Montgomery at Shrewsbury and the gargantuan Hugh of Avranches at Chester were extraordinarily ruthless lords who owed their authority to royal patronage and who governed the frontier with an iron fist. Acting largely on their own initiative, they and their allies launched punitive raids in south, mid- and north Wales and steadily picked off the most threatening Welsh dissidents. As we shall see, however, the Welsh were not easily vanquished, especially those who dwelt in the rugged and inhospitable upland ranges. The Norman marauders therefore focused their energies on establishing lasting military and territorial domination over the more fertile and productive arable lowlands of the borders and of south and east Wales. By the mid-twelfth century the country had become divided between *Marchia Walliae* (March of Wales), which lay under the control of marcher lords and, to a lesser extent, the English Crown, and *Pura Wallia* (Welsh Wales), the mainly northern and western areas which remained in the hands of independent Welsh rulers. The March was such a diverse and nebulous frontier region that the innocent incomer could never be certain whether he had entered Wales or not. It

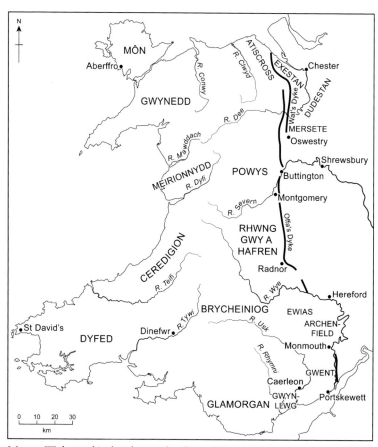

Map 4. Wales and its borders in the eleventh century: the eastern boundaries were in a state of flux, and were shaped and reshaped largely by changing military fortunes.

changed its shape according to the fortunes of both Crown and marcher lords, and also according to the vagaries of war. Marcher lords inherited and maintained exclusive powers and privileges which meant that they were not bound either by the king's writ or by English common law. Many of them positively revelled in their administrative and judicial independence. In 1250 one defiant marcher lord forced a royal messenger bearing a writ from Henry III to swallow both the writ and the seal. Buoyed by their own sense of racial supremacy and military invincibility, Norman lords extended their authority and possessions with the same eye for the main chance that characterized their expansion in the eastern Mediterranean, the Iberian peninsula and the shores of the Baltic. The most congenial river valleys and coastal plains in Wales thus began to resonate with the sounds of accents from Normandy, Anjou, Maine and Brittany. How tongue-twisting names like de Neufmarché, de Cantilupe and de Mortimer must have bemused monoglot Welsh speakers who found themselves living in a part of the country which was under alien rule and which was not Wales.

Although Norman power owed much to the proficiency of horsemen and crossbowmen, and to the devastating effects of siege weapons, the most vital cog in their military machine was the castle. This was an entirely new fortification in Wales, and it proved to be of critical importance in the most unstable and vulnerable regions. Initially, the unsophisticated, hastily constructed earthen works known as motte-and-bailey castles – some 600 in all – were not equipped to blunt the ambitions of determined Welsh insurgents, but when they were replaced by stone-built fortifications during the course of the twelfth century, the castle became the supreme symbol of military strength and colonization. Some of these refortified structures – the stone keep at Chepstow, the three-storeyed round tower at Tretower and the monumental great keep at Pembroke – were intended to terrify the Welsh and drive them into the most inhospitable mountain ranges. But even these strongholds were overshadowed by the forbidding military fortifications built by Edward I between 1277 and 1295 in order to achieve long-term security for the English realm and bend the Welsh princes to his will as their undisputed feudal overlord. A fully garrisoned, almost impregnable ring of stone castles, built at an astonishing cost of around £175,000 according to the blueprint of Savoyard master masons (notably Master James of St George), was constructed at selected sites in north Wales which had both strategic and economic potential to ensure that never again would the turbulent Welsh violate the king's peace. These impressive and intimidating monuments of military architecture compare favourably with any rival enterprise in Europe, but for the Welsh they were grim reminders that by the end of the thirteenth century they were assuredly a conquered people.

14. The enormously powerful Pembroke Castle, built in stone by William Marshall, was a symbol of conquest. Its late twelfth-century keep, with its huge cylindrical tower and stone dome, figures among its most notable architectural features. (Crown Copyright: Royal Commission on the Ancient and Historical Monuments of Wales)

The proliferation of castles was closely associated with the development of urban plantations, which were also agents of conquest because they housed incoming settlers, the overwhelming majority of whom were English and who, 'cowering under the skirts of their military protectors and sponsors', were just as prominent symbols of colonization as the fortifications which towered above them. Incomers, of course, had always settled in Wales, but the scale of the Anglo-Norman invasion, both military and civilian, was much greater than any previous incursion. Early urban plantations began to characterize the frontier and the coastal plains of the south, and when Edward I established an intimidating array of castle-boroughs in north Wales from 1277 onwards the country became even more heavily studded with deeply symbolic plantations which reminded people that a major shift had occurred in the balance of power. The all-conquering and predatory elite of settlers not only created walled towns in the shadow of castles but also established manorial

organization and demesne farming in favoured sites known as
'Englishries'. Pugnacious settlers from south-west England elbowed
aside peasants in southern Gower in order to set up a highly durable
anglicizing plantation known as *Gower Anglicana*. With the encouragement of Henry I, a Flemish colony led by Wizo and Tancard was
deliberately planted *c*. 1109 in the *cantrefi* (cantreds) of Rhos and
Daugleddau in south Pembrokeshire. As a piece of local ethnic
cleansing it was conspicuously successful, for the result was a dividing *Landsker* which, in time, had the effect of dividing the county
almost exactly between Welsh-speakers in the north and English-
speakers in the south. As late as the Elizabethan period, George
Owen of Henllys noted that whenever a Welshman crossed the
divide into 'Little England beyond Wales', he invited derisive cries
of 'looke there goeth a Welshman' as if he was a being from another
world. These highly exclusive and durable territories were power
blocs which provided further tangible proof that incomers represented the 'haves' of society.

The Church, too, was pressed into service as a tool of conquest
and a means of imposing an alien model. Paradoxically, Norman
barons who were ferocious opportunists in the secular domain were
not averse to being depicted as sponsors of muscular piety. But first,
Norman brooms swept clean. Having decided that hardly any part
of the native ecclesiastical tradition was worthy of preservation,
they eliminated the bulk of it. Indeed, in many respects, the impact
of the Normans on ecclesiastical life was even more dramatic than
the changes which they wrought in secular society. Throughout
Christendom they had a reputation as militant reformers, and in
Wales wholesale changes were instituted based on tried and tested
models within continental Europe. These changes proved to be every
bit as profound as those set in train at the time of the Protestant
Reformation.

Ecclesiastical reform was driven by powerful political imperatives.
When William the Conqueror embarked on his celebrated 'pilgrimage' to St David's in 1081, he was making a political statement
regarding the authority of Canterbury over Wales. The Normans
were determined to ensure that prelates and princes were unswerving
in their allegiance to Canterbury. Four territorial dioceses were
established, and these were underpinned by an infrastructure of

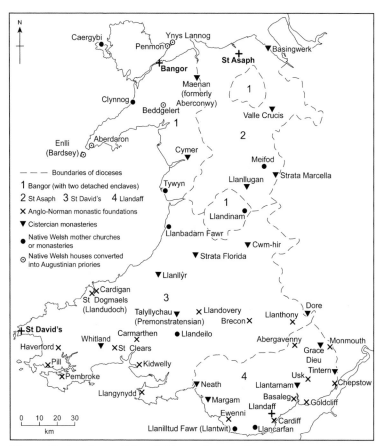

Map 5. During the twelfth and thirteenth centuries native monasticism in Wales was replaced by European monastic life, in which the influence of the Cistercians was paramount. This map shows the dioceses and monasteries of Wales *c.* 1300.

archdeaconries, rural deaneries and parishes. Pliant bishops were appointed to preside over changes in liturgy and to eradicate the names of Welsh saints in favour of saints of the Roman Church. Having ripped the heart out of the *clasau*, the Welsh bishops embarked on an impressive programme of building activity. The striking west front at Llandaff and the beautiful nave at St David's represent some of the finest examples of medieval architecture, and recent discoveries in the field of visual culture have revealed that the native Welsh were by no means insulated from the prevailing spiritual and intellectual impulses on the continent, or insensitive to artistic beauty.

Continental influences became a particularly powerful element in Welsh monasticism as Norman barons, who liked to think of themselves as soldiers of Christ, offered monks and nuns from Tiron, Savigny and especially Cîteaux the opportunity to make headway in Wales. The Benedictines – the Black Monks – were used as an instrument of colonial authority to squeeze wealth from hard-pressed people, and one of the most galling features of the times was the cynical manner in which churches, lands and tithes in Wales were stripped of their assets in favour of abbeys in Normandy and England. This vacuum was filled by the Cistercian order – the White Monks – whose followers were never associated in people's minds with castellated settlements because they searched for remote but congenial places 'far from the concourse of men', where they built monasteries of striking beauty in the Burgundian manner at places like Tintern, Strata Florida and Valle Crucis. Monks arrived from Clairvaux from 1140 onwards and settled at the fountain-head of the order in *Pura Wallia* at Whitland in 1151. Of over 600 Cistercian houses founded by the thirteenth century, fifteen were located in Wales, including two tiny nunneries, in which unremitting manual toil and devout worship were expected. Cistercians were single-minded people whose withdrawal from the public sphere did not prevent them from developing a dynamic mission which took them into virtually every Welsh kingdom and enabled them to become indigenized. Yet, for all their gifts, Cistercians were self-assured to the point of smugness, and those who regretted the use of the reformed Welsh Church as an arena for competing interests probably sympathized with William of Malmesbury's acerbic description of this order as the one which provided 'the surest road to heaven'.

Over a period of two hundred years, therefore, the Anglo-Normans planted within Wales diverse and intriguing configurations, including castles, garrisons, boroughs, lordships and monastic houses, which not only changed the landscape but also underpinned the body politic of the conqueror. However, three points need emphasizing. First, the task of subjugating Wales and converting

15. The early thirteenth-century west doorway to the Cistercian abbey at Strata Florida (the Vale of the Flowers) in Cardiganshire. Part of *Brut y Tywysogyon* was written in this abbey and several native rulers were buried in its grounds. It is believed that Dafydd ap Gwilym lies buried under a yew tree in the middle of the graveyard. (Crown Copyright: Royal Commission on the Ancient and Historical Monuments of Wales)

the people to the Anglo-Norman view of the world proved to be a curiously incoherent, uneven and protracted process which took the best part of two centuries to complete. Until 1282–3 the conquest was largely limited to the prosperous lowland areas, where castles, boroughs and manors proliferated, while in the rugged upland areas of the north and west, where would-be rebel native princes seethed and plotted, there were periods when the Welsh seized the political initiative and threatened to forge native Wales into a single political unit. Secondly, throughout this period the Welsh proved sufficiently adaptable and flexible to assimilate a variety of new fashions and styles and to tailor them to their own particular needs and aspirations. Ironically, their willingness to widen their horizons ushered in new opportunities to express their own national identity based on language, law and history. Thirdly, even though there were some native princes who harboured intensely ambivalent feelings towards the kings of England and the Anglo-Norman barons, overall there was a widespread sense of moral indignation about the brutal behaviour of gangs of sword-wielding Norman warriors. Welsh rejoicing knew no bounds when the much-hated Robert of Rhuddlan was assassinated by the followers of Gruffudd ap Cynan at Degannwy in 1093 and his severed head pinned to the mast of a ship. Welsh poems and romances bristle with accounts of how the sight of streaming gore, severed heads and bleeding lances was sweet revenge for the humiliations heaped upon them. A cloud of witnesses, voicing their contempt for the unwelcome invaders at different stages in this period, claimed that it was both necessary and legitimate for the Welsh to throw off the Norman yoke. In a moving lament on the upheavals caused by overbearing Normans at the end of the eleventh century, the influential cleric and man of letters Rhygyfarch complained: 'One vile Norman intimidates a hundred natives with his command, and terrifies them with his look ... Our limbs are cut off, we are lacerated, our necks condemned to death, and chains are put on our arms.' In 1163 the stubborn spirit of the Welsh was encapsulated in the brave words (recorded by Gerald of Wales) of an aged inhabitant of Pencader who informed Henry II that the Welsh, and only the Welsh, would answer to the Supreme Judge on behalf of 'this small corner of the earth'. More remarkable still was the groundswell of disaffection and resentment which emboldened the supporters of Llywelyn ap Gruffudd (d. 1282) to declare in 1255 that they would prefer to 'be slain in war for their liberty than suffer themselves to be unrighteously trampled upon by foreigners'. Eloquent resolutions of defiance of this kind against the oppression which weighed them down serve to remind us that even the fissured and fragmented Welsh were prepared to risk armed confrontation in the hour of need.

Yet, in such uneasy and turbulent times, when military and psychological pressures preyed on men's minds, a complex array of responses to the might of the Normans was elicited from native princes. These included masterly inactivity, artful procrastination, uneasy compromises, tetchy stand-offs, surly truces and overt resistance. Bold statements of defiance should not blind us to the fact that the Welsh were perfectly capable of accommodating the alien conquerors as well as betraying their own princes. During these strife-torn years, the resistance to the Anglo-Normans included instances of irresolution as well as courage, impracticality as well as idealism, selfishness as well as altruism. In a world where the colonizer and the colonized kept a wary eye on each other, loyalties fluctuated and alliances were hard, and sometimes impossible, to sustain.

Prudent alliances helped to blunt the edge of conquest and to encourage, at least for short periods of time, peaceful co-existence. Although Norman–Welsh marriages were, in the last resort, a tangible sign of submission to dominant incomers, they were also a means for both sides to extend their territorial authority and to cement political partnerships. The surviving evidence tells us little about the conduct or role of women in the processes of government, but some of them clearly exercised influence within family and dynastic networks. It would be too easy to write them off as marriage pawns in a political game run by men. Gerald of Wales tartly observed that his grandfather, Gerald of Windsor, had married the ravishing Welsh princess Nest (*fl.* 1100–20), daughter of Rhys ap Tewdwr, in order to make 'deeper roots for himself and his dependants in those parts', but the manner in which Nest inveigled many men, including the philandering Henry I, into her bed and the fact that she was a willing accomplice in her celebrated abduction from Cilgerran Castle by Owain ap Cadwgan of Powys in 1109 suggests that a sassy-tongued, resolute woman could wield considerable influence even in a testosterone-fuelled society. Even some of the greatest political figures of the times deliberately pandered to the English Crown and the alien aristocracy. The Lord Rhys of Deheubarth cultivated alliances with Norman colonists by arranging marriages for his sons and daughters with the families of FitzMartin, lord of Cemais, and Braose, lord of Brycheiniog, Builth and Radnor, thereby enabling him to extend the political influence of the house of Deheubarth. In 1205 Llywelyn ab Iorwerth (d. 1240) married Joan, the natural daughter of King John, and subsequently was at considerable pains to ensure that nearly all his children married into prominent aristocratic marcher families. At critical moments, women played an important role in the careers of influential Welsh princes. Senana, wife of Gruffudd ap Llywelyn (d. 1244), actively negotiated her headstrong husband's release from captivity, while Eleanor de Montfort, wife of Llywelyn ap Gruffudd, displayed a high degree of diplomatic finesse in mediating between her husband and Edward I during the latter stages of the Welsh wars of independence. Although their freedom of action was severely circumscribed, wise and opportunistic women were perfectly capable at times of challenging male prerogatives and achieving tactical successes.

Individuals who had a foot in both Welsh and Norman camps were bound to nurse ambivalent views about colonization. The classic example is Gerald of Wales, an exceptionally erudite and opinionated writer and churchman who, on the one hand, believed that Wales was 'a portion of the kingdom of England, and not a kingdom in itself' but, on the other, lamented the demise of the term 'British' (*gens Britannica*) at the hands of 'a corrupt word … now called Welsh (*Walensica*)'. Although he made great capital of the fact that he belonged both to the Welsh and the Normans, only a quarter of the blood coursing through his veins was Welsh. The great-grandson of the doughty warrior Rhys ap Tewdwr, he was the youngest of four sons born at Manorbier, Pembrokeshire, to William de Barri and Angharad. Able thus to boast of Norman and Welsh lineage, he could speak French, Latin, English and Welsh (though the last not fluently). As a product of marcher society, a royal clerk and an ecclesiastic, he had fingers in many pies. Gerald could not live without books and he was happiest in his study. He loved words, both spoken and written, and he used them with precision, wit and wounding clarity. As a mirror of the fraught Cambro-Norman world, his rich and diverse corpus of writings is of cardinal importance within a European context, but the fact that he was the first to publish works on Wales makes him a very special

16. Giraldus Cambrensis (*c.* 1146–1223) or Gerald of Wales was a prolific and colourful writer whose chronicles painted a unique picture of Wales under the Normans. He depicted the Welsh as warm, compassionate, eloquent, stubborn, inconstant and devoted to the defence of their country. (Syndics of Cambridge University Library)

figure. His *Itinerarium Kambriae* (Journey through Wales) (1191) and *Descriptio Kambriae* (Description of Wales) (1194) are remarkably sophisticated, albeit partial, pieces of ethnographic writing, and there is no doubt that our understanding of the late twelfth century would have been much the poorer had his works not survived. His shrewd eye for observation, his delight in anecdotal evidence and malicious gossip, and his interpretation of the ethnic and cultural tensions of his times have made him the most quotable of medieval commentators. His colourful diatribes against his many enemies were extraordinary, and he would have made a splendid tabloid columnist. He portrayed a people who subsisted on bread, oats, dairy products and meat, who practised transhumance and who were strangers to urban life. Hair was cut short and shaped around the eyes and ears, and teeth were so assiduously cleaned with green hazel shoots and woollen cloths that they shone like ivory. The Welsh were proud of their roots, frugal, thin-skinned, hospitable, music-loving, fickle, immoral and mendacious. Brave and determined warriors, they constantly pressed self-destructive buttons in their bid to protect their freedoms. Such observations, though not always truthful or reliable, were never less than entertaining.

Gerald of Wales was right to highlight political disunity among the Welsh. Like those of the Irish, their territorial ambitions were dogged by internecine strife, tribal feuds and succession practices which rendered them vulnerable to incursions by the marcher lords and the English Crown. Yet, largely because the military supervision exercised by the Anglo-Norman lords and the kings of England was generally loose and spasmodic, from time to time Welsh princes were able to recover the initiative, notably in west and north Wales. Whenever they sensed that the colonizers were distracted by events elsewhere or that the Crown was preoccupied by civil strife in England, nimble guerrilla fighters seized opportunities to raze castles and recover lands. Several substantial gains were registered during 1094–1100 and 1135–54, as valorous Welsh princes strove to cast off the Norman yoke. Gruffudd ap Cynan (c. 1055–1137), a warrior who harboured a grudge against Norman interlopers, returned from exile in Ireland to free Gwynedd west of the Conwy from the stranglehold imposed by alien lords and the forces of Henry I, while in the war-torn south-west his youngest daughter Gwenllïan, a beautiful princess so terrifyingly androgynous that she was likened by Gerald of Wales to the Queen of the Amazons, revealed remarkable martial prowess on the battlefield. Welsh soldiers in the legions of Deheubarth salivated at the prospect of fighting under her banner and she met her death with characteristically reckless courage during an assault on Kidwelly Castle in 1136, at a spot known to this day as 'Gwenllïan's field'. Such derring-do seized the popular imagination – 'Gwenllïan!' subsequently became a potent rallying cry, at least in folklore – and nourished the spirit of rebellion. However, whenever the Welsh proved too audacious for their own good, the kings of England displayed their military authority and refused to yield an inch from their conviction that the lords of Wales were duty-bound to do homage and fealty to the

Crown. Four expeditions into Wales by Henry II in the mid-twelfth century were high-profile reminders that the Welsh were his clients and, even if they did deliver their oaths of allegiance to the Crown through gritted teeth, there was no doubting their subordinate status.

Nevertheless, such setbacks did nothing to dampen the ardour of Owain Gwynedd (*c.* 1100–70), son of Gruffudd ap Cynan, and Rhys ap Gruffudd (1132–97), both of whom strove hard to resist the wholesale Normanization of Wales by turning Gwynedd and Deheubarth respectively into defensible kingdoms. How such rulers styled themselves, and expected others to recognize them, was of considerable importance. In his later years, Owain Gwynedd basked in the suffix Prince of the Welsh (*princeps Wallensium*), while Rhys ap Gruffudd, out of courtesy perhaps, became rather grandly known as 'the Lord Rhys'. The wise statesmanship of the former laid the foundations for the future pre-eminence of the house of Gwynedd, but the latter – hailed as 'conqueror of the mighty' – made the fatal mistake of siring eight legitimate and seven illegitimate sons, a recipe for dynastic discord following his death in 1197. With the kingdom of Powys reduced to impotence by internal feuds and the fissures induced by gavelkind, the initiative passed decisively to Gwynedd, thereby opening the way for a period during which the dream of an independent Wales took a giant step forward.

What, then, were the factors which enabled Llywelyn ab Iorwerth (*c.* 1173–1240) and his grandson Llywelyn ap Gruffudd (d. 1282), the two greatest rulers of medieval Wales, to believe that it was possible to foster a common sense of political unity in which the supremacy of Gwynedd as a miniature feudal state was assured and its rulers recognized by the English Crown as princes of Wales (*princeps Wallie*)?

Profound socio-economic changes occurred during the thirteenth century, and these had the effect of breaking down the isolation of communities. Although the geographical location of Gwynedd rendered it a power bloc not easily breached or conquered by Anglo-Norman armies, its people were much more mobile than ever before. Many Welsh soldiers responded to the call to serve in the Crusades or to serve the Crown in France, and merchants, traders and sailors travelled by land and sea to locations many thousands of miles from

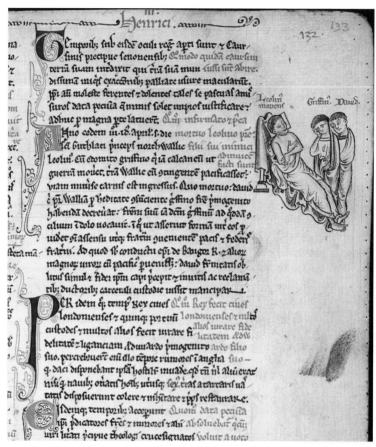

17. Llywelyn ab Iorwerth (*c.* 1173–1240), otherwise known as Llywelyn Fawr (Llywelyn the Great), was one of the wisest and most accomplished princes of Gwynedd. This posthumous depiction, by Matthew Paris, *c.* 1259, shows him with his sons Gruffudd and Dafydd. (The Master and Fellows of Corpus Christi College, Cambridge)

their native patch. The well-travelled, educated elite were keenly aware of the development of sophisticated feudal models within Europe, and there were good reasons for believing that *Pura Wallia*, too, could fashion a robust polity. Demographic growth was fuelling change. By 1300 the population of Wales had risen to 300,000, a figure not to be reached again until the early Stuart period. The climate was remarkably benign – the mean annual temperature was around two degrees centigrade higher than it is now – and this ushered in new opportunities for livestock farmers and town dwellers to bring more land into cultivation. By the end of the twelfth century slavery was becoming a thing of the past, and freemen, living in substantial homes on the fringes of open-field arable lands and common wastes, formed a majority within the population. Bondmen and women were throwing off their shackles in large numbers and adapting their lives to a new world in which free status brought greater security and self-esteem. In one of his more dubious generalizations, Gerald of Wales maintained that the Welsh were strangers to urban life and were content to live in flimsy wattled huts on the fringes of woodland. The truth is that between *c.* 1100 and *c.* 1300, the proportion of people living in towns in Wales increased from next to nothing to 10 per cent. While the most flourishing town plantations were located in Norman-controlled locations along the frontier and the coastal plains of the south, and where well-heeled alien burgesses were granted special privileges, the urban landscape of north-west Wales was also transformed. Boroughs were a catalyst for the economy of the hinterland. The main beneficiaries, of course, were colonizers, merchants and burgesses, but the socio-economic surge also brought commercial prosperity to small Welsh ports like Llan-faes, Nefyn and Pwllheli. Although no mint was established in Wales, increasingly complex monetary exchanges were instituted in Gwynedd, the cattle and wool trade was thriving, and by the mid-thirteenth century it could be argued that the economy of the Principality was more enterprising and flexible than that of the hidebound March.

The development of princely government in thirteenth-century Gwynedd was also strengthened by the building of stone fortresses in strategic locations. Both Llywelyns were keenly aware that castle-power and military technology were of critical importance. Aping their alien masters and also the castle-building programme of the Lord Rhys, the rulers of Gwynedd built their own castles, trained armoured knights, and deployed siege engines and catapults to discomfit and defeat invading forces. Of the two dozen or so Welsh castles which still survive in some form, a third were built in Gwynedd. Three of the most striking were Dolwyddelan (*c.* 1200), standing in rugged defiance in the landlocked mountain pass in

18. The ruins of Castell y Bere, built *c.* 1221 by Llywelyn ab Iorwerth, lie on a rocky mountain fastness in the Dysynni valley in Merioneth. Like several other native Welsh castles, it had elongated 'D' shaped apsidal towers at either end. (Crown Copyright: Royal Commission on the Ancient and Historical Monuments of Wales)

Nantconwy; Dolbadarn (*c.* 1200), located in the shadow of Snowdon, at the head of Llanberis Pass; and Castell y Bere (*c.* 1221), a fortress built on an isolated rock outcrop in the Dysynni valley. Each of these, and several others, were erected by Llywelyn ab Iorwerth at key strategic locations in order to defend the territorial limits of Gwynedd. His grandson Llywelyn ap Gruffudd made full use of this military inheritance and, for good measure, extended his showpieces by building Dolforwyn castle (*c.* 1273–7), a hilltop fortress over-looking the Severn valley and some distance beyond the frontiers of his native Gwynedd. Some of the architectural features of these monuments – especially the use of round towers and gatehouses – reveal that Welsh rulers had assimilated some of the techniques used by castle-builders in France. Moreover, the sophisticated tactics employed by the armed forces of the princes of Gwynedd were radically different from the ad hoc guerrilla raids practised in the twelfth century. Cannily using their knowledge of difficult terrain, which was entirely unsuited to heavy cavalry or snail-like machines, the Welsh forces proved hard to subdue.

Just as important as military security was a strong and efficient administration. Where once there had been fragmentation and incoherence, the governmental infrastructure of thirteenth-century Gwynedd was now underpinned by a high-powered cadre of administrators, lawyers and ecclesiastics bent on transforming their patrimony into a miniature feudal polity. This was no easy task: family loyalties were deeply rooted and old habits died hard. The princes of Gwynedd had no illusions about the size of the task, and they wisely assembled a raft of gifted and experienced mandarins who not only provided effective day-to-day governance but also offered a range of sophisticated diplomatic skills. Some of these gurus were figures of real substance, notably Ednyfed Fychan (d. 1246), seneschal of Gwynedd, whose abilities as a counsellor, negotiator and arbitrator proved indispensable to Llywelyn ab Iorwerth, and whose sons also enhanced the ministerial elite which formed the bedrock of the government of Llywelyn ap Gruffudd in the latter half of the thirteenth century.

As the princes of Gwynedd acquired a reputation for political maturity and vigour, they surrounded themselves with court poets known as *Gogynfeirdd* (Fairly Early Poets or the Poets of the Welsh Princes), who were not only remarkably skilful wordsmiths but also men with access to the corridors of power. So well versed were they in the art of propaganda and intrigue that they were capable of manipulating public opinion, especially at times of dynastic tension. The works of about thirty court poets have survived – a total of around 12,700 lines of poetry – and although many of them were clearly receptive to new ideas and fashions arriving from the continent, they prided themselves above all on being the heirs of the *Cynfeirdd* and thus the legitimate native remembrancers. It is surely no accident that the dynamic upsurge of Welsh poetry in the twelfth and thirteenth centuries was closely associated with the attempts of Welsh princes to stem the Anglo-Norman tide. Probably under the influence of French festivals or *puys*, the Lord Rhys inaugurated the eisteddfodic tradition by organizing at Cardigan Castle, in 1176, a cultural event in which poets and musicians entertained guests and

also competed against one another. Poets were not necessarily flat-
terers or cyphers. Cynddelw Brydydd Mawr (*fl.* 1155–1200), the
most prolific and accomplished of them, sang to all the major princes
of his age and insisted on being heard: 'Silence, bards! You shall hear
a bard.' He warned the Lord Rhys that he would both praise and
judge him, and his extraordinary poem *Breintiau Gwŷr Powys* (The
Liberties of the Men of Powys) was a ringing defence of community
interests against draconian rulers. By the thirteenth century, however,
bardic families closely associated with the Venedotian court became
sophisticated publicity machines on behalf of the cause of national
independence. Skilfully linking the glories of the past with the potential of the present, they raised the political stakes and ensured that a
special relationship existed between them and their princely patrons.
Dafydd Benfras (*fl.* 1220–60) dubbed Llywelyn ab Iorwerth:

> Llywelyn, the ruler of rulers,
> A gentle advocate in the council of the wise.

Llygad Gŵr (*fl.* 1258–*c.* 93) composed five stirring odes to Llywelyn
ap Gruffudd, in which he praised his arch-hero for resisting 'foreign
people moaning in an alien tongue'. Spurred on by the enthusiasm of
the bards, the princes of Gwynedd came to believe in their right to
suzerainty over the whole of Wales.

If the sonorous cadences of the court poets stiffened the resolve of
the Welsh princes, so too did the painstaking work of historians and
lawmakers. The key historical text was *Historia Regum Britanniae*
(*c.* 1139) by Geoffrey of Monmouth (*c.* 1090–1155), a Monmouth-
born Normanized Breton who used his considerable literary and
imaginative powers to concoct an entertaining pseudo-history of
the Britons, from the sack of Troy to the death of Cadwaladr the
Blessed in 682. Its plaintive, but often uplifting, theme focused on
the manner in which the Welsh had paid for their sins by losing their
sovereignty to the Saxons. Yet, he assured his readers, all was not
lost, for the Welsh prophecies referred to the restitution of lost rule,
of freedom from captivity and of the expulsion of heavy-handed
foreigners. In this colourful *jeu d'esprit*, Arthur occupied a central
role as a chivalrous warlord who would awaken and return to set the
Welsh free in their hour of need. Geoffrey's tales became hugely
popular in Wales, especially in Welsh-language versions known as

Brut y Brenhinedd, and Gerald of Wales was convinced that all of Wales believed that their priceless patrimony – the entire island of Britain – was eminently recoverable. This first major work to become a European bestseller certainly won a place in the hearts of Welsh princes and emboldened them to resist Anglo-Norman incursions. Llywelyn ap Gruffudd made stirring use of the glorious origins of the Welsh during his exchanges with Edward I and his emissary, Archbishop John Pecham, in the fateful year of 1282.

The princes of Gwynedd also had good cause to show respect and affection for the legal profession. Whereas in Scotland common law was modelled on English practices, in Wales (and Ireland) native law (except in Anglo-Norman marcher lordships) not only prevailed but also provided one of the most robust public symbols of the separate identity of the Welsh. The law of Hywel Dda became a malleable piece of living jurisprudence to be utilized and plundered by a variety of interested parties, including native princes and their counsellors. Redactors of the Welsh lawbooks unhesitatingly modified their material in order to further the political ambitions of Venedotian rulers. The terms *gens* and *natio* began to pepper the legal and historical record, as *cyfraith Hywel* became a beacon of hope for Welsh native rulers who cherished ambitions of driving out alien forces and of establishing Welsh supremacy within a united kingdom. Legal spin doctors within Gwynedd deliberately manipulated Welsh law in order to declare the superiority of Aberffraw (and by definition Gwynedd) over the other traditional princely courts of Dinefwr and Mathrafal. Far from being fixed and immutable, therefore, the Welsh laws were pressed into service to legitimize the status of the two Llywelyns and the dynasty of Aberffraw, and to promote within them a genuine commitment to the rights of a nation which was, in terms of its language, law, history and customs, different from England. Small wonder that Archbishop Pecham believed that the law of Hywel Dda, which he believed was immoral, had been inspired by the devil.

Nor was the Welsh Church immune to the rhetoric adopted by many of the advisers of Welsh princes. As we have seen, the dynamics of colonization included powerful pressure to acknowledge the supremacy of Canterbury. The year 1107 was significant in the ecclesiastical history of Wales, since it marked the first occasion on which a Welsh bishop (in this case Bishop Urban of Llandaff) declared unswerving allegiance to the Archbishop of Canterbury. Hand-picked fellow bishops were expected to follow his example. But whereas the abrasive Urban had a reputation for treading on people's toes, Bernard, bishop of St David's from 1115 to 1148, was more sensitive to the values cherished by the Welsh and more reluctant to be a suffragan of Canterbury. With extraordinary courage, throughout the 1120s he honoured the legacy of St David by publicly championing the independence of the Welsh Church. Although he fought in vain, his torch was seized in the late twelfth century by Gerald of Wales who, though three parts Norman, embarked on a vigorous but ultimately fruitless campaign which would have made him primate of the independent province of St David's. We can only wonder what heights Gerald might have scaled had he succeeded in acquiring autonomous status for the see of which he was so fiercely proud. But he died an embittered man in 1223. In reaction, the Welsh derived even greater comfort from their reverence for St David as a powerful iconic figure and from the significance of the diocese of St David's as an exceptionally holy and much-frequented centre of pilgrimage. 'Once to Rome is equal to twice to St David's' became a popular maxim. In north Wales, Owain Gwynedd, in whose mind Norman prelates were inextricably linked with an alien yoke and alien tongues (French and Latin), simply refused to entertain any Norman nominees, while Llywelyn ab Iorwerth loudly bemoaned the fact that the Welsh Church was increasingly staffed by non-Welsh speaking bishops and priests who could neither preach nor hear confession without the assistance of interpreters.

Champions of the Normanized ecclesiastical order also discovered to their dismay that the Cistercian order was not prepared to bend itself easily to their dictates. Whereas Cistercian monastic houses situated on the Welsh borders, like Basingwerk and Tintern, were associated with English influence and patronage, those which thrived in *Pura Wallia* were taken to their bosom by the Welsh. Indeed, the arrival of the Cistercians was a significant watershed in the intellectual and cultural life of Wales. Although the White Monks were remarkably efficient economic managers who reared enormous flocks of sheep and cattle, and became pioneers in lead and coal mining and foundry work, it was as guardians of the Welsh identity that they made their most profound impression. Within their isolated cloisters, talented clerical transcribers were instrumental in breeding a new confidence in the potential of the Welsh language and the historical traditions which it embodied. At this early stage, of course, since few people were literate or had access to books, ears were finely tuned to appreciate recitations, songs and declamations. The Welsh literary tradition owed much to the influence of *cyfarwyddiaid*, who were gifted storytelling experts on native culture and lore in much the same way as were the *filid* in Ireland and the *shennachie* in Gaelic Scotland. Little of this oral tradition survived, but most of that which was preserved was written down in monastic *scriptoria* and is as richly entertaining to the modern reader as it must have been to medieval audiences. The recent claim that the thrilling stories in the 'Four Branches of the Mabinogi' were written by Princess Gwenllïan around *c.* 1120–36 has been universally derided, and the work is much more likely to have been undertaken by a cleric in the late eleventh century. Whoever he was, this was the work of a consummate artist. These brilliantly vivid tales of giants, monsters and witches, of heroic deeds, treachery, miracles, mutilations and magic were a sharp reminder to alien warlords that the progeny of the first inhabitants of these islands had something of intriguing importance to contribute to European culture. In fact, the eleven richly diverse prose works, collectively known since mid-Victorian times as 'The Mabinogion', provided splendid grist for the capacious mill of storytellers in Wales as well as a stimulating field of study for the interplay of oral and literate modes in the production of written texts. Indefatigable transcribers also preserved knowledge of the past. Three of the four surviving Latin versions of the Welsh chronicles known as *Annales Cambriae* were written at St David's, Neath abbey and Whitland abbey by patient transcribers who had abandoned the Insular script in favour of the new miniscule script known as the Caroline script. Strata Florida, which gained such a special place in the affections of the Welsh when the Lord Rhys became its patron, played a key role in the compilation and dissemination of *Brut y Tywysogyon*, a laconic, plain-as-a-pikestaff account of the historical development of the Welsh people between 682 and 1282.

From the mid-thirteenth century onwards the Welsh were so clearly becoming aware of their identity that they were determined to save for posterity their most cherished literary works. For instance, the celebrated *Llyfr Du Caerfyrddin* (Black Book of Carmarthen) (*c.* 1250), described by a leading palaeographer as 'a slowly built-up work of love' by a 'headstrong eccentric', and devoted to religious and legendary themes, is the oldest surviving manuscript of poetry in the Welsh language. Cistercians were profoundly sympathetic to deeply rooted native traditions and to the Welsh language as a badge of ethnic distinctiveness through which the Welsh people could sustain their mythologies and express their spiritual and cultural ambitions. Since most Anglo-Norman settlers had a low opinion of the vernacular, this commitment was all the more significant.

Moreover, Cisterican abbeys were not reluctant to reveal their political colours. Native princely dynasties patronized them and showered them with gifts for several reasons: they provided safe havens in troubled times; monks offered hospitality, prayed for them and provided other favours in return for protection; abbots were used as emissaries and mediators during delicate political negotiations. In many ways, therefore, the Cistercian houses made common cause with Welsh princes and identified themselves with creative initiatives associated with nation-building. The liaison between the two Llywelyns and the White Monks was not an innocent or a reckless flirtation – it was founded on mutual respect. So deep was the bond that Llywelyn ab Iorwerth was buried in a monk's habit at Aberconwy abbey in 1240 and his grandson's headless torso was laid to rest at Cwm-hir abbey in 1282.

In many respects, therefore, it would appear that a strong tide was flowing in favour of the princes of Gwynedd in the thirteenth century and that there was every prospect of establishing a viable independent Welsh state. The brutal fact, however, is that these preconditions proved insufficient to sustain a Welsh feudal polity and, as we shall see, by 1284 the aspirations of the Welsh princes had been shattered in the most ignominious fashion.

When the dynasty of Deheubarth imploded following the death of the Lord Rhys in 1197, the pendulum swung heavily in favour of Gwynedd where Llywelyn ab Iorwerth, son of Iorwerth Drwyndwn (Flatnose), was determined to achieve rather more than the restitution of the territorial unity of the dynasty. Llywelyn ab Iorwerth made such an impression on Welsh annalists that he became known as Llywelyn Fawr (the Great). A shrewd, intelligent man, he capitalized on the internal difficulties of the Crown during the first two decades of the thirteenth century. Having married Joan, the natural daughter of King John, in 1205, he waited until his father-in-law was heavily distracted by baronial plots before arranging a series of prudent marriages between his daughters and powerful marcher lords. An adroit negotiator, his reputation for wisdom and avuncular style masked a ruthless streak. When William de Briouze was discovered *in flagrante delicto* with Llywelyn's wife, he had no compunction about hanging him in full public view near Bala in May 1230. By that stage, he was styling himself 'Prince of Aberffraw and Lord of Snowdon'. Very much in the mould of European princes in the feudal age, Llywelyn revelled in the task of constructing a principality of Wales. By taking advantage of fissures within rival Welsh dynasties, he imposed his overlordship over them. Politics is the art of the possible, and he was convinced that the time was ripe to bring about what would in our times be described as a modernization of the realm. He sought to deepen the bonds which brought the Welsh together by both brute force and the promise of favours, and he surrounded himself with all the requisites of a feudal polity, including a corps of trusted advisers and administrators, a robust army and a nest of fawning poets who believed that he was God's chosen instrument. Llywarch ap Llywelyn, 'Prydydd y Moch' (Poet of the Pigs), urged the warriors of Powys to recognize his authority on the grounds that to be ruled by a Welshman who symbolized the political and cultural inheritance of the people was infinitely preferable to groaning under the heel of foreigners.

Although Llywelyn ab Iorwerth was probably the greatest of rulers in medieval Wales, revisionist historians are less prone than their predecessors to praise his political achievements. It is certainly the case that that which he achieved fell short of what he had hoped for. His power base was distinctly fragile, and he failed to ensure that Welsh lords recognized that long-term security could only be achieved by paying homage to the prince of Gwynedd, rather than to the king of England. In many ways, his misfortune was to die too soon (even though he was sixty-seven at the time of his death in April

1240), for the succession of his son and designated heir, Dafydd ap Llywelyn, was contested by another son, Gruffudd, who had been born prior to his father's marriage to Joan. Whatever the imperfections of Llywelyn's polity might have been, however, it was still preferable to the dynastic insecurity and bloodshed which followed. Henry III, who was itching to flex his muscles, summoned Dafydd to meet him and his council at Gloucester, where he was obliged to do homage. Meanwhile, Gruffudd was locked up in the Tower of London from where, on St David's Day 1244, he fell to his death when the makeshift rope by which he planned to make his escape from his window broke during his descent. This stirred Dafydd into military action against the Crown, but his sudden death from natural causes (and without leaving an heir) in February 1246 ushered in damaging power struggles in Gwynedd and a further opportunity for Henry III to exploit these divisions and revitalize Anglo-Norman rule. Owain and Llywelyn, the two elder sons of Dafydd's half-brother Gruffudd, were in no position to resist the military might of the Crown, and at Woodstock in April 1247 royal ascendancy over Gwynedd was affirmed and all the lords of Wales were expected to do homage to the king of England. Such humiliations rankled deeply, but instead of welding together the Welsh they simply provoked further civil strife.

Eventually, Llywelyn ap Gruffudd emerged triumphant from a bloody, but critically important, battle at Bryn Derwin near Clynnog in June 1255. In order to avoid further bloodletting, he incarcerated his brother Owain for twenty-two years while he set about establishing a wider supremacy beyond the confines of Gwynedd. Although we know little of his personal qualities, Llywelyn seems to have been prone to caution and impulsiveness in equal measure. He might have lacked the wisdom and finesse of his grandfather, but he was just as committed to the task of state-building and of defending the rights and honour of his countrymen. Capitalizing on the relative weakness of Henry III, he penetrated Crown lands in north-east Wales before driving deep into Powys and Deheubarth in a self-proclaimed bid to free the Welsh from English bondage. By March 1258, with the exception of the perfidious Gruffydd ap Gwenwynwyn of northern Powys, every Welsh lord of any consequence was solidly arrayed behind Llywelyn, who now grandly styled himself 'Prince of Wales'.

More territorial gains followed, and by 1263 he had even won the allegiance of Gruffydd ap Gwenwynwyn. His moment of glory came in September 1267 when, by the Treaty of Montgomery, the English Crown recognized the principality of Wales and the primacy of Llywelyn ap Gruffudd as Prince of Wales. To that extent, and to his great delight, he had achieved a goal which had eluded his illustrious grandfather. The year 1267 is therefore a major historic landmark in Wales.

It could be argued that Llywelyn's achievement at Montgomery betokened royal weakness at that particular time, rather than a long-lasting gain for Gwynedd. When the weak and ineffectual Henry III was succeeded in 1272 by his son, Edward I, Llywelyn found himself pitting his wits against a ruthless strategist for whom any kind of power-sharing was anathema. From the outset, he was determined to make Llywelyn his vassal. The first king of England since 1066 to boast an English name, Edward I was a relentless celtophobe who set in train a process which eventually led to the political assimilation of Wales, Ireland and Scotland into a kingdom in which England reigned supreme. Eighteenth-century Welsh radicals never thought of him as being anything other than a monster, and some of them found great difficulty in resisting the temptation to pass water over his grave in Westminster Abbey. To Edward, the Treaty of Montgomery represented a slippery slope towards fragmentation and strife, and when Llywelyn deliberately antagonized him by failing to fulfil his promise to pay tribute and perform homage, explosive consequences were inevitable. He defaulted on financial dues, ignored five separate summonses to obey him and poured oil on the already rising flames by insisting on marrying Eleanor, daughter of Simon de Montfort, the king's sworn enemy. In response, in 1275 Edward served notice of his intention of thwarting the Welshman's ambitions by taking Eleanor hostage. Internal problems were also mounting. The macho posturing of Dafydd, Llywelyn's duplicitous brother, continued even after his plot to assassinate Llywelyn was exposed in 1274, and complaints from the heavily taxed and disillusioned people of Gwynedd were becoming increasingly clamorous. Once lost, trust and confidence are difficult to rebuild, and Llywelyn could never be certain of the support of other Welsh princes, and certainly not of his loose cannon of a brother. A war was likely to prove calamitous, since Llywelyn's financial resources were extremely slender. His maximum annual income of £3,500 was a derisory war chest to do battle with a powerful warrior-king like Edward, whose army was more than five times larger than anything Llywelyn could muster. This 'brave battle-lion', as his acolyte Llygad Gŵr dubbed him, probably underestimated Edward's military strength, and he was not disposed in any case to submit to the dictates of the Crown.

Since the touchstone of Edward's policy was unshakeable resolve, in 1276–7 he decided to settle accounts. A massive army (which included the renegade Dafydd in its ranks) took to the field, supported by a swift-moving fleet of ships which deprived Llywelyn of access to grain from Anglesey. Unable to feed his soldiers, Llywelyn was forced to submit. By the Treaty of Aberconwy in 1277 he was ordered to forfeit a large portion of his territories, forced to pay swingeing fines and reduced to the basically hollow status of Prince of Wales. This was a deeply humiliating and chastening blow, and the only crumb of comfort to be gained was the fact that Llywelyn had at least lived to fight another day. To underpin his military success, Edward built a series of powerful castles and installed his own servants in key military bases in Gwynedd. Selected strategic sites echoed to the sounds of timber-felling, rock-cutting, digging, scaffolding and wall-building as hundreds of perspiring masons, carpenters and diggers built intimidating symbols of English military strength at Aberystwyth, Builth, Flint and Rhuddlan.

The following five years witnessed much shadow boxing in the form of legal and procedural arguments, as well as a deepening sense of resentment among the hard-pressed Welsh regarding the high-handed behaviour of Crown officials and mounting tax extortions. Even Dafydd ap Gruffudd, dissatisfied with the modest rewards he had received from the Crown, was not prepared to endure further humiliations. Spoiling for a fight, on Palm Sunday 1282 he launched a lightning raid on Hawarden Castle. Other uprisings and disturbances, probably planned and co-ordinated, erupted in different parts of Wales. Although Llywelyn could hardly abandon his reckless brother or sit out the crisis, he prevaricated until mid-June when the death of his wife Eleanor whilst giving birth to his daughter Gwenllïan drove him, more in despair than expectation, to place himself at the head of a national rebellion. Incandescent with rage, Edward once more raised a massive army in order to administer the *coup de grâce* to Welsh hopes. Troops were deployed to conduct a search-and-destroy sweep of north Wales, and Anglesey was sealed off by the English fleet.

A truce was called and John Pecham, Archbishop of Canterbury, was dispatched to north Wales to mediate. It would be hard to imagine a less fitting emissary than Pecham, for this haughty, tetchy celtophobe believed that the Welsh law was an abomination to God. He also reckoned that the most effective means of civilizing the Welsh was to drive them forcibly into towns. To his eternal credit, Llywelyn informed him that his people were 'unwilling to do homage to any stranger with whose language, customs and laws they are unfamiliar', stirring words which have been rightly coupled with those enunciated in the Irish Remonstrance of 1317 and the Scottish Declaration of Arbroath in 1320 as exemplars of early nationalist sentiment. Not surprisingly, after three days of sharp exchanges, frosty silences and withering glares, the talks broke up in mutual recrimination. For some mysterious reason, Llywelyn then left his native redoubt for the Welsh Marches. There is a whiff of betrayal in the historical records, and it may be that he was tricked into venturing with his army from Snowdonia. The marcher barons, notably Edmund Mortimer, probably conspired against him and when, on 11 December 1282, he found himself separated from his army, he was assassinated, possibly by either Robert Body or Stephen de Frankton, close to the Irfon river at a place now known as Cilmeri, in Breconshire. There was to be no glorious last stand, just a shabby ambush on a cold December morning. Only those with the hardest of hearts would deny that this flawed but courageous Welsh prince deserved a better fate than death from a random assassin's lance in a remote woodland in mid-Wales.

Llywelyn's severed head was sent to London where, to hoots of derision from bystanders, it was crowned with a circlet of ivy and paraded on a pike through the streets. Whereas Llywelyn's demise had been swift, that of the captured Dafydd was as grotesque as could be imagined. He became the first Welshman to be hanged, drawn and quartered in England, and his head was exhibited with that of his brother on the White Tower. The unforgiving Edward

19. Following his death on 11 December 1282, the body of Llywelyn ap Gruffudd (Llywelyn the Last) was buried in the abbey of Cwm-hir in Radnorshire. His head had been cut off and was shown to Edward I before it was conveyed to London and raised on the Tower of London. (Hulton Getty Picture Collection)

made strenuous efforts to eliminate other key members of the family. Eleanor, Llywelyn's wife, had died in childbirth and her baby daughter Gwenllïan was spirited away to wither in the nunnery at Sempringham, where she died in 1337. Dafydd's two sons were consigned to the dungeons of Bristol castle. Having completed the unfinished business of 1277, Edward I ensured that an arc of castles – terrifying symbols of Anglo-Norman dominance – was built to keep the Welsh in check, and that the state-builders of Gwynedd were deprived of the *Croes Naid*, the sacred and highly cherished relic of the princely regalia of the Welsh. In 1326 Edward would also kidnap the Stone of Scone, the distinctive talisman of Scottish national identity. Llywelyn ap Gruffudd's name was allowed to drift into oblivion, and until the second half of the twentieth century it remained 'a picturesque irrelevance to the true stuff of nationhood'. Only recently has his career been the subject of a full-scale scholarly biography in both Welsh and English. The Welsh have never been enthusiastic about celebrating their hot-blooded historical icons.

This chapter began with an appreciation of the peerless Welsh historian J. E. Lloyd. One of his most penetrating contributions was to reveal that the historical and national significance of Llywelyn ap Gruffudd lay in the fact that he was both the *first* Prince of Wales and the *last* Prince of Wales (Llywelyn Ein Llyw Olaf). Welsh poets in 1282 were more deeply aware than any one else that a fateful and decisive blow had been struck at Cilmeri. The quest for political independence had come to an end and the Welsh were now a conquered people, left lost and rudderless as the waters of impending doom engulfed them. In a celebrated lament to the lost prince, Gruffudd ab yr Ynad Coch spoke of his inconsolable melancholy:

> See you not that the sea is lashing the shore?
> See you not the Judgment portending?
> See you not that the sun is hurtling the sky?
> See you not that the stars have fallen?
> Do you not believe in God, foolish people?
> See you not that the world is in peril?
> Ah, God, that the sea would cover the land!

In its pithiness, Bleddyn Fardd's rhetorical question was even more telling: 'Ys terfyn byd?' (Is it the end of the world?).

4

Pestilence, rebellion and renewal, c. 1283–1536

Hwch Ddu (Black Sow) and Chwilen Bwm (Beatle the Cockchafer) are two rough-hewn fictional characters in one of the most exuberant and successful Welsh-language novels of recent times. Written in the genre favoured by Boccaccio (who also makes a cameo appearance in the tale), *Pestilence* (*Y Pla*) (1991) recounts the odyssey of Salah Ibn al Khatib, a young Islamic student, who was dispatched from Cairo to assassinate the King of France at a time when the calamitous pandemic known as the Black Death was remorselessly pruning the population of Europe. During this picaresque adventure the student found himself in the upland demesne estate of Dolbenmaen in Eifionydd, at a time when the pestilence was threatening to destroy the socio-economic fabric of this small medieval community in north-west Wales. On his arrival, he was immediately dubbed the 'Dark One', a satanic figure whose presence boded nothing but ill for the traumatized peasants. The serf girl, Hwch Ddu, gloomily predicted that 'we'll be no more than flies on a bullock's arse, to be whipped by the devil's tail', a reminder not only of the transience of human life but also of the sheer impotence of men and women in the face of such a deadly, killing disease. Unfit for the squeamish, this harrowing tale offers a far more convincing insight into the plague-ridden world of fourteenth-century Wales than any conventional historical account based on official documents can provide. The pungent smell of death hangs over the community as the spitting, cursing, fornicating Welsh serfs gulp weird and wonderful doses of medicine in a vain attempt to ward off the pestilence. Nothing is sanitized, and by employing a fascinating variety of literary styles the author, Wiliam Owen Roberts, brings to life the most mind-numbingly devastating event in Wales in the later Middle Ages.

Over the past generation, the two hundred and fifty years which lie between two seminal statutes, the Statute of Wales (1284) and the first Act of Union (1536), have been the subject of intense debate and considerable revision. At a time when medieval studies in Wales are becoming increasingly unfashionable, this is a heartening development. There is every reason to believe that this ongoing work on political structures, socio-economic travails, and religious and cultural endeavours will eventually provide a fuller appreciation of the tensions and resentments between the colonizer and the colonized, the moments of high drama which characterized a great national rebellion, and the new and liberating forces which pointed the way to a more stable and less bloodthirsty society. The rich and complex tapestry of this period can be summarized, however imperfectly, in the following triad: pestilence, rebellion and renewal. Each of these themes will now be explored in turn.

As has already been hinted, the principal biomedical disaster in the history of Europe in this period was the arrival of bubonic plague in 1348–9. Although the outbreak of the *Fad Felen* (Yellow Plague) had caused severe panic in sixth-century Wales, nothing on the scale of the Black Death had ever been experienced before. Scholars are divided over its causes. The traditional view, now increasingly discredited, is that the water-borne carrier of the extraordinarily toxic bacillus *Yersinia pestis* was *rattus rattus*, the flea-bearing black rat which carried the deadly infection with disconcerting speed from the Asiatic steppes to the major trade routes of Europe. More recently the rat and the flea have been absolved, though the true cause of the plague still remains an open question. What is clear is that the deadly pestilence arrived in southern England in June 1348 and spread with terrifying swiftness in a north-westerly direction. During the winter of 1348–9, it launched a two-pronged attack on Wales by crossing the Severn and driving up the Tywi valley, wreaking fearful devastation in ports, along river valleys, in upland lordships and in borough towns. The suddenness with which it penetrated the hinterland

and snaked its way along the Marches and deep into Gwynedd was every bit as shocking as its brutish effects. Since the sources relating to the course and effects of bubonic plague in mid-fourteenth-century Wales are far less abundant than those for England, it is impossible to tell whether the whole of Wales was severely affected by plague clusters. Presumably, there were regional variations: the towns of north-east Wales certainly suffered heavier rates of mortality than the surrounding countryside, whereas the converse was true of Gwynedd as well as of commotes in Ystrad Tywi and Ceredigion. But wherever it raged, *y Farwolaeth Fawr* (the Great Mortality), as this pitiless scourge was called, caused catastrophic falls in the population. At least a third of the population – around 100,000 – appears to have been wiped out. The Black Death certainly lived up to its name and, as is the case with HIV and Aids in our times, the extraordinary scale of human loss and suffering anchored itself in the minds and memories of those who survived.

The dearth and brevity of contemporary comment are striking, and one suspects that the literate few had been struck dumb by the catastrophic novelty of this grim reaper. It was left to poets like Gruffudd ap Maredudd and Llywelyn Fychan to convey the suffering and grief endured by their loved ones as they were caught in a deadly sequence of fever, headaches, convulsions, vomiting and the ugly swellings or buboes which gave this particular brand of plague its name. In a notable poem, 'The Pestilence', which dates from the second half of the fourteenth century, Llywelyn Fychan memorably wrote of the 'eradicating phantom' which robbed him of five children, 'gentle darlings' whose lives had been cut short by 'the shilling under the armpit . . . smouldering like a red-hot coal', leaving him to grieve 'barely alive in a harsh world'. Medieval medicine was powerless in the face of this unstoppable scourge and even the Physicians of Myddfai, whose medical skills were admired far beyond their native north-east Carmarthenshire, had no answer to it. True to its democratic instincts, the plague carried off the rich and the poor, newborn children and greybeards, native Welsh and English incomers, abbots and priests. No one was immune to its ravages, and as it rampaged through Wales it left in its wake the stench of decomposing bodies, which were hastily buried by perspiring gravediggers. Traumatized survivors had no time to mourn the dead properly and, as they struggled to understand how this catastrophe had come about, they found some reassurance in the realization that this was a divine punishment which could only be assuaged by penitence and devout religious observance.

That which we know about the victims is suffused with poignant ironies. As far as we can tell, no prominent Welsh lords were struck down, but in the heavily colonized lordship of Dyffryn Clwyd, Denbighshire, English families like the Posterns, the Stalworthmans, the Meols and the Pilles, who had been attracted to north Wales by the assurance of fertile lands and handsome privileges, fell victim to the plague. It is entirely possible that the most celebrated Welsh-speaking casualty was the peerless poet Dafydd ap Gwilym, who perished *c.* 1350 together with the two women – the gentle dark Dyddgu and the sultry blond Morfudd – he had courted so assiduously. The ravages of the Black Death prompted the chivalrous Monmouthshire-born soldier, Henry, Duke of Lancaster, to compose a treatise entitled *Le Livre des seintes medicines* (Book of Sacred Medicines or Remedies), but by 1361 the pestilence had claimed him too. Who can imagine the feelings of terrified parish priests or friars who, as they ministered to the sick and dying, made themselves even more vulnerable to the ravages of what they believed to be a divine visitation? Perhaps, like Brother John Clynn, a Franciscan friar in Kilkenny, some of them composed, before death came, a moving record of the course of the pestilence 'in case anyone shall still be alive in the future and any son of Adam can escape this pestilence'.

Although the Black Death was a never-to-be-forgotten demographic watershed, it must also be recognized that, as a result of climate changes and famine, the population had been falling since the early fourteenth century. Winters had become colder and summers wetter, and harvest failures occurred more frequently. The exceptionally harsh famine which struck northern Europe between 1315 and 1322 was known as the 'Great Famine' and, coupled with the famine which stalked the continent in 1330–1, it caused heavy mortality. Moreover, it is likely that those who proved most susceptible to plague in 1349–50 were those whose immune systems had been gravely weakened during their famine-torn years as children. In several ways, therefore, the Great Pestilence markedly accelerated socio-economic trends which had already become apparent. Acting as a catalyst, it had both short-term and long-term consequences, and further deadly visitations in 1361, 1369, 1379 and 1391 provoked a sense of chronic insecurity among the populace. Indeed, it is not difficult to imagine why the fourteenth century was often called 'the epoch of tragedies'.

The bond population, which had traditionally huddled more closely together than the free, bore the brunt of the plague. Paradoxically, however, those bondmen who survived seized the opportunity to remove the chains which had bound them to the land. Voting with their feet, they abandoned holdings and townships in their droves. Tenancies became vacant, unharvested crops were left to rot, and mills and fisheries fell into ruin. In rural Cardiganshire, the plaintive cry rang out in 1349: 'there are now only seven and there used to be 104 tenants called gabularii who withdrew this year because of the pestilence'. This haemorrhage of labour sounded the death knell for the old feudal order based on the *gwely* and the *gafael*, and led to much greater social mobility. As the old way of life crumbled, a society began to emerge in which people were differentiated more by their wealth and status than by their kinship. The practice of commuting labour dues for money rents gathered momentum, the land market became more volatile and the rise of individualism, which was deeply at odds with the old tribal ways, proved to be advantageous to new social groups, especially the *uchelwyr* (gentry or squirearchy), who utilized the highly adaptable legal device known as the gage (*prid*) to acquire land, played the marriage market adroitly, and assembled compact new estates for themselves by occupying vacant bondlands or urban burgages and by purchasing Crown lands. This upwardly mobile class of ambitious and, for the most part, cultivated men became the new 'haves' of Welsh society.

As historians become more gender-conscious, the experience of women in this rapidly changing world is becoming clearer. Doors had been opened to property-owning women in the Crown lands by the Statute of Wales (1284), which introduced English land law, and such rights were extended to the marcher lordships by the fifteenth century. More interestingly, plague helped to release poorer women from some of the shackles of the past. In the wake of the Black Death, they became more prominent in the labour market as bakers, brewers, harvesters, spinners and weavers. Relishing the opportunity to articulate themselves in a masculine world in which they were still expected to be silent and invisible, sharp-tongued scolds, cursers and quarrellers mercilessly harangued males and other women. As old restraints were removed, women improved their rewards in urban communities, and in rural areas even the unskilled seized their opportunity at times of acute labour shortage. Although the odds remained heavily stacked against women, a mounting body of evidence suggests that their lot was improving.

The havoc wrought by plague was nowhere more evident than in ecclesiastical circles. In the diocese of Hereford, 43 per cent of the clergy were wiped out in 1348–50 and, although data for Wales are scarce, there is no reason to believe that the onset of plague did not wreak similar havoc on institutional and pastoral life in the Welsh dioceses. Deeply worried by human losses, archdeacons in St David's swiftly dispatched candidates for ordination to the diocese of Hereford in order to replenish their dwindling complement of clerics. The financial effects of the pestilence 'swept over ecclesiastical possessions like a hurricane'. Revenues plummeted disastrously, monastic houses found their numbers of inmates dwindling alarmingly, and some of them were obliged to withdraw the rents and services of their tenants. Such painful economic woes severely damaged the morale of the religious orders, the clergy and their parishioners.

Nothing, therefore, can disguise the plain fact that the Black Death was an event of extraordinary magnitude, and not until the word *cholera* struck a chill to the spine in the nineteenth century did the Welsh once more experience a virulent mass killer of this kind. By terrifying and slaying a third of the population (the overwhelming majority of whom were Welsh-speaking peasants) bubonic plague caused a profound human tragedy, the extent and effects of which are scarcely imaginable. The nightmarish round of soaring temperatures, coughing, vomiting, swelling in the armpit, neck or groin, as well as the futile cures, hasty burials and tolling church bells, left their macabre imprint on the popular mind. The subsequent proliferation of funerary monuments – tombs, brasses and sarcophagi – indicates the extent to which this lethal visitation reminded the survivors of the fragility of human life. Although many of the socio-economic changes wrought by the Black Death were the acceleration of deeply rooted forces already in motion, its ravages undoubtedly changed the face of medieval Wales.

It is against this background of famine, dearth and pestilence that we must set the response of the Welsh to colonial rule from 1282 onwards and their propensity to rise in rebellion, notably the national uprising launched by Owain Glyndŵr in September 1400. As we have seen, during the massive military offensive launched by Edward I in 1277 and renewed in 1282–3 an iron ring of formidable castles was built in coastal locations, in order to remind the Welsh of the power and authority of the English Crown. Edward's strength was an inescapable reality; so, too, was his brutish imperial view of the world. Even as the body of the last native Welsh prince lay decomposing in the abbey of Cwm-hir, efforts were made to ensure that the memory of him was erased and that as few people as possible would look back nostalgically to his heyday. Llywelyn ap Gruffudd's seals were melted down and *Y Groes Naid*, the cross-shaped reliquary formerly worn by the Welsh prince, was secreted to England where it eventually found a home at Windsor Castle. Later, even the reputed skull of St David was carried off to the Tower of London. On no account were the Welsh to be allowed to preserve symbols of their collective dignity or to develop their own brand of pomp and circumstance. Potentially troublesome heirs and relatives were closeted or eliminated, and as the reality of conquest became manifest so, too, did the bleak assessment of the Welsh annalists of the significance of 11 December 1282 – 'and then all Wales was cast to the ground'. Both military and ideologically, Caernarfon Castle figured prominently in the king's strategy. He was determined to make it a proud symbol of his imperial ambitions: its majestic walls were redolent of the Land Walls of Byzantium, its towers were crowned with imperial eagles and its golden gate inescapably con-jured up images of Constantinople. True to his reputation as a monarch of great vigour and strength, Edward I used this extraordi-nary monument (and other impressive fortifications) to remind the conquered Welsh of the determination of the Crown to retain for-ever its conquered territories in Wales and to bend the inhabitants of the Principality to his will. Many centuries later the modern poet Tony Conran wrote: 'This is where empire begins. / It's the dragon's tooth.'

Following the ruthless deployment of military power came political annexation. In March 1284 a contentious royal injunction known as the Statute of Wales was promulgated at Rhuddlan. In this remarkable document, it was made explicit that Wales was no longer a kingdom, a country or a principality. Divine providence had decreed that the land and people of Wales had been 'annexed and united the same unto the Crown of the aforesaid Realm [of England], as a Member of the same Body'. Gwynedd was divided into three new shires – Anglesey, Caernarfon and Merioneth – and placed under the control of a justiciar of north Wales based at Caernarfon. A new shire called Flint was created and joined to the county palatine of Chester. The existing counties of Cardigan and Carmarthen were recognized and placed in the charge of a justiciar based at Carmarthen, and the five Crown-held shires formed the new Principality of Wales, which remained in existence until the first Act of Union in 1536. This unambiguously colonial document also robbed Welsh laws of their treasured inheritance. Although in matters of inheritance *cyfraith Hywel* was allowed to prevail (except with regard to bastards and females, and in cases of personal litigation), in criminal cases the law of England – a law which Edward I believed to be more modern and sophisticated than anything the Celts could assemble – was to be followed. Only in the Marches did the king leave well alone. He knew perfectly well that powerful English magnates would look askance at any attempt to pick a fight or curtail their influence. As a result, these feud-ridden lordships, immune to the royal writ, became over time a byword for turbulence, disorder and a host of petty tyrannies. Thus, throughout this period Wales was a patchwork of Crown lands, royal lordships and either Welsh or Anglo-Norman baronial lordships. It was a recipe for disaffection and strife. Edward I had no illusions about the potential threat, especially from Gwynedd: in 1285 he referred to the Principality as a 'snake lying in the grass'.

Military conquest and political annexation also ushered in economic deprivation and dispossession. The Edwardian settlement brought about significant changes in patterns of urban settlement and land exploitation. The humiliation of alien plantation was best illustrated in the boroughs which, as bastions of loyalty to the English Crown, grew in the shadow of the castles. Here, the native

20. With eight massive round towers and barbicans at either end, Conwy
Castle, built between 1283 and 1287, was one of the great fortresses of
medieval Europe. It vividly illustrated the conquest of Wales by England.
(Crown Copyright: Royal Commission on the Ancient and Historical
Monuments of Wales)

Welsh were denied rights enjoyed by English burgesses. Indeed, they
were no-go areas for the uncivilized 'barefoot scrubs' who happened
to speak only Welsh, and those who sought to ply their wares as
traders were summarily ejected as 'foreigners'. Moreover, large
numbers of English settlers colonized not only royal and marcher
boroughs but also substantial tracts of land in the surrounding
countryside. Enticed by mouth-watering inducements – handsome
estates, favourable rents and privileged status – the retainers of the
Crown and the principal barons colonized large tracts of fertile
farming land in the Welsh lowlands. In north Wales, the surnames
of some of these groups of settler-gentry – Birkenshaw, Castleford,
Clitheroe, Davenport, Rossendale – give a pretty clear indication of
whence they came, and nowhere was discrimination against the
Welsh more evident than in the lordship of Denbigh in north-east
Wales, which became a distinctive Englishry peopled by incoming
English families from Cheshire, Lancashire, Yorkshire and Shropshire.

These incomers were preferentially treated and subsidized, and in order to make way for them Welsh tenants and serfs were cast out to boggy and infertile pastures elsewhere. When 2,600 men were dispatched to Beaumaris in 1295 to build an astonishingly sophisticated concentric castle, the entire population of Llan-faes was driven off the land and exiled to Newborough. Colonization involved exploitation and marginalization, and, not unexpectedly, the native Welsh chafed, bristled and bridled as shameless land-grabbing reduced them to a pitiable plight.

Political and administrative doors were also shut firmly in the faces of the Welsh. Following the conquest the native aristocracy, just so long as they refrained from mischief, were allowed to fade into obscurity, while those upwardly mobile gentry who at least pretended to be indifferent or hostile to the ideals which had fired the princes of Gwynedd tried to accommodate themselves to the new order. In order to win their allegiance, if not their hearts, Edward I was prepared to make them bailiffs, beadles or constables, but on no account was he willing to offer them key posts. Those who became justiciars, sheriffs and chamberlains were men of English or marcher stock. A climate of opinion was thus created in which the Welsh were believed by alien planters to be feckless, inconstant and subordinate beings, fit only for makeshift offices and hard labour. To civilize and pacify them, so it was thought, would be a great service to humanity. In order to survive and prosper, therefore, Welsh families entered the marriage market, procreated, and raised heirs and heiresses whose first allegiance was to the English Crown and who aped the values of the colonizer.

Subtle and not so subtle means were used to persuade the Welsh that it was in their interests to appreciate the law, order and stability which the new regime offered. In 1301, in a bid to strengthen the ceremonial appeal of monarchy, Edward, the eldest surviving son of Edward I, was made Prince of Wales. The young prince had been conceived and born at Caernarfon, which, many centuries later, became the venue for a revival of the long-lapsed ceremony of investiture in the summer of 1911 and again in 1969. Since 1301 the title 'Prince of Wales' has been held by twenty-one heirs to the English throne, few of whom ever visited Wales or laid any claims on the attention of posterity. The significance of 1301, therefore, lies in the fact that the ill-fated principality of Gwynedd was replaced by a royal dominion known as 'the principality of North Wales'. Had Prince Edward been more charismatic, it is possible that the interests and groups supporting the Crown might have increased, but following his ineffectual reign from 1307 and his abdication in 1327 there was no great sense of revulsion in Wales when his exasperated enemies slew him by thrusting a red-hot spit into his bowels at Berkeley Castle. The second, and far more effective, means of moulding the values of the Welsh and circumscribing their freedom to rebel was by using Wales as a convenient and dispensable recruiting ground for bowmen, spearmen and foot lancers. Military service in foreign lands became an attractive prospect and, from the point of view of the Crown, it was a valuable means of defusing tensions and dissipating the energies of angry or ambitious young men. The recruiter par excellence was the Black Prince, the son of Edward III, who was, even by medieval standards, a deeply repugnant figure who squeezed from Wales every available able-bodied soldier to serve the Crown in France. To their credit, the Welsh acquitted themselves well on the continent. At Crécy (1346), where Edward III and his outnumbered forces won an outstanding victory over King Philip of France by means of superior tactics and the skill of longbow archers, around 7,000 Welsh soldiers, dressed in distinctive green and white uniforms (the colours of the leek), fought like tigers. At Crécy and Poitiers (1356), several exceptionally skilful Welsh soldiers displayed the fortitude and ruthlessness which the Black Prince respected. Pride of place must go to Sir Hywel ap Gruffydd, whose striking sobriquet 'Syr Hywel y Fwyall' (Sir Hywel of the Axe) was a vivid testament to his bellicosity. During the post-Poitiers celebrations the Black Prince, deeply impressed by the fearful carnage wrought by the Welshman's battleaxe, reserved a special place of honour for it in the royal hall. Other outstanding soldiers – Sir Richard Gethin, Sir Gregory Sais, Gruffudd Dwnn and Mathew Gough – served the Crown on the continent with unquestioning devotion, and the presence of large contingents of Welsh soldiers in the French wars and also on battlefields in Scotland and Ireland meant that concepts of duty and obedience to the Crown took root.

Even so, there is no need to suppose that Welsh soldiers who saw the advantages of teaching sharp lessons to foreign foes were necessarily blind and unheeding about the wounds inflicted on their fellow countrymen by the Edwardian conquest. From the outset, Edward I had been under no illusions about the likely reluctance of the Welsh to yield to his demands. The rabble-rousing proclivities of the disloyal Welsh were well known and, whenever royal policy was implemented harshly, tensions simmered beneath the surface. How could the Welsh settle for their lot when their leaders were marginalized and humiliated, when there were tales of mass evictions and individual cases of dispossession, and when the storm-troopers of the king's cause and royal favourites in the Marches enriched themselves? Although they lacked the military strength to engage in sustained active resistance, they were not cowed by the might of the Crown. According to the author of the *Vita Edwardi Secundi*, written *c.* 1326, the Welsh still trusted in the prophecies of Merlin: 'Hence it is that the Welsh frequently rebel, hoping to give effect to the prophecy; but because they do not know the appointed time, they are often deceived and their labour is in vain.'

It is important not to oversimplify the causes which lay behind the sporadic revolts that prompted English officials to sigh with exasperation, 'the Welsh, you know, are Welsh'. Popular revolts were multi-causal events and the commitment of activists was not necessarily altruistic, even though they were acutely aware of past and present indignities. Many individuals felt bitterly cheated, among them Rhys ap Maredudd, lord of Dryslwyn in Carmarthenshire, who took such grave exception to the humiliations heaped upon him by Robert Tibetot, Edward I's justiciar at Carmarthen, that he rose in rebellion in June 1287 and remained at large until he was betrayed by four of his own men in April 1292 and hanged at York. A much more serious flashpoint occurred in 1294–5 when Madog ap Llywelyn, the aggrieved son of a dispossessed nobleman, provocatively styled himself 'Prince of Wales and Lord of Snowdon' and masterminded a rebellion which displayed signs of national co-ordination and planning. Even as he struck out against English rule by attacking Cardigan Castle in September 1294, his supporters in several other theatres of war were engaged in similar raids. Depleted English garrisons, caught by surprise, were placed under intense pressure and when the Welsh rebels penetrated the mighty (but as yet uncompleted) castle at Caernarfon and lynched the deeply loathed castellan Roger de Puleston, Edward I was forced to deploy heavily armed troops to rout the insurgents at Maes Madog in March 1295.

Not surprisingly, the famine years of 1315–17 witnessed serious outbreaks of popular discontent as well as appreciable social distress and loss of life. Overbearing and sometimes ruthless government administration aggravated matters, notably in the uplands of Glamorgan where the appointment of a brutish royal custodian, Payn de Turberville, was greeted with universal dismay. In January 1316 Llywelyn ap Gruffydd (Llywelyn Bren), lord of Senghennydd and a deeply cultured man (he owned a copy of the *Roman de la Rose*), attacked Caerffili Castle before inflicting considerable damage on other Crown fortifications and manors. Fears of escalation prompted Edward II to act swiftly and, rather than bring further suffering to his people, Llywelyn gallantly surrendered; on the orders of the younger Hugh Despenser, he was brutally executed at Cardiff Castle. The fact that he had attacked the boroughs of Glamorgan with such ferocious intensity reveals the degree to which Welsh lords resented the overtly racist policies of English administrators. During the mid-fourteenth century, relations between the Crown and the native community deteriorated alarmingly as royal officials not only bled Wales of men and money in order to prosecute war in France but also employed squalid tactics which pushed the Welsh beyond endurance. The increasingly odious violations perpetrated by the Black Prince and his servants caused particular disquiet, and soon they began to reap what they had sowed. In February 1345 Henry Shaldeford, attorney of the Black Prince in north Wales, was hacked to death at Bangor by a group of prominent Welshmen led by Tudur ap Goronwy of Penmynydd, Anglesey. This incident horrified English burgesses and led them to dramatize the threat to their security and well-being.

Discontent and resentment therefore manifested themselves in various ways and, sooner or later, a massive explosion was likely to occur. Wales was increasingly being treated as a kind of cash cow, and famine, pestilence and war simply deepened the profound sense of misery and insecurity among the populace. That terrible divine visitation, the Black Death, spread like a conflagration through most of Wales and the impact of this pandemic, which gave rise to

apocalyptic expectations, exacerbated the mood of racial dishar-
mony and resentment. Harsh royal and marcher rule, swingeing
taxes and bullying tactics meant that the government was running
extremely short of friends. Nor was the Church immune from these
pressures. One of the most striking symptoms of ecclesiastical
malaise was the effect of the appointment of non-Welsh bishops
and other absentee administrators on Welsh-born clerics, whose
standard of living and career expectations had already been blighted
by pestilence and economic slump. The Crown brazenly used dioceses in Wales as a means of rewarding their loyal servants and
simply ignored the chorus of complaints. Another symptom was
the willingness of clerics as well as laymen to heed the reassuring,
and yet potentially disruptive, prophecies of the Welsh bards. These
traditional cheerleaders of the national cause took advantage of the
changing socio-economic context by unleashing a torrent of prophetic verse which renewed expectations of a Welsh deliverer, who
would overturn the oppressive Saxon regime and restore his people
to their former exalted position.

The inspirational power of the vaticinatory tradition (*canu brud*)
was exemplified by the part it played in associating the widespread
longing for the restoration of Welsh honour with the adventurer
and mercenary Owain ap Thomas ap Rhodri, alias Owain Lawgoch
(Owain of the Red Hand), a Walter Mitty-like figure who reputedly
never set foot in Wales but who was the great-nephew of Llywelyn
ap Gruffudd. He thus had every right to project himself as the
rightful heir of Gwynedd and as the Owain most likely to restore
to Wales some of its lost glory. Between *c.* 1360 and 1403, a
'Company of Welshmen' who served the kings of France were led
by Owain Lawgoch (known to the French as Yvain de Galles) and
Ieuan Wyn (d. 1384), who was nicknamed 'le Poursuivant d'Amours'.
Unfortunately, although the former entertained hopes of recovering
his inheritance by French-assisted force of arms, his own appetite for
power never really lived up to the bardic propaganda marshalled on
his behalf. In 1372, sailing at the head of a fleet from Harfleur,
Owain Lawgoch failed to get beyond Guernsey, and subsequent
forays were also cut short. In the summer of 1378 a spy (inappropri-
ately called Lamb) in the paid service of the English Crown disposed
of this alleged traitor by fatally stabbing him at Mortagne-sur-mer,

21. At the instigation of the English, the Welsh mercenary and claimant as
Prince of Wales, Owain Lawgoch or Yvain de Galles, was assassinated by
one John Lamb at the siege of Mortagne-sur-mer in 1378. Yet, the Welsh
continued to believe that he would return with his red spear 'to drive the
Saxons like pigs into Cors Fochno'. (The British Library)

in Poitou. Thus did another Welsh son of prophecy bite the dust.
Undeterred, Welsh poets sharpened their quills and spread the message that Owain Lawgoch was asleep in a cave, awaiting his day of
destiny. So it came to pass that an adventurer, who had hitherto been
hardly more than an irrelevance, in death found himself elevated to
the status of cult hero.

Yet, that such fond hopes had been pinned on Owain Lawgoch,
the last in the direct male line of Gwynedd, was an early sign of the
coming storm. Within a heavily colonized society, native poets were
at once comforting and destabilizing voices which recalled the past
glories of a vanquished people and kept alive hopes of freedom.
Matters had come to a head by the 1390s as the ethnic, socio-
economic, political and spiritual strains became apparent. The disenchantment of being 'a nation of wretches like drunken crows' was
matched by a growing upsurge of anger and frustration which led in
1400 to the climacteric known as the rebellion of Owain Glyndŵr.

On 16 September, in circumstances rather less flamboyant than the investiture of Prince Edward at Lincoln in 1301, Glyndŵr was proclaimed Prince of Wales by a small group of avid admirers at Glyndyfrdwy, Edeirnion, in Merioneth. To the English, unprepared and distracted by dynastic issues, the revolt came like a bolt from the blue and for over a decade it represented the most serious threat to the security of the Crown since 1282–3.

It remains a fine judgement to what extent the personality of Owain Glyndŵr was the key factor in inspiring the Welsh to take up arms in a trial of strength which lasted much longer than anyone could have predicted and which brought Wales to the brink of independent status. An air of mystery has always surrounded him. We know not when he was born or when he died. Comets were said to have blazed at his birth and his dependence on the flashes of inspiration provided by Crach Ffinnant, his personal spin doctor and seer (*daroganwr*), reinforced his reputation as a man who had access to magical powers. Not for nothing did Shakespeare shower high praise on him and depict him as a figure 'not in the roll of common men'. But he was not an exotic bandit hero in the Pancho Villa or Che Guevara mould. Quite the opposite: this cultivated, affluent nobleman was descended, on his father's side, from the royal house of Powys and, on his mother's side, from the royal house of Deheubarth. He had served in English armies and, ironically, had spilled Celtic blood. He was well versed in the law. Poets showered praise on him and were convinced that he was the man of the hour. Everything we know about him suggests that he was an immensely attractive and accomplished leader of men. In the light of these qualities, it is easy to see why this champion of Welsh independence managed to inspire his countrymen to rise up against colonial rule and why he is still remembered with genuine affection and respect. As we shall see, Glyndŵr was keenly aware of the power of ideas, and he became the most impressive and eloquent defender of the right of the Welsh people to exist and to control their own identity. His grasp of diplomacy matched his military prowess, and the manner in which he retained the allegiance of his followers and the breathtaking boldness with which he led his soldiers transformed the morale of a people who had come to believe that glorious, and sometimes inglorious, military failure was deeply embedded in their blood.

Yet, for all his abundant gifts, Owain Glyndŵr could never have transformed what began as a localized private quarrel with his tetchy and stubborn neighbour, Lord Reginald Grey of Ruthin, into a national insurrection had he not emerged at a time when he could give voice to the unresolved tensions and material grievances which had made his fellow countryman feel like an 'alien in the land of his birth'. There were several immediate triggers. The political upheavals of the late 1390s, and especially the brutal murder of Richard II in 1399, had deeply angered his supporters in Wales, and they were determined to seize the opportunity to wreak vengeance on the usurping Henry of Lancaster. The exclusion of the leading Welsh squirearchy from the most prestigious civil offices in Wales, as well as resentment over swingeing seigneurial extractions, fuelled a deep sense of grievance and prompted many ambitious Welshmen to believe that success on the battlefield would leave them in a better position to take advantage of propitious economic circumstances. Conquest, dispossession and disenfranchisement were dispiriting forces and these, together with the effects of the ravages of pestilence and fiscal expedients, provoked considerable racial hostility. According to the modern poet R. S. Thomas, Glyndŵr heard in the songs of the poets:

> The sharp anguish, the despair
> Of men beyond my smooth domain
> Fretting under the barbed sting
> Of English law, starving among
> The sleek woods no longer theirs.

Glyndŵr clearly tapped powerful emotional currents in society and the revolt, which stemmed from years of accumulated frustration, resentment and anger, burst out as an unplanned but visceral act of defiance. The willingness of people from all walks of life – landowners, ecclesiastics, craftsmen, university students, labourers, women as well as men – to flock to his banner testifies not only to the personal charisma of the leader but also to the deep groundswell of disaffection which existed in late fourteenth-century Wales. Those morale-builders par excellence – the Welsh poets – ensured that Glyndŵr's cause filtered into a remarkably wide consciousness. In a rousing *cywydd*, Iolo Goch likened Glyndŵr to a mighty lion who 'will wreak bodily destruction on all men of bloodstained England'.

Surely the wheel of fortune would at last turn in favour of the Welsh as they expressed their burning sense of indignation in a national rebellion.

Although age-old inequities and humiliations suffered by the Welsh provided an ideal breeding ground for a revolt, the depth of feeling seems to have been greater in north and south-west Wales than in the more heavily Normanized and urbanized communities of south-east Wales. Glyndŵr might have cut an impressive figure in his native patch, but merchants in trading areas like Severnside and burgesses in long-established Anglo-Norman settlements believed that he and his followers were misguided and dangerous malcontents. Along the anglicized borders people viewed the uprising with apprehension or horror, and as plunder and pillage accompanied hostilities, deep antagonisms were aroused between the Welsh in north and south Wales. The jaundiced chronicler Adam of Usk, who believed that to be born in north Wales was a singular misfortune, flayed Glyndŵr, depicting him as 'another Assyrian [who] vented his fury with fire and sword in unprecedented tyrannies'. Not everyone, of course, actively participated, but as the uprising dragged on for a decade it became harder to preserve a studied neutrality. Yet, the overwhelming impression gained is that Glyndŵr's cause, notably in the early stages, was so compelling and the atmosphere of defiance so great that large numbers attached themselves steadfastly to this major national uprising.

From the outset, Glyndŵr stamped his personality as well as his authority on the course of the conflict. Indeed, he seemed to be fulfilling the Machiavellian maxim that a prince could be both fox and lion. By word and deed, he showed himself to be more daring and innovative than any previous deliverer. Emboldened by the support pouring in from all quarters, his military strategy was to tax the resources and patience of the lumbering English armies by organizing sudden and sporadic raids and ambushes by posses of marauders. Direct confrontation was avoided in favour of surprise hit-and-run affairs. We know little of the size and composition of Glyndŵr's armies, but they were evidently well motivated, robust and fleet of foot. English armies marched so noisily that the Welsh guerrillas were able to avoid sustained open combat by taking to the hills. Such tactics meant, of course, that the war could not be swiftly resolved by one mighty and decisive clash of armies. The poets claimed that even the stars were in his favour, and Glyndŵr himself had the knack of appearing as if by magic at the head of his troops in different parts of Wales, sacking castles, burning towns and giving momentum to local raids.

To their credit, the Welsh were not found wanting and some spectacular early military successes were recorded. The most notable occurred on Good Friday 1401, when a forty-strong band of Welsh insurgents, led by Gwilym ap Tudur of Penmynydd, astonishingly seized the seemingly impregnable fortress at Conwy. This audacious coup, achieved 'by deceit and guile' according to one startled chronicler, had the element of surprise which Glyndŵr's men used so effectively. This was followed in the summer by a resounding victory, masterminded by Glyndŵr himself, over a powerful royal army at Mynydd Hyddgen in the remote moorlands of the Pumlumon mountain range in mid-Wales. During the siege of the town and castle of Caernarfon in November, Glyndŵr's army unfurled his standard, a golden dragon on a white field. Wraith-like, Glyndŵr evaded capture and, undeterred by draconian penal legislation passed by parliament, he captured two key enemies – Lord Grey near Ruthin and Edmund Mortimer at Maelienydd – in 1402 and held them to ransom. Never one to set his sights low, he also sought to engage the support of the Irish and the Scots, urging them to make common cause with their kinsmen who despised the Saxons. He continued to press home his advantage in north, mid- and south-west Wales, leading English armies a merry dance as his fleet-footed forces swept into boroughs, border towns and castles. Unable to mount the massive invasions which Edward I had organized, Henry IV was hard pressed to keep his elusive adversary under surveillance. By 1403 the uprising had truly caught fire and the Crown had good cause to be seriously concerned. Whenever Glyndŵr raised his golden dragon banner, people flocked to his side to stiffen the rebel cause. Virtually the whole of Wales was in his hands. In the summer of 1404 the gods smiled once more on his cause as the fortresses of Harlech and Aberystwyth fell to his men.

Every national rebellion needs an ideology to buttress it, and at this stage Glyndŵr lent to the cause a special intellectual and moral authority which gave a powerful stimulus to the campaign. He turned

22. In 1916 David Lloyd George, Secretary of State for War, unveiled a 'National Valhalla of Welsh Notables' at City Hall, Cardiff. Among the ten Welsh heroes and one heroine (Boudica!) was a statue to Owain Glyndŵr as a representative of statesmanship and martial prowess. The sculptor was Alfred Turner. (Geraint H. Jenkins)

it into a crusade in which new ideas and possibilities were defined and discussed in a way that few could have imagined before 1400. Glyndŵr clearly believed that Wales had a glorious history and a proud culture, and he was determined that his people should be treated as civilized human beings. He spoke in national terms, he convened national parliaments at Machynlleth and Harlech in 1404, and he adopted the royal arms of the princes of Gwynedd. His great seal bore the challenging words: 'Owain Prince of Wales by the grace of God'. He was fortunate to be able to call on the advice of 'the equivalent of a modern think-tank', a team of gifted Welsh ecclesiastics led by Gruffudd Young, archdeacon of Merioneth, and John Trevor, bishop of St Asaph, who raised the ideological tone of the uprising, partly in order to prevent it from degenerating into squalid civil strife but mainly to raise the international stakes. In July 1404 a Franco-Welsh treaty was signed, and this was followed within a year by an intriguing tripartite indenture, a bold plan to break up England which, had it been realized, would have extended the political boundaries of Wales in an easterly direction. With the benefit of hindsight, we can see that the latter was a pipe dream, but at the time it symbolized the confidence of Glyndŵr. The climate was certainly favourable for new ideas and some lateral thinking. The most striking indication of the mature statesmanship of Glyndŵr and his advisers is to be found in the celebrated Pennal Letters of 1406, which are preserved in the Archives Nationales de France in Paris and which were visited by thousands of people when they were exhibited in the National Library of Wales at Aberystwyth in 2000. These letters vividly evoke the national vision of the revolt. Glyndŵr viewed himself as a prince in charge of an independent state, whose boundaries stretched far beyond Offa's Dyke to encompass towns like Hereford, Shrewsbury and Worcester, whose intellectual and administrative dynamic would derive from two universities (one in the north and one in the south), and whose spiritual authority would be nourished by an independent Welsh Church, with its own archbishop at St David's. By any standards this was a compelling blueprint of the Wales of tomorrow, and the glittering opportunities which it offered invigorated the campaign.

But even as these eye-catching proposals were unfolding, Glyndŵr's momentum was beginning to stall. By 1405 the Crown had awoken to the fact that the menace posed by Glyndŵr's armies had to be directly confronted. As support from the French and the Scots melted away, Glyndŵr's cause began to wilt alarmingly during 1406. Severe military reverses robbed him of the sustained impetus required to realize his ambitious international programme. The loss of the castles of Aberystwyth in 1408 and Harlech in 1409 were twin hammer blows from which he never recovered, and harsh vengeance was exacted when Glyndŵr's wife Margaret, two of his daughters and his grandchildren were captured and bundled off to the Tower of London. The superior resources and firepower of the Crown sapped the energies of Glyndŵr's battle-weary troops and the Anglo-French truce of November 1407 signalled the end of any hopes of practical and sustained French support. Glyndŵr's last major throw of the dice – a raid on the Shropshire border in 1410 – proved to be a catastrophic failure. Thereafter, the royal armies had little difficulty in snuffing out the dying embers of the rebellion, though some rebels were still resisting in 1415.

At no time during the course of the rebellion was the national leader betrayed by his people, and it is easy to appreciate why this extraordinary man commanded the respect of gentlemen as well as fighting men. High on the castle mound near the town of Llandovery stands a striking statue to Llywelyn ap Gruffudd Fychan (d. 1401) of Caeo, a gentleman who preferred to suffer the agony of public disembowelment and dismemberment rather than inform against his leader. Others, too, had suffered physical torment for the vision of an independent principality of Wales. After 1412 Glyndŵr mysteriously disappeared, but he outlived Henry IV and disdainfully spurned the offer of a pardon by his successor Henry V. He probably died *c.* 1416. Psychologically, the Welsh took a long time to come to terms with his defeat – perhaps they never have. Yet, the relentlessly optimistic bards believed that their redeemer had not perished: he had simply joined the ranks of the slumbering heroes who awaited a second opportunity to liberate the Welsh people. But whatever his fate might have been, Owain Glyndŵr deserves to be judged in the context of his high ideals and his success in sustaining a national uprising which tested the might and patience of the English Crown for a decade. His leadership, energy and resourcefulness had inspired his supporters and, by giving them a new sense of direction, he had offered them, however fleetingly, a taste of remedies for their many ills. Nevertheless, it is hard to know where his legacy lies and to assess the impact of the rebellion on the development of Welsh society. We can surely discount the much-quoted judgement by a leading Welsh historian – 'Modern Wales . . . really begins in 1410.' The map of Wales remained unchanged, and the Welsh, now condemned to a subordinate status by penal legislation, had once more been cowed into obedience, even though a deep well of acrimony and anger still remained. Virtually all hope of establishing a united, independent Wales under the leadership of a native prince had disappeared. There were to be no further major uprisings of this kind against the power of the Crown.

This brings us to the third theme which dominates the latter part of a period commonly described as an age of reconciliation and renewal. Freed from pestilence and rebellion, Wales found itself on the cusp of a new era in the post-Glyndŵr years. As we have seen, the Black Death took a heavy toll on the population and the Glyndŵr rising added to the general sense of economic misery. The litany of complaints were endless: harvests had been crippled, livestock slaughtered, trade disrupted; farms, mills and castles had been destroyed, churches and country homes pillaged. The catalogue of plunder and destruction was greatly exaggerated by Tudor historians, and the truth is that Wales did not suffer anything like the material devastation experienced in many parts of the continent during the Hundred Years War or even (in the Stuart period) the Thirty Years War. Of late, revisionist historians have softened the gloomy and distorted appraisals of Tudor chroniclers and have focused more convincingly on the more positive signs of recovery. These green shoots will be examined shortly, but it would be misleading to give the impression that old habits of oppression, rapacity and the spilling of blood were things of the past in fifteenth-century Wales.

It is difficult to over-emphasize the impact on Welsh sensibilities of the overtly racist penal code of 1401–2, which remained on the statute book until 1624. These laws reduced them to the status of second-class citizens in their own land; they were unable to bear arms, assemble for meetings, hold public office or acquire land and property in either English or Welsh boroughs. True, the canniest

Welsh discovered means of circumventing the penal provisions imposed by Henry IV, but their very existence was a running sore and there were always heavy-handed English administrators who seized every opportunity to remind them that the price to be paid for rising in rebellion was total disenfranchisement. Gone was the bullishness of the brave new world which Glyndŵr had promised, and to be shackled in this way was yet another sign of the consequences of daring to take up arms against royal authority.

This profound sense of disillusionment was aggravated by the fact that in the marcher areas little effort was made to clip the wings of unruly or self-aggrandizing lords. Indeed, as the fifteenth century unfolded the marcher lordships became a byword for murders, ambushes, bribery, corruption, piracy and cattle raids. The presence of over-mighty subjects in the Marches and the general breakdown in law and order meant that Wales remained a deeply fragmented society. No fifteenth-century monarch succeeded in imposing order and stability on this wretched haven for lawbreakers, and although the language of the poets and indeed the behaviour of the up-and-coming squirearchy strongly suggests that they were eager to encourage and sustain good government, selfish interests and factional influences dogged their every move. However much a poet like Tudur Aled might preach the virtues of peace and harmony as 'the balm of his community', and however loudly Welsh lawgivers might champion the merits of *cymrodedd* (compromise) and *cyfla-faredd* (arbitration), the sorry tale of factional feuds, warlordism, personal antagonisms and sheer lawlessness still prevailed.

Although the outcomes of dynastic disputes and family rivalries during the Wars of the Roses resonated throughout Wales, and although Welsh poets made a sumptuous meal of key battles such as those of Mortimer's Cross (1461) and Tewkesbury (1471), as they publicized either Lancastrian or Yorkist fortunes, these vicissitudes are not sufficiently important to detain us here. Far more significant was the way in which ambitious and ruthless individuals took advantage of the weakness of the Crown (especially under Henry VI), the threat from France and the strains created by factional rivalry to exercise an unusual degree of power. In an age of powerful Welsh barons, three stand out. The most ruthless of them was Gruffudd ap Nicolas (d. 1456), a potentate in south-west Wales

who, having been granted considerable latitude by the Crown, ruled
his province with an iron fist. Under Edward IV, Sir William Herbert
of Raglan (who became Earl of Pembroke from 1468) was every bit
as ruthless and dominant, even though he sought to mask his private
ambition by pious professions of concern for the well-being of the
visual arts and the public good. The third public figure, Sir Rhys ap
Thomas (d. 1525), the grandson of Gruffudd ap Nicolas, became
virtually the viceroy of south Wales in the late fifteenth century, and
his intervention in the run-up to the battle of Bosworth not only
proved decisive but also earned him rich rewards.

   To those familiar with horror stories about the effects of fifteenth-
century dynastic disputes, factional feuds and public disorder, it
may come as something of a surprise to learn that this was a golden
age for Welsh poetry. Cultural renewal was one of the more uplifting
features of this period, and poets were able to make themselves
heard because they were the representatives of the *uchelwyr*, the
most upwardly mobile social group and the most successful in
exploiting the fluid and advantageous land market. These shrewd
estate-builders grasped every opportunity to acquire lands and extend
their influence at a time when the old economic institutions – the
manor and the *gwely* – were disintegrating. For instance, a series of
prudent marriages proved to be the making of the Mostyn family,
whose landowners consolidated these lucrative matches by accumu-
lating lands and offices in four different counties in north Wales.
Progressive new families like the Bulkeleys of Baron Hill, Anglesey,
and the Wynns of Gwydir, Denbighshire, knew full well how canny
wheeling and dealing could create an opportunity to occupy vacant
bondlands or urban burgages, to purchase Crown lands and derive
profits from farms and local offices. Such families were well placed
to benefit from the increasing emphasis on cattle rearing and sheep
farming, and the ships which brought in a wide range of expensive
and exotic goods helped some of them to fulfil their compulsive need
to sustain an extravagant lifestyle.

   Even though many poets had every cause to feel frustrated and
resentful following the demise of Owain Glyndŵr, they were shrewd
enough to know that money could be made by pandering to the
vanity of the *uchelwyr*. These squires or gentlemen were just as
vulnerable to the blandishments of praise poetry and vaticinatory

verse as their noble forebears had been before 1282, though there is also strong evidence that they were well versed in the poetic tradition and were fully capable of discriminating between genuine bardic craftsmanship and empty rhetoric. The poetic tradition had survived the trauma of the Edwardian conquest, and the *uchelwyr* duly became the new custodians. From the mid-fourteenth century onwards, the *cywydd* metre, together with the system of assonance, alliteration and internal rhyme known as *cynghanedd*, became the vehicles by which the new society was portrayed. The man who regenerated Welsh poetry was Dafydd ap Gwilym (d. *c.* 1350), an incorrigible sun-worshipping, nature-loving womanizer who deserves to be ranked alongside his better-known contemporaries, Boccaccio and Chaucer. One of his modern translators refers to his 'blazing sensuousness', and the fact that he once sent a love messenger to the nunnery at Llanllugan indicates that an impish new spirit of humour and irony had taken root. The ubiquitous *cywydd* metre which he pioneered enabled poets to use their powers of visual imagination as well as their technical expertise, and his substantial corpus of 151 extant poems reveal that poetry could now be formal and bawdy, sophisticated and rough-hewn. Unquestionably the greatest of Welsh poets, Dafydd ap Gwilym's work ushered in a remarkable flowering in the bardic tradition.

Cywyddwyr in the post-Glyndŵr age became past masters at *dyfalu* (the proliferation of metaphors, personifications and autonomasia), at composing love poems and works of satire as well as unctuous praise poems. In this golden age, the finest practitioners were Dafydd Nanmor, Guto'r Glyn, Lewys Glyn Cothi and Tudur Aled. Under Tudur Aled, who died in 1526, the tradition of praise poetry reached its apogee and nine elegies marked his demise. Yet, these sophisticated men were perfectly aware of some of the major social and political changes of the times, as the massive corpus of vaticinatory poetry (*canu brud*) amply reveals. Conscious of the sinfulness of the times, the Welsh bardic Savonarola, Siôn Cent (d. *c.* 1430/45), foretold a bonfire of the vanities as he reminded his listeners that 'all men end by lying down'. There was nothing jovial about Siôn Cent, but among the class of inferior poets and minstrels – poets of inferior status bearing names like Ding Moel (Bald Thing), Hywel Lipa (Hywel the Feeble) and Ieuan Du'r Bilwg

(Black Ieuan the Billhook) – there was much traffic in open vitriol and gallows humour. Medieval Welsh satire was suffused with startling references to physical ugliness, bodily odours and fluids, and various obscenities. The poet Llywelyn Goch ap Meurig Hen of Merioneth admitted in his twilight years to have violated each of the Ten Commandments. Women, too, were familiarizing themselves with the intricacies of the poetic craft, and some of them confidently barged their way into male literary circles. Gwerful Mechain (*fl.* 1460–1502), a Montgomeryshire-born poet, composed some of the most sexually explicit poems in the Welsh language and gave as good as she got in bardic jousts with misogynist males. Had Dafydd ap Gwilym been alive in her heyday, he would surely have relished *Cywydd y Cedor* (A Poem to the Female Genitals), her defiant riposte to his chauvinistic *Cywydd y Gâl* (A Poem to the Penis).

Other significant literary developments were taking place as the Welsh endeavoured to defend, preserve and legitimize their native language and culture, and to diffuse it throughout society. Since poets were expected to travel the country and sing for their supper in gentry homes and religious festivals, it became all the more necessary to conserve the riches not only of Welsh poetry but also prose literature, chronicles and legal texts. Although the ear – as well as gestures and symbols – was more important than the eye, the written word was becoming more widely used, and from the mid-thirteenth century onwards there occurred not only an extraordinary upsurge in Welsh manuscript production but also a proliferation of written records which served the needs of seigneurial administration, land conveyance, private deeds and much else. Although the native tongue was the most distinctive badge of the collective identity of the Welsh, it was increasingly forced to compete in elite circles with Latin, French and English. In a turbulent and precarious world, preserving the past and recording the present became an urgent necessity, and this explains the feverish scribal activity among copiers and compilers. The perpetuation of the Welsh cultural tradition owed a great deal to the stewardship of the monastic houses. *Brut y Tywysogyon*, written by scribes at the Cistercian house of Strata Florida, has become a *sine qua non* for all medieval Welsh historians, while the Hendregadredd Manuscript, which began to be written at the same abbey *c.* 1300, is a treasurehouse for students of the poetic tradition. By the later Middle Ages, however, the torch had been taken up by lay patrons and scribes, and the upsurge in the transcription and availability of bardic grammars, legal texts, religious texts and medical writings indicates a powerful determination to ensure that Welsh culture should not be allowed to weaken and die. One of the most significant repertories of medieval Welsh prose was *Llyfr Gwyn Rhydderch* (White Book of Rhydderch), written *c.* 1350 by Rhydderch ab Ieuan Llwyd ab Ieuan of mid-Cardiganshire, while around 1400 Hopcyn ap Tomas of Ynysforgan in Glamorgan commissioned Hywel Fychan ap Hywel Goch of Buellt, together with two assistants, to produce the celebrated poetic and prose compilation known as *Llyfr Coch Hergest* (Red Book of Hergest), which is now in the safe keeping of the Bodleian Library. It was increasingly incumbent on the Welsh-speaking *uchelwyr* to maintain the cherished practice of householdership (*perchentyaeth*), an obligation which included not only social hospitality but also a delight in ancestry, honour and the cultivation of the native tongue. As a result, most champions of the interests of the Welsh language had more reason for confidence than had been the case at the turn of the thirteenth century.

Architectural historians have been at pains of late to remind us that the major collections of Welsh *cywyddau* coincided with a remarkable upsurge of rebuilding. As castle-building lost its primacy, domestic architecture enjoyed a period of revival in the post-Glyndŵr era and dendrochronological analysis has revealed that the 500 or so hall-houses which have survived were built between *c.* 1430 and 1580. These robust and handsome homes, built according to the increasingly dominant cruck-framed timber patterns, were tangible symbols of the growing wealth and power of the rising *uchelwyr* and also living proof of the enviable skills of Welsh craftsmen. In deference to the carpenter's craft, Welsh poets used to style themselves 'carpenters of praise'. New and enhanced standards of material comfort, greater privacy and more refined aesthetic tastes advanced the reputation of landowners who revelled in their role as the successors of the native aristocracy in Wales. The *plasty* (mansion) thus became an integral part of the patrimony of the progressive Welsh gentleman.

23. The remarkable Jesse Window, painted glass dating from 1533, at the Church of St Dyfnog, Llanrhaeadr-yng-Nghinmeirch, Denbighshire, probably survived because it was removed for safekeeping during the English civil wars of the mid-seventeenth century. (Charles and Patricia Aithie: Ffotograff)

In this fast-moving world, the Church, too, was forced to adjust to new circumstances and opportunities. The most vulnerable institutions were the religious houses which, badly affected by high taxation, pestilence and the depredations of soldiers and pillagers during the Glyndŵr rebellion, were hard put to maintain their number. Sharp reductions in the number of monks, rumours of idleness, complacency and immorality, and changing cultural perspectives left the monasteries ill-equipped to build a new future for themselves. As the decades rolled by, it became increasingly obvious that life within the cloister had lost its appeal in a world in which the renunciation of material well-being was becoming unpalatable. Soon the sun would set on these unique buildings. An equally significant change occurred in ecclesiastical policy from the mid-fourteenth century onwards. Local candidates for Welsh bishoprics were ignored in favour of papal or royal nominees, many of whom proved to be birds of passage. Not a single Welshman was appointed bishop of St David's between 1389 and 1496, or bishop of Llandaff between 1323 and 1566.

Yet, in spite of these deep-seated difficulties, in the period after *c.* 1440 the Church embarked on a remarkable process of recovery within local communities. A substantial church building programme of restoration was launched in a bid to make good the losses suffered during the Glyndŵr rising. Among the most impressive local initiatives was the reinvigoration of Welsh religious literature and the cult of the native saints. Saints were deeply loved because they were believed to be miracle workers who dispensed services unavailable elsewhere. Many sick or depressed pilgrims who had no hope of embarking on arduous journeys to Rome, Jerusalem or Santiago Compostela travelled to highly cherished sites associated with Welsh saints and saintesses in order to gain tangible assurance that God and the saints had not abandoned them to a life of agonizing pain and crippling decay. The impeccable exemplar was the Blessed Virgin Mary, and poets, especially those in Glamorgan, loudly sang the praises of her shrine in remote Pen-rhys in the Rhondda Valley. Such highly revered sites reveal that, in their search for salvation and reassurance, people were becoming more sensitive to the beauty of holiness in nurturing vernacular spirituality. The Church might have been tarnished by alien bishops, non-resident cathedral clergy, poorly educated parish priests and understaffed monasteries, but the proliferation of devotional paintings, rood screens, stained glass and tombed carvings in local churches – lovingly created or refurbished by skilled craftsmen and designed to highlight the imagery of the salvation cycle, the Virgin Mary, Christ's Apostles and the saints – does not bear out the traditional view that the Church was in the doldrums. Worshippers were clearly deeply attached to the rhythms of the liturgy and to saints, relics and sites, and it is significant that the 'sacrilegious' attack from the 1530s onwards on those practices which lay at the heart of the everyday religion of Welsh people caused more outrage and despair than any other initiatives mounted by Protestant reformers.

These significant and promising shifts in society were clearly linked to burgeoning wealth. The post-Glyndŵr recovery was reflected, as we have seen, in the emergence of a more vigorous and productive land market which liberated the unfree and pro- pelled the gentry to a position of strength, in the appreciable upturn in the cattle and cloth trade, and in the development of urban life. Although their size and economic fortunes varied considerably, towns were clearly offering a much wider range of services and commodities, and were exercising a growing regional influence. In spite of the colonial stigma associated with borough and marcher towns, the Welsh began to penetrate them in a bid to share in the benefits of trading in meat, wool and cloth as well as to sample some of the joys of good living. In the towns of south Wales in particular, ethnic antagonisms were now less apparent, and a greater measure of integration and reconciliation had occurred over time. Southerners had been much more ambivalent about, and even hostile to, Glyndŵr and his fellow insurgents, and they welcomed peacetime opportuni- ties to strengthen the economic base of towns by deepening com- mercial links, via the Severn Channel, with the West Country and especially the mercantile world of Bristol. In both north and south Wales substantial commerce with the continent developed, and even a cursory reading of Welsh poetry reveals that at lavish banquets pros- perous *uchelwyr* and burgesses had a hearty appetite for exotic fruit and vegetables, as well as expensive wines from Bordeaux, Burgundy and Bayonne. Even the workless and the rootless, who never stood to benefit handsomely from urban life, found themselves irresistibly attracted to the more convivial and lively towns where there were greater opportunities to improve their cheerless lot.

Modern assessments, therefore, suggest that when the latest Welsh deliverer threw his hat into the ring in 1485, the socio-economic

24. A terracotta bust of Henry Tudor, dated 1509–18 and attributed to Pietro Torrigiano. When, following the battle of Bosworth in 1485, he acceded to the throne as Henry VII, the Welsh believed that they had reclaimed 'the Crown of Britain'. (Victoria and Albert Museum)

prospects for Wales were much more heartening than had been the case at the beginning of the century. At the close of this period, then, we return to the drive to establish fuller British integration and to eliminate the violent spasms of disorder which were such an obstacle to the extension of the jurisdiction of the Crown over the whole of Wales. By 1483 Welsh poets were churning out prophetic verse as never before. The man of the hour, so they believed, was the sickly and reclusive Henry Tudor who, since 1471, had been living in exile in Brittany. The umbilical cord which bound this young Lancastrian pretender, who was by birth half English, one-quarter French and one-quarter Welsh, was his ancestry on his father's side. His paternal grandfather, Owain Tudor of Penmynydd, Anglesey, could claim descent from Cadwaladr the Blessed (d. 664), held to be the last native king of Britain (according to Geoffrey of Monmouth, it was to him that an angel had appeared to assure that, in the fullness of time, the Britons would be freed from Saxon thraldom). Unperturbed by the meagre fraction of Welsh blood which coursed through his nephew's veins or by the fact that, having been born at

Pembroke Castle and raised there and at Raglan, he had never set
foot in England, Henry's shrewd uncle, Jasper Tudor, used his many
contacts to turn him into a plausible Lancastrian claimant to the
throne. Determined to make amends for an abortive dry run in
1483, Jasper Tudor bolstered the confidence of this unlikely *mab
darogan* (son of prophecy) and sailed from Honfleur on 1 August
1485 with an army of 4,000 men. On his arrival in Pembrokeshire,
Henry assured the Welsh that ridding them of their 'miserable
servitudes' was his priority. The whole enterprise could easily have
sunk into black comedy and disaster, but as he tramped north to
west and mid-Wales, enlisting support with each passing mile, he
took heart from the effusive support of Welsh poets and the practical
assurances of fighting men. Late in the day, Sir William Stanley, the
most powerful magnate in north-east Wales, declared for him and
when two hours of heavy fighting began at Bosworth Field on 22
August, his brother, Lord Stanley, made a decisive military intervention which clinched victory. The Yorkist king, Richard III, was
beaten to death, his crown was retrieved from under a thorn bush
and was placed on the head of the semi-Welsh usurper. So began the
long and tumultuous reign of Tudor monarchs.

If the poets are to be believed, bliss was it in that dawn to be
Welsh. They unquestionably regarded Henry VII as one of themselves and lauded him for fulfilling ancient prophecies and for bringing the Welsh back on to the historical stage. But it is surely high
time to lay to rest the supposed Welshness of the new king and the
depiction of him by Tudor chroniclers as a latter-day Moses, sent to
free his people from bondage. True, he richly rewarded his loyal
Welsh champions: Rhys ap Thomas, knighted at Bosworth, became
de facto ruler of the principality of south Wales, while Jasper Tudor
became Duke of Bedford and chief justiciar of the Crown's dominions in south Wales. But, apart from some studied gestures like
adding the red dragon to the royal arms and naming his consumptive
son Arthur, he never threatened to overplay his hand in displaying
his Welshness. Paranoid in his fear and hatred of pretenders, he set
far greater store on eliminating bogus claimants and snuffing out all
efforts to dethrone him. He had little intention of avenging the
ancient wrongs of his countrymen or of elevating Welsh interests
above the need to establish stable government. Historians agree that

Henry Tudor was not an innovator. Conservative and perhaps miserly at heart, this curiously uncharismatic monarch pitched his ambitions at modest levels. A strong feeling soon emerged that he had not redeemed his many promises, and even the charters of enfranchisement, which he granted (or, to be more accurate, sold) between 1504 and 1507 to communities in the principality of north Wales and to certain lordships, could never rescue his reputation prior to his death in 1509.

Nevertheless, Henry Tudor's spectacular victory at Bosworth Field was a major landmark in the history of Wales because it confirmed that the destiny of Wales, as had been the case since 1282, was tied up with that of England. Curiously for a man pre-occupied with security, however, he did next to nothing to curb the power of the mightiest marcher lords, and this urgent task was left to his son Henry VIII (who never displayed the least sign of affection for Wales). In 1521 – by attainder and execution – the third Duke of Buckingham, the most odious representative of the Welsh marcher lords, was eliminated, and ten years later the hapless Rhys ap Gruffydd of Dynevor, the grandson of Sir Rhys ap Thomas, suffered the same fate for alleged acts of high treason. But the problem of fragmentation and lawlessness remained. Successive presidents of the Council in the Marches proved unable to stem the tide of cattle stealing, murders and felonies, and under the weak and corrupt presidency (1525–34) of John Vesey, bishop of Exeter, a greater priority was given to selling pardons than to cracking down on thieves and robbers. It became increasingly evident that this running sore could not be cured without depriving marcher lords of their jurisdiction. But not until the early 1530s did frustrated Welsh gentlemen, for whom political union was a beguiling attraction, begin to shower the king's chief minister, Thomas Cromwell, with requests for major administrative surgery. The 1530s was a crucial decade, not only in the history of Wales but also in the history of the British Isles insofar as it ushered in a new phase in the attempt to create a unitary British state. Having first softened up the Welsh by appointing a draconian bishop, Rowland Lee, to the presidency of the Council in the Marches in 1534 and by tightening the administration of justice by passing a raft of parliamentary statutes, in 1536 Thomas Cromwell introduced the first of two acts (his head had been removed by the time of the second in 1543) which united Wales to England, abolished the distinction between the Principality and the Marches, ushered in shire government and encouraged cultural integration by making English the language of government. All this was achieved with remarkable swiftness and with little opposition. How different was the muted response to the Act of Union of 1536 from the plaintive cries of grief experienced in 1282–3.

5

Early modern Wales, 1536–1776

In the twenty-seventh year of the reign of Henry VIII, a Putney-born state-builder set Wales on the path towards integration within a Greater Britain, a process which reached its conclusion with the Anglo-Scottish Union in 1707 and the Union of Great Britain and Ireland in 1800. Such a future, of course, was hardly discernible in 1536 to Thomas Cromwell, the king's chief minister and the architect of the Act of Union (1536), for he was essentially a ruthless pragmatist whose incorporation of Wales into England was part of an overall strategy of recasting diverse elements of the commonwealth into a unitary state. Although he was a master of the perfidious politics of his age, Cromwell was no stranger to Erasmian idealism nor did he lack creative intelligence. The cornerstone of his policy was the concept of 'unification', and he was determined to bring good governance to Wales. Cromwell went to the block at the command of his royal master in 1540, but by that stage he had begun a new drive to impose order and 'civility' upon the Welsh within an administrative and legal dispensation known as 'England and Wales'. His blueprint stood the test of time: the Act of Union remained on the statute books until 1993.

In the sixteenth year of the reign of George III, a Llangeinor-born philosopher, writing at a time when British authority in colonial America was disintegrating, published a pamphlet which provided the thirteen American colonies with a powerful ideological justification for rising in rebellion. *Observations on the Nature of Civil Liberty* (1776) enunciated the principle that every community had the right to govern itself. Grateful Americans showered the author, Richard Price, with praise, and five years later, in the company of George Washington, he was awarded an honorary degree by the University of Yale. No Welshman in this period made a greater impact on the wider world. Price's principal aim was to stiffen the resolve of Americans in their quest for liberty, but this one-man Glamorgan think-tank revealed to those with eyes to see that governmental structures throughout the world were not sacred unless they derived their sovereignty from the principle of self-government. There is nothing in this particular pamphlet to suggest that Price believed that Wales was 'for political purposes a separate community', but by implication he planted the notion that an ethnicity like Wales had the potential – if the people so wished it – to construct a separate national identity.

Both Thomas Cromwell and Richard Price were compelling figures, forward-looking men who believed that their plans, by sweeping away the old, would create room for a better future. In the intervening 240 years between the first Act of Union and a pivotal moment in the history of the New World in 1776, the Welsh people could not have failed to observe the process of political assimilation and the growing influence of state authority. In a bid to bring the king's subjects in Wales into 'amicable Concord and Unity', a fitfully sustained campaign was launched from the Acts of Union (1536–43) onwards to integrate the Welsh into a single British entity. Since the English – whether government officials, religious reformers or moralists – presumed superior wisdom in matters associated with 'civility' and 'politeness', it was thought prudent to ensure that a monoglot Welsh people living in 'rude' and 'dark' corners of the land should become familiar with the language and mores of the 'civilizing' English world. In what passed for wit in Grub Street circles, Wales was scurrilously depicted as 'the very testicles of the nation' and 'the very Rubbish of Noah's Flood', and its people as culturally and morally deficient. Crude and hostile caricatures of the bone-headed Welsh multiplied, and it was widely assumed that such a sleepy backwater stood in urgent need of a healthy dose of English law, Protestantism and civility. By setting out the ambition of 'reducing' the Welsh to English norms of behaviour, the preamble to the Act of 1536 voiced the determination to bring good governance to Wales by vastly extending the rights, laws, customs and speech of England. The theme of this chapter, therefore, is the extent to which the process of assimilation and integration succeeded and how far it entailed the suppression of a distinctive Welsh identity.

First of all, however, we must turn to the continuities which existed and were maintained throughout a period usually referred to as 'early modern Wales' or, more confusingly, as 'pre-industrial Wales'. Wales at this time was a federation of small communities in which people thought in terms of localities and counties rather than nations or kingdoms. The accidents of geography made for insoluble internal divisions: sharp contrasts existed between the thinly peopled mountain heartlands and the more heavily settled fertile lowland and coastal plains. North and south Wales were deeply divided by the nature of the terrain, and there were also long-standing historical demarcations within counties. Welsh speakers from north Pembrokeshire who ventured to cross the *Landsker* into the southern Englishry could still expect a dusty reception. By modern standards, the population was small and widely dispersed. At any given time in this period, more people lived in London than in the whole of Wales. The urban and industrial sector was small and a voyager into the past would have been forcibly struck by the predominance of the pastoral economy and the discomfort of travel by land. A journey through Wales, either on foot or horseback, was not to be undertaken lightly, and until the arrival of a railway network in the 1840s it was never easy to travel swiftly or safely. Wales possessed no institutions of statehood, no separate church, no universities, museums or conservatories, or any other recognizable cultural focus. In spite of its pretensions to being the provincial capital of Wales (Thomas Churchyard claimed 'It stands for Wales'), Ludlow was a wholly English town on the wrong side of the border, and from an economic viewpoint Chester, Shrewsbury and Bristol all had better claims to being surrogate Welsh capitals. Without its own Dublin or Edinburgh, Wales increasingly lost its gifted and ambitious people, most of whom were irresistibly attracted by the glitter of London's lights.

Yet, the power of localism meant that the first loyalty of the bulk of the populace was to the county, region or parish in which they had

25. Shortly before his death in 1568, the gifted Welsh Renaissance scholar, Humphrey Llwyd, completed the first accurate map of Wales. Entitled *Cambriae Typus*, it was printed for Ortelius as a supplement to *Theatris Orbis Terrarum* (1573). This map was printed fifty times between 1573 and 1741. (The National Library of Wales).

been born and bred. The fact that contemporaries referred to John Davies *Mallwyd* or Griffith Jones *Llanddowror* or William Williams *Pantycelyn* shows that celebrated figures as well as faceless people who seldom peep out of the historical record were closely identified with their place of birth or abode. Regional pride prompted George Owen of Henllys to compile his famous *Description of Penbrokshire* during the latter years of the Elizabethan period, and even though his views on druidism were bizarre Henry Rowlands of Llanidan had no difficulty in raising a large number of subscriptions from Anglesey people to enable him to publish *Mona Antiqua Restaurata* (Ancient Anglesey Re-established) in 1723. Within these small, tightly knit communities people jealously guarded distinctive and age-old practices, including customary laws, weights and measures, price structures, domestic architecture and folk customs, all of which strengthened networks of kinship and what poets liked to call 'local roots' and 'ties of blood'. This does not necessarily mean that rural communities were harmonious units. On the contrary, they were often riddled with petty antagonisms, quarrels and feuds. Strangers were coolly received, closely watched, and if they spoke no Welsh they were often sent packing with a gruff 'Dim Saesneg' (No English). Welsh jurors were reckoned to be more favourably disposed to their own than to outsiders, and during the civil wars Welsh foot soldiers were reputed to 'love not a stranger longer than he can tell them the news'.

Most people lived in an oral world, depending on narratives, anecdotes, songs and proverbs for information and entertainment. Indeed, a rich oral culture of storytelling was sustained on the hearth and in alehouses by humble rhymesters and remembrancers who provided people who had no access to formal or regular schooling with unforgettably rich narratives of the 'Treachery of the Long Knives', 'The Massacre of the Welsh Bards' and 'The Discovery of America by Prince Madoc'. Knowledge about the world outside was relayed by returning soldiers and sailors. 'Bring him a stool to sit on', it was said of Elis Gruffydd, a multilingual soldier and chronicler in Tudor Flintshire, 'and a mugful of beer warmed up and a piece of burnt bread to clear his throat, so that he can talk of his exploits at Thérouanne and Tournay.' On the other hand, in sheltered parts, belief in the Ptolemaic universe stubbornly persisted up to the eighteenth century, and confused plebeians grumbled loudly when the new Gregorian calendar was introduced in 1752. The conservatism and inertia of peasant life meant that belief in superstition, magic and witchcraft withstood the hammer blows of religious reformers. Since they fulfilled vital roles as healers, marriage bureaux, lost-property offices and intermediaries between witches and victims, the cunning man and the wise woman continued to entice, baffle and satisfy clients well into the twentieth century. Promoters of 'civilitie' were appalled by the use made by plebeians of Sundays, wakes and festivals as a release from the stresses of burdensome daily toil and as a means of displaying their athletic prowess in violent ball games, as well as their taste for gambling at cockfights, wrestling matches and cross-country races. Large sections of society in this period would have been surprised to learn that historians believe that Protestantism was a major engine of change. Popular culture within small communities proved to be extraordinarily resistant to change.

None of this conjures up a distinctively 'Welsh' dimension and clearly the most significant, visible and enduring badge of the ethnic identity of the Welsh was their native language. Nothing irritated English-speaking officials and moralists more than the fact that this hot-blooded, leek-eating and innately rebellious people stubbornly clung to their own language. Even at the end of this period probably as many as nine of every ten persons were monoglot Welsh-speakers, and although English words and phrases were infiltrating domains such as the law, commerce and fashion as well as daily habits of speech even at plebeian level, the natural daily medium of communication was Welsh. As we shall see, affection for the native 'British tongue' was deep and lasting, and it is hard for those who are familiar with bilingualism or trilingualism to understand and appreciate the intensity and passion with which a monoglot people viewed their vernacular tongue. In the foreign country which was early modern Wales, the otherness of its people lay in the native language. The King's English, claimed Thomas Llewelyn in 1768, was of no more consequence to the monoglot Welsh 'than to the inhabitants of Mesopotamia or Patagonia'.

Even so, it would be foolish to argue, on the basis of these largely unchanging continuities and the unflattering depictions so

assiduously peddled by 'civilizing' celtophobes, that early modern
Wales was a provincial backwater characterized by monoglottism,
inertia, illiteracy and poverty. In fact, it was a period of dynamic
socio-economic and cultural change. Demographic growth, the
movement of goods and people, the emergence of a British Atlantic
economy, the drive towards assimilation and integration, the introduction of bible-reading Protestantism and the intellectual challenge
posed by humanism and other cultural initiatives were critical developments from which certain sections of society derived great benefits.

The tempo of socio-economic change increased as the population
began to grow and as Wales became sucked into a capitalist Atlantic
economy in which the London market, overseas trade, war and
slave-trading predominated. Over the period as a whole the population more than doubled, rising from around 225,000 in the 1540s
to around 489,000 by 1780. Overall the growth was piecemeal and
haphazard, but two specific spurts seem to have occurred: the first
between the Union and the civil wars, and the second from around
1740. Mortality crises caused by harvest failures and killing diseases
such as bubonic plague, typhus and smallpox continued to prune
local populations and to nourish the melancholy preoccupation with
death in the literature of the period, but, as the economy grew
stronger, rising birth rates and in-migration led to the emergence
of denser concentrations of populations in towns and ports in fertile
and low-lying coastal communities and in burgeoning industrial
parishes. There were greater numbers of people on the move and
many of them travelled long distances to fulfil their aims. Drovers,
harvest-labourers, beggars, garden girls, ardent evangelists and
footloose gentry sons were among the most prominent wayfarers.
London, the largest city in Britain, was the major target – one
Merioneth youth believed that it was 'the primary point in the geography of the world' – and the young flocked there in a bid to make
their fortune. Drovers earned a good living by ushering hardy Welsh
cattle to London markets and post-Union opportunities led to a
haemorrhage of gifted young people: bereft of academic institutions,
Wales lost around 2,000 students who registered at the universities of
Oxford and Cambridge between 1570 and 1642, and even though
Jesus College, Oxford, founded in 1571, was ringfenced for the benefit of the Welsh, most of these graduates never returned to Wales.

Demographic growth and economic hardship also meant that there was no shortage of able-bodied Welshmen capable of fighting as soldiers, sailors and mercenaries. Ironically, the first to define the 'Brytish Empire' in oceanic rather than territorial terms was the London-Welshman John Dee, the celebrated Elizabethan philosopher-magician who claimed descent from Rhodri Mawr and who insisted that the glorious deeds of adventurers like King Arthur and Prince Madoc meant that the Welsh had better claims to territories in the New World than anyone else. As a result, the mobile Welsh, driven out by hunger or ambition, became heavily involved in 'a multi-faceted, kaleidoscopic swirl of enterprise' which included planters, merchants, soldiers, sailors, mercenaries and indentured servants. Trade, colonization and plunder were closely intertwined. For their sins, the Welsh played an ignoble part in the colonization of Ireland by joining 'improving' English-style settlements and putting to the sword 'unruly' Catholics who stood in their way. More admirable were attempts to establish Welsh settlements beyond the seas, though some of these were gimcrack affairs. Having abandoned a wild and woolly plan to set up a Welsh colony at St Helena, in 1617 Sir William Vaughan of Llangyndeyrn, Carmarthenshire, founded a settlement called 'Cambriol' for his compatriots in Newfoundland. He claimed in *The Golden Fleece* (1626) that God had reserved the island for the ancient Britons, though he failed to add that the same deity was prone to confound human expectations. Much later, from the 1680s onwards, peace-loving Welsh Quakers sought spiritual refuge and economic betterment in William Penn's 'Holy Experiment' in Pennsylvania. But the Welsh were also present in numbers among the multi-ethnic class of traders, slavers, mercenaries and pirates who criss-crossed the Atlantic in search of untold wealth. Imperial rivalries and trading opportunities expanded the horizons of Welsh migrants and increasingly brought them into contact with the Atlantic coasts of Europe and Africa, the Caribbean islands and the eastern ports of North America. Sir Henry Morgan, the most celebrated buccaneer in the world in the late seventeenth century, is a classic case of a Welsh poacher turned imperialist gamekeeper. Having emigrated to Barbados as an indentured servant in the late 1650s, this hard-drinking, swashbuckling soldier of fortune, whose strategic insight enabled him to sack Portobelo,

Maracaibo and (where Drake had failed) the golden city of Panama, received a knighthood from Charles II, was appointed lieutenant-governor of Jamaica and died an extraordinarily wealthy man in 1688. Morgan thus carved out a place in history as one of the earliest begetters of the British empire. During the golden age of piracy in the early eighteenth century, the trans-oceanic exploits of Bartholomew Roberts, the Pembrokeshire-born Black Bart, who plundered, burnt and sank several hundred Spanish and Portuguese ships, became the stuff of legend long after his defeat and capture by a British naval squadron in 1722. Demographic pressures and beguiling economic opportunities thus enabled the Welsh to play a full part in the movement of labour, the traffic of goods (legal and otherwise) and the appropriation of land.

In order to accommodate and feed the rising population, major changes were set in motion within post-Union Wales. Extensive tracts of woodland were cleared to create new farmlands and much arable land was enclosed. By the end of the Elizabethan period, the traditional manorial lands had been hedged and the Welsh clanlands had all but disappeared. Environmentalists bemoaned the assaults on woods and forests by cultivators, enclosers and industrialists, and as sheep became more numerous than cattle on upland pastures, young trees were swiftly destroyed. By the eve of the industrial revolution, travellers into Wales could not fail to notice the deforested nature of the landscape, though there were still, notably in the Rhondda Valleys, densely wooded areas. Closely associated with this major ecological change was the demise of the ancient practice of transhumance. The traditional *hafod* and *lluest*, smallholdings which had served as temporary upland pastures, increasingly became permanent homes in order to meet the growing needs of the livestock economy. Cattle and sheep were critical to the success of the economy, not least because hard-pressed farmers required the gold and silver coins brought home to Wales by drovers and other middlemen to pay rents, taxes, tithes and other dues. Livestock sales in the great markets of Barnet and Smithfield ensured a supply of ready cash, and the Welsh economy derived further benefits when the Irish Cattle Act (1666), which denied entry to Irish livestock, provoked welcome price rises for the sale of store cattle.

Following generations of neglect, from the mid-seventeenth century tillers of the soil with modest capital to invest began to practise
rotation and cultivate new crops (turnips, clover, sainfoin) to add
to the staple fare of oats, rye, wheat and barley in mixed farming
regions. From 1755 onwards county agricultural societies introduced 'scientific' methods of cultivation and rewarded improvers
who farmed efficiently. If farmers in the less congenial upland ranges
were inactive, this was because they had no spare capital or incentive
to improve their properties and increase productivity. The most
adaptable small farmers, however, found part-time or seasonal
work in the craft, woollen, fishing or mining industries, where extra
shillings helped to placate rent-collectors. Risk-taking was out of
the question and, at times of extreme demographic pressure or inflation, small farmers were often reduced to the ranks of landless labourers, with few prospects of recovery. As a result of such pressures,
somewhere between a quarter and a third of the population found
themselves locked into the labouring classes, where life was nasty,
brutish and short. From dawn to dusk, these stunted, weather-beaten,
poorly paid serfs were hewers of wood and drawers of water, involved
in the 'tillinge of the lande, burneinge of Lyme, digginge of coles, and
other slaveryes and extreame toyles'. Women working on the land
were expected to perform arduous physical tasks, to help with milk-
ing and brewing, and to spin wool and knit stockings at night. Living
on bread, cheese, porridge and oatmeal in tiny, verminous hovels, the
labouring sorts had few rights, and it is not surprising that they
poached rabbits, hares and birds on gentry estates or bloodied the
noses of Puritan or Methodist evangelists who sought to eradicate
their hard-earned recreations. In times of dearth and exceptionally
high mortality they, too, were forced to hit the road in search of
food and employment, though once they began to consort with footloose and unscrupulous vagabonds, beggars and ne'er-do-wells they
were liable to be arrested, whipped and escorted back to their parish
of birth or last known place of settlement. Although governments
encouraged immobility and inertia, the effects of population pressure
and merchant capitalism kept people on the move.

Increased mobility, the infusion of capital from outside Wales, the
stimulus provided by Atlantic trade and the demands of successive
wars (especially in the eighteenth century) meant that enterprising

men were prepared to set aside time, energy and resources to strengthen the under-capitalized industrial profile of Wales. Not surprisingly, as government prospectors, joint-stock companies and individual entrepreneurs provided the capital, none of the profits was pocketed by the Welsh. The monopoly exercised by the Shrewsbury Drapers' Company between 1562 and 1624 meant that the profits of the woollen trade in mid-Wales, a domestic industry in which thousands of spinners, carders, weavers and fullers prepared copious supplies of coarse cloth, gloves, socks, caps and wigs, dribbled out of Wales. But once this monopoly was broken, Welsh weavers, fullers, knitters and merchants were given a new lease of life and, to some extent, were free to control their destiny by selling their wares to distant colonies. By the mid-eighteenth century, the demand for 'Welsh plains and cottons' on the international market was so great that it transformed the purchasing power of woollen manufacturers in small domestic industries in the counties of Denbighshire, Montgomeryshire and Merioneth. Even King George III, though he never visited Wales, wore Welsh stockings.

In the immediate post-Union period, a surge of enterprise also occurred in the exploitation of minerals. Incorporated by royal charter in 1568, the Society of Mines Royal encouraged highly skilled German miners and metallurgists to extract copper, gold, silver and zinc, but individual initiatives also bore fruit. By the 1620s Hugh Myddelton was reputed to be gaining monthly profits of £2,000 from lead mines he leased in mid-Cardiganshire, while Thomas Bushell was authorized to establish a royal mint at Aberystwyth castle in 1637. A general shortage of fuel led to a sizeable expansion in the coal industry which, by 1688, formed around 90 per cent of Welsh exports. It was around this time that Sir Humphrey Mackworth, a Shropshire-born technophile with autocratic and risk-taking tendencies, not only brought the lead mines of Cardiganshire out of the doldrums but also seized opportunities to develop coal mining and the smelting of imported lead and copper in the Neath/Swansea area, thereby ensuring that by the 1730s it was the greatest metallurgical centre in the world. Hard on its heels as a developing metalworking centre was north-east Wales, where Holywell was the major focus by the 1770s. At this stage, too, there emerged Thomas Williams, 'The Copper King', who, on the basis of the rising mineral power of the copper mines at Parys Mountain, Anglesey, showed a refreshing willingness to give the industrial giants of England a run for their money. This self-made millionaire was thoroughly capable of intimidating his rivals, and Matthew Boulton dubbed him 'a perfect tyrant [who] will screw damned hard when he has got anybody in his vice'. Lewis Morris, a barrel-bellied Crown steward who urged the Welsh gentry to invest in the lead mines of Cardiganshire (he called them the 'Cambrian Peru') rather than 'choose to rummage the East and West Indies for Money', was deeply conscious that the wheels of the Welsh economy were increasingly being oiled by merchant capitalists from the north of England, the Midlands, Bristol and London, whose affluence was based on colonial ventures, privateering, slave trading and war-driven manufacturing. But there was no sense of outrage as Wales found itself drawn into a world of greed, excess and skulduggery in which the lion's share of the spoils went to English-born investors.

External capital certainly catalyzed the iron industry in northeast Wales and the northern uplands of Glamorgan. Prolonged and expensive wars, the transfer from charcoal to coke smelting, and the provision of blast for smelting iron from Boulton and Watt's steam engines all laid a platform on which hard-nosed adventurers from England improved efficiency and acquired sizeable profits. These were not men to be toyed with. John Wilkinson – 'mad Iron John' – made a small fortune at Bersham, close to the populous town of Wrexham, not only by ruling his workforce like a grenadier but also by providing the armed forces with superior cannon, grenades and shells. But even his impressive enterprise was eclipsed by the extraordinary arc of ironworks – the celebrated 'labyrinth of flames' – established at Cyfarthfa, Plymouth, Penydarren and Dowlais in the mineral kingdom around Merthyr Tydfil. Here, from the 1760s onwards, pig-iron production soared as mercantile capital supplied by John Guest (Shropshire), Anthony Bacon (London) and, most of all, by Richard Crawshay (Yorkshire) – a self-made, tyrannical ironmaster whose wealth and egotism did not endear him to his employees – set it on the path to becoming the greatest centre of iron production in the world.

By most European standards, Wales was an extremely lightly urbanized country. In the mid-Tudor period the largest, 'fairest' and 'most civil' towns of more than 1,500 people were Carmarthen, Haverfordwest, Brecon and Wrexham. But, reflecting the sluggish nature of the economy, the overall proportion of urban dwellers was scarcely more than 10 per cent of the total population. The norm was Lilliputian: towns comprised some two or three hundred inhabitants, were subject to fluctuating economic fortunes and lacked truly urban facilities. Castle towns, having lost their military function, simply stagnated, and even those market towns with a growing range of commercial and professional services remained small, shabby and nondescript until, during the late seventeenth century, they acquired specialisms and new retailing, leisure and cultural functions. Over the bulk of this period Welsh towns, and indeed rural inhabitants, were inextricably tied into the economies of the regional urban 'capitals' of Wales which lay within striking distance on the other side of Offa's Dyke. Farmers and manufacturers in north and mid-Wales looked to Chester and especially Shrewsbury (the premier marketing centre for Welsh cloth and a conduit via the Severn for iron producers) for their salvation, while Bristol was known as the 'great Mart of south Wales'. The Welsh towns which did best were dependent on the transforming effects of industrial growth or quickening maritime activity in the Irish Sea and the Atlantic. Carmarthen benefited from its flourishing port as well as its status as the headquarters of the Welsh printing industry from the 1720s onwards, while Swansea experienced an exceptional surge of expansion as the principal manufacturer of copper in Britain. By the 1740s, long before its reincarnation as 'the Brighton of Wales', Swansea was an unrivalled Copperopolis. Yet, by the time of the first official census in 1801 less than 15 per cent of the total population lived in towns of over a thousand inhabitants. Early modern Wales was a land of rural dwellers, but over time its economy had become more diverse and more closely intertwined with the new Atlantic community.

The socio-economic integration of Wales within England was at least indirectly a consequence of the Acts of Union 1536–43, a programme of legislation which was part of a much larger package designed to bring diverse peoples living in vulnerable peripheries like Ireland and Calais, as well as counties palatine such as Chester and Durham, under royal authority. Unity, uniformity and administrative efficiency within all parts of the realm were central to the strategies of the chief policy-maker, Thomas Cromwell, in the 1530s. Cromwell was convinced that Wales, with its unprotected coastline and unruly marcher lordships, was a serious security risk and an obstacle to his aim of establishing a more effective and progressive system of government. His ideals coincided with the aspirations of the Welsh gentry, who were equally determined to be rid of the marcher lordships and to share the benefits of English common law and a voice at Westminster. Yet, far from being a bilateral measure carried out with widespread approval on both sides, the Union was a crude piece of annexation. Although the gentry were for the most part supportive, hardliners like Rowland Lee, who had grave misgivings about giving the Welsh any measure of self-regulation, were strongly opposed, and we can be sure that those below gentry status had no hand in the formulation of the terms. Curiously, the Welsh bards were conspicuously silent on the issue and, by all accounts, the statutes seem to have been engineered and implemented painlessly. Only in hindsight, especially on the occasion of the four hundredth anniversary of the 1536 Act, did nationalist historians highlight what they believed to be the most contentious and unwelcome pieces of legislation in the history of Wales.

Although Henry VIII expressed his 'singular zeal, love and favour' towards the Welsh people in the preamble to the 1536 Act, the whole tenor of the legislation was hostile towards the so-called 'sinister usages and customs' which were emblematic of the otherness of Wales. Such obstacles to the development of 'civil' government undoubtedly included the brutal private jurisdictions and so-called liberties which made the marcher lordships a blot on the landscape, but they also included the Welsh laws and the vernacular, a speech singled out as being 'nothing like nor consonant to the natural mother tongue' known as English. Hastily assembled, the 1536 Act was something of a dog's breakfast. There was clearly a pressing need to sweep away the marcher lordships and establish internal unification by means of shire government. Wales was divided into thirteen shires, six of which – Anglesey, Caernarfonshire, Merioneth, Flintshire, Carmarthenshire and Cardiganshire – had already been in existence since the Statute of Wales in 1284 – and the seven new counties carved out of the defunct and unlamented

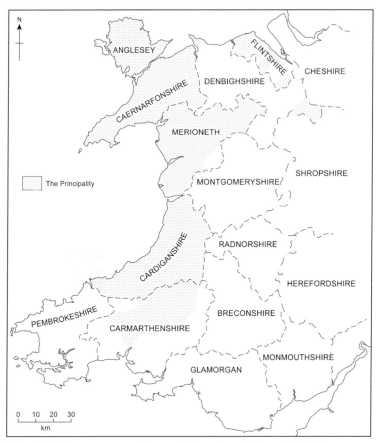

Map 6. In the twenty-seventh year of the reign of Henry VIII Wales was incorporated, by the 1536 Act of Union, into England. 'England and Wales' would become a common refrain thereafter. In place of the old marcher lordships, there were now thirteen shires. The border established between Wales and England has survived to our times.

marcher lordships were Denbighshire, Montgomeryshire, Breconshire, Radnorshire, Monmouthshire, Glamorgan and Pembrokeshire. English common law displaced *cyfraith Hywel* and English became the official medium of law and administration, and no monoglot Welsh-speaker could henceforward hold office. Parliamentary representation was extended both to the shires and boroughs of Wales, thereby permitting twenty-seven voices to be heard at Westminster.

In several respects, the 1536 Act was imprecise and confusing. The process of shiring was not immediately implemented and at one stage the setting up of a new Principality for the benefit of Prince Edward was seriously contemplated. But by the time the second Act was passed in 1543 – a measure which comprised 130 clauses and which dotted the 'i' and crossed the 't' in a more systematic way – the counsel of the Brecon-born administrator and scholar Sir John Prise, who had married a niece to the wife of the executed Thomas Cromwell, had evidently been heeded. The apparatus of English shire government – justices of the peace, sheriffs, coroners and constables – was introduced, and English principles of land tenure (primogeniture) replaced partible inheritance (gavelkind). Significantly, Wales was granted until their abolition in 1830 a system of higher courts distinct from that of England: these were the Courts of Great Sessions, whose function was to hear criminal, civil and equity cases. Four circuits were set up in each corner of Wales, and the courts were charged to administer English law during six-day sessions held in spring and autumn. The Council in the Marches, first established in 1471, was granted statutory authority as an administrative and judicial body, while the administration of county affairs and minor criminal cases were entrusted to local justices of the peace within the Courts of Quarter Sessions.

Historians have traditionally described the Tudor settlement of 1536–43 as 'Acts of Union', but it could just as easily be argued that 'Acts of Assimilation' would provide a more accurate indication of the integrative process at work. The key phrase in the preamble to the 1536 Act is that Wales henceforth was to be governed 'in like form' to England. Both politically and administratively, it was made part and parcel of England. There remained, nonetheless, curious and irritating anomalies. In a seemingly arbitrary way, the settlement of the political boundary had the effect of isolating several robust communities of Welsh speakers on the 'wrong' side of Offa's Dyke. The severance from Wales of these linguistic enclaves meant that 'the Welsh toong', according to the Tudor historian David Powel, 'is commonlie used and spoken Englandward'. Just as disconcerting was the failure to include Monmouthshire within the system of the Courts of Great Sessions (it was dispatched to the Oxford circuit of the English Assize Courts), thereby necessitating in many subsequent statutes and elsewhere the use of the annoyingly misleading phrase 'Wales and Monmouthshire'.

The key to the successful implementation of the Union were the Welsh gentry, who now embarked on a mutually supportive partnership with the Crown and central government. Tudor monarchs tickled the vanity of the gentry by associating them, both historically and practically, with the interests of the Crown. In the striking phrase of the Elizabethan commentator George Owen, the Welsh became 'Magistrates of theyr own Nation'. In a very real sense they were offered a stake in developing 'civil' government, and there is no doubt that, without their willing co-operation, the state would not have been in a position to create a politically unified realm or promote a new social programme based on the 'civilizing' influence of English law and administration. The story was very different in Ireland, where the response to so-called 'civilized' norms and integration was incandescent rebelliousness. As the Irish became more fractious, the Welsh became more benign. Thomas Cromwell and his successors had shrewdly calculated that those in Wales who stood to benefit from the Tudor settlement would happily promote the process of assimilation. The gentry themselves, of course, were not paragons of virtue and some of them were the worst possible enemies to good order and government. No one familiar with Tudor and early Stuart court records would deny how frequently cases of bribery, corruption and jury-rigging disfigured Welsh life or how often factional rivalries led to skirmishes, duels and violent affrays on the streets. Pre-Union abuses and malpractices did not vanish overnight, and turbulent squires did not always devote themselves to the public good. Yet, George Owen was probably right to point out that no sensible person at the end of Elizabeth's reign would have hankered after the days of the marcher lords, when a substantial portion of Wales had been a cauldron of hatreds and divisions. The strikingly large number of civil and criminal cases coming before the Court of Great Sessions up to the mid-seventeenth century indicates that the Welsh, even though monoglot speakers suspected that the use of English was an attempt to mystify and intimidate them, were happy to make use of the principal royal court in Wales. But Owen's claim that Tudor rule had 'brought Wales to great Civilitie' was a good deal more contentious. What is certain is that the leaders of

Welsh society were far too closely bound up with the Tudor settlement to contemplate stepping too far out of line or, even more
improbably, rising in rebellion.

   The rise of the Welsh gentry is one of the most striking features of
this period, and the Union legislation unquestionably opened new
windows of opportunity for them. Implicit within the fundamental
social division between *bonedd a gwrêng* (gentry and commonalty)
was the deep-seated belief that prosperous gentlemen who could
boast extensive acres of land and a reputable ancestry were people
to whom God had awarded privileged status and who deserved
unswerving obedience and respect. This was a society based on
inequality, deference and paternalism, and once the Union had
declared that they would be the principal beneficiaries the Welsh
gentry embarked on a variety of stratagems, not all of which were
legal, designed to extend their domains and enrich their coffers.
They acquired monastic lands, enclosed extensive pieces of waste,
forest and common land, and arranged propitious and lucrative
marriage settlements. The latter could cut both ways: Katheryn of
Berain, the Denbighshire granddaughter of a bastard son of Henry
VII, married four times and was famously known as 'the Mother
of Wales'. But in the main, the marriage market was governed by
males. Although the native tradition of partible inheritance was
reluctant to beat a hasty retreat in post-Union Wales, progressive
gentry families were strongly in favour of primogeniture because it
encouraged the building up of compact, permanent estates. Thus it
was that the resident Welsh gentry – the Bulkeleys of Anglesey, the
Mostyns of Flintshire, the Vaughans of Cardiganshire, the Mansels
of Glamorgan and many others like them – extended their holdings,
built grand houses, sat for portrait-painters, hired genealogists (and,
less often, household poets) and sent their sons to grammar schools,
universities, the inns of court and, if they promised to behave themselves, to widen their horizons still further by embarking on a Grand
Tour of Europe. Inevitably, in the long run the landed elite came to
believe that whereas English was a high-prestige language eminently
equipped for government, law and administration, Welsh was a
barley-bread tongue fit only for peasant use on the hearth and at
fairs and markets. They equated civility with speaking English
and, as the period unfolded, the incomprehensible jabber of the

'mountain' Welsh increasingly offended the 'polite' sensibilities of elites in highly gentrified counties like Glamorgan. Although it is important not to pre-date the anglicization of the Welsh elite, with every passing year from the mid-seventeenth century onwards those who presumed superior wisdom in such matters believed that 'civilized' people spoke English. Many gentlemen publicly endorsed political and cultural integration. Sir William Vaughan, the promoter of one of the most ill-judged chapters in the history of Welsh settlements overseas, besought the English to recognize that old divisions were receding and that 'our green leeks, sometimes offensive to your dainty nostrils, are tempered with your fragrant roses'. Sir William Maurice of Clenennau, whose prolix speeches in the House of Commons rendered him a figure of fun, flattered to the new Stuart dynasty by addressing James I as 'King of Great Britain'.

Almost without exception, therefore, the Welsh gentry could be relied upon to rally to the establishment. Their economic wealth buttressed their political power within their localities, and it was in their interests to exercise the coercive powers of the state and maintain subordination among the deferential, unrebellious Welsh. Since electoral contests could prove to be ruinously expensive, most sensible gentlemen were at pains to avoid them by arranging beneficial gentlemen's agreements which pretended to be means of preserving the peace of the county. When a contested election could not be avoided, freeholders and burgesses were marched to the polls by their masters and were left in no doubt about what was expected of them. Although Welsh MPs were exasperated by the financial demands of Charles I and the heavily 'popish' liturgy promoted by his ally, Archbishop William Laud, during the 1630s their ingrained loyalty to the throne meant that the Crown was not abandoned in its hour of need in 1642. Outside Pembrokeshire and parts of Denbighshire, support for parliament at the outbreak of the civil wars was extremely tenuous, and a sheaf of decisively pro-royalist petitions, promising unwavering loyalty to Charles I, was a fair reflection of Welsh sentiments on the eve of hostilities, even if the counties themselves were not on an effective war footing. Mercifully, Wales never became a major theatre of war, but it was strategically important and the king in particular milked it for men, resources and money for all he was worth. In fact, he overplayed his hand in mustering fighting men by coercion and by permitting his armies, who were notorious plunderers and sickness-bearers, to ravage at will. Having forfeited his popularity, Charles found that 'ambidexters' (as they were called in south Wales) became increasingly reluctant to take to the field, and growing bands of war-weary neutralists and peacemakers in Glamorgan revolted against royalist armies who disrupted the livelihood of drovers and clothiers. Yet, Wales did not become a significant focus of attention until disenchanted parliamentarians in Pembrokeshire offered their services to the beleaguered king in the Second Civil War in 1648. During a formidable contest at St Fagans on 8 May 1648, however, Colonel Thomas Horton's seasoned troops put the insurgents to the sword and, ironically, the participation of the Welsh and others in a futile bid to revive the royalist cause probably sealed the fate of the king.

As we have seen, the Welsh in medieval times were no strangers to the practice of eliminating men with royal blood coursing through their veins, but their descendants in Stuart times were of a different ilk. Not only the gentry but also the bulk of the populace were horrified when the Lord's Anointed, the defender of the rights and privileges of all his subjects, was publicly beheaded outside the Banqueting Hall in London in January 1649. A deep sense of desolation fell over Wales, and for more than a century Welsh literature was replete with barbed references to 'king-killers' and 'murderous Roundheads'. For the overwhelming majority of Welsh people, the Cromwellian republic was 'a monster without a head', and local governing elites found themselves elbowed aside by armed blacksmiths, millers and tailors who, together with radical Puritan saints and administrators, acquired a reputation for racketeering, petty corruption and bribery. Most of the accusations were levelled against Colonel Philip Jones who, having become 'a sort of unofficial minister for Wales' among Oliver Cromwell's chosen few, was reckoned by royalists to have become a wealthy man through the misuse of public office. Not until the twentieth century, when charges of public corruption were often levelled against local politicians, was Wales riven so badly by corruption scandals. Voicing the despair of loyalists, Welsh poets poured vitriol on aliens, strangers and low-born men whose sharp swords and bullying tactics had turned their world upside down.

The short sharp shock of republican rule left an indelible imprint on people's minds, and even in the mid-eighteenth century commentators referred to the 'late troubled times' as if they had occurred the previous year. Never were church bells rung more joyously in Wales than on the occasion of the return of Charles II in May 1660, and the popular revulsion shown towards regicides like Colonel John Jones, Maesygarnedd, who was hanged, drawn and quartered, shows the depth of loyalty which remained towards the Crown. For Welsh royalists, revenge was sweet and the practice of politics once more became dominated by powerful landed families who had no difficulty in controlling a tiny Welsh electorate which never exceeded 25,000 people. The Eatanswill world of patronage, jobbery and corruption meant that party divisions, in the traditional sense of Whig versus Tory, were meaningless as the privileged few continued to frown on contested elections and, when necessary, used bullying stewards and agents to ensure that even the most cussed voters obeyed their landlords at the polling booths. In this climate of fear and suspicion, the 'old leaven' of radical Puritans were purged within the borough towns and efforts to 'civilize' the Welsh and reform their manners were even more rigorously implemented. Although several gifted Welshmen rose to high political office under Charles II and James II, Welsh parliamentary politics became a desultory affair. The 'rage of party' which characterized political life under the later Stuarts was replaced by an oligarchic system whose arbitrary and unrepresentative nature meant that the politicization of the nation lay far in the future. So entrenched was political integration and so somnolent were the Welsh that in 1746 parliament declared, without fear of offending the Welsh, that whenever the word 'England' appeared in any piece of legislation it should be read as including 'Wales' also. Even Welsh Jacobites, who noisily toasted the Pretender behind closed doors until the small hours, were conspicuous by their absence when long-awaited rebellions broke out in 1715 and 1745. Jacobitism in Wales is the sorry tale of the dog which barked a good deal but never bit.

The politics of oligarchy were closely associated with changes in the balance of wealth and power from the Restoration onwards. The prevailing trend was for land to gravitate into the hands of a tiny number of massively wealthy landowners. Gravely weakened by their curious failure to produce male heirs or crippled by mortgages, the native gentry slipped down the social scale and some of them sank without trace. In the 1770s Thomas Pennant noted that traditional gentry homes were being swallowed by 'our Welsh Leviathans'. This shift was best exemplified in gentrified Glamorgan, where many of the elite families were more prosperous than the minor nobility of France or Italy. With monotonous regularity, famous old estates fell into the eager hands of a new ruling class of absentee titans. Old patriarchs, whose local esteem in Tudor and Stuart times had been based on ancestry, *noblesse oblige* and a sense of cultural allegiance, had now been replaced by new parasites who, in Iolo Morganwg's caustic phrase, were no better than 'pimps, panders, whores and toad eaters'. Growing numbers of social commentators deplored the political attitudes of powerful absentee non-Welsh-speaking landowners who employed agents and stewards to enforce manorial rights, enclose common land and intimidate recalcitrant voters. By the time of the American war, the gulf between the 'haves' and the 'have-nots' was greater than it had ever been. Little wonder that a more progressive style of politics was emerging from Dissenting academies and masonic lodges where 'friends of liberty' assembled. But Old Corruption was still very much alive and kicking, and the gentry class never doubted for a moment the benefits of Union.

Did all this mean that the Welsh had sunk into denial and paralysis? Having been hustled down avenues which robbed them of their political and legal identity, did they simply close their eyes and ears? Were they content to be marginalized by the insensitivities of the political classes and prostrate themselves before the English model? For answers to these questions we need to explore the effects of the Long Reformation and the nature of cultural change. The Reformation in Wales is best considered over a long timescale as a succession of reforming missions from *c.* 1536 to the high watermark at the end of the eighteenth century (some would say even to the great religious revival of 1859). Winning the hearts and minds of the Welsh to the Protestant faith could not be accomplished overnight, and throughout the early modern period commentators, moralists and reformers, many of whom ascribed superior status to the 'civilized' English tongue, were scathing about what they believed to be the social isolation, lamentable communications and slow-moving economy of this 'dark', 'barren' and 'popish' land. Whatever the truth of the matter, it swiftly dawned on Welsh promoters of the Reformation and defenders of Welsh selfhood that the presence of a vernacular liturgy was absolutely crucial.

Initially, the Reformation did not come to Wales as a result of a blinding revelation experienced by a Cymricized Martin Luther. It was imposed by a powerful monarchy through acts of state and came about less because people were dissatisfied with medieval Christianity than because of the political and financial needs of Henry VIII. The first decisive change occurred in 1533–4 when the king severed ties with Rome and made himself, by the will of parliament, supreme head of the Church in England. He then cast his beady eye on a vulnerable but wealthy target – the monasteries and friaries – and resolved to be rid of them. His trusty minister, Thomas Cromwell, organized an orgy of licensed vandalism worthy of the Taliban at their worst. By 1540 the entire Welsh complement of forty-seven monastic houses had been dissolved and church property, as well as deeply cherished shrines and effigies, had been stripped away and fed to the flames. This turned out to be the prelude for even more wanton destruction of the old order in the Edwardian period, a transformation carried out so swiftly that it provoked widespread bitterness and resentment. Yet, despite predictions of a likely uprising led by champions of the Old Faith, there was no Welsh equivalent of the Pilgrimage of Grace or any executions or burnings on a large scale. A cleric in north Wales bravely claimed that if Henry VIII ever ventured to Snowdonia 'he would souse [him] about the ears till he had made his head soft enough', but the Welsh gentry and clergy, mindful of the king's foul temper and reluctant to forego some of the rich spoils likely to come their way in the wake of the dismantling of the pre-Reformation church, obeyed the royal will, paid lip service to the new Protestant regime and got on with their lives. Catholic poets grumbled about 'the faith of the English', but once Mary I had died childless in 1558 and been replaced by her Protestant half-sister, Elizabeth I, the Protestant crusade could begin in earnest.

The critical question at this stage was whether the state was prepared to endorse the notion that political unity and uniformity could best be defended by taking steps to ensure that Welsh did not

become the formal language of Protestantism. It had already signalled its intentions by replacing the Latin liturgy with English
bibles and prayer books, but those who were more closely involved
with the massive task of making Protestantism a living reality to a
largely monoglot and illiterate people and who were determined to
guard against the possibility of a Catholic resurgence argued
strongly in favour of adopting Welsh as the official medium of
public worship throughout Wales. In the event, representation at
the highest political level by three highly gifted Protestants from
north Wales – Bishop Richard Davies, Humphrey Llwyd and
William Salesbury – persuaded the government that the souls of
the Welsh could be saved more swiftly through the medium of
Welsh. This astonishing volte-face paved the way for the epoch-
making Act of 1563, which ordered the translation of the Scriptures
into Welsh. This had the effect not only of empowering and energizing the 'rude' and 'contemptible' vernacular in the religious domain
but also of safeguarding its future prospects as a living tongue.
Salesbury's flawed version of the Welsh New Testament in 1567
was not at all well received in Welsh churches, but William
Morgan, vicar of Llanrhaeadr-ym-Mochnant, completed in 1588 a
Welsh version of the complete Bible which was a startlingly fine
literary masterpiece. The impact of the Welsh Bible in grounding
the Protestant faith in Wales cannot be over-emphasized. In Ireland,
Protestantism was propagated in English and inevitably smacked of
colonialism. In Wales, the presence of a Welsh bible and prayer book
in every parish church meant that the New Religion lost its alien
image. Indeed, in his preface to the Welsh New Testament in 1567,
bishop Richard Davies maintained that the Welsh were a chosen
people who, by rejecting the 'false' and 'polluted' Catholic religion
in favour of the 'true' apostolic faith which had been brought to them
by Joseph of Arimathea shortly after Christ's death, were now experiencing its second flowering in a Welsh Protestant environment.
Among other things, therefore, in the long run Protestantism became
a key conduit for the expression of cultural nationalism in Wales.
Without the Welsh Bible, the Reformation would have been a transient phenomenon imposed on an unwilling and resentful populace.

    As the series of draconian anti-Catholic legislation amply reveals,
Elizabeth was not prepared to tolerate religious pluralism or anyone

Y BEIBL CYS-
SEGR-LAN. SEF
YR HEN DESTA-
MENT, A'R NEWYDD.

2. *Timoth.* 3. 14, 15.

Eithr aros di yn y pethau a ddyfcaift, ac a ymddyried-
wyd i ti, gan wybod gan bwy y dyfcaift.
Ac i ti er yn fachgen wybod yr fcrythur lân, yr hon
fydd abl i'th wneuthur yn ddoeth i iechydwria-
eth, trwy'r ffydd yr hon fydd yng-Hrift Iefu.

Imprinted at London by the Deputies of
CHRISTOPHER BARKER,
Printer to the Queenes moft excel-
lent Maieftie.

1588.

26. In September 1588 the first printed Welsh bible was published in
London. The work of William Morgan (1544/5–1604), vicar of
Llanrhaeadr-ym-Mochnant, Denbighshire, it proved to be a triumphantly
successful work which enabled Protestantism to flourish in the native
tongue. (The National Library of Wales)

who stirred up disaffection. Her long reign was punctuated by invasion scares and plots, and local magistrates were regularly ordered to exercise the strictest vigilance. Welsh Catholics in exile, especially at Douai, Milan and Rome, worked tirelessly in training missionaries, and brave recusant families sheltered them in priest-holes or guided them to obscure caves where clandestine printing presses helped to sustain the increasingly forlorn hope of restoring the Old Faith. Although only two Catholics – Richard Gwyn at Wrexham in 1584 and William Davies at Beaumaris in 1593 – were martyred during the reign of Elizabeth, this does not mean that the deeply ingrained habits of Catholic piety were eliminated. Thanks largely to the financial and moral succour provided by powerful families like the Marquis of Worcester (one of the principal funders of the royalist cause during the civil wars), and from 1622 by the Jesuit college at Cwm, Herefordshire, Catholicism retained robust support along the Welsh Marches even though it was increasingly associated in the minds of the Welsh with foreign rule, oppression and treason. By the 1630s, however, only octogenarians would have retained even the faintest memory of life under a Catholic ruler, and the prospects of sustaining a vigorous Counter-Reformation in Wales had receded alarmingly.

Mercifully, the rivalry, however uneven, between the two religions did not provoke a flurry of prosecution for witchcraft. In fact, Wales was spared the malevolent horror of the European witch trials. There were no professional witchfinders, and antagonisms against recusants were not sufficiently acute to stir up feelings against 'heretics' of any kind. Only five suspected witches were put to death, the first of whom, Gwen ferch Ellis, was publicly hanged in Denbighshire in 1594 for allegedly bewitching several neighbours. By all accounts, the state was so heavily preoccupied in prosecuting and executing thieves in Wales that it had little time to focus on demonology. Local people were more likely to vent their spleen on sowers of discord and strife, and during the heyday of cases of verbal and written slander (1570–1670) Welsh courts echoed to the sounds of colourful accusatory words such as 'y bastard bingam' (thou spayfooted bastard), 'cornworwm brwnt' (foul cuckold) and 'yr hen butain gaglog' (you old draggle whore). Belief in witchcraft never faded, but the good sense and humanity of neighbours meant that killing innocent people was judged to be far more reprehensible than bringing actions for slander.

It was one thing to snuff out Catholics and curb witches, but if Protestantism was to become a living reality the clergy needed to be jolted into preaching the Word vigorously. Hotter Protestants, known as Puritans, offered a more vivid sense of right and wrong by preaching the virtues of Calvinism. John Penry, an angry young Breconshire man, had the temerity to warn Elizabeth that God would use the Spanish Armada to punish her for neglecting to reform a church which was riddled with 'dumb dogs' who were either too lazy or worldly to disseminate saving knowledge. For mainstream churchmen, separatism was anathema and when Penry opted for the more radical and dangerous alternative to worshipping in parish churches and refused to recant, he became the first Welsh Puritan martyr in May 1593. The fact that this young man left behind a widow and four tiny daughters called Safety, Comfort, Sure Hope and Deliverance lent added poignancy to his demise. Yet, Penry was a peripheral figure who attracted little support and even less sympathy during his brief career. The killjoy element implicit in godly Puritan discipline was unattractive and, without a preaching ministry, it was hard to instruct flocks. There were no obvious disciples to follow in Penry's footsteps until the eve of the civil wars, when William Wroth founded a separatist Independent church at Llanfaches, Monmouthshire, in 1639 and masterminded a vigorous programme of itinerant preaching. This was led by gifted and energetic Puritans like Walter Cradock, Morgan Llwyd and Vavasor Powell, whose names loom large in the story of how separatist churches in Wales claimed the right of the individual to interpret scripture and to find his or her own way to God's truth. But although London-Welsh Puritans funded the first octavo Welsh Bible in 1630 and the catchy, but unmistakably Puritan, verses composed by Rees Prichard, vicar of Llandovery, exercised a profound oral influence and an even greater printed one by running to fifty-two editions between 1658 and 1820 under the title *Canwyll y Cymru* (The Welshmen's Candle), Puritanism found it hard to shake off its image as an alien plant. It appealed chiefly to affluent middling sorts in border towns and ports, where bilingualism was developing and where attachment to the Crown was weakest.

As crude and hostile caricatures of the Welsh accompanied the parliamentary campaign during the civil wars and as zealous ministers began to turn the world upside down by encouraging sectarians like the Baptists, Fifth Monarchists, Quakers and Ranters to promote their unfamiliar and potentially explosive teachings, radical saints strove to introduce on a much larger scale the 'civilizing' benefits of the Puritan gospel. As in Cornwall, parliament was viewed as 'the party of Englishness' in Wales, and moderate opinion as well as the traditional elites were alienated when, under the terms of the Act for the Better Propagation of the Gospel in Wales (1650), supposedly unfit clergy were replaced by zealous preaching ministers and sword-waving republicans, who not only threatened to establish a rigid rule of the saints but also to undermine the popular culture and festivities held dear by those whom they sought to convert. In vain did Morgan Llwyd, a supremely gifted (but often impenetrable) writer, seek to persuade Welsh readers that the demise of 'unhappy Charles' was a harbinger of the second coming of Christ and a fair deal for all under the Puritan regime. To the Welsh, state-sponsored Puritanism and its associated radical sectarianism were abhorrent, and Henry Vaughan, the greatest of Welsh metaphysical poets, feared that this represented 'a thick black night' rather than 'a glorious day-spring':

Arise O God, and let thine enemies be scattered, and let those that hate thee flee before thee. Behold the robbers are come into thy Sanctuary, and the persecuters are within thy walls. We drink our own waters for money, and our wood is sold unto us. Our necks are under persecution, we labour and have no rest. Yea, thine own Inheritance is given to strangers, and thine own portion unto aliens.

The Puritan propagation, conducted in an atmosphere of bitterness and recrimination, aroused widespread hostility and fear, and when the Merry Monarch arrived in 1660 churchmen looked forward to the opportunity to pay off old scores.

The return of the monarchy and the restored Church of England presaged hard times for Puritans (or Dissenters, as they were called from 1662 onwards), and the governing elites used their best efforts to eradicate them altogether. The Clarendon Code, a draconian series of penal statutes, was designed to inflict as much suffering and humiliation upon past enemies as possible. Malcontents and republicans were swiftly rounded up and incarcerated. Among them was Vavasor Powell, who was locked up for the best part of ten years and still went to meet his Maker while singing 'A Roundhead I will be'. In the year 1662, 130 Puritan ministers were ejected from their livings, but the rigorous implementation of the penal code was largely determined by the willingness of magistrates to proceed against Dissenters. Even those who did bestir themselves discovered that nimble separatists took advantage of flaws and anomalies in the legislation or evaded capture by worshipping in remote caves or farmhouses. Baptists, and especially Quakers, made light of living 'under the Cross', and the latter endured exceptionally brutal treatment without ever resorting to retaliation or anger. Yet, there were limits even to their patience and when William Penn opened a door of mercy to beleaguered Friends, many hundreds of them sailed from 1682 onwards to the New Jerusalem in Pennsylvania where 'the Welsh Barony' offered the promise of liberty of conscience and peaceful fellowship. But there was no escape for proselytizing Catholic priests, five of whom were hunted down and barbarously executed in 1679. Not until the passing of the Toleration Act of 1689 did old enmities begin to soften, but even afterwards Dissenters remained a disenfranchised minority. Yet, 'the Lord's free people', as they liked to call themselves, proved to be a lively leaven in the lump, especially among book-reading craftsmen and artisans in thriving urban centres. Thanks to the likes of Stephen Hughes, 'The Apostle of Carmarthenshire', a compelling Independent minister who disseminated thousands of Welsh bibles, translated Bunyan's *The Pilgrim's Progress* into Welsh and made *Canwyll y Cymru* a major bestseller, both the reading habit and independent thinking were fostered among the minority of people who enjoyed reading and wrestling with the scriptures and other godly books.

More ominous were growing signs that churchmen and Dissenters who were anxious to foster literacy and good works were prepared to renege on the spirit of the Act of 1563 which had made Welsh the language of Protestantism in Wales. During the period of Puritan propagation in the 1650s, English-medium schools had been established and, when the voluntary movement known as the Welsh Trust (1674–81) took up the torch, Puritan morality and the drive towards literacy became inextricably associated in the public mind with anglicization. English, too, was the dominant medium in the ninety-six schools established from 1699 onwards by the Anglican-sponsored Society for the Promotion of Christian Knowledge (SPCK), and this dovetailed neatly with the apparent desire of the leaders of the established church to deCymricize the institution. During the eighteenth century, the epithet 'Anglo bishops' (*esgyb Eingl*) was coined to describe absentee English bishops, birds of passage who denied preferments to Welsh-speaking clergymen and whose inability to read even the most elementary Welsh rendered them unfit for office. An English proctor, representing a disgraced clergyman in Anglesey in the early 1770s, smugly claimed that Wales was 'a conquered country, it is proper to introduce the English language, and it is the duty of the bishops to endeavour to promote the English, in order to introduce the language'.

Faced by the calamitous prospect of an anglicized established church serving the pastoral needs of a predominantly Welsh-speaking people, an alternative bottom-up strategy was devised by those who believed that the success of the Reformation in Wales was in jeopardy. A major turning point occurred in 1695, when printing spread to the provinces and Shrewsbury became the headquarters of the Welsh printing trade under the remarkably enterprising printer, publisher and almanacker Thomas Jones. In 1718 the first official printing press on Welsh soil was established in the tiny village of Trerhedyn in the Vale of Teifi, and three years later the first of several flourishing publishing enterprises was set up in Carmarthen, the commercial 'capital' of south-west Wales. The first printed Welsh book had been published in 1546, but by 1699 only around 220 Welsh-language books had seen the light of day. By contrast, over 2,600 Welsh books were published during the course of the eighteenth century, a figure which compares extremely well with, for instance, the mere 70 titles published in the Scottish Gaelic language before 1800. This appreciable flow of mostly pious books clearly helped to nourish a new respect and affection for the printed word, to improve literacy rates and to assist those who were fired by a burning zeal for saving souls.

The emergence of a substantial book-reading public, however, stemmed largely from the extraordinary success of Welsh-medium circulating schools established between 1731 and 1776 by Griffith

Jones, rector of Llanddowror in Carmarthenshire, and his affluent benefactress, Madam Bridget Bevan of Laugharne. This asthmatic, melancholy clergyman, with a high reputation as a powerful evangelist, distanced himself from the discredited policy of the SPCK of imparting a knowledge of English by teaching the three 'Rs' by rote. In its place, he devised a remarkably flexible and effective Welsh-medium system of peripatetic schools tailored to the needs of humble, illiterate people. The enterprise was rudimentary, but therein lay its strength. With the financial support of those who had their hands on the strongest social levers and the co-operation of his fellow clergy, Jones assembled on virtually a shoestring an army of teachers (both male and female) and urged them to concentrate on teaching the 'vulgar sorts' to read the Bible and the Church catechism in their native tongue. Determined to acquire the reading habit, farmers, craftsmen, labourers, wives and children flocked to parish churches, barns and farmhouses which, by the 1750s, echoed throughout Wales to the sounds of adult and infant voices chanting the alphabet, spelling words, repeating the catechism and reciting scriptural passages. Jones found that it was possible for both young and old to acquire reading fluency within six to eight weeks, and his annual report, *The Welch Piety*, is replete with tales of wizened septuagenarians and poor, ragged children joyfully mastering the alphabet. The whole enterprise was informal, flexible and so highly effective that, in 1764, Catherine the Great dispatched an emissary to appraise the scheme. It is reasonable to suppose that, by the 1770s, around half the population of Wales could read, and this dramatic upsurge in literacy rates both revitalized church life and strengthened the native tongue.

Advances in schooling went hand in hand with a programme of evangelization which could also legitimately claim to be of, and by, the people. From 1735 onwards Welsh Calvinistic Methodism emerged and transformed itself from being a spontaneous, inchoate group of enthusiasts into a robust movement of twice-born Christians, energetically dedicated to the cause of bringing Satan's kingdom tumbling down. Led by its self-styled commander-in-chief Howel Harris, a carpenter's son from Trefeca, Breconshire, Daniel Rowland, a silver-tongued clergyman from Llangeitho, Cardiganshire, and William Williams, the legendary hymn-writer

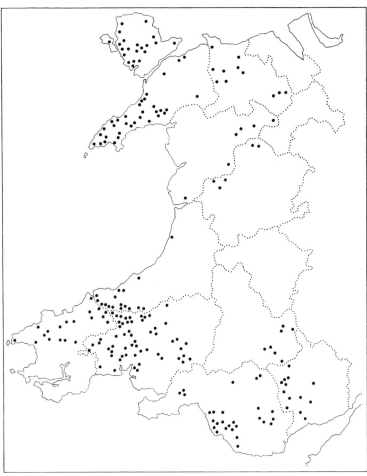

Map 7. From the 1730s Griffith Jones, an Anglican clergyman from
Llanddowror, Carmarthenshire, launched a remarkably successful
educational scheme based on circulating schools in which adults and
children were taught to read in the Welsh language. This enterprise not
only substantially increased levels of literacy but also greatly strengthened
the native tongue. The map shows the location of the circulating schools
by 1756–7.

27. The principal standard-bearer of the Calvinistic Methodist cause in Wales was Howel Harris (1714–73), a carpenter's son from Talgarth, Breconshire. This famous profile, revealing a piercing eye and a jutting jaw, conveys the essence of a man who was driven by a sense of divine mission 'till to pieces I fall'. (The National Library of Wales)

from Pantycelyn, Carmarthenshire, the movement precipitated extraordinary Pentecostal scenes and prospered mightily in mid- and south-west Wales, where the circulating schools were most numerous. Griffith Jones never formally associated himself with Welsh Methodism, but the 'heap of Boys', as Harris dubbed himself and his equally youthful colleagues, idolized him and sought to emulate his itinerant preaching zeal and pastoral work. These young evangelists, not noted for their theological insights, relent- lessly focused their minds and hearts on salvation through spiritual rebirth. The principal epicentre was Llangeitho, a Welsh Halle which witnessed scenes of great excitement – singing, weeping, convulsions, trances – as Daniel Rowland, who attracted pilgrims

28. William Williams (1717–91) – the 'Sweet Singer' – was the greatest of
Welsh hymnologists. He, more than any other, became the voice of
Methodism in Wales. The rich vividness of his scriptural imagery helped to
bring spiritual joy to thousands of people. He claimed to have travelled 'four
times the world's circumference' in the cause of Methodism. (The National
Library of Wales)

travelling on foot, on horseback and by boat, brought these 'Welsh
Jumpers' to fever pitch. The young evangelists delighted in striking
'bright and fiery sparks' in the hearts of hearers and then assembling
converts in exclusive, tightly knit society meetings in which spiritual
small-group therapy was undertaken under the watchful eye of
mentors. Methodism's irresistible combination of open-air sermons,
individual introspection and fervent hymn-singing proved especially
attractive to farmers, craftsmen and artisans. It also made a particular
point of encouraging young women to unburden themselves and
acquire reading skills. The prolific Williams Pantycelyn counselled
concupiscent society members on marital issues and, in his ground-
breaking *Cyfarwyddwr Priodas* (A Guide to Marriage) (1777), he
depicted female converts as lively, intelligent and self-improving

women. A quarter of the letters contained in the Trevecka Collection of Calvinistic Methodist correspondence were either by, or to, women, and this literary traffic provided them with a means of establishing closer contacts with both the international and local evangelical communities. As early as 1750 there were 428 Methodist societies, four-fifths of which were located in south Wales. As a force for spiritual and communal bonding, these cells were of growing significance.

The champions of Welsh Methodism liked to claim that it took Wales by storm, but in fact its growth was uneven, molecular and determined largely by the extent to which its young leaders were prepared to drive their bodies to the point of exhaustion. Their own foibles sometimes let them down. In 1750 Howel Harris was formally expelled by his colleagues, who had become thoroughly exasperated by his domineering ways, his heretical views and his eye for the opposite sex. Riven by factionalism until Harris re-entered the fold after a major revival at Llangeitho in 1762, the movement made little progress in north Wales before the 1770s and evangelists who braved the market towns of Gwynedd more often than not returned home nursing bruised bodies inflicted by mobs who took exception to strolling evangelists with unfamiliar accents and unpalatable messages. Methodism gained a reputation for bigotry, hypocrisy and philistinism, and the propaganda which poured from the presses reveals that it aroused the same fears and antagonisms as Jacobitism. Its leaders were not over-burdened with humour, and the movement as a whole did not add to the gaiety of the nation. But by focusing on bible reading, individual and collective piety, and the subjective awareness of sin, Methodist reformers brought to the Welsh people a fuller appreciation of the implications of the Protestant religion. Methodism revitalized church life and injected new vigour into Dissenting causes. As a result of the heroic and selfless efforts of the people themselves, the Welsh-language Reformation had not only come of age by the end of this period but a sense of national consciousness had also become deeply grounded in the Welsh Protestant identity.

This brings us finally to how the Welsh addressed the problem of defending and reinvigorating their native language and literature. Two separate, and very different, initiatives were launched in this period. The first – rather more highbrow than the second – was sustained by cultural patriots of gentry stock in the period up to 1660, when the Vale of Clwyd in Denbighshire became the cradle of Welsh humanism. Here, as early as 1547, William Salesbury, the most learned and prolific Renaissance scholar in Wales, urged his countrymen to seek learning in their mother tongue:

Unless you wish to become worse than animals ... seek learning in your language. Unless you wish to be more unnatural than any nation under the sun, honour your language and those who honour it.

Salesbury was under no illusions about the task ahead. Planting the urban and courtly culture of the Renaissance in a poor, pastoral society which had no affluent patrons, printing presses or academic institutions in which the Welsh could gain intellectual stimulation was surely likely to prove impossible to achieve. Following the death of Tudur Aled in 1526, the bardic tradition had entered a period of decline during which the *cywydd* became old-fashioned, if not redundant. Political developments boded ill: when the notorious 'language clause' in the 1536 Act of Union relegated the vernacular to a subordinate status, the Welsh gentry increasingly rode the crest of fashion by ensuring that their sons learnt to speak English fluently and acquired the polished cultivation denied them in rural Wales. Pinched by inflation, they became reluctant to employ household bards and when eisteddfodau were convened in 1523 and 1567, they applied pressure to ensure that unlicensed wandering poets and minstrels with a reputation for composing subversive satire were excluded from the bardic profession. The psychological effect of discovering that English was now unquestionably the language of opportunity and advancement was striking. It accelerated an intellectual 'brain drain' from Wales and encouraged potential writers in Welsh to use more 'civilized' tongues. For instance, William Thomas, who taught Edward VI, was the author of the first Italian grammar. Siôn Dafydd Rhys, the Catholic humanist, chose to write in Latin in order to reveal to the peoples of Europe the glories of his native tongue, but others yearned to be more acceptable to the English. Post-Union Wales found itself producing growing numbers of socially ambitious, effete Welshmen – later dubbed 'Dic Siôn Dafyddion' by satirists – who, from vanity, shame or a growing sense of inferiority, affected an English accent and despised the vernacular. Not unusually, the Welsh were often their own worst enemies. Most of the poets, for instance, proved mulishly stubborn, preferring to trade in trite, conventional flattery than using their professional skills to convey the glories of the Renaissance.

The net result, at least in publishing terms, was small. By shunning the printing press, secretive Welsh bards penned their own obituaries. By 1660 the days of the *penceirddiaid* (chief poets) had long passed. Prose writers proved to be more flexible and, thanks largely to the splendid writings of the uncrowned king of the Welsh Renaissance, Dr John Davies, Mallwyd, polished works of scholarship emerged in the fields of grammar and lexicography. The publication of the Welsh Bible was a prodigious achievement, not least because it turned a sacred book which had been viewed as a symbol of the majesty of the English Crown into an emblem of Welsh nationality. The year 1588 has very different resonances for the Welsh speaker than for anglophones. The work of remembrancers like David Powel of Ruabon, author of *The History of Cambria now called Wales* (1584), meant that the national glories of the past were not entirely forgotten. Another Denbighshire man, the polymathic Humphrey Llwyd, ensured that the first printed map of Wales appeared in the trailblazing atlas *Theatrum Orbis Terrarum* (Theatre of the World) (1573), published by the Dutch geographer Abraham Ortelius. Among others with a high European profile were the peerless Elizabethan magus John Dee, the remarkably versatile Tenby-born mathematician Robert Recorde, who invented the 'equals' sign, and the Caernarfonshire epigrammatist John Owen, who was better known on the continent than was Shakespeare. But the harvest of Welsh-language humanistic works proved to be depressingly slender, and the death of the distinguished lexicographer John Davies in 1644 signalled the end of the humanist effort to bring to Wales the new Renaissance Europe.

The second initiative came in the early eighteenth century, when groups of lively and ambitious middling sorts responded decisively to the growing feeling that Wales was in danger of losing its literary and historical traditions forever. Despite the best efforts of the calligrapher John Jones of Gellilyfdy and the antiquary Robert Vaughan of Hengwrt, to assemble, copy and protect valuable

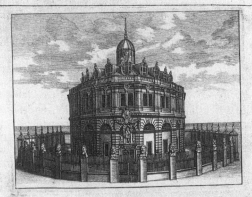

Archæologia Britannica,

GIVING SOME ACCOUNT

Additional to what has been hitherto Publifh'd,

OF THE

LANGUAGES, HISTORIES and CUSTOMS

Of the Original Inhabitants

OF

GREAT BRITAIN:

From Collections and Obfervations in Travels through
Wales, Cornwal, Bas-Bretagne, Ireland and *Scotland.*

By EDWARD LHUYD M.A. of *Jefus College,*
Keeper of the ASHMOLEAN MUSEUM in OXFORD.

VOL. I.
GLOSSOGRAPHY.

OXFORD,
Printed at the THEATER for the Author, MDCCVII.

And Sold by Mr. *Bateman* in *Pater-Nofter-Row, London* : and *Jeremiah Pepyat*
Bookfeller at *Dublin.*

29. *Archaeologia Britannica* (1707), one of the major publications of the age, demonstrated that the Breton, Cornish and Welsh languages enjoyed a common Celtic origin. The author, Edward Lhuyd (1660–1709), keeper of the Ashmolean Museum at Oxford, was a polymath of international repute. (The National Library of Wales)

Welsh manuscripts from the ravages of mildew and mice, a sense of
crisis prevailed towards the latter years of the seventeenth century.
The God-fearing Welsh almanacker Thomas Jones reckoned that
the Almighty had nearly 'blotted us out of the Books of Records'.
The instinctive reaction of scholars was to turn to the ivory towers of
Oxford for salvation, especially when the peerless Edward Lhuyd, in
his impressive *Archaeologia Britannica*, presented the first convincing demonstration of the common Celtic origins of the Breton,
Cornish and Welsh languages. It would not have passed unnoticed
that this affirmation of Celticity occurred in the year of the union of
England and Scotland, but since Lhuyd died two years later and
none of his successors was of the same calibre, cultural patriots in
Wales turned to the native printing presses and to London-Welsh
communities for inspiration. The culture of print provided a host of
new opportunities for poets, almanackers, ballad-mongers and play-
wrights. Popular ballads, sold by hawkers and chapmen, catered for
the public demand for the profane as well as the religious. Interludes
(*anterliwtiau*) offered thrilling theatrical experiences in the open air.
The leading light was Thomas Edwards (Twm o'r Nant), the 'Welsh
Molière', whose earthy compositions included sharply satirical and
humorous cameos of the likes of 'Penny-pinching Siôn', 'Fornicating
Foulk' and 'Sir Tom Tell Truth'. The bardic tradition was also given a
new lease of life as it became a more popular and democratic activity
among farmers and craftsmen; it even welcomed women into its
hallowed ranks. Welsh history came alive on the pages of *Drych y
Prif Oesoedd*, a work by Theophilus Evans which not only rescued the
national history of Wales from the condescension of English writers
but also provided the reading public with a bold, rollicking version of
the past in their own tongue. His epic tale greatly enhanced the self-
confidence of the Welsh, and by the end of the Victorian period at
least twenty editions had been published.

   Celtomania and druidomania began to prosper as never before and
were encouraged by London-based societies like the Cymmrodorion
(1751) and the Gwyneddigion (1770), whose leaders were determined to restore what they believed to be the oldest living literary
language in Europe to its former glory. Led by the redoubtable
Morris brothers of Anglesey, notably Richard, a clerk in the Navy
office, and Lewis, a Georgian Mr Fix-it, a circle of scholars

Newydd oddiwrth y Seêr:
NEU
ALMANAC am y Flwyddyn 1684,
yr hon a elwir blwyddyn naid.
Yr hwn ſy gyflawnach, a helaethach nag yr un ar a
wnaed o i flaen ef. Ag ynddo a Tyſtiolaethwyd,
mae 'r Gymraeg iw 'r Jaith hynaf, ar Jaith oedd
gyntaf yn y Bŷd.
Hereunto is added; A direction to *English* Scholars,
ſhewing them by a plain and eaſie way, how to pro-
nounce and read *Welch* perfectly.
O wneuthuriad Tho. Jones, *Myſtriwr yn Sywedyddiaeth.*
5 y pumed argraphiad neu breintiad.

*Eu oed-
tan iw
36.*

Argraphedig yng-haerludd, ag ar werth gan yr
Awdwr yn *Black-Fryers, Llundain,* 1684.

30. The cheapest and most heavily thumbed Welsh publications were the
annual Welsh almanacs, the first of which was published in 1680 by the
colourful printer, publisher and almanacker, Thomas Jones (1648–1713),
whose many enemies derisively referred to as 'the Sweating Astrologer'.
(The National Library of Wales)

developed a new passion for discovering, transcribing and preserving Welsh manuscripts. The growing interest in romanticism and primitivism meant that in no part of Britain was the antiquarian imagination more widely encouraged than in Wales. Evan Evans's *Some Specimens of the Poetry of the Antient Welsh Bards* (1764), a Welsh equivalent of James Macpherson's Ossianic writings, was a literary landmark in the recovery and interpretation of the Welsh poetic tradition and, although its significance was lost on the rank and file of Cymmrodorion members (who, alas, preferred wine, women and song to the muse of the *Gogynfeirdd*), the more progressive and self-consciously Welsh members of the Gwyneddigion Society became pacesetters in the publishing world and also promoters of Welsh eisteddfodau. The most distinctive of the early Welsh Romantics was Iolo Morganwg, who was a frequent visitor to London from 1773 onwards. When not engaged in rancorous

31. In market squares or inn yards, public performances of Welsh interludes attracted noisy but appreciative crowds. These rough-and-ready plays, riddled with obscene gestures, moral judgements and satirical barbs, championed the lot of the underdog. The prince of interlude writers was Thomas Edwards (Twm o'r Nant), who was widely fêted as 'the Cambrian Shakespeare'. (The National Library of Wales)

feuds with other writers (mostly from north Wales), he set himself the task of creating an idealized past by composing literary and historical forgeries of great daring and originality. In the fullness of time, his ideas and writings not only bolstered the indigenous culture but also heightened the sense of nationhood. By the 1770s, therefore, Welsh writers from a wide variety of backgrounds were rallying strongly in support of the native language and delighting in rediscovering the literary and historical treasures of the past.

The development of an urban sector and trading centres, new patterns of ownership, the culture of print and the commercialization of leisure fuelled this popular Welsh-language cultural renewal. At its head lay the middling sorts, people who proudly dubbed themselves 'Cambro-Britons' or 'Ancient Britons' in order to affirm their standing as the first possessors of the British isles, as the speakers of the senior 'British' tongue and as the guardians of the authentic 'British' history. 'We are the Aborigines' was the song of the Cymmrodorion. Cultural patriots, mindful of slights and injuries suffered in the past, were no longer prepared to be viewed as bondmen to English cultural superiority. True, some of the movers and shakers in Georgian Wales were prone to sport dual identities. Howel Harris trumpeted the virtues of 'Great Britain' and proudly wore the livery of the Breconshire militia during the Seven Years War, but his principal mission was to save the souls of the native 'old Britons'. Pandering to the English came easily to Lewis Morris, but he revelled in being counted a 'proud hot Welshman'. Many Cambro-Britons were steeped in the scientific language of empiricism, were reading the works of Locke, Newton and Herschel, and indulging in patriotic discourse. Even as Richard Price was assembling 'friends of liberty' around him in the mid-1770s, the Welsh were civilizing themselves in the vernacular and feeling a stronger sense of their own identity than had been the case since pre-Union days. The climate of opinion was changing, and enhanced self-esteem was encouraging a new mood of optimism.

6

A crucible of the modern world, 1776–1900

In late Georgian Wales, Cardiff was a small, modest, down-at-heel market town nestling in the shadow of a ruined castle. Cattle and swine roamed the streets, and the main function of the town was to distribute agricultural goods from surrounding rural areas and manufacturing goods from West Country ports. It was a Tory stronghold and the 1,871 inhabitants enumerated in the 1801 census, most of whom spoke Welsh, bowed to the will of the Bute family. By 1900, however, Cardiff had become, by some distance, the most populous town in Wales and the gateway through which millions of tons of coal travelled in railway wagons to the holds of steam-powered ships in its impressive docks. Prosperous colliery proprietors, shipowners, merchants and bankers basked in Cardiff's reputation as the coal metropolis of the world. It had elected Liberal MPs between 1852 and 1895, and did so again from 1900 to 1910. This dynamic, heavily anglicized and cosmopolitan urban conglomeration had increased its population a hundredfold, and its reward in 1905 was to be granted city status. Fifty more years would pass before it was officially recognized as the capital of Wales, but from 1871 onwards no other town could legitimately challenge its primacy. This astonishing transformation epitomized the changing geography and socio-economic experience of large parts of Wales.

Over this period, Wales changed more swiftly and dramatically than in any previous era in its history. As it entered the age of mass population, technology, urban living and industrial employment, a new society was born which was markedly different from that of the

past. The population grew by leaps and bounds, startling professional statisticians as well as lay observers, and the demographic profile
of Wales became heavily skewed in favour of the industrialized
and urbanized counties of south Wales. Transport improvements
changed the pace and rhythm of life to such an extent that distances
which had once seemed immense were now reduced sharply. As an
excited correspondent reported in the *Welshman* in 1846: 'this is the
age ... of Railways and Steam appliance of all kinds. Science is
putting on her full strength, knowledge is not running but flying to
and fro.' It is true that many people living in remote rural parts clung
tenaciously to old ways and lived out their lives in the harshest
poverty, but even those who dwelt in such sheltered communities
must have been aware of the quickening pace of daily life and of
expanding geographical horizons. Blast furnaces and forges, rolling
mills, smelting houses, deep coal mines, slate quarries and sprawling
industrial townships were changing the landscape, and Wales, on
the strength of its reputation as a producer of iron and steel, copper,
coal and slate, became one of the principal workshops of the world.
As railway and telegraphic links improved, news travelled more
swiftly within Wales and across its boundaries and, for the most
part, life became more diverse, challenging and complex than ever
before. Marching under the banner of what was called 'Progress'
was an exhilarating experience for those who benefited from technological advances and who admired Samuel Smiles's bestselling
work *Self-Help*, a truncated Welsh-language version of which was
published at Tonypandy in 1898. But there were losers as well as
winners in this bustling new economy, and in both rural and industrial Wales there were people for whom malnutrition, disease and
early death were part of their wretched lot in life.

At the heart of this great explosion of energy lay a demographic
transformation, the size and pace of which were unprecedented.
Stunned by a graph revealing the spiralling growth of numbers,
one modern historian exclaimed: 'Is there a peak more jagged in
Snowdonia?' Over the period as a whole the population more than
quadrupled, rising from *c.* 489,000 in 1780 to 1,189,000 in 1851,
and to 2,015,000 by 1901. Only during the decade 1861–71, a
period when the iron industry was in decline, did the intercensal

percentage change of population growth fall below 10 per cent. The key to the increase lay in extraordinarily high fecundity and birth rates, and mounting numbers of in-migrants. As a result, the centre of gravity within Wales changed decisively. By the end of the Victorian period, more than half the population lived in the industrialized counties of Glamorgan and Monmouthshire. Successive censuses bore witness to a marked drift from rural communities. Whereas around four-fifths of the population lived in rural areas in 1801, by the eve of the First World War that proportion had plummeted to a fifth. The percentage of males occupied in mining and quarrying soared from 16.9 per cent in 1851 to 31.7 per cent by 1911. Unlike the experience of their early modern forebears, the Welsh in this period became movers rather than stayers. The expansion of population and new commercial developments meant that there were more hands to work, more mouths to feed and more people moving from place to place.

The livelier traffic of people was made possible by new modes of transport which increasingly changed the pace and rhythm of people's lives. In 1805 Iolo Morganwg famously declared: 'every part of Wales has an easy and direct communication with London, but north and south Wales have no more intercourse with each other than they have with the man in the moon'. As a committed Welsh nation-builder, Iolo was prone to make sweeping statements, but in this case he was not necessarily wrong. Wretched internal transport facilities and the drive towards establishing a modern unitary state meant that the Welsh had always been pulled eastwards, but the need to bring in industrial capital and move goods more swiftly changed the priorities and meant that they were now able to colonize different parts of their own country. Intensive turnpiking from the 1770s led to improvements in the foundations and surfaces of roads, and although bumpy rides continued to plague disgruntled travellers, stage coaches and mail coaches hastened the movement of people and goods. Canal-mania reached its peak during the turbulent 1790s: sizeable capital investment led to the building of four major canals (Glamorganshire, Monmouthshire, Neath and Swansea), all of which gained a reputation as cheap, efficient and reliable carriers of raw material and as relaxing means of carriage for human travellers. Vigorous commercial and industrial expansion encouraged some of the greatest engineers of the age to display their inventive genius. The Scots engineer Thomas Telford left a permanent mark on the built environment of north Wales. In collaboration with William Jessup, he constructed the remarkable Pontcysyllte Aqueduct at Llangollen between 1795 and 1805, the highest navigable canal aqueduct (306 metres) ever built. Telford's greatest masterpiece was opened in 1826: the Menai Suspension Bridge, which joined Anglesey to the mainland of Wales, was not only the first chain-link iron suspension bridge but also had an unprecedented span of 580 feet. In 1857 Crumlin Viaduct Works, which built spectacular and complex spans in countries as diverse as Brazil, Italy and India, erected the finest bridge in the South Wales Coalfield across the valley of the Ebbw river at Crumlin. The building of reservoirs also changed the face of the landscape and provided opportunities for Victorian water engineers to display their expertise and ingenuity. The river Vyrnwy was dammed from 1881 in order to provide soft mountain water for the inhabitants of Liverpool. Likewise, the river Elan was dammed from 1882 to slake the thirst of the people of Birmingham. The politics of health loomed large, but not until the mid-twentieth century did the appropriation of water collected in Wales become a controversial political issue.

Meticulously planned enterprises like these certainly caught the public imagination, but the most significant changes came with the age of steam locomotion. By refashioning the landscape and travelling at great speed, snorting steam express trains seemed to epitomize the spirit of the age. The *haiarnfarch* (ironhorse) became a cultural icon which transformed the economic prospects of the Welsh, reduced class barriers and helped them to develop their own cultural institutions. Wales can lay claim to the first load-carrying steam locomotive: Richard Trevithick's engine, travelling at a princely five miles an hour, made its maiden journey from Penydarren, Merthyr, in 1804. Several decades went by, however, before the railway mania seized the imagination of the Welsh. Between 1840 and 1870 over 1,400 miles of railways were built in Wales, and no means of transport proved more effective in accelerating rural migration than 'the Charon of the industrial century'. Railways penetrated deeply into the countryside and established particularly dense networks in the South Wales Coalfield, where

Map 8. Since the early sixteenth century coal had been mined in south Pembrokeshire, while the coal industry of north-east Wales enjoyed prosperity from the eighteenth century onwards. But the major centre of the coal industry in Wales from the nineteenth century onwards was the South Wales Coalfield. Here 'King Coal' reigned supreme. (Crown Copyright: Royal Commission on the Ancient and Historical Monuments of Wales)

they proved to be critical to the success of the swiftly expanding coal export trade. The railway boom created small armies of perspiring navvies who, with picks and shovels, bent their backs in digging tunnels, building bridges and embankments, and laying hundreds of miles of railway tracks which linked together market centres, industrial towns and tourist resorts. Railways broke down age-old habits of isolationism and, in particular, released thousands of agricultural workers from a life of grinding poverty. Thanks to the railways, the have-nots sought their Welsh El Dorado in the south. For the carrying of freight and passengers, the railways had no rivals on land.

Steam also replaced sail on the oceans, thereby opening up opportunities to seafaring communities and long-distance travellers. During the course of the nineteenth century wooden vessels propelled by sail or oar were largely replaced by steam-propelled, ocean-going merchant ships built from iron and steel in major shipyards and powered by steam coal from the Rhondda. In 1851 the Royal Navy committed itself to using the fine quality steam coal of south Wales, a decision which accelerated demand for the Welsh 'black diamonds' from all parts of the world. Dock facilities in Cardiff, first provided by the second Marquess of Bute in 1839, were extended and improved regularly up to 1907, as fleets of modern tramp steamers specialized in the 'coal out, grain home' trade. By the 1880s it was claimed that the port of Cardiff was so tightly packed with ships that it was possible to walk across the docks on the decks of the moored vessels. Although the sea took a heavy toll in ships and seamen, seafaring extended the horizons and enriched the experiences of master mariners and sailors. Old salts told and retold tales of narrow escapes during perilous voyages around the Horn, of burials at sea and (sotto voce) of dubious encounters with fast women in drinking dens in exotic locations like Bombay, Guadeloupe, Rio and Rangoon. Seafaring encouraged ethnic and cultural interaction: steam vessels brought into Wales groups of Arabs, Greeks, Chinese, Spaniards and Italians who formed distinctive ethnic minorities. By the same token, as we shall see, the relative ease and speed of travel by sea meant that acquiring a new life beyond the seas was a more attractive prospect than ever before to the poor and the not so poor.

It is difficult to over-emphasize the importance of industrialization and urbanization in nineteenth-century Wales. The tragic story of Ireland in the wake of the Famine of 1845–9 is a stark reminder of how the fate of the Welsh might have been very different had Wales remained a predominantly rural society. Whereas the impoverished Irish had no choice but to emigrate or starve, from the 1790s the Welsh were able to capitalize on new opportunities of employment in their own burgeoning industrial and commercial districts or find opportunities across the border in England. The initial pacesetters were the iron and copper industries. The former was largely located in areas of bleak moorland on the rim of the South Wales Coalfield, stretching broadly over a twenty-mile radius from Hirwaun to Blaenafon. Iron ore, coal, limestone and water were in plentiful supply in these parts, and the infusion of metropolitan capital from the 1770s and the demands of war with France after 1793 provoked a dramatic upswing in production. The epicentre of the iron industry was Merthyr Tydfil, where flaming labyrinths dominated the industrial landscape and where a highly mobile skilled workforce strengthened Welsh primacy in ironmaking by developing a 'Welsh method' which removed carbon impurities from molten iron. By the mid-nineteenth century a string of iron towns dotted along the northern outcrop of the coalfield was producing 40 per cent of the total output in Britain. Most of the iron rails used throughout the world were manufactured at furnaces in Cyfarthfa, Dowlais, Ebbw Vale and Nant-y-glo. John Hughes, the son of a Cyfarthfa engineer, showed the kind of inventiveness and tenacity which brought him wealth and plaudits on a wider stage. Having devised the 'Hughes Stringer', a robust mounting for heavy naval guns used on iron-clad battleships, he established a hugely successful series of ironworks in a new settlement in the Donetz Basin in the Ukraine which came to be known as Hughesovka (Yuzovka). Copper and brass, while yielding untold environmental pollution, also offered speculators a reliable means of enrichment both in the Swansea/Neath area and around Holywell in the north-east. In the copper-rich county of Anglesey, Thomas Williams, a shrewd attorney, became virtually a millionaire by outmanoeuvring his rivals in the Midlands and Cornwall, and by establishing lucrative strategic partnerships between his impressive Parys Mountain copperworks in Anglesey and shipping agents in south Wales. By the mid-nineteenth century most of Britain's copper and over half of that of the world was being refined in the 'Copperopolis' which stretched from Pembrey (Carmarthenshire) to Tai-bach (Glamorgan) along the southern coastline.

A second phase in the industrialization of south Wales occurred from the 1850s onwards, as 'King Coal' deposed the ironmasters. The famous old ironworks of Plymouth and Penydarren closed in the 1870s. The Dowlais Company transferred its steel production to East Moors in Cardiff in 1891, leaving Cyfarthfa as the sole, but much diminished, giant. The future clearly lay with coal. The

32. The valley of Rhondda Fawr in Glamorgan was the epicentre of the
steam coal industry in the latter part of the nineteenth century. Chains of
settlements, with terraces of working-class houses, became a distinctive
feature of industrial life. (Crown Copyright: Royal Commission on the
Ancient and Historical Monuments of Wales)

sinking of extraordinarily deep shafts in the Rhondda Valleys produced a series of frenzied 'coal rushes' during the second half of the
nineteenth century which turned lush rural pastures and woodland
into a huge conglomeration of sprawling industrial and urban settlements. The astonishing demand for steam coal, improved railway
and port facilities, the more extensive use of mechanical power and
the formation of massive coal combines like the Cambrian, Ocean
and Powell Duffryn meant that the output of coal increased nearly
tenfold between 1854 and 1900. No longer was coal simply a
handmaiden to iron: it was the major player in the industrial profile
of south Wales. Rhondda's population leapt from *c.* 2,000 in 1851
to over 113,000 in 1901. The emergence of the Bessemer converter
in 1856 and the Siemens 'open-hearth' method, pioneered at
Landore in 1867, opened a new chapter in steelmaking, especially
at Dowlais, Ebbw Vale and Tredegar in south Wales and at
Hawarden in the north-east, while in the western parts of the
South Wales Coalfield, Llanelli became a renowned 'Tinopolis' as
the tinplate industry eclipsed the copper-smelting trade. By 1889
ninety-six tinplate works were producing over half a million tons of
tinplate, though the adverse effects of the McKinley tariff imposed
by the American Government in 1890 proved to be a major setback
to the industry. Yet, even though Wales, at least in the eyes of
statisticians, was not reckoned to be a meaningful economic unit,
the available data reveals that its overall economic development
between *c.* 1860 and the First World War was swifter than that
of England or Scotland. The giant coal companies prospered
mightily: the output of Powell Duffryn doubled to nearly two
million tons between 1870 and 1900, while David Davies's Ocean
Coal Company witnessed a rise in production from just over a
million tons in 1880 to 2.5 million by 1900. For affluent coalowners, wealth begat more wealth during these expansionary years.

Although the South Wales Coalfield forged far ahead of its coun-
terpart in north-east Wales, in terms of production export markets
and manpower, the smaller industrial enterprises of mid- and north
Wales were still very much part of the mainstream of British capitalism. Steam-driven machinery transformed the woollen industry of
mid-Wales, and there was every prospect in the early nineteenth
century that a manufacturing centre like Newtown – a town

33. The number of Welsh people employed in coal mining peaked at around 232,000 in 1913. Welsh coal, such as that produced at the Lewis Merthyr Colliery, Trehafod, helped to power the world. Such pits are now a rarity in south Wales, though visitors to the Rhondda Heritage Park can take guided tours through the shafts of this colliery. (National Museums and Galleries of Wales)

described as 'the Leeds of Wales' – might be able to compete with the West Riding of Yorkshire. Such opportunities, however, were spurned, and the major beneficiaries were the thriving woollen factories of the Teifi Valley in south Cardiganshire, which prospered by producing shirt and underwear flannel for the mining families of south Wales. Such developments partly compensated for reduced production in the once thriving lead mines which, by the mid-nineteenth century, had become so vulnerable to the booms and slumps of the markets that investors withdrew their capital. Non-ferrous industries such as lead, copper, zinc and brass were vital to the economy of Flintshire, and the iron empire at Bersham, close to the bustling town of Wrexham, remained at the cutting edge of technology. The bituminous coal seams of east Denbighshire and Flintshire were also vigorously worked. In the north-west, the most striking industrial growth occurred in the slate-quarrying districts of Gwynedd where the Penrhyn family owned the third largest estate in Wales, to which they added substantial profits from exporting slate.

In these communities, slate quarrying was the lifeblood of the economy and was responsible for 93 per cent of the total British output by 1882. It was also a peculiarly Welsh industry. Nine of every ten quarrymen at Blaenau Ffestiniog in 1891 were monoglot Welsh speakers, and it was taken as read that none but the native speaker possessed the innate gift for handling and chiselling slate. Hundreds of tons of Welsh slate were shipped annually through Port Penrhyn and Porthmadog to slate roofs all over the world.

Swift urbanization proved to be grist to the pockets of industrialists and also satisfied the aspirations of demoralized rural migrants. During the Victorian period, the urban geography of Wales was transformed. In 1811 only Carmarthen, Swansea, Merthyr and Wrexham could boast a population in excess of 5,000 people, but by the census of 1901 over 50 per cent of the population of Wales lived in towns. By this stage, five major urban centres dwarfed all others: Cardiff (164,333), Rhondda (113,735), Swansea (94,537), Merthyr (69,228) and Newport (67,270). In the early part of this period, the iron town of Merthyr made all the running: to the astonishment and alarm of visitors, this Welsh 'Samaria' reflected the results of dramatic demographic growth and industrial development as well as providing a focus for working-class consciousness. Its population of 7,700 in 1801 mushroomed sixfold to 46,378 in 1851. With its myths and martyrs, and its reputation as a hotbed of drunkenness and crime, Merthyr acquired such a distinctive reputation in the eyes of its own people that the essentially rural ambience of the late eighteenth century suddenly seemed to be no more than a distant memory. But even Merthyr's remarkable demographic expansion was eclipsed by the rise of Cardiff. Fewer than two thousand people lived in Cardiff in 1801, but within a century its population had leapt to 164,333, an extraordinary transformation which enabled it to become in all but name the capital city of Wales from the 1870s onwards. Although modern Cardiff owed its image to the enormously prosperous Scottish magnates, the Bute family, its economic strength derived from its booming coalfield hinterland and in particular the seemingly limitless supply of high quality steam coal in the Rhondda Valleys, which was exported to coal bunkers as far afield as Buenos Aires, Bombay and Port Said. Once the town's thrusting bourgeoisie of bankers, merchants and shippers had successfully challenged the powerful monopoly of the

Tory Butes, Cardiff overtook Merthyr as the largest town in Wales from 1871 onwards, and the diverse, dynamic and cosmopolitan character of this 'Chicago of Wales' set it apart from all other urban communities in Wales. By 1900 dynasties of shipowning families were dispatching over 13 million tons of coal in most years, as well as other minerals, in powerful steam-driven liners to distant ports all over the world.

As a result of these spectacular developments, Wales was not only repeopled but it also kept its own people. Industrialization and urbanization precipitated remarkable internal migration, mostly to the South Wales Coalfield but also to the North-East Wales Coalfield and to the slate-quarrying districts of Gwynedd. Happy to abandon the scythe for the mandrel and the chisel, unskilled labourers poured into the new industrial townships, where the prospects of lucrative work and a more exciting and unpredictable lifestyle were irresistibly attractive. Mercifully, therefore, the demographic haemorrhage which blighted nineteenth-century Ireland was averted, and migration flows in Wales, at least until the 1870s, had the effect of strengthening the indigenous language and its associated culture. Had Wales not experienced large-scale industrialization, far greater numbers of its people would have been forced to emigrate. The South Wales Coalfield acted as 'a cauldron of rebirth' for the Welsh language during the first seven decades of the nineteenth century, and even as late as 1891 Glamorgan boasted the largest concentration of Welsh speakers (320,072) in the whole of Wales. But as the 'vast black Klondyke' of the Rhondda sucked in migrants like a giant hoover, growing numbers of them came from the West Country and further afield. A distraught Nonconformist minister feared that English-language culture was 'rushing in upon us like mighty irresistible torrents', and during the latter years of Victoria's reign the influx of English-speaking migrants certainly had a detrimental effect on the fortunes of Welsh. Language boundaries were constantly shifting in these teeming communities, but the prevailing trend was for monoglot Welsh-speakers to become bilingual and for monoglot English-speaking incomers to resist acculturation. In the overwhelmingly Welsh-speaking slate-quarrying districts of north-west Wales, however, the reverse was true. Welsh was reckoned to be the sole authentic language of the truly skilled quarryman and, as the popular verse went, 'the rock does not understand English'.

As this process unfolded, the South Wales Coalfield in particular became a dynamic social, economic and cultural melting pot in which people of very different backgrounds co-existed. Apart from the Welsh themselves, the largest group of incomers were from England. The numbers of English-born people living in Glamorgan rose from 70,711 in 1881 to 194,041 in 1911, most of whom were pleased to discover that the Welsh kept a welcome in the hillsides. The influx of ethnic minorities, however, sometimes provoked friction and violence. For the most part, Irish incomers in the post-Famine period fared badly. Stereotypes of them as ragged, feckless, drunken 'Papists' abounded, and a long tradition of hostility towards them culminated in the horrifying Tredegar riot of July 1882, in which fifty Irish homes were wrecked. The Irish were consigned to unskilled jobs and overcrowded hovels, and were subjected to vicious assaults by those who believed that Catholicism and moral decay went hand in hand or who saw anyone who lived in the 'Little Ireland' communities as undercutters and blacklegs who flouted accepted codes of behaviour. Undeterred, the Irish maintained a distinctive collective identity and were said in 1892 to have been 'as Irish in heart as though born in Cork, or Waterford or Tipperary'. Jews were targeted during disturbances in Merthyr at the time of the 1898 strike, but for the most part they were easily assimilated into urban society. Italian caterers from the 1890s onwards, soon to be followed by specialists in ice cream, were warmly embraced. The Butetown district of Cardiff was a particularly striking focus of multi-racialism and cosmopolitanism.

Meanwhile Welsh-speakers, especially the young, were deserting rural communities in droves. During the last two decades alone, around 160,000 people left the Welsh countryside, large numbers of whom settled in the towns and cities of England, notably Merseyside, Teesside, the West Midlands and London. The major rail and road arteries ran from east to west, and during periods of acute economic distress people were prepared to travel considerable distances in order to improve the quality of their lives, even if the price to be paid was eventual acculturation and assimilation. Locomotion dispatched them swiftly to thriving urban cities across

Offa's Dyke, though such was the attraction of London that, in the early part of this period, poor young women known as 'The Garden Girls' would annually trudge over two hundred miles from west Wales in search of employment and precious shillings in the gardens and parks of the capital. 'Who would ever stay in Wales?' asked the London Welshman Edward Charles as he celebrated the social opportunities which the 'Great Wen' offered to the upwardly mobile as well as to those who yearned for intellectual stimulus, colour and excitement. Welsh-language societies were formed to promote Welsh letters and stimulate patriotic zeal through eisteddfodau and gorseddau, though it became increasingly apparent that the second and third generations found it almost impossible to retain the daily language of their forefathers. Integration into a wider Britain and its empire was a high priority among those who prospered in London and, although Nonconformist ministers in Wales sought to stem the flow to the metropolis by conjuring up the image of a sinful Babylon, nowhere in Wales could match London for sheer productivity, wealth and cultural diversity.

In north Wales, however, the eastward diaspora was towards Liverpool, which became a surrogate capital for the Welsh bourgeoisie who believed in the Protestant work ethic, self-help and competition. Among these typical Smilesian figures was Owen Owen, a tenant farmer's son from Montgomeryshire, whose sharp eye for advancement turned his drapery business into a remarkably successful venture, while Carmarthen-born Sir Alfred Lewis Jones, a former cabin boy, became a shipping entrepreneur sufficiently wealthy by 1900 to be able to purchase the British and African Steam Navigation Company for £800,000. Emblematic of these successes was the majestic Princes Road Chapel, built in 1868–71 and dubbed the 'Welsh Calvinistic Methodist Cathedral of Liverpool', which was largely funded by affluent Welsh-born builders, merchants and bankers. On Sundays, handsomely dressed and accoutred men, twirling their moustaches and accompanied by wives in soft and lustrous silks, cut impressive figures. Welsh migrants in this 'metropolis' of north Wales formed a much more cohesive group than their counterparts did in London, and the constant inward flow of less well-to-do people to the timber yards, cotton factories and building works of Merseyside preserved a Welsh identity. Liverpool became a lively centre for Welsh-language publishing, especially for newspapers like *Yr Amserau, Y Cymro* and *Y Brython*, and, following the National Eisteddfod held in the city in 1884, the Liverpool Welsh National Society was founded to foster what it referred to as the national interest of Wales. In 1896 Tom Ellis argued in *Young Wales* that Liverpool provided a metropolis for north Wales which served as a counterpoise to the influence of Cardiff in the south-east.

In an age of conquest, trade and empire, as well as voyage and settlement to distant parts of the globe, the fortunes of many Welsh people became ever more dependent on the seas around them. As we have seen, the Welsh were not averse to leaving home and settling overseas. But some of them had no choice. When Britain lost its American colonies in the early 1780s, Australia was earmarked as an appropriately far-flung and uncongenial home for criminals. Some of the first reports of life in the Antipodes were supplied by David Samwell, a Denbighshire-born surgeon who accompanied Captain James Cook on expeditions to the South Pacific. Samwell used to regale the London Welsh with hair-raising tales of cannibalism (he also witnessed the murder of Cook), of dusky Hawaiian beauties he had impregnated and of the intriguing land dubbed 'New Wales' (later to become New South Wales) by Cook. From 1787, therefore, this new penal colony became the destination for criminal exiles. Over the following three generations, around 2,200 Welsh convicts, male and female, found themselves dispatched on notorious 'hell ships' on a perilous four-month journey to the other side of the world, during which the sea, sickness and disease took a heavy toll of lives. Vulnerable convict girls were sadistically abused on these journeys and, on their arrival, were assigned to abusive masters and put to work in a harsh and unforgiving environment. By the mid-nineteenth century, however, Australia was viewed by the Welsh as a land of opportunity rather than a place of exile. The Victorian gold rush of the 1850s attracted energetic prospectors and Welsh families determined to make a fresh start. Tales of gold-rich streams and shining nuggets proved irresistible to those with a sense of adventure, and a powerful Welsh presence was established at Ballarat, the epicentre of the gold country, where the number of Welsh-born emigrants rose from 1,800 in 1851 to 9,500 in 1861. The gold rush was a particularly liberating experience for

Joseph Jenkins, a celebrated Welsh swagman who left his native Cardiganshire in 1868 and recorded in vividly detailed diaries his encounters with Aborigines and his forthright reactions to the notorious Ned Kelly gang, whose depredations prompted him to warn his countrymen that 'No honest man should set foot in Australia.' By *c.* 1900, however, some 13,000 Welsh-born people were living in Australia, a minority of whom struggled, in the teeth of impossible odds, to sustain a coherent and identifiable Welsh ethnic identity. Local newspapers and magazines reveal that Welsh settlers grappled with definitions of Welshness, but the primary focus of their affection was the eisteddfod, which served as a respiratory chamber for a culture with few prospects of a share in the fruits of progress.

For Welsh people with dwindling reserves, itchy feet and lofty ambitions, America was the unrivalled land of opportunity, and it figured prominently in the literature and imagination of the Welsh throughout this period. Credulous romantics were drawn to it by the unlikely prospect of discovering the Mandans, a tribe of white-skinned Welsh-speaking Indians often referred to as the Madogwys (Padoucas), who were reputedly the descendants of Madoc, the mythical son of the medieval prince Owain Gwynedd who had discovered America in 1170. This legend became highly fashionable among London-Welsh political radicals in the 1790s and, even in the mid-Victorian period, to challenge its authenticity was to invite opprobrium. But there were other, more important incentives than Madoc and the Mandans. The American Revolution had stimulated a new political consciousness, and the prospect of freedom from religious and political discrimination was music to the ears of Welsh Dissenters. Having stood on the ruins of the Bastille, the Baptist minister Morgan John Rhys emigrated to the 'Land of the Free' in 1794, where he established a Welsh settlement at Beulah in the Allegheny mountains, Pennsylvania. Land hunger in a period of economic crisis prompted growing numbers of tenant farmers and craftsmen to embark on the arduous 3,000-mile journey in the hope of emulating the old Quaker dream of establishing an exclusive homeland across the seas. 'Mr Go-to-America (alias Lover of Wealth)' was excoriated by stay-at-home Nonconformist ministers like Christmas Evans, who warned all such travellers against abandoning their native land, but the opportunity of acquiring cheap land and peace of mind made overwhelming sense to suffering farmers and labourers, and was certainly well worth a few weeks of seasickness and several months of *hiraeth* (homesickness). Some emigrants set off on brigs, barques or schooners from small ports like New Quay or Cardigan, and the concentration of settlers in the fertile lands of south-east Ohio was so high that the region became known as 'little Cardiganshire'. Most people, however, travelled to Liverpool in order to cross the Atlantic on larger and speedier steam-driven ships. The opportunity of earning a profitable livelihood on the rich pastures of the American prairies was hard to resist, and promotional campaigns by enthusiastic advocates of emigration helped to excite the interest of those in search of self-betterment. One of the most persuasive voices was that of Samuel Roberts, a fiercely independent and radical Nonconformist minister from the heart of Montgomeryshire: his moving accounts of landlord coercion in the 1850s persuaded many tenants that America offered them the only feasible escape route. Roberts and his associates bought 75,000 acres of rich and fruitful land in Tennessee, an ill-starred enterprise which ended in bitter acrimony and financial disaster.

Highly skilled and industrious Welsh coal miners, puddlers and steelworkers were also irresistibly attracted to the 'Promised Land'. The number of Welsh-born people living in the United States of America increased appreciably from 29,868 in 1850 to 100,079 in 1890. More than a third of the latter were located in the anthracite coalfield of Pennsylvania, where the city of Scranton could boast the largest concentration of Welsh people living outside England and Wales. Other industrial conurbations like Pittsburgh, Carbondale and Wilkes-Barre were attractive destinations to underpaid colliers living in wretched conditions and plagued by irregular employment, undercutters and strike-breakers. From the mid-nineteenth century, therefore, emigration was predominantly industrial in character although, since America was such a huge melting-pot, it made no difference to the prospects of either rural or industrial emigrants of maintaining their ethnic identity. To their great credit, Welsh settlers founded over 600 chapels in America and published a much larger corpus of Welsh-language books and periodicals than is commonly recognized. One of the most substantial publications was *Hanes y Gwrthryfel Mawr* (History of the Great Rebellion)

(1866), a bulky volume of over 600 pages which interpreted the American Civil War (1861–5) through the prism of the Welsh-American experience. Following this calamitous war, the American government became even more determined to mould all settlers into one nation, and second-generation Welsh immigrants, despite their fond attachment to the chapel, the eisteddfod and singing festivals, were more likely to know the words of 'My Old Kentucky Home' than 'Hen Wlad fy Nhadau' (Land of my Fathers). All attempts to resist cultural assimilation were doomed to fail, and even the likes of Samuel Roberts saw no future for the Welsh language in the new, interconnected cosmopolitan world. By 1900 even Y *Drych* (The Mirror), the most successful and long-lasting Welsh language newspaper of its day in America, confessed that the writing was on the wall: 'The way to perpetuate it [i.e. the Welsh eisteddfod] ... is to join it with the Stars and Stripes and place it under the special patronage of "Uncle Sam".' For the most part, Welsh colonists readily and confidently embraced the mores of 'Uncle Sam', and no one begrudged their right to respond to their cultural dilemma by becoming fully Americanized.

One lone visionary, however, resolved to discover a haven for beleaguered Welsh speakers outside their native land. A native of Llanuwchllyn, Merioneth, Michael D. Jones has long been recognized as one of the fathers of modern Welsh nationalism and one of the most implacable opponents of anglicizing trends. His experience of living in Cincinnati convinced him that the cultural assimilation of Welsh-speaking emigrants was occurring so swiftly in North America that a more distant, virgin territory was required for an autonomous Welsh settlement. Haunted by the spectre of the demise of Welsh and mindful that deference to speakers of English was one of the besetting sins of his countrymen, he dreamed of establishing a 'Nova Cambria' in the largely unexplored province of Patagonia in Argentina. One of the great adventures in Welsh history was launched on 24 May 1865, when around 150 intrepid Welsh emigrants set off from Liverpool on a tea-clipper, the *Mimosa*, to a remote part of South America which has stimulated memorable travellers' accounts from the days of Charles Darwin to Bruce Chatwin. Initially, the emigrants' hopes were deflated by the harsh realities of climate and terrain. Nevertheless, in this bleak and inhospitable environment, made all the more hazardous by hostile Indians and other marauders (Michael D. Jones's son was allegedly murdered by Butch Cassidy and the Sundance Kid), the Welsh settlers began to earn a modest living and established the trappings of a self-governing, Welsh-language colony. From the outset there was an illusory air to this brave enterprise, but it nevertheless proved to be far less susceptible to linguistic erosion than its critics had predicted. Over the best part of three decades, Welsh was the official language of administration, law, commerce, religion and education. The Patagonian adventure gripped the public imagination and, although Spanish gradually deposed Welsh as the language of the sons and daughters of the Mimosian settlers, the robust and determined core of Welsh speakers in the colony to this day will not lightly abandon Michael D. Jones's dream.

However intriguing and sometimes wholly admirable the saga of Welsh emigration might have been, in numerical terms it was a relatively modest affair. It certainly pales by comparison with the overwhelming majority of people who resisted the temptation to seek a new future for themselves and their families over the western horizon and who chose to stay in their native land and face the challenges of living in an expanding and class-ridden society. Writing in the mid-1860s, the great popular orator and peace activist Henry Richard maintained that the 'normal condition of the Principality is one of profound calm, rarely ruffled even by a breath of popular discontent'. Richard's aim was to trumpet the alleged achievement of Liberal Nonconformity in creating a law-abiding and civilized people, but his interpretation is not borne out by the evidence. During this period, dependable old Wales grew some pretty sharp horns. Indeed, not since pre-Union days had it posed such a serious threat to the British state.

The fundamental problem in the countryside was the maldistribution of wealth. By the latter years of the eighteenth century, many landed estates had fallen into the hands of absentee landowners who, if they were not already English, swiftly adopted metropolitan values and distanced themselves from the native culture and the tongue spoken by the vast majority. Property, wealth and influence became heavily concentrated in the hands of a tiny number of landed families who stood aloof from their social inferiors. It had always been taken for granted that such privileged people would live in attractive houses, enjoy unimaginably high standards of comfort, breed racing horses and gallop through the countryside in pursuit of hares and foxes, but it was also expected that they would seek to promote social harmony and take a sympathetic view of the plight of tenants during periods of economic hardship. But the relationship between landlords and tenants became increasingly strained as the years unfolded, especially as hard-hearted stewards and agents violated the traditional code of conduct which had previously bound the two social groups together. Writing in the turbulent 1790s, William Jones, a self-styled Voltairean heretic who farmed inhospitable land on the Wynnstay estate in Montgomeryshire, launched a blistering attack on those who expected deference from the have-nots but who sucked their tenants dry: 'these rapacious cormorants, not satisfied with open racking, frequently join the fox tail to the bear's claw and make use of base circumventions to fleece us more effectually ... and if we happen to complain of our hardships, we are immediately told in a true Aegyptian phrase "that we are idle" '. Insecurity of tenure prevailed as tenants groaned under the weight of high rents, tithes and other dues. Lacking ready capital, they were unable to carry out necessary improvements, let alone implement what they derisively called 'new-fangled' agricultural methods. Under the strains of the French war, shortages of grain and the enclosure of land produced a spate of violent protests which forced each local militia to stay on its toes. Following the agricultural boom of the war, during which landowners were the main beneficiaries, post-1815 Wales became even more unstable. A succession of wretched harvests and a rash of enclosures aggravated the plight of rural dwellers. Tenant farmers saw no hope of improving their daily lot, as the pressure of demographic growth began to bite. The Poor Law Amendment Act of 1834, which refused outdoor relief to able-bodied men and compelled parishes to build workhouses, was bitterly opposed, and when tithes were commuted into money payments from 1836 onwards, the sense of injustice deepened. Observers noted with monotonous regularity the 'extreme misery' of small farmers and agricultural labourers who were increasingly forced to rely on private charity and public relief. Over much of the

34. From 1839 to 1844 Rebecca and her daughters not only destroyed the much-loathed tollgates set up by the turnpike trusts in rural south-west Wales but also sent threatening letters to landowners, committed acts of arson, and punished adulterers, thieves and pilferers by using 'shaming' devices like the *ceffyl pren* (wooden horse). (The National Library of Wales)

latter part of the nineteenth century, pictures taken by John Thomas, the most celebrated Welsh Victorian photographer, provide haunting images of expressionless, shrivelled people – paupers, servants, beggars and urchins – who endured heartbreaking penury and mental anguish in rural slums.

Class divisions and tensions stalked rural Wales, and the faultlines in the south-western counties were starkly identified by Thomas Campbell Foster, a correspondent of the *Times*: 'the oppressed, the abject and the cringing; and the oppressive, the tyrannical and the haughty'. Indeed, this overpopulated area became a powder keg awaiting a spark of tinder. Whereas the antienclosure riots had involved relatively small numbers of people in isolated bursts of violent protest, by the late 1830s rural grievances were expressed in much more sophisticated and clandestine ways by large numbers of men who blackened their faces, wore women's clothes and swore allegiance to a redresser of wrongs known as 'Rebecca', whose scriptural legitimacy was to be found in Genesis 24:60. The legendary Rebecca Riots of 1839–44 did not constitute a mass movement – they were confined largely to the counties of Carmarthenshire, Cardiganshire and Pembrokeshire, and were fomented by small farmers – but they created a huge public stir and intense excitement. Over the years, a deep sense of indignation, anger and frustration had simmered in these counties. Whereas food rioters in the past had openly pillaged boats and stores, Rebecca vented her wrath either by pulling down gates and barriers (many of which had been illegally erected) which had placed a heavy burden on toll-payers carrying lime or butter from parish to parish, or on the deeply loathed workhouses known as the 'Welsh Bastilles'. The 'Lady', as the ubiquitous anonymous horsewoman was known, became the self-styled upholder of 'the people's law', the spokeswoman of the helpless, the wronged and the dispossessed.

When Rebeccaites stalked the countryside at night, local communities echoed to the sound of bloodcurdling yells, horns, firearms and rockets. Sinister tactics, including threatening letters, lurid posters, rick-burning and machine-breaking, were employed. Men of property went to some pains to avoid inciting the Lady's anger in case they were visited at midnight, but agents, informers and clergymen were regular victims of bitter attacks. One of Rebecca's greatest triumphs was the assault on the Carmarthen workhouse in June 1843, but it also acquired a reputation for using the *ceffyl pren* (wooden horse), the Welsh version of the *charivari* or skimmington ride, as a means of shaming and punishing adulterers and thieves. The deployment of large numbers of troops had no discernible effect, largely because an impenetrable wall of silence protected the insurgents and allowed them to destroy hundreds of toll-houses, gates, bars and chains, as well as commit a diverse range of nocturnal outrages with impunity. Even the promise of lucrative rewards failed to persuade anyone to volunteer to give evidence against them. 'They know everybody, and see everything', complained a hapless policeman dispatched to Rebecca's stamping grounds in 1843. The attacks peaked during the summer of 1843; emboldened by their success, some of the mobs became dangerously violent, and a small hooligan element resorted to the most disagreeable strong-arm tactics. The chief culprits were John Jones (Shoni Sguborfawr), a former prizefighter whose fists were as large as shovels, and David Davies (Dai'r Cantwr), a ballad-monger with a taste for capricious and violent behaviour. Both men had scores to settle and used Rebecca as a cloak for their nefarious deeds. But there were also more orderly, though just as angry, mass meetings (conducted in impenetrable Welsh to all but the participants) at which petitions to the Queen and parliament were drawn up, and deputations were sent to negotiate with landowners and government commissioners.

Once the authorities realized that these determined rural guerrillas were unlikely to yield, legislation was ushered through parliament to ameliorate grievances arising from the heartily despised tollgates and the poor law. Amid a welter of recriminations, the thugs who had sullied the good name of Rebecca were bundled off to Van Diemen's Land to reflect on their misdeeds. The railway boom meant that young agricultural labourers, who were poorly paid and often abominably treated by farmers, were able to escape to the teeming industrial townships of south Wales. As a result, the numbers of farm workers declined by 46 per cent between 1851 and 1911. But small tenant farmers were locked into a more rigid social structure which, unless they were brave or desperate enough to emigrate, rendered them vulnerable to the depredations of stewards and agents who seldom troubled to understand their needs or difficulties. The writings of the Nonconformist minister and farmer Samuel Roberts of Llanbryn-mair, Montgomeryshire – *Farmer Careful of Cilhaul Uchaf* (1850) and *A History of Diosg Farm* (1854) – provided graphic examples of how annual tenancy arrangements had created a mood of insecurity and distrust. The rising tide of Welsh emigrants in the 1850s confirms the widespread sense of disaffection in the countryside. The cycle of protest and agitation continued. Gangs of poachers terrorized gentry estates, and cases of arson and disorderly behaviour continued to catch the headlines. Recent studies have revealed the surprising extent to which the brutalizing effects of rural poverty led to a spate of cases of infanticide, incest, suicide, wife-beating, prostitution and theft. In 1848 the North Wales Lunatic Asylum was opened in a bid to cope with growing numbers of mentally ill or handicapped people. Although rural Wales (except perhaps in 1843) was never as unstable as Ireland, it was no Arcadia.

A severe agricultural depression and steepling price rises in the 1870s deepened the sense of injustice felt by tillers of the soil and

35. One of the finest nineteenth-century Welsh photographers was John Thomas (1838–1905), who earned his living by taking pictures of celebrities and common people. This striking photograph of individuals at the almshouse at Cerrigydrudion, Denbighshire, was taken *c.* 1890. (The National Library of Wales)

forced them either to depend even more heavily on close-knit, mutually supportive groups in which labour 'debts' were redeemed at harvest-time or to leave for America, Canada and Australia. Large-scale mechanization did not occur on Welsh farms until the twentieth century, and opportunistic Liberal Nonconformists exploited opportunities to conflate the land question and the tithe issue. By the 1880s it was the farmers of north-east Wales, drawing their inspiration from the tactics of Rebecca, who showed the fire in their bellies. On 23 August 1886 a banner headline in the *Daily News* read: 'The Tithe War in Wales'. During these disturbances, rioters armed themselves with sticks and staffs, bulls were let loose, and auctioneers and tithe-collectors were severely beaten. Speaking on their behalf, one Liberal politician deplored the 'money wrung from these poor, hard-driven farmers . . . to provide champagne and claret for the common room of the wealthiest colleges in the world'. For much of the nineteenth century, therefore, rural Wales was a cockpit for riots, disturbances and violent crime. Small wonder that its population was shrinking.

Industrial communities were also laced with individual and collective examples of injustice, suffering and protest. Working people struggled to find ways and means of improving their living and working conditions within a capitalist society in which ironmasters and coalowners were hell-bent on increasing their own material gains, and who had no intention of promoting the interests of their workforce. Land and minerals were the great sources of wealth for a caucus of titans who lived in great opulence. The fortunes of the Bute family, who owned over 100,000 acres of land, were greatly enhanced by profits from the high quality steam coal which was dispatched from Cardiff to distant ports. Flaunting his wealth gave John Patrick Crichton Stuart, the third marquess of Bute, untold pleasure: he employed William Burges, a remarkably gifted architect with a taste for medieval splendour, to transform his home, Cardiff Castle, into an eclectic romantic residence. By contrast, instilling fear and apprehension was uppermost in the mind of the Crawshay family, whose huge furnaces dominated Merthyr's landscape. Richard Crawshay – 'Moloch the Iron King' – was a ruthless, self-made man who epitomized the vileness of rampant capitalism. Even his fellow ironmasters dubbed him the 'Tyrant'. In 1825 his son, William, built a feudal-like castle at Cyfarthfa so that he could gaze down at the toiling masses below. Not many were able to boast, as did Taliesin Williams, the son of Iolo Morganwg, that he never cringed before the Crawshay and Guest families. Nor did the slate

THE SAXON: "AM
I ON THE RIGHT
WAY FOR BANGOR?"

THE WELSH DEACON:
"ISS, SURE.
GO ROUND THE
CHWITH AN'
TROI I LAWR
LON LLECHI-
LLWYDION TILL
YOU COME
AT TY MARI
TOMOS, AN'
THEN CROSS
AFON TROBWLL,
AN' —— "
(EXIT SAXON)

36. As the 'age of locomotion' brought greater numbers of people into Wales, visitors found themselves in communities where Welsh was the predominant, if not the only, tongue. Cartoonists swiftly seized on their bewilderment. (The National Library of Wales)

barons of Gwynedd seek to win the affection of quarrymen. In the very heartland of Gwynedd, where the dreams of Llywelyn ap Gruffudd had crumbled, the Penrhyn family built a mock-medieval castle, designed by Thomas Hopper in the revived Norman style, where the paranoid George Sholto Gordon Douglas-Pennant, second Baron Penrhyn and the owner of the largest slate quarry in the world, held quarry workers in utter contempt. He once referred to the Welsh as 'a nation of liars' and utterly rejected the notion of collective bargaining. Such extravagance and hostility meant that industrialized regions were deeply divided societies.

By contrast, working families who settled around the ironworks and collieries of the South Wales Coalfield began a long and anguished struggle to improve their lot and to acquire a certain measure of political self-consciousness. Some, of course, were immeasurably better-off than they had been in wretchedly deprived and overpopulated rural communities. The puddlers and rollers who worked in extraordinarily hot conditions in the furnaces and forges of Merthyr were well paid, as were those colliers who prided themselves on their skills and stamina. Agricultural labourers, too, were beguiled by reports of higher wages and opportunities for greater freedom and self-expression. By 1841 Merthyr figured among the fifty largest towns in Britain and its workplaces hummed with activity. But, in general, life for most people was a daily battle against deprivation, disease and death. Migrants were initially accommodated in temporary wooden huts or hastily built stone houses in the squalid frontier townships and only subsequently, when the coal rush began, were long rows of small terraced houses built into the valley slopes below slag-heaps of waste. Not until after 1870 were many towns prodded into launching public health initiatives and, even when some of the most appalling social slums came under the critical gaze of sanitary inspectors, who pinched their noses as they tiptoed through the squalor, improvements were often left to local discretion. The lack of regard for personal hygiene, overcrowding, poor sanitation and sheer malnutrition positively encouraged the spread of infectious diseases. Typhus and tuberculosis (or phthisis, as it was then called) were grim reapers, and from 1832, cholera – the scourge of Asia – pruned families with terrifying swiftness. Healthy rats and emaciated people were the hallmark of the smoky frontier towns, and the weak and the young were easy targets. In 1852 the average life expectancy in Merthyr – a rumbustious, populous town likened to Sodom and Gomorrah by Nonconformist ministers – was seventeen and a half. Even in the last decade of the nineteenth century, one in every twelve infants under five in the Pontypridd Registration District died of killing diseases like measles, pneumonia and dysentery. The workplace was unimaginably hazardous. Colliers faced daily hazards – roof falls, explosions, shaft-winding accidents – and some catastrophes, notably the explosion in 1894 which killed 290 men at the Albion Colliery, Cilfynydd, traumatized even hardened mining communities. During hot summers, the smells emanating from cesspools, privy pits and rivers were unbearable. Noxious vapours were hard to avoid: the stench of sulphur hung heavily over the copperworks around Swansea, and respiratory diseases – pneumoconiosis in the pits and silicosis in the quarries – enfeebled or killed the strongest of men. One of the most striking features was the spectacular increase in recorded crime. Cases of theft, drunkenness and assault meant that heavy police activity, regular street patrols and surveillance of public houses were required in towns like Cardiff, Merthyr, Newport and Swansea. Fagin and his urchins would have prospered in the 'China' district of Merthyr, an intimidating bastion of vice and crime where 'Emperors' and 'Empresses' (leaders), 'Rodnies' (juvenile offenders) and 'Nymphs' (prostitutes) roamed the streets.

In the circumstances, it is hardly surprising that working people were often roused to anger and violent protest. From the revolutionary years of the 1790s onwards, the industrial valleys of south Wales became a breeding ground for class hostility and militancy. The authorities were deeply shocked by the activities of the 'Scotch Cattle' in Monmouthshire in the 1820s, a covert group of daring workers who waged a war of terror against blacklegs. Violence was also prevalent in Merthyr, where the plebeian workforce bore the brunt of coercive measures which were instituted by ironmasters and supported by magistrates during times of food riots, strikes and disturbances. Many people did not so much question existing ideas or institutions as rail against the excesses of the system – the truck system, for instance, was used by unscrupulous ironmasters to compel workers to accept payment in the form of cheques or tokens in lieu of cash wages – and seek militant ways of putting things to right. Severe economic depression from 1829 sent working people in droves into the arms of the fledgling trade unions in order to protect themselves against intimidation, a trend which was further reinforced by growing support from politically minded shopkeepers and merchants, many of whom were steely Unitarians. Matters came to a boil in May/June 1831, when the industrial oligarchy of Merthyr and the forces of the Crown were challenged in a startling armed rising. Cries of 'Cheese with bread' and 'Reform' rang out through the town, and on the hills above the first red flag displayed in Wales was raised when rioters slaughtered a calf and besmeared a flag with its blood. Radical Dissenting ministers, including Thomas Evans (Tomos Glyn Cothi), whose reputation for inflammatory deeds dated from the 1790s, egged on the rioters, while Anglican parsons wrung their hands in horror. The debtor's court was sacked and set alight, and troops dispatched from Brecon were confronted outside the Castle Inn. More than two dozen demonstrators were killed and seventy wounded as the authorities sought to suppress the violence with ferocious intensity. Two supposed ringleaders were singled out for punishment. Lewis Lewis (Lewsyn yr Heliwr), a huntsman, was sentenced to transportation to New South Wales, though he was subsequently (and mysteriously) reprieved. The other, Richard Lewis (Dic Penderyn), a miner, was not so fortunate. Wrongly accused of wounding a soldier, he was sentenced to death and publicly hanged outside Cardiff gaol in August. Even as the noose tightened around his neck he continued to maintain his innocence, and his final plaintive cry 'O Lord! This is an injustice' haunted the dreams of the assembled throng for many a year. By executing Dic Penderyn, the authorities ensured that this otherwise unexceptional man became apotheosized into a working-class hero.

Undeterred by this setback, working people at Merthyr and elsewhere renewed their efforts and determination to shape events by pursuing the cause of trade unionism. By a curious irony, however, the co-operative movement, heavily laced with millenarian hopes (which the Newtown-born socialist and factory reformer Robert Owen advocated), failed to leave as strong an imprint on Wales as it did elsewhere. As the slights and humiliations caused by the failure of the Reform Act of 1832 and the Poor Law Amendment Act of 1834 to meet the needs and aspirations of the working class began to fester, growing numbers threw in their lot with Chartism, a working-class movement which culminated in a major armed rising. The celebrated Six Points of the People's Charter – manhood suffrage, the secret ballot, equal electoral districts, the abolition of property qualification for MPs, the payment of MPs and annual parliaments – was a familiar blueprint for all Chartists. But, if we view the movement in the context of the vision and commitment of its Welsh participants rather than as a strand in the political activity and strategy of the British campaign, certain features can be discerned which gave it a special volatility. Welsh Chartism was strongest in the south-east, and by the late 1830s there had emerged in the South Wales Coalfield thousands of tough-minded ironworkers, colliers and artisans who, mindful of the electrifying effects of the Merthyr rising and impatient for radical change, formed a broad alliance against employers, tradesmen and officers of the law. Their discourse was shot through with the antagonisms of class and ethnicity. As the publicist 'Junius' put it, the dominance of the state and the

37. On 4 November 1839 thousands of Welsh Chartists marched to Newport, where they were fired on by the 45th Regiment stationed at the Westgate Hotel. This insurrection was the bloodiest battle on mainland Britain during the nineteenth century. (The National Library of Wales)

coercive measures imposed by alien ironmasters meant that the Welsh proletariat were 'bound by laws, oppressive and tyrannical by nature'. As in the case of Rebecca's children, there was a powerful sense of solidarity within the ranks of working people, and some of the strongly anglophobic sentiments expressed by some of them betokened a deep-rooted antipathy towards wealthy and oppressive strangers who had reduced them to humiliating impotence. Songs like *Liberty's Address to the Welsh*, published in the spring of 1839, called on the enslaved to destabilize mercantile capitalism:

> Burst your shackles – and be free!
> Sons of Cambria! – follow me!

Significantly, too, advocates of legal and constitutional agitation were increasingly marginalized by those who espoused 'physical' force. A former mayor of Newport, John Frost, and a Carmarthen solicitor, Hugh Williams, both of whom were thoroughly upright and decent men, were unable to keep in check more impetuous radicals like William Price and Zephaniah Williams, who believed that theirs was a fight for freedom and a noble cause worth dying for. The latter in particular was bent on taking over the ownership of mines and instituting a workers' republic in Britain, by force of arms if necessary. While those who favoured moral persuasion focused on peaceful petitioning, a far greater body of workers advocated more decisive action. Arms, powder and cannon were requisitioned and stored in secret places in the hills. The 'physical' force wing thus prevailed, and on 3–4 November 1839 around 7,000 Chartists from the heads of the valleys, many of them armed with guns, pikes and knives, set off in three columns from different starting points and marched towards Newport. The Newport rising was the largest and most impressive political confrontation between government and working people in nineteenth-century Britain, and even torrential rain and some unforeseen hitches en route did not dampen the mood of high expectation. Scholars have disagreed over the aims and objectives of the insurgents, and Welsh Chartism as a whole offers an interesting study of how historians examining the same kinds of evidence can come to different conclusions. Was the march on Newport simply meant to be a mass demonstration? Was it designed as a wake-up call for militant Chartists elsewhere in Britain? Or was it an attempt, as Zephaniah Williams strongly maintained, to establish a republican government? Wherever the truth may lie, things went disastrously wrong on the fateful morning of 4 November when troops guarding the Westgate Hotel at Newport opened fire on the marchers who returned fire before dispersing in confusion, leaving twenty-two bodies behind. A distraught Frost fled as soon as blood began to flow, but, following a humiliating and painful mass treason trial, the three leaders of the march – John Frost, William Jones and Zephaniah Williams – were transported to Van Diemen's Land. Of the three, only Frost returned.

It has often been mistakenly assumed that the collapse of Welsh Chartism ushered in peace and tranquillity. But the truth is that the bloody encounter at Newport, and to a much lesser extent the take-over of the mid-Wales town of Llanidloes by aggrieved Chartist textile workers (also in 1839), became the stuff of legend and an inspiration for others. The tradition of militancy and martyrdom invigorated trade union activity in the iron and coal communities and, even though peaceful bargaining figured more prominently in negotiations between employer and employee, the threat of violence and disorder was never far away. No one should underestimate the readiness of the Welsh in this period to involve themselves in riots, physical intimidation and crime. As we shall see, the authorities were deeply troubled by what they believed to be the sinister nature of the South Wales Coalfield and the potential rebelliousness of militant Welsh-speakers. Yet, as greater numbers of working people were brought into the world of politics and as a much enlarged electorate emerged, the trend was for masters and men to achieve a certain modus vivendi based on the recognition of mutual interests. William Abraham (Mabon), who became the first Welsh miners' MP in 1885, was an emollient figure who succeeded in preserving the idea of trade unionism during the strikes and defeats of the 1870s, as well as bowing to the demands of coalowners for a sliding-scale system in which wage rates were determined by the price of coal. Wales itself had begun to nurture its own wealthy coalowners like David Davies, W. T. Lewis (Lord Merthyr) and D. A. Thomas (Lord Rhondda). Davies is a particularly interesting example of a self-made man who made his reputation as a sawyer, a bridge-builder and a railway contractor before becoming the chief colliery proprietor in the Rhondda and the developer of Barry docks. Yet, the volatility of markets and the intransigence of old-style capitalists such as Lord Penrhyn continued to give rise to confrontations and disputes. In 1896–7 a bitter and prolonged strike occurred as the quarrymen of north Wales refused to accept their allocations of rock and unsuccessfully challenged the might of the Penrhyn family. In April 1898 a 'Great Lock-Out' in the South Wales Coalfield, prompted by opposition to the sliding-scale system, involved over 100,000 colliers and their families. Defeat proved hard to bear, but the setback radicalized the workforce and led to the formation of the South Wales Miners' Federation in October 1898, a body which was determined to preach and practise the virtues of solidarity.

Many of those who threw in their lot with Rebecca, who marched under the banner of Chartism, and who defied the wishes of ironmasters and coalowners, were firmly grounded in the scriptures and were avid supporters of the Sunday school movement. Any student of religion in mid-Victorian Wales cannot fail to be impressed by the remarkably high levels of religious observance among common people as well as affluent middling sorts, and by their willingness to channel their creative energies into spiritual matters. Nonconformity (as Dissent was known by the 1850s) became the voice of the majority of worshippers. When the results of the first and last census of religious worship, held on Sunday, 30 March 1851, were published, they revealed that the Welsh far outstripped the English: 57 per cent attended a place of worship in Wales, compared with 39 per cent in England. Moreover, in terms of worshippers, the Church of England in Wales was outnumbered by four to one: 80 per cent of those enumerated on that particular Palm Sunday in Wales were Nonconformist chapel-goers. Wales could boast 2,813 chapels by this stage, and by 1905, as the population spurted upwards, the number had increased to 4,280. Small wonder that the champions of Welsh Nonconformity believed that the 1851 census provided incontestable proof that no nation in the world could match Wales for sheer religious vitality. In the vanguard were thousands of Calvinistic Methodists, Independents, Baptists and Wesleyan Methodists; the most aggressive of these claimed to be advocates of a Welsh-speaking majority no longer satisfied by an established church led by English-speaking squires, absentee bishops and penurious clergymen whose performance in the pulpit left much to be desired. Unable, perhaps unwilling, to adapt its archaic machinery to accommodate demographic shifts, industrial and urban growth, and the vigorous competition provided by Nonconformist denominations, the Anglican Church was thrown on to the defensive. At the beginning of this period, it was still held in some affection (even by Calvinistic Methodists) as 'The Old Mother' (*Yr Hen Fam*), but by mid-Victorian times its detractors crudely dubbed it 'the Alien Church' (*Yr Eglwys Estron*). How had this transformation come about?

First of all, Nonconformists enjoyed crucial advantages over their Anglican adversaries. Dogged by structural weaknesses, maldistribution of wealth, absenteeism, non-residence and pluralism, the unreformed church was no match for the growing Nonconformist denominations which catered for the needs of their members by building chapels in accessible locations. Denominational rivalry was unquestionably a spur to chapel-building, especially after Thomas Charles of Bala summoned up the courage to protect the interests of Calvinistic Methodism by severing its links with the established church in 1811, a deed from which his great mentor, Daniel Rowland (d. 1790), had recoiled. During these heady years a new Welsh chapel was opening every eight days, and the fact that so many ministers and elders were prepared to run the risk of incurring huge debts is a measure of their confidence. Gone were the days of the tiny meeting house or secluded chapel. Considerable funds and energy were now expended on building massive chapels which were meant to serve as 'ornaments to the locality'. Designed by professional architects, chapels sporting impressive exteriors and elaborate internal decoration bore witness not only to the desire of worshippers to praise God but also to the superb gifts of Welsh craftsmen. The proliferation of such buildings brought a new and dynamic energy to Nonconformity and fired the imagination of its leaders.

As the established church lost its self-confidence as well as its role as the guardian of the Christian faith, Nonconformity displayed its flexibility and dedication by directly serving the needs of the people. Pious men of humble stock became princes in the pulpit as the expanding world of Nonconformist culture offered clear opportunities for ministerial success. By the mid-nineteenth century Wales could boast around 2,000 Nonconformist preachers. Congregations were often driven into paroxysms of delight as the pulpit superstars preached extempore, using dramatic gestures, biblical dialogues, melodrama and burlesque to enliven their performances. Worshippers trembled whenever the one-eyed Welsh Baptist minister, Christmas Evans, fixed them with his piercing Cyclopian gaze, while the thunderous voice and penetrating eyes of Edward Matthews, Ewenni, were likened to two furnaces 'emitt[ing] sparks at the congregation'. A powerful dramatic element permeated the preaching style of John Elias, an autocratic figure in Calvinistic Methodist circles whose congregations swayed before him like reeds in a storm. Such strong-willed men generated considerable *hwyl* (enthusiasm) as they urged listeners to escape the fires of eternal damnation by giving their souls to Jesus. When Henry Rees, the most celebrated Calvinistic Methodist preacher of the mid-Victorian years, died in 1869, a battalion of 4,000 mourners trudged three miles in procession to his burial place on the Menai Straits. Potters and artists commemorated these iconic figures by producing ceramic figurines, sculptured busts and oil paintings which signified that Nonconformity and religious diversity had come of age. No picture by the photographer John Thomas sold better than his striking depiction of '74 Famous Men of the Welsh Pulpit', and it was a common assumption that these gifted word-smiths had been singled out by God to achieve great things.

Likewise, it was openly acknowledged that the missionary enter-prises of these itinerant or settled preachers were swept along by an irresistible revivalist tide. Evangelical preaching in vast, open-air meetings offered not only the means to salvation but also passion and excitement akin to that of a modern rock concert. Revivalist preachers seemed to be in perpetual motion, embarking on preach-ing tours on foot, on horseback and, from the 1840s, on trains. Untroubled by the shock waves occasioned by Darwinism and mounting biblical criticism, they were determined to make Wales an impregnable bastion for the Nonconformist faith. Local revivals often had electrifying effects and, as the numbers of converts multi-plied swiftly, Wales became known as a 'land of revivals'. Such outbreaks of enthusiasm were sometimes triggered by temperance issues or outbreaks of the dreaded cholera. 'How can ye escape the damnation of hell?' cried David Rees of Llanelli, as the ravages of cholera ripped through industrial communities in 1849. Ministers invariably saw the 'finger of God' in the revival movement, and public demonstrations of praise were never more evident than when the greatest revival of all broke out in 1859. Indirectly inspired by the American revivalist movement, the 1859 revival was initially associated with the extraordinary preaching missions of Humphrey Jones and David Morgan in Cardiganshire, but as expressions of religious fervour gained momentum it spread to all parts of Wales. Nonconformity may have benefited from as many as 110,000 new converts, and had the 1851 religious census been held two decades later its results would surely have confirmed that the 1860s marked the high point of chapel-going in Wales. Moreover, the effects of the 1859 revival proved to be much more profound and long-lasting than those of its better-known successor in 1904–5.

Nonconformity also offered more than spiritual joy and fulfil-ment. Through its Sunday schools, it nurtured a book-reading peo-ple. From the 1790s Thomas Charles of Bala, the son of a tenant

farmer from Carmarthenshire, devoted the bulk of his time to
founding Sunday schools and distributing saving literature sponsored by the British and Foreign Bible Society, a body which he
helped to found in 1804. Charles's own *Geiriadur Ysgrythyrawl*,
an enormous four-volume scriptural dictionary published in
1805–11, became one of the most heavily thumbed works in
Nonconformist circles. Welsh printing presses teemed with religious
literature. By producing, buying, distributing and reading thousands
of Welsh-language bibles, catechisms, primers and hymn books, the
Sunday schools stimulated literacy among the young and the old, the
rural dweller and the urban migrant. *Trysorfa y Plant*, a magazine
for Sunday school children, was selling 45,000 copies per month by
1881. Enrolments in Sunday schools were staggeringly high. In 1901
more than a third of the inhabitants of the Rhondda were registered
in Sunday schools, and these socially inclusive, democratic seed-
beds of Nonconformity acquired their own heroes and heroines.
People all over the world are familiar with the charming story of
Mary Jones, a determined young peasant girl who, in the spring of
1800, walked barefoot from Abergynolwyn to Bala in Merioneth
(a journey of some 25 miles) to buy a bible from Thomas Charles, a
bible which she not only read every day for sixty-two years but large
parts of which she also committed to memory. Where else but in
Wales could travellers encounter seasoned colliers sitting by the
roadside discussing complex theological subjects like 'How to reconcile the sovereignty of God with the responsibility of man'? The
Sunday school became a popular institution in Wales, and the early
socialist David Thomas reckoned that its nation-wide organization
was as robust and effective as the American Standard Oil Company.

Welsh chapels were also alive with other attractions – penny
readings, prayer meetings, the Band of Hope, bible classes, eisteddfodau and hymn-singing festivals – which deepened spiritual bonds
and filled the social calendar in a world riven with disease and
violence. The hymns of William Williams, Pantycelyn, continued
to enrich the spiritual experience of worshippers, and from 1806
onwards the image-laden hymns of Ann Griffiths of Dolwar Fach,
Montgomeryshire (which had been memorized by her maid-servant
and recorded), showed that women, too, were capable of expressing
profound religious truths. By Victorian times Wales was acquiring a

reputation as the 'Land of Song', as music-making captured the popular imagination. A major turning point occurred in the revival year of 1859, when John Roberts (Ieuan Gwyllt) published *Llyfr Tonau Cynulleidfaol*, a book of Congregational hymn tunes which, by encouraging four-part singing, stimulated Welsh congregations and choral societies to develop the ability to sing hymns in a rousing fashion, an art which became broadly characteristic of the nation. Printing presses clattered noisily, churning out thousands of melodies, test pieces and song sheets, and music shops sold pianos, violins, organs, banjos and piccolos in growing numbers. Brass bands and string bands began to flourish, and soloists like Lewis William Lewis (Llew Llwyfo), Robert Rees (Eos Morlais) and Edith Wynne attracted an ardent following. The harmonium and the piano displaced the harp as the new fashion for choral singing – both mixed choirs and male voice choirs – took root. At national eisteddfodau, mouth-watering prizes were offered and Welsh choirs swiftly established a reputation not only for musical virtuosity but also for doggedly refusing to lose with good grace. The volatile conductor, Dan Davies of Merthyr, was known as 'the Wellington of choral singing'. Such men were both feared and revered. When Griffith Rhys Jones, a blacksmith known as 'Caradog', led his South Wales Choral Union, a 456-strong choir, to victory at the Crystal Palace in 1873, the people of Aberdare proudly built a bronze statue in his honour. A substantial collection was made to enable Joseph Parry, a former pit-boy from Merthyr, to return from America to develop his skills as the most eminent of Welsh composers, an investment which bore rich fruit. Nonconformists were exceptionally well placed to encourage the tradition of popular choral and congregational singing, and the singing festival (*cymanfa ganu*), where hymns were sung with gusto and where those who had gained proficiency in the tonic sol-fa notation were awarded certificates, became enormously popular.

Well has it been observed that mid-Victorian Wales, at least outwardly, was 'respectable, religious [and] petty bourgeois in style and aspiration'. Although the common people found the chapels attractive, a special affinity emerged between the affluent and upwardly mobile bourgeoisie and the Nonconformist religion. Pious middling sorts – tradesmen, merchants, bankers, shopkeepers and farmers – viewed old-fashioned Puritan virtues such as industrious-ness, self-help, sobriety and respectability as a progressive cause in a society bedevilled by unrest, drunkenness and secular pleasures. The traffic in liquor in Wales was astonishing: there were 506 drinking places in Merthyr alone in 1854, and Ellen Sweeney of Swansea, who was convicted of drunkenness for the 156th time in 1880, was not considered to be an unusual case. Sobriety did not come easily to the Welsh working class, and when the Welsh Sunday Closing Act was passed in 1881 there was no great sense of enthusiasm for it outside middle-class temperance and sabbatarian circles. Nonconformity encouraged upward social mobility and, although the middle classes believed that saving souls was critically impor-tant, they also reckoned that people of taste and discernment like themselves were entitled to improve their own lot and that of others. Some of them saw very clearly that the evangelical wing of Nonconformity had several blind spots, especially on matters relat-ing to political and legal rights. The conservatively minded John Elias used Calvinistic theology as a means of snuffing out what he believed to be the spirit of rebellion, but following his death in 1841 more progressive middle-class Nonconformists campaigned strongly on issues such as tithes, church rates and burial rights. In towns like Merthyr and Swansea, civic 'boosters' and religious reformers deployed the temperance movement, the police and the press as a means of regulating urban spaces and 'civilizing' the feckless working class, whose apparent obsession with gambling, drinking and fighting was repugnant to them. Having imposed upon themselves a regime of strict self-denial, these reformers waged war on the demon drink by establishing coffee taverns, literary societies and workmen's libraries. Assamese tea was vigorously marketed in Nonconformist circles from the mid-Victorian period onwards.

The stress on self-improvement dovetailed neatly with the ethos of imperial Britain. Affluent Welsh Nonconformists were so confident that God smiled upon them that they dispatched gospel-bearers to India, Madagascar and Brittany to convert heathens to Christianity. In 1841 the Calvinistic Methodists launched what became a hugely successful missionary campaign in north-east India, as a result of which readers of denominational magazines became as familiar with the topography of the Khasi Hills as they were with their own local terrain. Moreover, they basked in the achievements of 'Christian soldiers' who served Victoria on distant battlefields and in those of missionaries (many of whom were women) who risked their lives in a bid to save the souls of benighted peoples of different coloured skin. By 1901 the Khasi Christian community numbered 16,000 and was so heavily steeped in the doctrines of Welsh Presbyterianism that an incredulous reporter, sent to Shillong, noted that they had 'adopted Welsh Methodism with scarcely a variant'. That these peoples could also sing a Khasi version of 'Land of my Fathers' is another indication of how unpredictable the effects of cultural imperialism could be.

The successes of Nonconformity, both at home and abroad, should not be allowed to obscure the fact that a good many of its champions became rather too heavily preoccupied with wealth, social position and respectability. Those who jostled for primacy as elders in the 'big seat' (*sêt fawr*) in chapels became sitting targets for lampoonists. By exposing the sham and hypocrisies of 'respectable' chapel-goers, the satirist David Owen (Brutus) and the novelist Daniel Owen debunked the notion of Wales as an unblemished land. It comes as something of a surprise to find devout editors of Nonconformist denominational magazines filling their columns with advertisements for bizarre birth control methods and other products for the benefit of those suffering from 'the errors and indiscretions of youth'. Some of the heaviest investors in shares in shipping companies were canny Welsh Nonconformists, and in the quarrying districts there were strong rumours that ministers and deacons who had signed the teetotal pledge were regularly availing themselves of clandestine supplies of beer. The desire to 'get on' prompted many well-to-do Welsh-speaking ministers from the 1870s onwards to collude with those who believed that Welsh was an obstacle to improvement. As a result, the linguistic and spiritual needs of monoglot English in-migrants were accommodated within specially built chapels known as 'English causes'.

Nor should we swallow, hook, line and sinker, the exaggerated claim made by Henry Richard – the quintessential Welsh Liberal Nonconformist – that the Welsh nation was synonymous with Nonconformity. There was clearly a large section of the public who cared nothing for organized religion. The religious census of

1851 revealed that half the population had not darkened either church or chapel on the appointed date, and the number of those who neglected public worship increased as the century wore on. In his classic realist novels, Daniel Owen not only exposed the double standards and sanctimoniousness of upwardly mobile chapel-goers but also drew attention to the forgotten underclass of undesirables who cocked a snook at formal religion: 'there are yet hundreds who know no more of the gospel than of the strangest thing in the world. There are dark and filthy back streets where poverty, wretchedness and evil abide and beget themselves anew year after year.' Many such people were contemptuous of the notion that commercialized entertainment – fairs and festivals, gambling booths, cockfights, prizefights, 'magic lantern' shows and drinking dens – were sinful pursuits. The rise of leisure facilities and recreational codes offered people a much wider range of choice during leisure hours and even on the Sabbath. Whereas working people in north-east Wales took association football to their hearts from the 1870s onwards, the mining communities of south Wales nurtured an undying passion for the oval ball. Those who believed that many of the harmless, traditional folk customs of a once 'merry Wales' had been fatally undermined by the 'sour spirit' of Nonconformity were more likely to welcome the boom in alternative leisure facilities, and Darwinism, secularism and atheism were undoubtedly gaining ground by the 1890s. A general sense of weariness in Nonconformist circles helped to create a deep crisis of faith and a widespread sense of foreboding.

It is more than a little ironic, too, that the established church, so bitterly excoriated by Nonconformist propagandists, was experiencing a striking resurgence by this stage. One of the enduring myths about Victorian Wales is that Anglicans failed to put their house in order and that it was the church of a minority. Initially, the established church had certainly been timid and slow to respond to massive socio-economic changes, but over time the influence of the Oxford movement, vigorous patronage by landowners, and new initiatives by bishops and clergymen brought about a wave of rebuilding and refurbishment which transformed the prospects of the Anglican cause. By 1906 it boasted 193,081 worshippers, the largest single religious community in Wales. Paradoxically, at the very time Nonconformists were vigorously pursuing the cause of disestablishment, 'the old traitress' (*yr hen fradwres*) was embarking on a period of renewal. While Anglicanism could never hope to recapture its traditional drawing-power or impose its will on the majority, it could look forward to better times.

The depiction of the established church as a traitress had stemmed largely from the bitterness and anger occasioned by the Treachery of the Blue Books (*Brad y Llyfrau Gleision*), a seminal event in 1847 which shaped the future of political and cultural life in Wales for several generations. In Ireland, the Great Famine had proved to be such a traumatic experience that a massive diaspora followed. A million people died and another million emigrated, while those left behind witnessed an 'awful, unwonted silence'. In sharp contrast, at around the same time the Welsh exploded in incandescent rage when three young, monoglot English-speaking, Oxford-trained law graduates called Johnson, Lingen and Symons inflicted on them probably their greatest moment of public shame by portraying them as a source of moral contamination. In 1846 these commissioners had been sent into Wales, at the behest of parliament, to examine the condition of education. They set about their tasks with brisk zeal. Written and verbal evidence, collected mainly by Anglican assistants, enabled them to produce a hefty report in three volumes which caused such a huge stir that its publication became a defining moment in the history of modern Wales.

Ironically, the comments of the commissioners on the state of education, though predictably harsh, were close to the truth. There were too few schools, their resources were pitiful and teachers were poorly trained. Over the preceding decades suspicion and rivalry between church and chapel, and especially between champions of state intervention and advocates of voluntarism, had been at its most bitter in the field of education. The absence of large-scale commitment to improving standards was, as the commissioners rightly noted, all the more regrettable since the Welsh themselves, especially those who frequented Sunday schools on a regular basis, showed every sign of being hungry for education. Had the commissioners simply confined their comments to such matters, their report would scarcely have excited much attention or left a profound mark. But they gratuitously exceeded their brief by traducing the morals and language of the people: the Welsh were liars and cheats; their women were primitive and unchaste; they clung to an absurd vernacular and an outmoded culture which kept them 'under the hatches'. The report not only exhibited the most deplorable denial of dignity and respect for the people of Wales but also betrayed a failure to appreciate that a language which was not English could embody different concepts and relationships that enabled the Welsh to see the world in a different way. To the commissioners, however, lack of English had led to 'manifold evils' such as perjury and civil disobedience, which could only be remedied by a sound dose of anglicization and modernization. Such sentiments were music to the ears of a government which believed that the English language was the language of modernity, progress, conquest, empire and commerce. The Welsh, for their part, were left reeling in bewilderment and anger.

From 1847 onwards the air was thick with accusations, counter-accusations and recriminations, as the Welsh sought to come to terms with this public humiliation. The psychological effects of the indictment prompted different social groups to respond in different ways. Markers were set down for the future, as some began to ponder whether the price to be paid for their 'otherness' was either to be disregarded or loathed as an immoral and degraded people. Others, seething with rage, raised their voices boldly.

Nothing discomfited the middle-class Welsh more than to be counted a 'lesser' people, and there was thus a growing tendency among them to pander to the assumption of English superiority and to crave the approval, if not the affection, of their nearest neighbours. The dread of further disgrace or shame meant that they colluded with the sponsors of the charges by vowing to exorcise the rebelliousness of the past and to anglicize their countrymen as swiftly as possible. In a staggering piece of self-delusion, the poet William Williams (Caledfryn), who had previously given evidence in favour of Nonconformity to the commissioners, now proclaimed that the principles espoused by Voltaire or Tom Paine had never been expressed in Welsh and that his countrymen had never risen in protest or rebellion. An overwhelming desire for respectability and acceptance, coupled with a growing commitment to utilitarian values, prompted them to promote Darwinism, scientific inquiry and

38. The artist Hugh Hughes expressed the sense of national outrage against the report known as 'The Treachery of the Blue Books' by publishing a series of cartoons in *Pictures for the Million of Wales* (1848). This caricature shows 'Dame Wales' tossing the egregious English commissioners into the sea. (The National Library of Wales)

the English tongue. In their eyes, the most effective way to avoid future collective humiliation was to suppress the use of Welsh in key domains. Within the National Eisteddfod – the annual Welsh-language showpiece – the educationist Hugh Owen pandered to the vanity of the 'best people' by conducting the proceedings of the

'Social Science Section' in English from 1862 onwards. When a programme of school-building was instituted by the Education Act of 1870, a nationwide system of elementary schooling was launched. Its path, however, proved anything but smooth. To Her Majesty's Inspectors, bilingualism in schools was a 'difficulty' rather than an opportunity and, since Welsh was increasingly equated with ignorance and backwardness, parents were perfectly happy for brutal sanctions to be invoked against pupils who used Welsh in elementary schools. The use of the 'Welsh Not' – a wooden plaque hung around the neck of pupils who deigned to use Welsh at school – was a humiliating reminder of the subaltern status of the native tongue, and those who sought to promote a distinctive educational system for Wales were sidelined. Pupils were taught to learn and regurgitate notes about heroes like Alfred, Wellington and Nelson, to sing 'Hurrah for England', and by Edwardian times to wrap the Union Jack around themselves on Empire Day. While the Irish were victims of their history, the Welsh were starved of their own past. At both primary and intermediate level, discrimination against the Welsh language and its culture was so acute that Y Punch Cymraeg, the Welsh equivalent of Punch, dubbed the educational infrastructure 'the silent machinery to Anglicize the Welsh'. Even a leading Oxford-trained scholar like Sir John Rhŷs, who had been born and bred in a monoglot Welsh rural environment, seldom published in Welsh and came to believe that his native tongue should be left to die in peace, while the Western Mail claimed loudly that Welsh speakers who clung to monoglottism would remain 'narrow-minded and clannish and ignorant'. In short, those who were determined to get on in the world viewed Welsh as the language of potato soup, straw beds and peripatetic minstrels. In such circles, 'Welsh does not pay' became a popular catchphrase.

Groups of cultural patriots, however, stubbornly refused to worship at the altar of Progress. From the 1770s onwards, highly intelligent and versatile craftsmen and artisans had set themselves the task of recovering the lost or abandoned cultural traditions of Wales and creating a more attractive image for its people. Authors, poets, artists, musicians and myth-makers strove to rescue Wales from the condescension of the English, to rid it of its provincial 'non-historic' status, and to foster a distinctive romantic identity. Styling themselves 'ancient Britons' or 'valorous Celts', they lay great store by primitivism, druidism, ancient lore, music and pageantry. Thomas Gray's poem, *The Bard* (1757), seized the imagination of artists like Paul Sandby and Thomas Jones, Pencerrig, who depicted one of the last surviving harpist-bards about to leap to his doom into the 'foaming flood' of the Conwy river as the dastardly Anglo-Norman troops closed in. This image of the Celtic bard fixed in the public mind the notion that poets, priests and Druids in the Celtic past had long white beards, flowing robes and melancholy songs to sing. The presiding genius among these myth-makers was the Glamorgan stonemason, Iolo Morganwg, arguably the most gifted, complex and intriguing figure in the annals of Welsh culture. Although he has often been dubbed a rogue and a charlatan, he was a serious scholar and almost certainly the best-read man in the Wales of his time. Throughout his long and chequered life, he never lost his affection for 'the old happiness' (*yr hen ddywenydd*) – his charming description of the study of the language, literature and history of Wales. His literary forgeries were so convincing that he successfully passed off his own poems as the authentic work of the fourteenth-century poet Dafydd ap Gwilym and persuaded the London-Welsh literati to publish them in the year of the French Revolution. In June 1792 he conducted the first ceremony of The Assembly of the Bards of the Isle of Britain (*Gorsedd Beirdd Ynys Prydain*) on Primrose Hill, London. This druidic court, a theatrical event steeped in quasi-masonic rituals and Jacobin symbolism, was designed to give one of the forgotten peoples of Europe a new and enhanced sense of their identity and worth. By July 1819 Iolo had realized another dream when, at the age of seventy-two, he succeeded in incorporating the Gorsedd into the annual round of provincial eisteddfodau sponsored by the Cambrian Society.

The revitalized eisteddfod survived Iolo's death in 1826 but, under the influence of gentry patrons and Anglican clerics, from the 1830s it increasingly yielded to the intrusive demands of the English tongue and the flood of British patriotism which enveloped Wales following the Blue Books controversy. Most eisteddfodic poetry was so turgid and verbose that common people found solace in the tear-jerking stanzas of John Ceiriog Hughes (Ceiriog). It was left to a small, but noisy, band of idiosyncratic Victorian Druids to hold fast to the dreams and ambitions of Iolo Morganwg by assembling at each solstice and equinox at the Rocking Stone on Pontypridd common under the stewardship of the likes of Evan Davies (Myfyr Morganwg), the proud owner of 'the Druidic Mundane Egg' which he alleged had been worn by a succession of druidic high priests in Wales since time immemorial. Not to be outdone, the redoubtable William Price, a disciple of Iolo and a fiery druidic Chartist whose beard stretched to his waist, used to dress in a white jacket, a scarlet waistcoat, emerald green trousers and a fox-skin hat during these eye-catching ceremonies. His unconventional behaviour reached its peak in 1884 when, having publicly burnt the body of his infant son (named Jesus Christ), he successfully established in court the legality of cremation. Such wild and eccentric activity infuriated the Welsh middle class, but uncritical antiquaries like John Williams (Ab Ithel) and a new generation of painters and sculptors celebrated the Welsh Druid-bard and proved to be a useful counter-balance to those who sought to promote the use of English in eisteddfodau.

Rather more significant was the manner in which the post-1847 furore opened new doors for women. What outraged the Welsh most were the gratuitous remarks made by the three commissioners on the standards of morality of their women, who were portrayed as a licentious lot, obsessed by 'courtship on beds' or 'bundling', a practice supposedly encouraged by nocturnal meetings organized in the name of Nonconformity. Parts of Wales (notably Anglesey) were said to be 'universally unchaste', and it was alleged that illegitimacy rates were soaring. Growing numbers of writers spoke out vigorously on behalf of females. Rather than react with shame or penitence, Welsh women and their male champions furiously rebutted the charges. In a biting satire entitled *Artegall* (1848), Wales's first female historian, Jane Williams, Ysgafell, defended their honour, while in 1854 R. J. Derfel – a travelling salesman-cum-poet-cum-playwright – penned a forthright drama which drew on narratives associated with the 'Treachery of the Long Knives' in the days of the perfidious fifth-century traitor, Vortigern. But although unfounded allegations were not allowed to pass unchallenged, the damage to the reputation of women had been done. Never before had the female population of Wales been publicly defamed in a government-sponsored report. The calumnies were a godsend for sniggering London newspapers, and crude jokes about 'Welsh whores' with the morals of alleycats were delivered with even greater relish than before. In the face of this onslaught, Nonconformist ministers led by Evan Jones (Ieuan Gwynedd), editor of *Y Gymraes*, the first Welsh-language periodical for women (1851–3), sought to exorcise the ghost of 1847 by depicting the quintessential Welsh woman as an 'angel of the hearth', a symbol of Nonconformist purity and the embodiment of godliness, sobriety and thrift. One of the principal sponsors of this periodical was Augusta Hall, Lady Llanover, who, from the 1830s, had promoted a romantic image of the docile Welsh peasant woman dressed in a national folk costume, complete with cloak, bedgown and tall Welsh hat.

The reality was rather different. There might have been angels in pious, middle-class households, but most women were tied to the milk churn, the spinning wheel and the washing place. The patriarchal view of women still prevailed, and men were determined to keep them in check. It was not uncommon in some parts for a husband to place a halter around the neck of his wife and sell her in the local market. Although women were barred from working underground after 1842 (as indeed were under-tens), they remained a reservoir of cheap labour in the fields, manufactories and domestic service. The pit brow lasses who, in their heavy dresses or trousers and hobnail boots, carried out such onerous and dangerous tasks as tipping coal, moving wagons and filling barges, were so heavily disfigured by dirt and smoke that they were scarcely distinguishable from men. There were plenty of obstreperous women who never read domestic conduct books or listened to sermons, and whose reputation as scolds, bawds and witches aroused fear among their neighbours. Unwanted offspring were disposed of as desperate, but determined, single mothers chose to kill their babies rather than face penury and shame. Crews of sailors from all parts of the world lusted after the whores of Tiger Bay, and the heavily frequented brothels of the 'China' district in Merthyr were a law unto themselves.

In a variety of ways, women were insisting on their right to be seen and heard. They took an active part in corn riots and the defence of common rights, and seized the initiative in organizing the shaming (and often menacing) rituals which embarrassed errant husbands or lovers. In coastal villages bereft of mariners for many months, women learned how to be independent by bringing up families single-handed, while in militant industrial regions they knew how to wreak vengeance on wife-beaters and blackleg miners. They participated in anti-slavery, anti-Corn Law and temperance movements, formed local Chartist cells and expressed their views in Sunday school classes. Once the dust had settled following the 1847 controversy, they increasingly began to enter the public sphere as suffragists. Sarah Jane Rees (Cranogwen), a strong-willed schoolmistress, preacher, lecturer and sailor, provided a platform for Welsh bluestockings and proto-suffragettes in the periodical *Y Frythones* (The Female Briton) (1879–89), and no journalist did more to champion feminism than John Gibson, editor of the *Cambrian News*. As late as 1885 Gibson still feared that women were 'either slaves or are legally, socially and politically non-existent', an abject state of affairs which prompted him to publish *The Emancipation of Women* in 1891. Attitudes were nevertheless changing. The Welsh Intermediate and Technical Education Act of 1889, one of the most admirable pieces of legislation in Victorian times, opened new doors to both sexes. Equality was given to women in the burgeoning university colleges: a woman was the first to graduate at Cardiff, and one of three students at Bangor in its inaugural year (1884) were women. Even less well-to-do and gifted women were benefiting from schooling by this stage, and the percentage of females signing a marriage register with a mark fell from 69.5 in 1845 to 5.3 in 1900. Most of all, women were seizing new opportunities by the end of the nineteenth century to participate in politics. When the Welsh Women's Liberal Union assembled at Newtown in 1896, the words 'We *will* have the vote' were emblazoned above the stage.

The 'Treachery' of 1847 also served a creative purpose by stimulating and channelling the political consciousness of the Welsh. For much of the early part of this period, Old Corruption remained alive and well. General elections were held irregularly, and the great majority of men (and all women) were ineligible to vote. Planting the ideology of democracy was a protracted process. The early drivers of change were tippling, pipe-smoking Jacobin sympathizers in London, Denbighshire and Merthyr who read and idolized Tom Paine and who became doughty champions of free speech. These *citoyens du monde*, led by irrepressible Unitarians like Iolo Morganwg, John Jones (Jac Glan-y-gors), Thomas Evans (Tomos Glyn Cothi, who was locked up for sedition in Carmarthen prison for two years) and Morgan John Rhys (a Baptist minister who stood on the ruins of the Bastille and also lectured American republicans on the evils of slavery), stood up to the bully-boys of the 'Church and King' mobs and strove to awaken the Welsh from their political slumbers during the turbulent 1790s. Their noisy activities brought dividends as middle-class radicals joined them in campaigning for manhood suffrage, the ballot, and the removal of civil and religious disabilities by petitioning parliament. But the auguries remained gloomy. Despite a robust defence of the Courts of Great Sessions – the last vestige of Welsh 'separateness' – this institution was abolished in 1830, and when the misnamed 'Great' Reform Act was passed in 1832 it brought few tangible rewards for the Welsh. The number of parliamentary seats was increased from 27 to 32, two of which were awarded to the swiftly growing boroughs of Merthyr and Swansea, but the numbers of those who entered the pale of the constitution as voters were derisory. As we have seen, large groups of working people chose to express their grievances and aspirations outside the formal boundaries of politics, but the clarion calls which appealed to the constitutionally minded middle-class radicals were 'Agitate' and 'Organize'. The cult of violence was repugnant to pressure groups like the Anti-Corn Law League and the pro-disestablishment Liberation Society, both of which sought to educate the Welsh to think about politics in a mature and sophisticated way. But progress was slow until the commissioners of 1847 provoked such a deep sense of outrage that the Welsh were jolted into unprecedented political activity. When elections did occur thereafter, the turnout rates were high and the degree of participation increased appreciably as the century wore on.

At this stage, and for the rest of the century, the press became an extremely powerful moulder of opinion. Over the nineteenth century as a whole, in excess of 10,000 separate Welsh-language publications appeared, and an even greater tide of print in English.

Innovations in technology, the expansion of transport, new postal services, the removal of stamp duties and the seemingly insatiable demand for reading matter transformed the prospects of the radical cause from the 1850s onwards. The world of journalism flourished, and some of the finest reporters and editors – William Rees, Thomas Gee and John Gibson – were men of considerable political gifts as well as successful businessmen. Not even agnostics doubted that the press was 'the most powerful engine under God', and readers of *Baner ac Amserau Cymru* (Banner and Times of Wales) (1857–), the *Western Mail* (1869–) and the *South Wales Daily News* (1872–) became better informed and less likely to accept that problems did not disappear for being ignored.

To the landed gentry and affluent industrialists, however, 'Reform' was a hydra-headed monster to be resisted at every turn, and it became increasingly apparent that pressure groups could only achieve so much, and that the critical issue was the extension of the vote. The 1867 Reform Act more than doubled the number of Welsh voters from 61,575 to 126,571 and opened the way for what was optimistically hailed as an *annus mirabilis* in the elections of 1868, during which memorable victories were recorded by Liberal candidates. In many ways, however, it was business as usual: most Welsh MPs, whatever their political colours, were still drawn from elite social groups. Even so, the rallying cry 'A country is mightier than the lord' enabled Liberal candidates like Henry Richard at Merthyr, who was widely respected as the 'apostle of peace', to depict their masters as cruel, oppressive tyrants who could never represent the true interests of the Welsh people. For the first time in their history, tenant farmers, quarrymen, colliers and tinplate workers had participated in a truly popular campaign and had decided the results of elections in key rural and industrial constituencies. Landlords retaliated by victimizing and evicting recalcitrant tenants and, although the Ballot Act of 1872 eased tensions, the balance of power did not tilt decisively towards Liberalism until the large-scale extension of the franchise was secured by the Representation of the People Act (1884) and the Redistribution of Seats Act (1885). Appreciable numbers of the working class gained the vote and, in the 1885 election, all but five of the thirty-five parliamentary seats were captured by Liberals. Portraits of Gladstone and Henry Richard adorned parlours in farmhouses and cottages, and a new generation of energetic and compelling young Liberal MPs like David Lloyd George and Tom Ellis championed the cause of aggrieved Nonconformist tenants, anti-tithe militants, campaigners for disestablishment and all those who believed that the diversity and special needs of Wales required recognition. With the creation of elected county councils in 1889, the political hegemony of the local squires came to an end.

Out of the Liberal ascendancy grew the 'Young Wales' movement and the first serious calls for 'Home Rule for Wales'. As early as the 1770s romantic myth-makers and cultural patriots in Wales had come to the conclusion that a national library to safeguard literary treasures, a national academy to preserve folk customs and a national university to nurture a confident cultural elite were fundamental desiderata if Wales was to retain a semblance of its past glories. Iolo Morganwg devised the Gorsedd of the Bards in 1792 as a means of projecting a new vision of history, of a nation reborn in radical liberty. In 1776 the Welsh word for patriotism (*gwladgarwch*) had been coined and by 1798, a year of rebellions, the Welsh equivalent of nationality (*cenedligrwydd*) had entered the vocabulary. But two generations passed before, in the post-1848 period often called 'the springtime of nations', the more significant word nationalism (*cenedlaetholdeb*) informed political discourse. 'Land of my Fathers' (*Hen Wlad fy Nhadau*), composed in 1856 by two Pontypridd patriots, was adopted as a national anthem in national eisteddfodau from the mid-1870s, and Welsh periodicals in the late Victorian period were littered with vacuous phrases such as 'Wales must believe in itself' and 'the spirit of national awakening'. The writings of Robert Ambrose Jones (Emrys ap Iwan), whose European sensibility stimulated new interest in Wales as a 'nation' and who coined the Welsh word for self-rule (*ymreolaeth*), condemned the abject servility of the Welsh. When the good name of the Welsh was impugned following the controversial 1891 census, by no less a figure than the Registrar General, who claimed that Welsh speakers were liars and cheats, the old warrior Michael D. Jones swiftly mobilized public support. Around a million people spoke Welsh by the close of the century, and there was every reason to believe that the native tongue had the potential to become, both numerically and socially, a powerful influence in contested spheres like politics, law, education and science as well as in its traditional domains – the hearth, the workplace, the chapel and the eisteddfod. Ominously, however, by 1901 the numbers able to speak Welsh had fallen below 50 per cent. Wales had become a land of two languages.

But although most people probably saw themselves, first and foremost, as Welsh, appreciable numbers also identified themselves with the modern unitary British state. Liberal politicians, for instance, were not much interested in acquiring a separate state for Wales. Some of them might have flirted with the notion of 'home rule', but they yearned most of all for self-esteem and parity with the English. At critical moments, the Young Wales movement failed to mobilize support among the commercial and urban communities of south Wales between 1886 and 1896. Likewise, the aim of the university movement, propelled from the mid-1860s by energetic, even ruthless, Welsh-speaking Liberals, was to ensure that the first University College of Wales – established in 1872 in a half-completed neo-Gothic hotel on the seafront at Aberystwyth, and sustained by hard-earned pennies and shillings from miners and quarrymen – would serve the whole of Wales, but age-old forces of particularism, especially the antipathy between north and south Wales, scuppered the notion of a unitary Welsh university. Although a degree-conferring national federal university was eventually established in 1893 and projected itself as the 'people's university' set up 'in and for Wales', its future development was vitiated by centrifugal interests.

A sense of Britishness was an integral part of the Welsh who shared the ambitions and ideals of imperial torchbearers and who played their part in a morally indefensible campaign of land theft, exploitation and enslavement. At the time, of course, to be part of the imperial adventure was a matter of great pride rather than shame to leading Welsh Liberals and to the soldiers and sailors who extended British colonial rule in wars against Afghans, Zulus and Indians. By the end of the Victorian era, the British empire constituted one-fifth of the world's landmass and no one cheered louder than the Welsh when the seemingly indestructible Queen Victoria – the 'Great White Mother' – celebrated her Golden Jubilee in 1887 and her Diamond Jubilee in 1897. Henry Morton Stanley (his real

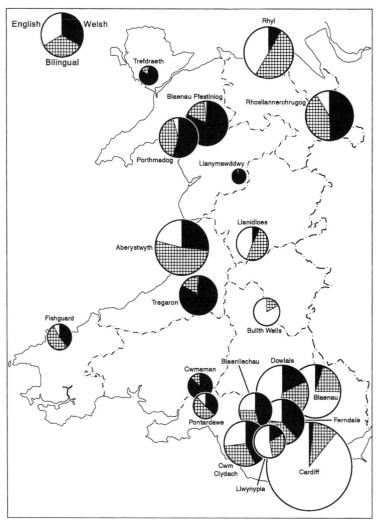

Map 9. The 1891 census was the first of its kind to provide data on the prevalence of the Welsh language. It showed that the best part of a million people spoke Welsh, but that bilingual speakers and monoglot English speakers were in the majority in the industrial and urban areas of south Wales and the borderlands. This map indicates the rich linguistic kaleidoscope which had emerged in different parts of Wales. (University of Wales Centre for Advanced Welsh and Celtic Studies)

name was John Rowlands), an illegitimate army deserter and journalist born in Denbigh, nurtured a colonizing zeal which brought
him fame as the discoverer of Dr Livingstone on the shores of
Lake Tanganyika in 1871 and as the hero of the Emin Pasha relief
expedition. Among those determined to play his part in the new
imperial democracy of Britain was the educationist and writer
O. M. Edwards who, on the one hand, sought to 'restore the Old
Country to its former glory' by publishing readable magazines for
the idealized *gwerin* (folk) but who also, on the other, called on his
countrymen to rejoice in the great imperial enterprise which firmly
located Wales on those maps coloured red in children's books.
'Honour the flag [Union Jack], my fair child', he reminded the
young, 'it's a fine old flag ... Remember every day, as you say
your prayers, that you are a subject of the Crown of Great Britain.'

In 1900 Keir Hardie, a Scotsman, was elected by the people of
Merthyr to represent them in parliament as the first Socialist MP in
Wales. A year later Queen Victoria, who had spent only seven nights
in Wales during her long and popular 64-year reign, passed away. As
far as we can tell, there was no connection between the two events,
but both in their way signalled the end of an era.

7

Wales awakening? 1901–2006

King Edward VIII was one of the few English monarchs who managed to combine an air of effortless superiority with the common touch. In November 1936, amid much cheering, hymn-singing and some grovelling, this glamorous playboy visited the derelict Dowlais ironworks, whose flaming labyrinths had until recently lit up the skies above Merthyr since the late eighteenth century. Keenly aware that Baldwin's government had virtually washed its hands of its responsibility to alleviate the social wounds caused by poverty, malnourishment and unemployment, the king moved among the people, pressing the flesh and visibly expressing his sense of shock and disbelief. There is no reason to believe that he was not speaking from the heart when he uttered the words, 'something must be done', a comment which passed into the folklore of Welsh working-class history. Nothing was done, however, and following a brief reign of ten months and nineteen days Edward VIII abdicated in order to marry a twice-divorced American. To most adult males in the South Wales Coalfield, whose lives had been disfigured by long-term unemployment and deprivation, this episode simply confirmed their belief that both kings and governments did not care a fig about their plight.

By contrast, the public mood in the pre-war years had been markedly different. All the evidence seemed to point to blooming material prosperity and vitality. The Welsh were bursting with confidence. In 1901 the editor of the *Western Mail* waxed lyrical about Wales's economic prospects: '[Wales] is one of the brightest and

39. Born in Manchester in 1863, but unmistakably Welsh, David Lloyd George served as Chancellor of the Exchequer (1908–15) and Prime Minister (1916–22). A splendid orator, he once declared: 'A fully equipped Duke costs as much to keep up as two Dreadnoughts, and Dukes are just as great a terror, and they last longer.' (The National Library of Wales)

most truly civilized spots in the Queen's dominions ... with the black mineral pouring into the lap of Cardiff, Newport, Swansea and Llanelli, where the argosies of the nations await its arrival to convey it to the remotest parts of the earth.' The Welsh collier, mythologized by writers as a warm-hearted, humane hero, symbolized the triumphant rule of King Coal. By the eve of the Great War, the South Wales Coalfield employed 233,000 miners who produced

56.8 million tons of coal per annum. The buoyancy of the coal industry fuelled demographic growth and, as expectations were raised, new entrepreneurs emerged. In 1902 the rather forbidding industrialist Sir Alfred Moritz Mond opened the largest nickel works in the world at Clydach, an investment which soon began to yield results. But the production of coal held centre stage. 'In peace and in war', cried Lloyd George, 'King Coal is the paramount Lord of Industry.' Production methods were changing swiftly and the pace of life in centres of global importance was quickening. Cardiff, which achieved city status in 1905, was 'swimming on the tide, and the world (it appeared) lay at its feet'. Nothing, so it seemed, could hold back the progress of the Welsh.

In the political domain, too, there were excellent grounds for optimism. Liberalism was riding high, and its leaders expressed a strong desire for recognition and equality within the British framework. Champions of the small but growing Labour movement sensed a new dawn. The air was still punctuated with cries of 'Home rule for Wales', an aspiration which sat comfortably with pride in the British empire. There were over a million Welsh speakers by 1911, and Liberal patriots like O. M. Edwards deliberately used the printed word as a means of restoring what they reckoned to be the lost honour of the Welsh people. Christopher Williams, who believed that the investiture of the Prince of Wales at Caernarfon in 1911 boosted the renewed sense of nationality, celebrated the new mood of optimistic expansion with his striking painting, *Wales Awakening*. The first national buildings in Wales – The National Library of Wales at Aberystwyth and the National Museum of Wales at Cardiff – were erected following a royal charter in 1907 and became not only conspicuous for the beauty of their architecture but also for providing unrivalled treasure-houses for Welsh culture. Even Providence seemed to be smiling upon the Welsh. Wales resonated to the sounds of religious revival in 1904–5, and heartfelt cries of 'Bend us, O Lord' spread like wildfire through town and countryside as worshippers became convinced that wondrous things were unfolding. In this brash, male-dominated society, powerful personalities caught the eye. The fiery populist Lloyd George delivered platform speeches with all the passion of a pulpit giant, while the equally fiery socialist Keir Hardie was an icon to those who

40. In 1911 Maesteg-born Christopher Williams (1873–1934) was
commissioned by George V to prepare a commemorative painting of the
Investiture of Edward, Prince of Wales, at Caernarfon. In the same year he
began painting the above work, *Deffroad Cymru: Wales Awakening*, which
expressed the growing national sentiment of the Edwardian age.
(Caernarfon Town Council)

championed working-class representation and social equality. In such heady times, touches of eccentricity were cherished. Robert Scourfield Mills (alias Captain Arthur Owen Vaughan, alias Owen Rhoscomyl, alias 'the Kid'), an outrageous braggart whose *Flamebearers of Welsh History* (1905) was a bestseller, scripted the bizarre National Pageant held in Cardiff castle in 1909. The intoxicating whirl of activity spread to the sporting field. Billy Meredith, the Chirk-born footballer, was the first superstar of 'the people's game', while the peerless and equally zany goalkeeper Leigh Richmond Roose was fêted by hosts of admirers. In an atmosphere of unbearable tension, the Welsh rugby team conquered the undefeated New Zealand All Blacks at the Arms Park, Cardiff, in December 1905. Some Jeremiahs, admittedly few in number, foretold a day of reckoning, but the vast majority of social commentators revelled in the *joie de vivre* of the times and the success of their countrymen. As we shall see, however, this early twentieth-century optimism was in many ways a great facade. Mesmerized by the economic boom, and by their unexpected appearance on the world stage, the Welsh inadvertently fostered the illusion that all was well.

Charting the course of Welsh history in such a complex and tumultuous era as the twentieth century is not an easy task. The mass of documentary material – personal papers, books, newspapers, oral testimony, audio and film recordings, internet sites – is stupefyingly large and far greater than anything available for earlier periods. For present purposes, therefore, this discussion focuses on four discrete, yet interlocking, themes: social and economic change; war and peace; the cultural fabric; and the political pattern.

Although it is easier for us to discern the social and economic realities which lay beneath the surface in pre-1914 Wales, the rhapsodic outbursts of the Edwardians were clearly misplaced. The principal Achilles heel of the Welsh industrial base was its failure to develop secondary industries. Although coal exports were booming and realizing excellent results, the over-emphasis on this single industry in south-east and north-east Wales meant that the narrowness of the infrastructure left it vulnerable to fierce competition from international rivals. It also had the effect of locking Wales out of 'the great international industrial learning race'. Coalowners and iron

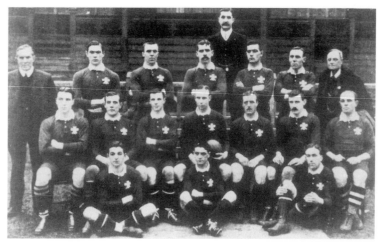

41. Before a partisan crowd of 47,000 at Cardiff Arms Park, a try by Welsh wing Teddy Morgan enabled the Welsh Rugby XV to defeat the all-conquering All Blacks of New Zealand on 16 December 1905. The *Western Mail* described it as 'the hardest, keenest and most vigorous contest ever waged between two representative teams on the football field'. (The National Library of Wales)

and steel masters, wedded to outdated business methods and loath to diversify, were too preoccupied with making fat profits. A second weakness was the increasingly skewed demographic profile of Wales. By 1911 around two-thirds of the total population lived in Glamorgan and Monmouthshire. The influx of Welsh working-class families and a huge surge of in-migrants from the West Country meant that the industrial and urban geography changed so swiftly that Wales was unable to respond to the opportunities posed by new technology and employment prospects caused by shifts in world demand. Thirdly, Edwardian Wales was marked by a high degree of economic inequality. Most working-class people lived in small, overcrowded houses without lavatories, baths or piped hot water. Work was labour-intensive, and whenever the breadwinner was cast into the ranks of the unemployed there were always too many mouths to feed. There were no sickness benefits to support the unemployed. Infant mortality was an inescapable part of daily life, and in the poorest communities thousands of young children were, as the pious put it, 'called to Jesus' prematurely. Of those who survived, few stayed on at school beyond the age of fourteen. Although diphtheria, measles and scarlet fever wiped out many of them, the biggest killer was tuberculosis, the 'great white plague'. On average, one in eight died at the hands of this grim reaper. Its deadly effects were keenly felt in the countryside, especially in the western rural communities: in 1915 Cardiganshire, which had an unenviable record of high infant mortality, blindness, lunacy and dental decay, was described as 'this shockingly backward county'. Women, who were still second-class citizens, regularly fell victim to tuberculosis or maternal mortality and, for those who survived, life was a daily battle to keep body and soul together.

It is no coincidence that the three seminal figures in the creation of the British welfare state – Lloyd George, Aneurin Bevan and James Griffiths – were Welsh, for there was a growing desire among the Welsh people in favour of setting up a free or heavily subsidized system of welfare. By doggedly pursuing a class-oriented strategy based on the provision of state welfare benefits designed to improve the lot of the common people, Lloyd George became a figure of adulation who richly deserves his place in the pantheon of social reformers. Never a friend of aristocrats and landowners, in an array of dazzling speeches Lloyd George exposed the grotesque advantages enjoyed by the wealthy. In 1908 he introduced the Old Age Pensions Act which provided between 1s. and 5s. a week to people over the age of seventy. His controversial 'People's Budget' in 1909 infuriated peers and precipitated a constitutional crisis, while the National Insurance Act (based on the German model) which he introduced in 1911 was a watershed in welfare legislation. In the eyes of his admirers the 'Welsh Wizard' could do no wrong, and during his premiership after 1916 he enhanced his reputation by extending the provision of pensions and unemployment insurance, and by funding a major housing programme. Just as Lloyd George symbolized the nation's will for victory during the Great War, so did he represent the much broader quest for social justice.

The windfall profits provided by the Great War soon disappeared as international competition for coal, the growing preference (not least by the Admiralty) for oil and the declining export trade dampened the spirit of optimism. The mood darkened as the 'Geddes Axe' of 1922, a worthy rival to the sword of Damocles, ushered in severe cutbacks in public expenditure. The vast army of coal miners – 271,000 of them in 1920 – now found themselves entering a period of economic slump which was as bewildering as it was traumatic. The iron and steel industry also fell on hard times: the massive, historic Cyfarthfa works closed its doors in 1921. The woollen mills of the Teifi Valley did likewise, as foreign and domestic demand collapsed. The boom in housing ended in 1924 and women, whose expectations had been raised by new job opportunities during the Great War, were once more enslaved to the kitchen, the wash tub, the mangle and the front doorstep. The expectations of men who had survived the horrors of the Western Front were cruelly dashed by a combination of harsh global economic forces and sheer ineptitude or lack of compassion on the part of stony-faced politicians and mandarins at Westminster. From 1925 onwards unemployment rates began to spiral uncontrollably and, following the Wall Street Crash in 1929, many parts of south Wales became an exemplar of 'life on the dole' at its worst. With the possible exception of Northern Ireland, unemployment rates were higher in inter-war Wales than in any other part of Britain.

Revisionist historians remind us that not all parts of Wales did badly in the years of depression and that the degree of privation fluctuated widely. Urban communities with a more diverse and flexible occupational structure were better able to ride out the storm. Blessed with much greater disposable income, the middle classes in places like Llandudno, Cardiff, Swansea and Tenby were able to afford motor vehicles and electrical goods. By 1938 there were as many as 81,320 licensed private cars and 24,375 motor-cycles in Wales. Parts of north-east Wales, where employment in steel, house-building and the production of rayon boosted incomes, became net importers of population. Even in the South Wales Coalfield there were pockets of prosperity, especially in the anthracite and metal-based industries in the western quarters. Whereas the percentage of unemployment was 51 per cent in Merthyr in 1935, it was lower than 14 per cent in the Amman Valley. Swansea was one of the main beneficiaries of the appreciable increase in the export of anthracite coal in the inter-war years. Increased mobility also meant that tourist resorts fared well.

But the well-heeled were a minority, and the fact remains that an uncomfortably large percentage of the population in both town and country was seriously disadvantaged by the slump. Nothing could be further from the truth than the notion that rural Wales was insulated from the depression. It is true that freeholders benefited from the sale of gentry estates after the Great War, and loud cheers were certainly heard at auctions whenever Welsh tenants were able to buy the holdings of petty tyrants. No one can blame them for rejoicing in the demise of the ruling class which had blighted the lives of the propertyless before outliving its own social functions. The number of owner occupiers increased fourfold between 1909 and 1943, but with the return of peace in 1918 the boom in agriculture collapsed and the ensuing depression wiped the smile off the faces of farmers who had benefited from the land sales boom. Farm prices plummeted as Britain became a dumping ground for international food surpluses. Like returning soldiers, farmers spoke bitterly of the 'great betrayal' which had left them at the mercy of the free market. Although the Milk Marketing Board, established in 1933, and the introduction of fat cattle subsidies a year later offered lucrative possibilities, farmers who were mortgaged to the hilt, and morbidly suspicious of besuited 'experts' who urged them to improve grass-lands and the quality of their stock, were loath to experiment. Nor were they prepared to invest in machines: by 1939 there were fewer than 2,000 tractors in Wales. Agricultural workers living in cottages unfit for pigs and who somehow subsisted on starvation wages began to leave for America and Canada in ruinous numbers. Disease, deprivation and premature death were rampant in inter-war rural communities. Thanks to dilatory and penny-pinching local authorities, the incidence of tuberculosis remained deplorably high and when the Committee of Inquiry into the Anti-Tuberculosis Service in Wales, chaired by the Liberal MP Clement Davies, published a scathing report in 1939 it was met with a profound sense of shame and anger.

No amount of revisionism, moreover, can alter the fact that the bitter years of depression also caused great suffering to thousands of people in the South Wales Coalfield. A region which had produced the finest steam coal in the world and high-quality steel which spanned the globe was brought to its knees by an unparalleled social and economic malaise. The statistics tell a bleak story. Between 1921 and 1939, 241 collieries were closed down. Dowlais, the cornerstone of the iron and steel industry, was so severely strained by economic pressures after the Great War that it eventually admitted defeat in 1930. Other more modest steelworks and tinplate hand-mills succumbed in swift succession. Unemployment levels had soared to over 27 per cent by July 1930 and worse was to follow. In localized black spots, the rates were catastrophically high: 93 per cent of the insured population of Blaina was unemployed in 1932, and 61 per cent of the breadwinners at Merthyr were similarly disadvantaged by 1936. Some of the most poignant images of suffering were captured by film-makers in realist documentaries which focused on queues of unemployed men, hunger marches and soup kitchens. Nothing was more memorable than the scenes in Ralph Bond's film *Today We Live* (1937), which depicted unemployed miners scavenging for coal with their hands and with wooden rakes on wind-swept slag heaps. Those who were gainfully employed in collieries had long been aware that the industry was being run with callous disregard for human safety. 'There is blood on the coal, there will always be blood on the coal', wrote Bert Coombes, an English-born miner who settled in the Vale of Neath. Memories were still fresh of the appalling disaster at the Universal Colliery, Senghennydd, on 14 October 1913, when 439 miners lost their lives and scores of widows and dependent children were left behind. The inquest verdict – accidental death – was an obscene denial of the truth. A similar sense of public outrage followed the explosion which ripped through Gresford Colliery in Denbighshire on 22 September 1934, killing 266 workers, the worst calamity to befall the North-East Wales Coalfield. Following a grossly mishandled inquiry, the colliery's management was absolved of blame. Even where pits had been closed, for many years afterwards people lived out their lives against a background of risk, suffering and death, and with the consequences of negligence and error. On 21 October 1966, a waste tip moving with the speed of an avalanche engulfed the mining village of Aberfan, killing 144 people, including 116 schoolchildren. The events of that day remained burned in the memory of the Welsh, not only because of the slaughter of the innocent but also because the National Coal Board refused to accept responsibility for the disaster.

Economic slump triggered a severe demographic malaise in the inter-war years. The birth rate fell appreciably from 29 live births per 1,000 of the population of south Wales in 1920 to 15 live births per 1,000 in 1940. This was accompanied by an eastward exodus on a biblical scale. As a result of voluntary, assisted or enforced migration, Wales lost the vital energies of young and gifted people in large numbers. Between 1920 and 1939, over half a million people left Wales in search of employment in the Midlands, south-east England or abroad. Never was there a more apt title for an anthology of poems than Idris Davies's *Gwalia Deserta* (1938). Those who left often experienced a deep sense of loss, displacement and alienation, among them thousands of young Welsh girls who went to work as domestic servants in London. With pardonable exaggeration, the novelist Gwyn Thomas referred to this large-scale outward migration as 'a Black Death on Wheels'.

It is salutary to recall that during these years, governments believed that economic fluctuations and their social consequences were acts of nature beyond the control of man. Even after the economist J. M. Keynes called for the setting up of a major public works programme in 1936, Baldwin's Conservative government and suspicious civil servants were not much interested in intervening on behalf of people living in a region with a rather sinister reputation for harbouring militants, communists and other malcontents. Deflationary policies prevailed, even though the price to be paid was massive unemployment and human misery. There may well be some truth in the argument that the British government actually preferred to pay the unemployed for not working rather than stimulate economic growth as Franklin D. Roosevelt's New Deal programme had done in America. Some experiments, launched as if south Wales was some kind of passive laboratory, were crass and ill-conceived. The transference of surplus labour to parts of England, for instance, was vigorously opposed, and when the Special Areas Act was instituted in 1934 it failed to provide sufficient resources to remedy structural problems. Aneurin Bevan scornfully dubbed the policy 'an idle and empty farce'.

Yet, it would be a mistake to believe that government inertia paralysed the energies and the will of working people in south Wales. While it is true that long-term unemployment knocked the stuffing out of older males, what shines through in this bleak age is the 'bravery of the simple, faithful folk'. The historian Glanmor Williams, who was raised in Dowlais, referred to working people as 'willing to share their last crust with others and marvellously brave and supportive of one another in adversity'. Far from being passive and stoic bystanders, working people raged against the pitiful response of successive governments and actively campaigned to improve the quality of their own lives. Local Medical Aid Societies provided medical treatment. The Tredegar Medical Aid Society, for instance, served the needs of around 95 per cent of the town's population in the 1920s and inspired Aneurin Bevan to address inequalities in health care. Voluntary groups like the Quakers and the Salvation Army helped to alleviate suffering, but if ever a group of people deserved a better deal from life, it was the women of south Wales. In the home, they were resourceful and resilient: scrimping and saving, they made a little go a long way and made a point of keeping their houses (including doorsteps) meticulously clean. Even the alarmingly high mortality rates in their midst did not deter them from venting their anger against the means test and the transference policies of the government. On 3 February 1935 around 300,000 people – an extraordinary figure – marched against the humiliations of the means test. Women figured strongly among them, as did Communists, and the degree of unity achieved by working-class families in these spontaneous demonstrations imprinted itself on the collective memory.

Not until 1945 did the will for change and a desire to fuel the productive capacity of the people become apparent. With a comfortable majority to sustain them, the Labour governments of 1945–50 and 1950–1 were able to pursue a vigorous reform programme based on a planned economy, a major extension of public ownership, full employment and enhanced social welfare. This government proved to be one of the few administrations which managed to translate aspiration into achievement. As far as Wales was concerned, two aspects of its portfolio were of critical importance. The first was the drive for economic growth and full employment. The travails of war had fortified the case for Keynesian intervention and social reconstruction, and the nationalization of key industries – mines, railways, road haulage, docks, electricity, gas, iron and steel – was a striking departure from the past. There was particularly widespread public rejoicing when the coal industry was brought into public ownership in 1947, and new employment opportunities in coal, iron, steel and building meant that unemployment levels had fallen sharply to 3 per cent by the autumn of 1951. The economy became much more diverse as new factories were set up – Hoover at Merthyr, British Nylon Spinners at Pontypool and Hotpoint at Llandudno – and the skill-base enhanced. It seemed to many commentators that a new Wales was being born.

The second change in public attitudes focused on health and welfare. As early as 1942 the Beveridge Report had changed perceptions by encouraging people to think in terms of a welfare rather than a warfare state. Two Welshmen in the Labour government were charged with helping to create a more just and caring society. Aneurin Bevan and James Griffiths were both former miners whose democratic socialism had been forged during the 'locust years' of the slump. Both had first-hand experience of life on the dole and of the need to protect the poor and the sick from the cradle to the grave. As Minister of National Insurance, Griffiths introduced new family allowances and protection for injured and disabled industrial workers. Most importantly, his National Insurance Act (1946) was inspired by what he had seen and experienced:

It is not security that destroys, it is insecurity. It is the fear of tomorrow that paralyses the will, it is the frustration of human hopes that corrodes the soul. Security in adversity will, I believe, release our people from the haunting fears of yesterday and make tomorrow not a day to dread but a day to welcome.

Griffiths was a fundamentally decent man whose goal was to see people live longer and healthier lives. His better-known and more colourful colleague, Aneurin Bevan, Minister of Health, possessed genuine star quality. A mesmerizing speaker, he teased and taunted the Tories, wrongfooted elitist members of the BMA (British Medical Association) by 'stuffing their mouths with gold', and insisted that the National Health Service, which came into effect on 5 July 1948, would be free to all at the point of delivery. Bevan was lionized in Wales for his achievement and a great surge in demand for spectacles, dentures and other welfare provision followed this legislation.

BRITAIN'S QUADS: *First family album picture*

42. The role of two Welsh Labour politicians – James Griffiths and Aneurin Bevan – in laying the foundations of the welfare state was celebrated in the *Daily Herald* on 6 July 1948, the day after the National Health Service came into effect. (The National Library of Wales)

When the Conservatives came to power in 1951, they accepted that there could be no return to the horrors of the 1930s. Thus, no risks were taken and no long-term plans were implemented. The overall pattern which emerged was that the economic base, traditionally dominated by coal, iron and steel, became a more diversified and service-based economy. Until 1973, a period often depicted as the 'Stop-Go Cycle' era, unemployment remained low and standards of living rose. Farmers prospered as never before as the Hill Farming Act (1946) and the Livestock Rearing Act (1951) provided grant aid and subsidies which enabled even embattled hill farmers to make a decent living. By contrast, hopes of a second 'industrial revolution' faded as the coal industry continued to shrink: the workforce declined to 47,000 by 1970. Instead, investment was directed towards the steel and tinplate industries where new giants were created. Following the formation of the Steel Company of Wales in 1947, the chief beneficiaries were the massive new works built at Margam in 1951 and two new strip-mill works built at Trostre (1953) and Felindre (1956). The huge new Spencer steelworks at Llanwern (1962), substantial investment in the blast furnaces of Shotton, and the Esso oil refinery at Milford (1960) showed that the nostrums of Keynesians had not perished, even if the boom eventually petered out during the 1970s. Such advances could not have occurred without transport improvements. Although the entire railway track mileage was virtually halved following the infamous Beeching Report of 1963, the development of the M4 corridor and the completion of the Severn Bridge in 1966 revived the economy of south Wales and tied it ever more closely to the wider British economy. White-collar workers had cause to be grateful for attempts to counter-balance job losses in the traditional industries. The Royal Mint came to Llantrisant, the Passport Office settled at Newport and the Driver Vehicle Licensing Agency found a congenial home at Morriston, Swansea, where, ironically, car-theft rates rocketed thereafter.

The upshot, as Harold Macmillan reminded them, was that the people had never had it so good. Improved care and nutrition, inoculation against poliomyelitis and the availability of antibiotics led to improvements in life expectancy. Suburban housing, council estates and high-rise flats provided visible evidence of the upturn in the economy and of growing affluence among middle-class and working-class sectors. A range of creature comforts and consumer durables – vacuum cleaners, washing machines, fridges, telephones and televisions – relieved housewives from hours of drudgery and tedium, and greater spending power meant more cars (upwards of 600,000 by 1971) and more frequent vacations abroad. As a result, there were many more Joneses to keep up with. Sexual attitudes and behaviour changed rapidly from the 'swinging sixties' onwards. Although sex was still a taboo subject in sheltered communities, the young rejected conventional sexual morality in increasing numbers. Outside disapproving evangelical circles, the loss of virginity prior to marriage no longer carried any stigma. Illegitimacy rates increased, abortion became more widely available and, thanks to the parliamentary efforts of Leo Abse, MP for Pontypool, homosexuality was viewed in a more tolerant light. Changes in the educational structure fuelled the cultural revolution. In order to correct the deplorable lack of investment and the prevailing inequalities within education, Welsh universities in the post-Robbins era opened their doors to an unprecedented expansion of student numbers, many of whom volubly expressed their views on censorship, war and hidebound attitudes. Moreover, by committing themselves to a system of comprehensive schooling, local authorities bade farewell to the divisive effects of the dreaded 11-plus examination which had prevailed since the Education Act of 1944. Most significant of all was the greater independence and control over their lives achieved by women from the 1960s onwards. Greater numbers of women were employed in factories, warehouses and shops, as well as in professional services, and this led to changing lifestyles and rising expectations. For the most part, however, their jobs were in low-paid, part-time, semi-skilled sectors, and even at the close of the century, as the historian of women in modern Wales has glumly pointed out: 'The old gender hierarchy remains – with men on top.'

Two events in 1973 heralded the demise of the 'long economic boom'. In January, Britain became a fully fledged member of the European Economic Community, a seminal event which, nevertheless, did not solve deep-seated problems of economic management. Hard on its heels came the formation of the cartel known as the Organization of Petrol Exporting Countries (OPEC), which dealt a mortal blow to international economic stability by quadrupling the price of oil, sending inflation soaring and precipitating the so-called 'winter of discontent' of 1978–9 during which hospitals were picketed, dead bodies lay unburied and rats gorged themselves on mounting piles of rotting food and rubbish. Keynesianism was in disgrace and when the standard-bearer of the New Right, Margaret Thatcher, took office in 1979 the icy winds of monetarism began to blow across Wales. The 'Butskellism' which had prevailed for most of the post-war period was discarded in favour of a commitment to the acquisitive individualism advocated by right-wing gurus like Friedman and Von Hayek. This was an agenda which favoured the rich and the enterprising. Government controls were removed, and in the brave new competitive world industries were left to work out their own salvation or were deliberately starved of resources.

Admirers of the Thatcher era – and there were certainly beneficiaries in Wales – claimed that she made industry leaner, fitter and more competitive. Moreover, the working class and lower middle class were beholden to her for giving them the opportunity to buy their homes at discount prices. Home ownership in Wales soared by 30 per cent between 1979 and 1990. But the heavy price of locking Wales into a world of monetary restraints was crippling unemployment, a soaring housing market, rural and industrial unrest, and a remorseless dismantling of the social bonds which held society together. As might be expected, the Welsh, whose natural inclination had always been to encourage good neighbourliness and to support the weak and the infirm, scoffed at Thatcher's preposterous claim that there was no such thing as society.

The Thatcher *blitzkrieg* exacted a heavy toll in the countryside. Farmers faced profound and diverse pressures. Incomes were falling and costs were rising so swiftly that a sharp reduction occurred in the number of farms of fewer than 50 acres. Already groping to find a way forward through the thicket of bureaucratic procedures associated with the Common Agricultural Policy, farmers were heavily clobbered by two serious outbreaks of foot-and-mouth disease in 1967 and 2002, and the BSE crisis in the 1990s. Further sustained pressure was imposed by the growing demands on them to embrace organic methods of farming, embark on ecological initiatives and cater for visitors, ramblers and campers. By 1999 only 5.2 per cent of the entire Welsh workforce was employed in agriculture, and suicide rates within the farming community were twice the national average. The era of the archetypal farmer, made famous in the poems of R. S. Thomas and the paintings of Kyffin Williams, was drawing to a close. Rural inhabitants in general found themselves deeply divided over issues such as fox hunting, wind-turbine technology, and the social and cultural effects of the closure of village shops and post offices. Most critical of all was the effect of inequalities of opportunity and wealth on the young and the poorly paid. In-migration, of course, had preceded the Thatcher era, but under her leadership it swiftly gathered momentum. As young people left the rural heartlands in droves, they were replaced by well-heeled in-migrants – retired people, commuters, second-home and holiday-home owners – who took advantage of the free market to buy properties at modest prices in the most scenically attractive parts of Wales or within travelling distance of Manchester, Chester or Bristol. One sociologist referred to 'a million on the move' as the indigenous population was replaced by non-Welsh-born incomers whose wealth and earning capacity sent house prices soaring far beyond the reach of low-earning local people. Outraged language activists freckled prominent landmarks with defiant slogans such as 'Wales is not for Sale' (*Nid yw Cymru ar Werth*) and 'Hold your Ground' (*Dal dy Dir*), and daily conversations in rural areas became infested with references to 'locals', 'incomers' and 'white settlers'.

With abundant supplies of North Sea oil to buttress their tight fiscal policy, the Conservatives deliberately ran down the traditional smokestack industries and robbed the unions of their power and influence. The miners' strike of 1984–5 was a deeply traumatic experience which led to massive pit closures. By 1992 only four collieries were still open in south Wales and, three years later, in a defiant riposte to the now-deposed Thatcher, Tower Colliery at Hirwaun, the last surviving deep mine in Wales, was bought from British Coal by the workforce. Other staple industries fell victim to international competition. The boom in steel and tinplate from the 1960s, which had been galvanized by a seemingly insatiable demand for consumer-durable goods, collapsed in the anti-Keynesian world of the 1980s: by 1990 steelworks at Ebbw Vale, East Moors, Brymbo, Dowlais and Felindre had all closed. The steelworks town of Port Talbot, fêted in its heyday as 'Treasure Island', was rechristened 'Giro City'. One social scientist pointedly entitled a volume which he published in 1987, *Wales is Closed*. The mood of disenchantment was palpable. Networks replaced neighbourhoods as people's lives became more fragmented, rootless and atomized.

The restructuring of the economy proved to be a painful and sometimes humiliating process within what was already a depressed labour market. Lying at the foot of the average earnings league in Britain, Wales was an enticing destination for foreign-based companies specializing in electronics, chemicals and vehicle component assembly. With the aid of the Welsh Development Agency, sunrise industries replaced sunset industries, notably along the M4 corridor, in Alun and Deeside, and in Wrexham. By 1991, 67,000 workers were employed in foreign-owned manufacturing companies, the overwhelming majority of which came from America, Europe and the Far East and which paid relatively low wages to their employees. Hand in hand with this trend came the privatization of public utilities. The marketplace was introduced into health care, and the same right-wing philosophy meant that comprehensive schooling came under fire. From 1997 New Labour under Tony Blair embarked on a so-called 'Third Way', which proved to be a grave disappointment to those who hoped to see plans for the redistribution of wealth. Wales's unenviable reputation as a low-skill and low-wage manufacturing economy, though attractive to external investors, continued to betray an alarming under-use of natural resources and potential. Not surprisingly, the National Assembly for Wales, established in 1999, set itself the goal of using structural funds from Europe to bridge the economic divide between, on the one hand, the prosperous areas around the M4 corridor and the A55 in north Wales and, on the other, the black holes of unemployment, deprivation and low skills which characterized life in the valleys of south Wales, in north-west Wales and west Wales.

Over the century as a whole, major socio-economic changes had occurred. By the time of the 2001 census, most of the 2,903,000 people living in Wales were healthier, taller, more literate and more likely to live much longer than their Edwardian forebears. The landed gentry no longer ruled the roost. Society was more diverse, more egalitarian and more complex in its social patterns. The welfare state, improved housing and wider consumer choice meant that growing numbers of people had never enjoyed such affluence. Derelict shipping and industrial premises had been renovated, and out-of-town retail parks catered for car-borne shoppers as consumerism took off. Greater sensitivity to environmental and industrial pollution meant that the landscape in post-industrial Wales was dotted with green zones, wooded recreational areas, country parks, heritage centres and marinas. No parts of Wales enjoyed the benefits of economic regeneration more than Cardiff Bay and the Swansea Maritime Quarter, both of which expanded beyond recognition from the mid-1990s onwards. Women were much more prominent in the labour market than ever before, and most people had greater access, via the internet and electronic mail, to a wide and diverse range of information. Much greater social and sexual independence meant that promiscuity, cohabitation, one-parent families, divorce, remarriage and homosexual relationships were more prevalent than they had been two generations earlier. The gap between the affluent and poorest parts of Wales continued to widen, and the Welsh Assembly Government set itself ambitious targets for removing the economic disjunction between east and west Wales in its strategy document, *A Winning Wales* (2005).

Many of the changes discussed above were brought about against a background of war or the fear of war. When the twentieth century dawned, Welsh soldiers were embroiled in a time-consuming and expensive war against the two tiny Boer republics of the Transvaal and Orange Free State. Although the relief of Mafeking in May 1900 captured the popular imagination, the task of protecting imperial interests and of breaking the spirit of heavily outnumbered, but extremely nimble and strong-willed, Boers on the veldt proved to be rather more difficult than military strategists had imagined. Considerable media coverage was devoted to the protracted guerrilla campaign, which involved the use of armoured trains and concentration camps, and Welsh newspapers discovered that there was an alarming public thirst for graphic images of the war. Photographic journalism meant that the Welsh became keenly aware of the progress and conduct of the war, and as hostilities dragged on political passions were roused. Champions of Britain's status as a great power found nothing to admire in the actions of the 'traitorous' Boers, and during the 1900 election only ten Liberal candidates were critical of the war. Initially, in urban and industrial communities the imperialist tide ran strongly, and pro-Boer sentiment came largely from the likes of David Lloyd George (on grounds of policy) and Keir Hardie (on pacifist grounds). Lloyd George came close to being lynched by angry mobs at Birmingham town hall in December 1901 and was referred to by local Unionists as 'this most virulent anti-Briton'. Not for the first or last time in his life, Hardie was treated as a pariah. Bloodying the noses of pro-Boers gave Unionists considerable satisfaction, though the folly of waging a war which cost around £220 million forced many of them to temper their jingoism. The war became increasingly unpopular, and there was widespread relief when the weary Boers eventually surrendered on 31 May 1902. 'All wars are horrible', wrote Lord Salisbury shortly before the Boers capitulated, but he could never have predicted the almost unimaginable horrors and senseless carnage which would follow twelve years later in the Great War. Putting the Boers to the sword was a mere picnic compared with the inferno of gunfire, shells, poison gas and brutalities which attended this total war. Indeed, some of the swagger which had accompanied military campaigns in the past vanished once it was realized that war on a truly grand scale was a hideous ordeal.

Yet, when war with Germany was declared on 4 August 1914 seasoned strategists and commentators had little inkling of what lay in store. The general view was that this necessary war would bring decisive victory by Christmas, but in the event four Christmases were to pass before hostilities ended. Over a period of four years the Welsh, especially servicemen, were plunged into the first large-scale industrialized war in the history of the world, an armed conflict which slaughtered, maimed and incapacitated thousands of people. Although Wales did not produce a latter-day Aneirin or a Cynddelw Brydydd Mawr to convey the pathos of war and inspire its warriors, it could rely on the rhetorical powers of Lloyd George. This sharp-witted, cottage-bred solicitor had already displayed a blend of charm and cunning in advancing the Liberal cause, and with the outbreak of war he sensed the mood of the times. In several impassioned speeches, brimming with scriptural invocations and skewed versions of the history of Wales, he called on his countrymen to rise to the challenge in a spirit of selfless patriotism. At national eisteddfodau, he tugged at the hearts of his admirers by promising that the age-old martial spirit of the Welsh would bring untold blessings to one of the 'little five-feet high nations'. His trusted ally, the Revd John Williams, Brynsiencyn – derisively dubbed 'Lloyd George's chaplain' – had no qualms about dispatching raw recruits to what he considered to be a holy war that the Prince of Peace himself would have sanctioned. 'Be men. Stand up boldly for your country, your freedom and your God', he cried, as he reproached those who were slow in coming forward. The old Welsh proverb *Gwell angau na chywilydd* (better death than dishonour) was bandied about freely, and leading Welsh academics, who might have been expected to know better, maintained that Germany had sold its soul to Lucifer. A new Welsh division of the army was set up in November 1914 and a regiment of Welsh guards was established a year later. From January 1916 all single men aged 18–41 were liable for conscription, and by May this provision also included married men. The upshot was that, according to the official record, 272, 924 men (21.52 per cent of the male population) served in the armed forces during the war. Many of them fought bravely as they endured the constant pounding of shells, the chattering of machine-gun fire, the screams of the wounded, and the stench of dead and disfigured bodies.

To their consternation, Welsh servicemen found themselves led by generals whose thinking was blighted by an outdated view of modern warfare and technology. Preoccupied with old-fashioned concepts such as gallantry and with launching large-scale (but ultimately futile) offensives, they exposed thousands of men to the most horrifying conditions imaginable at the Somme and Passchendaele battles. Some 35,000 Welshmen lost their lives during the Great War, and many more thousands were wounded or crippled. By December 1916 Lloyd George had become Prime Minister and, by bringing energy, vigour and decisiveness to the war effort, he confirmed his reputation as a man who got things done. But his failure to remove Field Marshall Sir Douglas Haig remains an indelible blot on his performance as premier. He turned a blind eye to Haig's asinine strategy on the Western Front and, contrary to the version he presented in his memoirs, he failed to address the problems of the war economy until the lamentable effects of the Passchendaele offensive had become clear. By then, terrible casualties had been suffered in the principal theatres of war. The poet R. Williams Parry, who by his own admission was the most gormless of soldiers, wrote poignantly of 'the wrench of losing the lads'. Among the fallen was the poet and writer Edward Thomas, a man who had counted himself 'mainly Welsh' and who was killed at the battle of Arras in 1917. Another was Leigh Richmond Roose, the prince of Welsh goalkeepers, who had been described in his pomp by an admiring fan as 'this wondrous Hercules'. But pride of place was given in the pantheon of fallen heroes to the young Welsh-speaking Trawsfynydd shepherd Ellis Humphrey Evans – better known by his bardic *nom de plume* Hedd Wyn – who was mortally wounded in northern France on 31 July 1917. Five weeks later he was declared the winner of the chair at the National Eisteddfod held at Birkenhead. The vacant chair, draped in black during the ceremony, became a symbol of sacrifice, and thereafter Hedd Wyn became a cult figure: more elegies were composed in memory of this shepherd-poet than any other twentieth-century poet, and a striking bronze statue was erected in his honour and unveiled near his home in Trawsfynydd in 1923. Some of his poetry stands comparison with the greatest war poets of his age:

> Woe that I live in this dire age,
> When God on far horizon flees . . .
> The lads' wild anguish fills the breeze,
> Their blood is mingled with the rain.

At home, the pressure to 'do one's bit' was intense. Farmers responded enthusiastically to incentives to increase production by bringing unused acres into cultivation and, as War Office contracts poured in, the Welsh textile industry prospered as never before. The demand for coal and steel was insatiable, and one of the beneficiaries of the increased opportunities for work were women. As gender barriers were temporarily lowered, women seized the chance to wear trousers and carry out roles traditionally reserved for males. They invigorated the war effort by becoming munitionettes in engineering works and factories or by serving as conductresses, policewomen and postworkers. The Women's Land Army was established in 1917, and Welsh farmers soon discovered that landgirls were enthusiastic allies at the plough, in potato fields, and in tending sheep and cattle. By acting as ambulance workers and nurses, they had first-hand experience of lives tragically affected or cut short by war. Those employed in asylums were deeply shocked to encounter mentally disturbed soldiers whose grotesque dreams and nightmares plunged them into long-lasting melancholy and despair. In the enforced absence of husbands, married women struggled to cope with food shortages and other privations, and the onset of an influenza pandemic in the autumn of 1918 rendered their malnourished children even more vulnerable. And as long as the war continued, they lived in daily dread of a telegram from the War Office bearing sad tidings of the loss of a husband or a relative. The Great War, therefore, did little to enhance the status of the 'new women' and,

43. The death of the young Merioneth shepherd Ellis Humphrey Evans (Hedd Wyn) at Pilkem Ridge in July 1917, shortly before his poem 'Yr Arwr' (The Hero) won the chair at the National Eisteddfod of Wales at Birkenhead, epitomized the horror of the Great War. On 11 August 1923 a memorial by Leonard Merrifield was unveiled in his native village of Trawsfynydd. (University of Wales Centre for Advanced Welsh and Celtic Studies)

with the coming of peace, they were swiftly urged by the government to return to their domestic duties and to replenish the lost or wasted generation with as many bouncing babies as possible.

Not everyone, of course, was able to share the common enthusiasm for teaching the Kaiser a sharp lesson. Those with German connections or with a reputation for disloyalty were treated with special vigilance and, at times, little mercy. The German scholar Hermann Ethé, whose stupendous grasp of languages was matched only by his ability to consume large quantities of alcohol, was branded a traitor and hounded out of Aberystwyth by a furious mob carrying the Union Jack. The animus against Irish republicans was just as acute. In the aftermath of the Easter rising of 1916, over 1,800 Irishmen, including Michael Collins and Dick Mulcahy, were interned without trial at a camp in Fron-goch, Merioneth. The initiative, however, rebounded on the government, for one of the most heavily Protestant Nonconformist communities in Welsh-speaking Wales now sported a fertile seedbed for Irish revolutionaries. Among others who refused to comport themselves as British patriots were those who could not be shamed or intimidated into enlisting and those conscientious objectors or anti-war campaigners who were stigmatized as spineless cowards. Keir Hardie was shouted down at Aberdare shortly after the declaration of war: 'Turn the German out!' was the cry. Ithel Davies, a farm labourer from Montgomeryshire, was placed in a straitjacket whilst in custody in Mold and was badly beaten by prison officers. George Maitland Lloyd Davies, a former soldier who was locked up in four different prisons, literally refashioned the sword given to him as an officer with the Royal Welsh Fusiliers into a sickle which he displayed in his office at the Fellowship of Reconciliation in London. Some of Wales's principal Welsh-language writers – D. Gwenallt Jones and Lewis Valentine – were so profoundly affected by their wartime experiences that their lives were never the same again. Others, unable to mourn or express the inexpressible, buried their private pain and grief.

By a peculiar irony, the Great War also proved to be the making of some notable individuals by enabling them to strike out in new directions. Although the war devastated the lives of thousands of individuals, it also ignited the spark of enterprise in some cases. When Margaret Haig Mackworth, daughter of Lord Rhondda and a suffragette of unusual strength of character, survived the sinking of the *Lusitania* in 1915 she made it her mission to improve the lot of women by becoming commissioner of Women's National Service in Wales. Tremadog-born T. E. Lawrence became an international celebrity during the war by concocting astonishing tales of his exploits as 'Lawrence of Arabia'. David Ivon Jones, a grocer's son from Aberystwyth, believed that the Great War was an imperialist enterprise which would paradoxically usher in the triumph of the proletariat. Having defected from Calvinist Methodism to Unitarianism, his quest for truth and social justice took him to New Zealand, where he became a socialist, to South Africa, where he became a communist activist, and to Soviet Russia, where he translated the works of Lenin and celebrated the new socialist state before his own death in 1924. 'Nothing certain stands nowadays', he wrote, 'and none can live above the ferment of the times except by fossilization.' Given the opportunity, Jimmy Wilde, the 'Tylorstown Terror', would have relished landing blows on the Kaiser, but he was happy to bring international recognition to Wales by winning the flyweight championship of the world in 1916. War was certainly hell for combatants, but it also released and galvanized creative energies.

There was an overwhelming sense of relief when peace returned in 1918. Celebrations were muted, but Lloyd George the war leader was fittingly granted his meed of praise. Although his tactical nous had been suspect, he had been hailed as the man of hour by his countrymen ever since his appointment as Minister of Munitions in November 1915 and as Prime Minister in December 1916. In O. M. Edwards's journal, *Cymru*, he had been depicted as a valorous leader in the Arthurian mould, defending the realm against the barbarian Huns. To Lloyd George's great credit, he never underplayed or discarded his Welshness at Downing Street and nothing filled the Welsh with greater pride than the knowledge that the 'Welsh Wizard' had successfully prosecuted the war against the might of Germany. He was thus portrayed as the saviour of the nation, 'the man who won the war'. His brilliant wartime speeches (even Hitler was astonished by them), especially his references to rejuvenating the tiny nations, had struck a powerful chord and, as a man of action, he had clearly inspired people to meet the challenge. But the jubilation was also heavily tinged with sadness and an aching feeling, which Lloyd George himself must have experienced, that a generation of brave and gifted young men had been lost. For the best part of a decade after the war, thousands of crosses, cenotaphs and obelisks were erected in towns and villages to honour the fallen and to remind future generations of their sacrifice, and from Armistice Day 1918 onwards Welsh people assembled annually in their localities to pay tribute to the dead. As a result, war remained an intrinsic part of the collective national memory of the people. As poets and writers found their voices, too, misgivings about war multiplied. Three pieces of literature stand out: David Jones's famous war epic, *In Parenthesis* (1931), D. Gwenallt Jones's semi-fictional *Plasau'r Brenin* (The King's Mansions) (1934) and *Traed mewn Cyffion* (Feet in Chains) (1936), an evocative depiction by the novelist Kate Roberts of the impact of war on quarrying communities in north-west Wales.

As the number of wireless owners and newspaper readers proliferated during the inter-war years, popular opinion became preoccupied with the growing threat posed by communism and fascism and in particular with the need to stand up to Hitler and Mussolini. Led by the Revd Gwilym Davies, as early as 1922 the Welsh League of Nations Union campaigned vigorously for disarmament, co-operation and peace. 'Love, not War – *Hedd nid Cledd*' (Peace not a Sword) was the watchword of the North Wales Women's Peace Council, and when the famous Peace Ballot was held in 1935 the Welsh overwhelmingly upheld the principle of collective security. In a bid to indoctrinate the young, from 1922 the Welsh League of Youth revived the pacifist tradition by celebrating the work of Henry Richard in Victorian times and, as a gesture to international friendship, it arranged that an annual Welsh children's goodwill message was transmitted to the children of other lands. In September 1936 a sensational event occurred in the Llŷn Peninsula when three prominent Welsh nationalists, fired by strong pacifist ideas as well as cultural considerations, set fire to an RAF bombing school, a deed which convulsed Welsh-speaking Wales but which was eclipsed in the South Wales Coalfield by the response to communist–fascist rivalry in Spain. As Lewis Jones's novel *We Live* (1937) reveals, the challenge of defeating fascism in Spain prompted Welsh communist miners to take up arms. Around 70 per cent of the Welsh contingent who served in the International Brigades were members of the Communist Party, but many more individuals and families contributed pennies, shillings and tins of milk to relieve the sufferings of the Spanish people. The deeds of some of these volunteers acquired a heroic flavour. In a hostile setting, the trafficking of Captain David Jones of Swansea – popularly known as 'Potato Jones' – and the gallantry of Harry Dobson, a stalwart of the

British battalion in Spain, became the stuff of legend. Such diversions, however, were dwarfed by the threat from relentless Nazi aggression. On 1 September 1939 a ranting demagogue called Adolf Hitler sent his troops into Poland, and two days later Britain and France went to war with Germany. More misery, death and destruction lay in store.

The Second World War proved to be as much a test of the resolve of civilians as it was of the power of the armed forces. Patriotic catchphrases abounded: people were urged to 'be prepared', to 'pull together', to 'dig for victory' and to 'keep smiling through'. Wartime propaganda fuelled the notion of shared commitment and selflessness. Even as planes droned above and sirens wailed, adversity brought out the best in people and they huddled around the wireless to listen to the rousing speeches of Winston Churchill. The Welsh might not have loved Churchill – his name had been anathema to working people since his infamous intervention at Tonypandy in 1910 – but for the most part they were prepared to sweat, toil and shed blood in order to thwart Hitler's plans. Far more than was the case in 1914, going to war against Germany was believed to be a just cause. Newspaper reports portrayed the retreat from the shores of Dunkirk and the Battle of Britain as one of our finest hours. Both of these were mythical interpretations, but they helped to sustain morale. Jeering the broadcasts of William Joyce ('Lord Haw-Haw') raised spirits, and Ivor Novello, the Cardiff-born actor, playwright and songwriter whose song, 'Keep the home fires burning', had been a huge success in the Great War, caught the popular mood once more with his tear-jerking song, 'We'll gather lilacs'. Dylan Thomas's film *Wales – Green Mountain, Black Mountain* (1942) was a graphic reminder in cinemas of what was at stake and, although the bulk of the populace knew nothing of the death camps and the systematic slaughter of the Jews, films like *The Silent Village* (1943), which recreated in a Welsh-language context the destruction by the Germans of the Czech Village of Lidice, showed that Nazism was a brutal ideology. Strong cups of tea and cigarettes helped to ease anxieties and, even in the darkest hours, cheerfulness kept breaking through. The Swansea-born comedian Harry Secombe, who served with the Royal Artillery, developed an unrivalled expertise in blowing raspberries at the enemy, impersonating Hitler and developing bizarre comedy routines with Spike Milligan. The overwhelming message conveyed in print and on the air, however, was that the Welsh, as British citizens, were fighting for survival against a common enemy and that people from all walks of life were expected to 'do their bit'. But although the vast majority pledged their full support to the war effort, presented a united British front, and provided many examples of heroism and gallantry, the so-called Dunkirk spirit did not prevail in all quarters. There were deep-seated stresses and strains which cannot be overlooked.

The first flashpoint manifested itself as a result of the way in which the demands of the wartime state undermined traditional social networks by directing labour and moving people. Thousands of Welsh men and women from diverse backgrounds were mobilized to join the armed forces and to work for long, energy-sapping hours on the land, in factories and in war industries. The refusal of the army to consider allowing Welsh fighting men to serve under Welsh officers in their traditional regiments provoked outrage, as did the conscription of young unmarried women and their removal on 'slave trains' to the Midlands and the South of England. Within Wales, too, conflicts were generated by the temporary liberation of women. By 1943 Welsh women workers outnumbered their male counterparts as they swarmed to well-paid jobs producing explosives, shells and detonators. 'Where *is* Mrs Jones going?' asked one poster which showed a determined young lady joining the army of munitionettes. Their world turned upside down, women enjoyed the liberating results. Barrack square drilling transformed timid country girls into confident and immaculate soldiers, and factory workers, determined to play their part in toppling Hitler, now believed that there was more to life than bearing children, scrubbing backs and serving meals. This shift aroused fear and resentment among males. Coal miners were enraged to learn that munitionettes were rewarded with higher wages and their wives, too, deplored the way in which these feisty upstarts flaunted their wealth by buying powder, lipstick and silk stockings. As 'good-time girls' swarmed around American soldiers in local camps, Nonconformist ministers rushed to moral judgements and prayed for a speedy return to full-blown domesticity. The prospect of a furtive romance prompted lonely married

44. The Welsh photographer Geoff Charles (1909–2002) donated his collection of 120,000 negatives to the National Library of Wales. Among his finest images are photographs of evacuee children arriving at Newtown railway station in Montgomeryshire shortly after the outbreak of the Second World War in 1939. (The National Library of Wales)

women to throw caution to the winds and, not surprisingly, the incidence of venereal diseases and illegitimacy increased appreciably.

The movement of people into Wales also caused widespread upheaval and alarm. Thousands of women and children were evacuated from bomb-threatened urban centres in England to 'safer' parts of rural and urban Wales, only to find that the welcome in the hillsides, at least initially, was distinctly chilly. Female evacuees whose lifestyle was rather different from that of their hosts had no qualms about drinking and smoking heavily in pubs and swearing like troopers. Welsh families that set great store by godliness and cleanliness were horrified to discover that many of the poor and tearful children who had been dispatched, suitably labelled, from danger zones in England suffered from head lice, impetigo and scabies, and were also utterly devoid of table manners. Tales of bedwetting, bad language and shocking behaviour were doubtless amplified, and by all accounts most children eventually settled down, enjoyed the more placid rhythms of rural life and even learnt Welsh. Inward migration also caused disenchantment within the ivory towers of the University of Wales. Working-class students at Aberystwyth and Bangor resented the toffy-nosed, affluent student evacuees who arrived from the University of London, and only when some of them began to display aptitude as fire fighters, anti-gas operators and entertainers were they accepted into the fold.

The wartime government also tested people's loyalties by curtailing individual rights and liberties, and by victimizing innocent people. The number of conscientious objectors was recorded as 2,920 in 1945, and some of them made it their business to ensure that their voices were heard loud and clear, even though such action adversely affected their careers. In 1941 the anti-war protester Iorwerth C. Peate was deprived of his post as keeper of the Department of Folk Life at the National Museum of Wales, and only by steadfast lobbying at the highest levels was his reinstatement effected. With his flat cap, walrus moustache and bow tie, T. E. Nicholas was a familiar figure in Aberystwyth, where he practised as a dentist. A former member of the Communist Party of Great Britain and celebrated as a man of peace who loathed fascism with all his heart, he and his son were imprisoned on the preposterous pretext of being in possession of a few paper flags bearing the Swastika. Under Defence Regulation 18B, which allowed arbitrary power of detention, they were held in prison for nearly four months, during which time Nicholas composed Welsh sonnets on prison toilet paper.

Wilful infringements of civil liberties also accompanied the appropriation of large tracts of land by the War Office. An explosion of rage occurred in 1940 when the military seized over 40,000 acres (60,000 hectares) of land on the Epynt Mountain in Breconshire and summarily ejected over 400 people from farms occupied by Welsh-speaking families for generations. In language riddled with geopolitical rhetoric and imagery, defenders of organic Welsh communities loudly voiced their protest. The Quaker poet Waldo Williams believed that the invasion of troops into the Preselau area in Pembrokeshire, which farmers used to winter cattle, was a threat to the values of civilization: 'Let us guard the wall against the beast, let us guard the well against the mire.' The nationalist party, Plaid

Cymru, officially washed its hands of this 'English war', but its neutral stance did it considerable harm. At a time when Welsh-language broadcasting was drastically curtailed and when the National Eisteddfod was in the doldrums, it was relatively easy to accuse nationalists of disloyalty. When a by-election for the University of Wales seat in parliament was held in 1943, mandarins within the university and elsewhere argued that a vote for Saunders Lewis, president of Plaid Cymru and a convicted arsonist, would not only be an endorsement of fascism and treachery but also allow Lewis the opportunity to succeed where Guy Fawkes had failed.

There is also compelling evidence that efforts to control consumption buckled under the strain of wartime needs. Although food producers were encouraged to expand outputs of crop and livestock products, in order to encourage equality of sacrifice a programme of consumer rationing was introduced to reduce popular access to food, clothing and petrol. In the event, however, stubborn farmers in the more sheltered rural parts refused to implement what they believed to be unrealistic quotas or cereal targets imposed by the County War Agricultural Executive Committees, whose shrill admonitions often fell on deaf ears:

> Farmers! Plough now by day and night.
> Play your part in the fight for right.

Magistrates found themselves dealing with a growing number of cases involving the slaughter of animals and infringements of black-out regulations and petrol rationing. The black market flourished as retailers, farmers and spivs discovered loopholes in the system and conducted illicit, small-scale barter and exchange operations. Cardiff, Newport and Swansea had a hard core of experienced forgers and racketeers who dealt with impunity in coupon-trafficking, burglary and fraud.

Yet, circumstances dictated that only by uniting in a common cause could victory be achieved. The majority understood this only too well and adversity brought out the best in people, especially as military casualties mounted (some 15,000 were killed during the fighting). But whereas the victims in the First World War had been mostly military personnel, on this occasion civilian casualties were much heavier. Aeroplanes transformed war into a test of air power as well as conquest on the ground, and those living in key urban or industrial communities became targets for large-scale aerial bombardments. Thanks to the Luftwaffe, bombs seriously damaged large parts of Butetown, Deeside and Newport, but the brunt was borne by Swansea, which lost its major architectural features during the 'Three Nights Blitz' on 19–21 February 1941. The 'People's War' dragged on until May 1945, and during the intervening years the will to win remained strong. When hostilities ended, tears of joy were shed, bonfires were lit, streetlights blazed gloriously and crowds danced happily in the streets. The bloody and devastating consequences of war in Wales, however, were eclipsed when an atomic bomb, grotesquely nicknamed 'Little Boy', was dropped on Hiroshima on 6 August 1945. Future developments would occur in the shadow of the destructive power of the atomic bomb and the impending nuclear arms race.

From 1949 until 1963 males from the age of eighteen were liable for two years of national service and thus found themselves either subjected to hours of aimless square-bashing in training camps or dangerous active service in zones of combat like Korea, Egypt and Cyprus, where many were killed or wounded. For some, military service was palatable because it instilled self-discipline, but for others discharge papers could not come too soon. In the post-war period the world became a smaller, darker and more perilous place, and bitter struggles on the issue of nuclear disarmament emerged, especially when Aneurin Bevan reversed his stance by championing the British nuclear deterrent in 1957. The presence of so many artillery ranges, training camps and nuclear power stations on Welsh soil meant that Wales had not been so heavily occupied by external military personnel since the Cromwellian republic. Not surprisingly, therefore, it developed an amorphous peace movement comprising humanists, ecologists, civil libertarians, feminists and pacifists. A familiar and iconic figure in the era of CND (Campaign for Nuclear Disarmament) protests from 1958 was Bertrand Russell, who was born in Monmouthshire and died in Merioneth. The annual march to Aldermaston always sported a large and vociferous Welsh contingent, and by the 1980s there was a huge upsurge of feeling against American Cruise and Trident nuclear missiles. All the while local peace groups redoubled their efforts, deriving much of their impetus from the strong Welsh presence among peace-loving women at Greenham Common in Berkshire. Following the horrifying Chernobyl disaster in April 1986, rain-clouds bearing radioactive material burst over north Wales, con-taminating pastures and reservoirs, and reminding the populace of what might easily occur at nuclear power stations like Trawsfynydd in Merioneth or Wylfa in Anglesey.

Much to the chagrin of peace campaigners, the Falklands War was waged in April 1982 in a belated but futile attempt to arrest post-imperial decline in Britain. A massive armed fleet was dis-patched to South America to rescue the Falkland Islands (Malvinas) from Argentine invaders, a perilous enterprise in which Welsh soldiers risked their lives and also faced the possibility of exchanging fire with Argentine soldiers descended from the Patagonian migrants who had left Wales in Victorian times. Such poignancies cut no ice with the Prime Minister, Margaret Thatcher, and George Thomas, Speaker of the House of Commons, rattled sabres in support of the 'Iron Lady' by declaring: 'We are still a tough little race.' The ambiguities of this verbal slippage did not occur to him, but the view of the war was rather different in Wales from that of the thunderous jingoism of Conservative politicians and the editor of the *Sun*. Thirty-two members of the Welsh Guards died and in his moving autobiography, Simon Weston, who was severely burned when Argentine sky hawks attacked the *Sir Galahad* at Bluff Cove in May, described his colleagues, enveloped in flames, 'jerking and writhing to a silent tune of death'. Even so, he and his fellow Welsh Guards strongly believed that it was their duty as soldiers to defeat aggression and defend the honour of Britain.

Unlike the small and protracted wars of the imperialist ventures in Victorian and Edwardian times, early twenty-first-century wars waged by the superpowers deployed massively destructive firepower which could bring hostilities to a swift conclusion, but which were also capable of inflicting huge casualties as well as causing 'shock and awe' among civilians. This made the Iraq war of March–April 2003, in which Britain played the role of junior partner to America, a profoundly unsettling affair. Welsh people served and died in a cause which not only heightened instability within Iraq but also led to the proliferation of terrorist attacks elsewhere. Protesters claimed that the war was both illegal and immoral, and shortly before hostilities broke out tens of thousands joined anti-war marches on the streets of Cardiff and London. Even at the end of this period, therefore, the issue of war and peace continued to concentrate the political mind in Wales. Yet, it remains the case that anti-militarism has been a cause for the minority. Throughout their history, the Welsh have never been reluctant to go to war or to support hostilities.

The cultural changes which occurred during the course of the twentieth century were as profound as any other major social development. Arguably the most striking cultural feature of the period was the massive decline in the number of Welsh speakers. At the time of the 1901 census, 929,824 people (around 50 per cent of the population) spoke Welsh and, in an era when Britain was the greatest power on earth and English the dominant language, it was perfectly possible for people in Wales to live their lives almost entirely through the medium of Welsh. In *y fro Gymraeg* (the Welsh heartland), well over 80 per cent spoke Welsh and the native tongue was a robust, living language in the domains of the hearth, neighbourhood, religion, popular culture and even politics. Indeed, the absolute numbers of Welsh speakers was still rising and reached its zenith of 977,366 by 1911, by which stage bilingualism was fast becoming the norm. Thereafter, Welsh embarked on a downward spiral which was not reversed until 2001. The increasing use of English knocked it off its perch and reduced its prestige value. Two world wars inevitably took their toll on Welsh speakers, and in the inter-war years, when adverse living conditions scarred the lives of working people, thousands of young and active Welshspeakers were uprooted. As many as 66 per cent of the out-migrants to England were under the age of thirty, and between 1921 and 1951, for instance, the Welsh-speaking population of the Rhondda plummeted from 69,000 to 31,000. Over a longer time span a substantial in-migration of working people, professional classes and retired people from England, most of whom were not assimilated linguistically, meant that the English language spread remorselessly westward. Aided by the arrival of the telephone and especially the wireless, the television and the mass media, it penetrated all parts of Wales. From the Edwardian period onwards there were compelling incentives to acquire and use English at the expense of Welsh. English-medium schooling became the norm as the wide-spread assumption that English was the language of 'getting on' struck deep roots. 'Welsh does not pay' and 'No good fiddling about with Welsh' were familiar refrains in times when making ends meet was reckoned to be more important than language main-tenance and nation-building.

Welsh speakers experienced an intense feeling of loss, displace-ment and alienation as successive decennial census figures brought further rude shocks. By 1951 the percentage of Welsh speakers had declined to 29 per cent. Adult Welsh monoglots were as rare as gold sovereigns in the Cambrian mountains, and in English-speaking towns in south Wales the native language was viewed as a badge of ignorance. In the public eye, Welsh was virtually invisible. It is true that even before the Great War steps had been taken by a variety of patriotic cultural societies to bolster faltering confidence in Welsh, and that by 1940 the Welsh League of Youth, a voluntary nationwide society for Welsh-speaking children, was the largest youth movement in Europe. But these initiatives could not counter the powerful English-language steamroller, and by the late 1950s the odds against the survival of Welsh were stacking up ominously.

It was around this point that Saunders Lewis reappeared in the public arena to take up the cudgels once more on behalf of his embattled tongue. In a celebrated radio broadcast delivered in February 1962 and entitled *Tynged yr Iaith* (Fate of the Language), he prophesied that, should current trends continue, Welsh as a living language would perish by the dawn of the twenty-first century. His message was unambiguous: linguistic decline could only be rectified by unorthodox political means. This was an act of great moral bravery on Lewis's part. His call to non-violent arms inspired young Welsh speakers, and within a matter of months *Cymdeithas yr Iaith Gymraeg* (Welsh Language Society) had been founded by articulate and determined activists who pledged themselves to transforming the prospects of their native tongue. The year of 1962 signalled the entry of Welsh into the political sphere, as frenzied activity of the Welsh Language Society raised the political temperature in Wales and divided opinions. Although these young activists (whose numbers never exceeded

45. Playwright, poet, literary critic, novelist and politican Saunders Lewis (1893–1985) was one of the most versatile and controversial figures in twentieth-century Wales. 'Small as he was', said R. S. Thomas of him, 'he towered.' This is a cartoon by Tegwyn Jones. (Tegwyn Jones)

2,000) acknowledged their debt to the non-violent civil disobedience practised by Ghandi and Martin Luther King, the haunting words of the Welsh philosopher J. R. Jones – 'the experience of knowing … that your country is … being sucked away from you, as it were by a rapacious swallowing wind, into the hands and possession of another country and civilization' – provided the impetus which prompted them to pose a severe challenge to the establishment. Local authorities and custodians of the law floundered as protesters devised ingenious stratagems to outwit them. Monolingual English road signs were daubed with green paint, television masts were climbed, court proceedings were disrupted, and many marches and demonstrations were held in the full glare of television cameras. Lord Hailsham famously called them 'baboons', but this kind of non-violent direct action provided the political dynamic which paved the way for linguistic regeneration. No modern movement did more to revive the fortunes of Welsh. It set in train a series of significant developments: bilingual road signs and administration, enhanced legal rights, Welsh-medium educational provision from nursery schools to university level, Welsh-language broadcasting on radio and television, and two Welsh Language Acts in 1967 and 1993, both of which fell short of expectations but which none-theless provided a major psychological boost for the language, not least by establishing a Welsh Language Board to promote greater use of the native tongue. Other initiatives bore fruit. With the establish-ment of the Welsh Books Council in 1962, state subsidy and the professionalization of the book trade meant that the volume of Welsh-language publications increased prodigiously from 308 in 1975 to 583 in 2004. Even more striking was the proliferation of local Welsh-language newspapers (*papurau bro*) from the early 1980s, an enterprise which stimulated language renewal at parish-pump level.

As a result of sustained public protest, financial subsidies, self-help and behind-the-scenes lobbying by well-disposed Welsh politi-cians, the tide of language decline eventually began to turn. The 2001 census figures revealed that the total number of Welsh speak-ers – 582,358 (20.8 per cent of the population) – had begun to rise for the first time since 1911. Its sunniest message was a striking upturn in the number of Welsh speakers in the 3–14 age bracket, and there were also signs of appreciable growth among the upwardly mobile professional classes who, no longer ashamed of Welsh, viewed it as a passport to lucrative job opportunities. Psychologi-cally, the figures also indicated an unwillingness to accept that the language was doomed to perish. Yet, it remains to be seen whether the Welsh will still be able to choreograph the survival of their native language. By the end of the century, the traditional tightly knit rural Welsh-speaking heartlands had become a shadow of their former selves, an alarmingly high proportion of Welsh speakers were lin-guistically isolated, and fragmented networks of Welsh speakers in urban areas were plainly an inadequate substitute for robust Welsh-language communities. Whether the loudly trumpeted aim of the Welsh Assembly government of developing a fully bilingual Wales will prove to be anything more than a pious and unachievable

46. Cymdeithas yr Iaith Gymraeg (The Welsh Language Society), founded in 1962, embarked on a highly successful campaign of civil disobedience in Wales in order to secure official status for Welsh in the public sphere in Wales. Committed to non-violent direct action, its members were mostly young, well-educated, middle-class people who believed strongly that 'a nation without a language is a nation without a heart'. (The National Library of Wales)

declaration of intent is also a moot point; those familiar with the history of other Celtic languages will need no reminder of the ability of politicians to allow minority languages to die by stealth. Most critically of all: how will the Welsh language cope in an increasingly globalized environment in which rapid technological change, mass communications and multinational corporations determine cultural patterns? It is against this background that the fate of Welsh, currently the strongest of the six Celtic languages, will continue to unfold.

In 1957 the prolific novelist Islwyn Ffowc Elis published a science-fiction novel entitled *Wythnos yng Nghymru Fydd* (A Week in the Wales of the Future), in which he depicted a Wales which had become a province of Western England – a kind of *Wallia Geriatrica* – in which no Welsh was spoken. As we have seen, such a scenario, however far-fetched, had been averted by the close of the century. Yet, it remained true that the twentieth century had witnessed the emergence of the English language as the predominant language in Wales. If time was running out for Welsh, the fortunes of English were ineluctably improving as the decades rolled by. At the cusp of the twentieth century Wales was absorbing incomers at rates akin to those experienced by the United States of America. Most incomers came from England and settled in the booming industrial and urban regions of the south. By 1914 they constituted a sixth of the total population. They were not necessarily antagonistic towards the Welsh language, but as a rule the English do not easily acquire languages other than their own, especially when the social pressures upon them to do so are relatively weak. As English became the lingua franca among the Welsh-born working class in the industrial south, it was dinned into many more heads that learning Welsh was a futile exercise. Greater mobility, tourism, the mass media, out-migration, in-migration and the eventual collapse of the smoke-stack industries all favoured the incursions of the English language. For most people, it was an inevitable and welcome development which broadened horizons and sharpened cultural tastes. By the 2001 census, nearly four-fifths of the population of Wales were monoglot English-speakers and around 590,000 people (22 per cent) living in Wales had been born in England. Over the course of the century English had become a truly global tongue in the field of advertising, business, diplomacy, politics, scholarship, sport and leisure, and the new information and communication technologies were underpinned by Anglo-Americanism.

From the industrial revolution onwards, Wales had also played host to incoming ethnic minorities who enriched society and culture

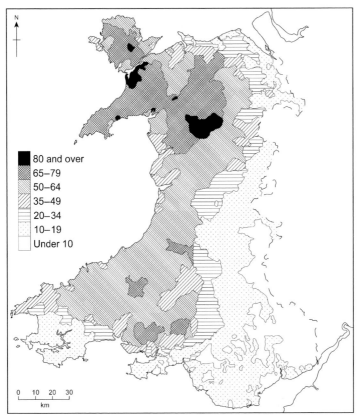

Map 10. The percentage of the population able to speak Welsh in 2001.
A hundred years earlier, a dominant core in which over 90 per cent of the
population spoke Welsh could be identified. By 2001 the Welsh-speaking
heartland had shrunk appreciably and the growth-points lay among the
urban middle class and those aged 3–15.

even as they grappled with the dilemmas and problems of belonging.
Of late, historians have devoted greater time and energy to examining
the issues raised by ethnicity and cultural diversity. Families of
Spanish ironworkers and coal miners settled in south Wales, as did
incomers from Italy who set up restaurants, cafes, ice-cream parlours
and chip shops. The cosmopolitan community of Tiger Bay included
West Indians, Arabs, Greeks, Chinese, Indians and Scandinavians,
most of whom revelled in the challenges offered by one of the greatest

coal-exporting ports in the world. It would be a mistake to deny that flashpoints did not occur. In times of dearth and unemployment, it was easy to accuse foreign-born people of stealing jobs or cornering the market. In 1911 Jewish shopkeepers in Tredegar became the objects of visceral hatred because they were thought to have rack-rented tenants and overpriced goods, and in Cardiff in 1919 black people working or living in the docks were attacked by angry mobs. But in absolute terms, the number of aliens was relatively small and, for the most part, division over the respective advantages of the Welsh and English languages were more apparent than racial tensions. Even by 2001 the ethnic minority population of Wales, though markedly more diverse than ever before, was still relatively small. Of the 62,000 non-white ethnic minorities in Wales (2.1 per cent of the total population), the highest concentrations were to be found in Cardiff, Newport and Swansea, which meant that the degree to which the Welsh were a tolerant people had yet to be put to the test. It is true that the Wales of 2006 is a much more multicultural and tolerant society than that of 1906; its liberal, middle-class citizens campaigned strongly against racism in the anti-apartheid era and, in the latter decades of the twentieth century, over the treatment of asylum seekers. But only a foolish person would claim that prejudice and discrimination did not and do not exist in Wales. Ethnic minorities remained marginalized in Welsh politics, and most non-white icons like Colin Jackson, Ryan Giggs and Colin Charvis were associated with sport rather than the corridors of power. A fundamental shift in *mentalités* will be required if we are to appreciate fully the implications of multiple identities for the Welsh identity, and the best starting point for the reader might be *Sugar and Slate* (2002), the riveting autobiography of Charlotte Williams, the daughter of a white Welsh-speaking mother and a black father from Guyana.

Fears for the future of the Welsh language and the aspirations of English speakers also profoundly exercised writers in both languages, and provoked an extraordinarily impressive upsurge in creative writing. The federal University of Wales was often criticized for being overly elitist, but it nonetheless offered a congenial Abraham's bosom upon which most leading Welsh-language writers could rest either as graduates or lecturers. At Bangor, the intellectual stimulus came from the pedagogue and purist John Morris-Jones, who prided himself on being the chief academic cock-of-the-walk in north Wales. He set daunting new orthographical and academic standards by publishing *A Welsh Grammar* (1913) and by demonizing the Gorsedd of the Bards and the bogus mythology of Iolo Morganwg. At Cardiff, W. J. Gruffydd, a cantankerous gadfly, thrived on stimulating bad-tempered debates in his journal, *Y Llenor* (The Writer), while at Aberystwyth a constellation of poets – T. Gwynn Jones, T. H. Parry-Williams and D. Gwenallt Jones – became some of the most vocal proponents of modernism. At Swansea, the multi-gifted playwright, poet, novelist and literary critic Saunders Lewis bestrode the Welsh-language literary world like a colossus. From the mid-1920s cultural nationalism began to express the more creative and regenerative potential of the Welsh, though often at the expense of intolerance of differences.

These differences surfaced when a new generation of writers reminded them that the dragon had two tongues. The substantial influx of an English-speaking workforce into south Wales from the 1890s, the proliferation of English-language secondary schools and the growing stigma attached to Welsh meant that several writers living in industrial and urban south Wales wrote poetry and fiction in English. Some of their writing was elegiac and sentimental, but most of it mirrored the class-based social and political struggles of the times. This flowering of literary voices was dubbed 'Anglo-Welsh' writing, even though the group's house journals – *Wales* (1937–) and the *Welsh Review* (1939–) – were unambiguously titled. The gritty realism of Lewis Jones's powerful novels, the rumbustious depictions of the lives of mining families by Jack Jones, the acerbic wit of Gwyn Thomas and even the cloying sentimentality of Richard Llewelyn's bestselling novel, *How Green Was my Valley* (1939) – which went through twenty-eight impressions in five years – indicated that English literature in Wales also had the capacity to adapt, change and reinvent itself. Bristling with ambition, the cherubic, feckless poet Dylan Thomas became an international icon. Despairing of provincialism, he left Cwmdonkin Drive in Swansea for the bohemian haunts of London, where he established his reputation as a poet but where his insecurity also manifested itself in heavy drinking and philandering. His magical 'play for voices', *Under Milk Wood*, sonorously narrated by Richard Burton and broadcast in 1954, a year after the poet's death in New York, was an instant success, and other memorable lines from his poetic *œuvre* such as 'And death shall have no dominion' and 'Do not go gentle into that good night' still resonate loudly in a world troubled by fear and strife.

But even though writers in both linguistic camps had much in common – the poetry of Gwenallt, the furnaceman's son whose verse had the strength of wrought iron, breathes the same spirit as the communist-inspired novels *Cwmardy* (1937) and *We Live* (1939) by Lewis Jones, while the short stories of Kate Roberts and the novel *Un Nos Ola Leuad* (One Moonlit Night) (1961) by Caradog Prichard offer scintillating fictional depictions of industrial communities – relations were more than strained. Harsh and unforgiving words were uttered: Welsh-language writers tended to consider Anglo-Welsh writing impoverished and second-rate, while the latter derided the parochialism of blinkered Liberals and nationalists. Bridges were not built until Welsh-speaking writers like R. S. Thomas, Emyr Humphreys and Gillian Clarke, who had been raised in anglicized parts of Wales and who wrote in English, abandoned pejorative labels like 'Anglo-Welsh' and 'English writers in Wales'. The Welsh Arts Council (subsequently the Arts Council of Wales), founded in 1967, became a major patron of literature in both languages, and the publication of *Cydymaith i Lenyddiaeth Cymru* and its English equivalent *The Oxford Companion to the Literature of Wales* in 1986 publicly celebrated the fact that hatchets had been deeply buried. Wales had become a land united and divided by two languages. Literary critics now sensibly referred to 'internal differences' and 'corresponding cultures', as well as to the virtues of inclusiveness and collaboration. In both languages, the post-1945 period was marked by a chorus of new voices. This was reflected in the revival of *cynghanedd* and free-metre poetry (in Welsh), a long-awaited breakthrough in the careers of feminist poets, and a wave of joyous, satirical and ironic post-modern fiction and fantasy which were significant contributions in their own right to the self-understanding of the Welsh. The divisions of the past faded, and writers in both tongues revelled in 'a new and rainbow-like modernism'. One lingering, sobering thought remains: had twentieth-century Wales been a fully fledged nation with international clout, would writers of the calibre of Saunders Lewis, Emyr Humphreys and R. S. Thomas have been rewarded with a Nobel prize for literature?

Historically, there had always been organic links between Welsh literature and the Christian religion, but it soon became clear that the latter was just as vulnerable to the unanticipated stresses and strains of modern society. Just as the mother tongue began to wither, so did Christian worship. Yet, the Edwardians would not have recognized the woeful and bedraggled state of organized religion in Wales at the beginning of the twenty-first century. Nonconformist leaders in particular believed that wholesale spiritual regeneration had been sparked off by the religious revival of 1904–5, the last great upsurge of revivalism in modern Wales. Although the first stirrings predated his emergence in the public eye, the revival was spearheaded by Evan Roberts, a 26-year-old former miner from Loughor, Glamorgan, who embarked on seven missionary campaigns in the company of several attractive young women, who helped him to 'carry the fire' around Wales by conducting prayer meetings, singing and sometimes preaching. The columns of the reporter 'Awstin' in the *Western Mail* fuelled the fervour by publishing the confessions of hardened sinners and testimonies of healings. The Lord's 'glorious work' prompted heavy drinkers to outlaw alcohol, rugby players to embrace the bible rather than the oval ball, and blaspheming colliers to mend their ways by organizing makeshift pentecostal meetings underground. Singing the signature tune of salvationism, 'Here is love vast as the ocean' (*Dyma gariad fel y moroedd*), thousands fell into the arms of Jesus. Indeed, never were the hymns of William Williams, Pantycelyn, or those of Sankey and Moody, sung with greater fervour. A powerful visionary element within the movement was enhanced by tales of strange lights, miracles and the casting out of devils. By the beginning of 1906, however, the spiritual fire had already burned itself out. Many of the newly converted remained in the fold of the chapels, but many more lost their faith or returned to their old ways. As one lapsed convert cruelly observed: 'the revival was the swan-song of the old religious tradition in Wales ... the consumptive's flush of death'. An exhausted Evan Roberts withdrew from public life and died in Cardiff in 1951. But Nonconformists, who thrive on nostalgia, nursed fond memories of the godly passion of the last great Welsh revival of 1904–5.

As the ferment of expectation faded, Nonconformists resumed their sectarian war over disestablishment. In many ways, the final stages of this bitter and unedifying struggle were played out in a political rather than a religious arena. Vicious political infighting – Lloyd George locked horns with the Bishop of St Asaph – and stalling tactics by the House of Lords meant that the necessary legislation was not in place until 1914, at which time war intervened. Six years elapsed before the four Welsh Anglican dioceses were able to form a separate and independent province. Nonconformist rejoicing was muted in 1920, partly because disestablishment turned out to be a blessing in disguise for churchmen. Much of the ground lost to Nonconformity in the mid-Victorian period had already been regained and, freed from the shackles of Canterbury, the Welsh Church was in a position to strike out in new directions, recruit gifted men to the episcopate and make a conscious effort to integrate into Welsh society.

It is important not to predate the decline of Welsh Nonconformity. On the eve of the Great War there was a chapel for every 400 persons living in Wales, and around 20 per cent of the total population was a Nonconformist communicant. But the good intentions of its religious leaders were confounded by a series of events over which they had little control. Four years of unremitting war and sacrifice led to a mood of disenchantment. The appetite for religion dulled, especially among returning soldiers who had witnessed brutal, calculated destruction on the continent. Their disillusionment was shared by the writer Caradoc Evans, whose satirical works, *My People* (1915) and *Capel Sion* (1916), about the alleged tyranny and hypocrisy of the Nonconformist chapels caused widespread outrage. 'Wales is a country of secret sins', he declared cryptically, and much of the Welsh resentment against the so-called 'Anglo-Welsh' writers can be attributed to the callous manner in which he pilloried chapel-goers. Chapel-going was increasingly associated with discredited Liberalism, and young people could be forgiven for believing that the labour movement, with its vision of social justice and brotherhood, was better equipped to enable them to survive and prosper in times of need. Far fewer of them were now prepared to be cajoled or bullied into listening to hell-fire sermons or singing gloomy hymns, and in some cases their disillusionment ripened into cynicism or atheism. Out-migration on a massive scale carried thousands of young and active worshippers beyond Wales, and those who remained were scarcely convinced or reassured by the flaccid social gospel preached by their ministers. In the light of these adverse circumstances, it is remarkable that Nonconformist membership figures held up so well in the inter-war years.

The Second World War contributed heavily to a widespread loss of faith and as, from 1945 onwards, people became more affluent, more mobile and more sceptical of traditional teachings, churches and chapels were no longer judged to be indispensable social and cultural foci within communities. Membership slumped alarmingly within the mainstream Nonconformist denominations, and many chapels were left with a rump of ageing worshippers, enfeebled and fearful for the future. In Anglican circles, too, hopes of growth were dashed and even in Catholic communities the old missionary zeal was ebbing away. In adversity, mainstream Christians resorted to ecumenism – the last resort of the embattled – but this proved to be a case of too little too late. Towards the latter decades of the century it certainly failed to counter the advances of evangelicalism, pentecostalism and Catholicism, and especially the emergence of non-Christian religions – Islam, Hinduism, Sikhism and Buddhism – all of which gained modest ground in urban communities. By the dawn of the third millennium the unthinkable had occurred: Wales had become a post-Christian society. By 2005 the percentage of active Christians had fallen to around 6 per cent of the total population. Ironically, according to the 2001 census, some 72 per cent of the people of Wales still declared themselves to be Christian, but they were clearly not prepared either to worship or toil on behalf of the faith they professed. It is not so much that the Welsh turned against Christianity; they simply preferred to do other things.

The diminished role of Christianity had important cultural implications. In the past, religion had represented the sense of community which lay at the heart of socio-cultural life, but it now became the case that the Christian witness no longer played a key role within localities or the political nation. Churches and chapels could no longer assert a moral authority or expect to be heeded on matters such as abortion, divorce and homosexuality. Freedom, equality and social justice were judged to be more important emblems of

Welshness than religious faith. Post-modern Wales had little regard for the pieties of the past and, despite the best efforts of conservationists, places of worship which were once thronged with Christians were closed down, left to crumble into ruins or converted into private homes, warehouses, garages, cinemas, pubs and casinos. As religious observance declined, the Nonconformist ethos or 'conscience' was abandoned. Its ebbing influence became manifest when the traditional 'dry' Welsh Sunday was abandoned from the 1960s onwards in favour of the opening of public houses, cinemas and shops on the Sabbath. Most consumers were pleased to be liberated from such constraints, but the loss of Sunday schools, pulpit sermons and scriptural readings meant that teachers and writers could no longer refer to the Gadarene swine, the waters of Babylon or even a doubting Thomas, and expect to be understood. Fervent rugby fans were more likely to be conversant with Max Boyce's 'Hymns and Arias' than with the majestic hymns of Williams Pantycelyn. This mostly silent cultural transformation marked one of the most decisive breaks in the history of Wales.

In some ways, it is surprising that life and vigour had not been drained out of religious denominations in Wales much earlier. From the Great War onwards, the emergence of what would come to be called the mass media capitalized on the disillusionment of people with the old ways and on the greater number of leisure hours at their disposal. As radio, television and cinema entered the burgeoning public sphere, the cultural landscape changed dramatically. This coincided with a period in which the Welsh press was largely eclipsed by the proliferation of mainstream metropolitan newspapers which misrepresented or discounted issues of Welsh interest. Throughout the century Wales was dogged by the absence of a thriving independent newspaper industry, based and financed in Wales, and dedicated to fostering passionate and critical debate about the cultural and political dilemmas of the times. Into this void stepped broadcasting. Under its gimlet-eyed director general, John Reith, the BBC began transmitting programmes in 1922 and became a public corporation four years later. Reith had no doubt that his principal responsibility was to ensure that the wireless would act as a vehicle for promoting a 'British' view of the world. Using 'standard' English, presenters and commentators with cut-glass accents brought events such as royal weddings, coronations, jubilees, rituals and festivals into Welsh living rooms. It amused Reith to make racist comments about Celts and, tit for tat, his corporation was dubbed the 'Big Bumptious Concern' by the Welsh, who deplored the baneful effects of metropolitan provincialism. Intensive lobbying was required before Wales was grudgingly granted its own Welsh Region in 1937, an initiative which exercised a profound influence on people's minds and tastes. Writers and broadcasters seized the opportunity to nurture a more distinctive and democratic style of broadcasting which met, though not fully, the needs of a bilingual society.

From the 1950s television became the dominant medium. Since the BBC continued to reflect traditional values and the culture of an elite, the advent of commercial television in 1955 (Television Wales and the West followed in 1958) was a mortal blow to its monopoly. The subsequent media revolution totally undermined the BBC's hallowed role as the arbiter of popular taste and culture. The devolutionary instinct, allied to the growing demand for new and competitive modes of expression during the cultural revolution of the 1960s, released further creative energies. The cultural mission of Welsh broadcasting was greatly enhanced by the advent of BBC Wales and Harlech Television (or HTV) by 1968 and, as a heartening range of different agendas emerged, separate radio channels for Welsh-language and English-language listeners were launched by the BBC in 1977. The swell of nationalist fervour and the campaigns of Welsh-language activities meant that television was singled out as a symbol of the problems which afflicted the ailing native tongue. A failure of vision on the part of the Conservative government in September 1979 prompted it to renege on its earlier promise to authorize the setting up of an all-Welsh channel. Such a channel would have satisfied those who were determined to secure the transmission of a coherent range of Welsh-language programmes on a separate channel and those who were perfectly happy to consign such a service to what they hoped would be an innocuous ghetto. However, when Gwynfor Evans, honorary president of Plaid Cymru and the chief icon of the modern nationalist movement, vowed to fast unto death unless the government honoured its pledge, the Conservatives capitulated and the new channel,

Sianel Pedwar Cymru (S4C), began broadcasting in November 1982. That such extreme tactics were employed in what might be considered a trifling cause can appear baffling, even alien, to outsiders, but the new channel became a tangible symbol of cultural renewal. In its early years, it commanded an appreciable and rising audience by displaying considerable ingenuity in its use of resources. It encouraged a thriving independent production sector and committed itself to widening the range and improving the quality of Welsh-language programmes. Its viewing figures reached a peak in 1996. Thereafter, the effects of the wider availability of digital and satellite television prompted its executives – to widespread alarm – to deCymricize the content of programmes by encouraging language degeneration and a much stronger element of bilingualism in order to improve ratings within the new multi-channel environment.

Much to the disapproval of pious Nonconformists, from the inter-war period onwards the Welsh became enthusiastic patrons of the cinema. In lavish new 'dream palaces' and itchy flea-pits, people escaped from the drudgery of their daily lives to gaze in wonder at glamorous Hollywood stars. To some degree, both the radio and the cinema provoked a revival of interest in the more homely, but still vibrant, amateur chapel- and eisteddfod-based theatrical activity, but black-and-white motion pictures were simply irresistible. By the mid-thirties there were more cinemas per head of the population in south Wales than in any other part of Britain. 'Thank God for the pictures', cried working-class viewers as they laughed at the antics of Charlie Chaplin and Buster Keaton, and salivated over Clark Gable and Greta Garbo. Although matinee idols were invariably Hollywood-based, and although film directors were prone to see Wales through the prism of a fictional, idealized America, Welsh-based films like *The Proud Valley* (1939) – which starred Paul Robeson as a black American stoker in the Welsh valleys – movingly expressed the strong community spirit which characterized life in the industrial townships. Moreover, gifted documentarists vigorously defended the integrity of these communities by portraying the sufferings of the poor and the unemployed in a gritty, radical and innovative manner. But gifted young actors from relatively humble backgrounds were obliged to make for London in order to achieve fame. Some were entrapped by the tiresome music-hall stereotypes of the Welsh which passed for comedy in the eyes of the Ealing Studios, but a sprinkling of them became truly international stars. The most brilliant was Richard Burton, an exceptionally handsome and well-read miner's son from Pontrhydyfen, Glamorgan, whose peerless speaking voice and natural air of authority set him apart from others. Another mesmerizing figure in the modern era was Anthony Hopkins of Port Talbot, who rejected Wales and London's West End for life in California as an actor and a director. His Oscar-winning performance as Hannibal Lecter in the film *The Silence of the Lambs* (1991) was loudly acclaimed as Wales basked in the fame of another of its departed sons. Only cynics begrudged his success, for the indigenous Welsh film industry, starved of resources and bereft of ideas, offered few avenues of opportunity or advancement, even though films like *Milwr Bychan* (1986) and *Hedd Wyn* (1992) were well received. Hollywood ruled still, and the feel-good factor engendered in the *fin de siècle* age of celebrities, instant stardom and tittle-tattle meant that the *Western Mail* could publish photographs of the actress Catherine Zeta Jones on a daily basis without ever considering the urgency of the need to redefine and reassess the role of the indigenous Welsh film industry.

By contrast, from the 1940s in particular, the musical world strove to stay abreast of new developments in funding and technology as well as changing sensibilities. Until then, Wales's reputation as the 'Land of Song' had been based on performances, in chapels and eisteddfodau, of choral music which were stronger on passion and drama than on technical excellence. The development of musical literacy had been poorly co-ordinated and critical perspectives had been at a premium. New sources of subsidy, radio, television and the recording industry all stimulated and sustained a new wave of amateur and professional music-making. The National Eisteddfod of Wales, rejuvenated by the imposition of the all-Welsh rule in 1950, exercised a powerful influence on young musical talent, not least in the field of folk music and *cerdd dant*, with the latter becoming a less extemporaneous, more codified art form. The Eisteddfod was also a nursery for outstandingly gifted soloists. The Welsh National Opera company (WNO), founded in 1946 and bankrolled largely by the Welsh Arts Council, catered for well-heeled middlebrow audiences by hosting opera productions which developed native singers, both within the ranks of its remarkable chorus and as individual performers in their own right. That such a small nation could raise and venerate the likes of Stuart Burrows, Margaret Price, Geraint Evans and Gwyneth Jones is worthy of comment. Safely ensconced from November 2004 onwards in its lavish home at the Wales Millennium Centre in Cardiff, the WNO capitalized fully on the powerful presence and sumptuous voice of the baritone Bryn Terfel, whose success on the international stage brought great lustre to the name of Wales. Post-war Wales also witnessed the emergence of internationally renowned composers: Daniel Jones, William Matthias and Alun Hoddinott demonstrated an intensely individual and imaginative virtuosity which in many ways was authentically Welsh. The opening of the Welsh College of Music and Drama in Cardiff in 1949 was another major step forward, insofar as it nurtured young composers and singers dedicated to promoting a diversity of musical tastes and communicating these across frontiers and languages.

Above all, the impact of the post-war 'baby boom' left its imprint on popular musical tastes. The young ignited and sustained a powerful pop music revolution which, as in the case of film, derived from the American example. Bill Haley took Cardiff by storm in 1957 and the 'Mersey sound' of the Beatles soon penetrated all parts of Wales in the gyrating sixties. Transistor radios blared out rock 'n' roll in homes and public places, and Mary Hopkin's song, 'Those were the days', caught the public mood. The plaintive and satirical songs of the Welsh-language troubadour Dafydd Iwan fired the imagination and touched the soul of his fellow activists. Singers like Shirley Bassey and Tom Jones, who made their reputation in the 1960s, were still giving fresh-faced tyros lessons in longevity and style well into the twenty-first century. Another great reservoir of vibrant youthful energy was tapped in the 1990s, a decade which epitomized the 'Cool Wales' image and which played a significant role in defining the modern Welsh identity. Within a homogenized global musical culture, Welsh rock bands bearing exotic names like Manic Street Preachers, Catatonia, Super Furry Animals and Stereophonics became international stars without ever compromising the languages, accents and muscular sounds which were peculiarly Welsh and to which they were evidently deeply attached.

Unexpectedly perhaps, there was also a certain distinctiveness about Welsh taste in fashion. The liberal and frivolous aspect of the 'swinging sixties' appealed to those with sartorial ambitions. Everyone took their cue from London and it was there that Mary Quant, metropolis-born but of Welsh parentage, won worldwide fame as a promoter of miniskirts, hot pants, coloured tights and rib sweaters. Much later, Laura Ashley, who hailed from Merthyr and settled in mid-Wales, set tongues awagging in London with her distinctive floral patterns and designs. When her business was floated on the stock market in 1986, it was valued at over £200 million. Welsh males, too, tried to express changing moods and aesthetics in an exuberant manner. David Emanuel co-designed the wedding gown worn by Diana, the ill-fated Princess of Wales, at her marriage in 1981, while Julien Macdonald made frocks for famous models from as little fabric as possible. Although the world of fashion was a source of fascination or bewilderment to many, Welsh involvement at this level reflected a new awareness of consumer tastes and marketing as well as a more general sense of cultural self-confidence.

Long before fashion experts gained a high degree of visibility, the Welsh had stiffened their self-esteem by delighting in the sporting achievements of their heroes. A nation may not live by sport alone, but from late Victorian times sporting prowess helped to define the Welsh identity, not least by making it less British. One of the major causes of the decline in religious observance was the rise of leisure and the growing popularity – and in time commercialization – of sport. The old world of rural pastimes and pursuits fell into slow but unmistakable decline as the opportunities which the modern economy and lifestyle offered for organized team sport, at local and national levels, multiplied dramatically. Sport thus played its part within a rich matrix of cultural forms and, by helping to 'bring alive a sense of "otherness"', it enabled both participants and supporters to express a sense of national identity. This was especially important in the post-1945 era when, thanks to extensive coverage by press, radio and television, virtually no one could remain insulated from major sporting events.

Although organized team sport began to be taken very seriously, there was still room for the individual cyclist, whippet-racer, pigeon-fancier and foot-runner. But none of these could earn a poor working-class boy the fortune which boxing offered. Boxing was often a squalid and brutal affair, but it offered hungry youngsters an avenue of escape and the prospect of good money. It also commanded a large and loyal following. Some of the finest Edwardian boxers lived in south Wales. Freddie Welsh won the lightweight championship of Britain in 1909, the extraordinarily popular and successful flyweight Jimmy Wilde, a world champion, lost only four contests in his career, and when the bantamweight folk hero 'Peerless' Jim Driscoll was buried in 1925, Cardiff virtually closed down as thousands of mourners assembled to pay tribute to 'the prince of Wales'. Although the Welsh specialized in little men with dancing feet and quick hands, bigger boxers were also idolized. The thousands of Welsh people who listened intently to the radio commentary in August 1937 of the clash between the ex-miner Tommy Farr and the American heavyweight Joe Louis went to their graves believing that their favourite had been robbed. Hard luck and tragic stories abound in boxing, as the post-war careers of unfortunate pugilists like Joe Erskine and Johnny Owen confirm.

But socio-economic configurations and the seemingly unslakeable thirst for large-scale spectator sports meant that team sports moved to centre stage. From late Victorian times onwards rugby football and association football appealed strongly to the mass of the populace. Rugby initially derived its impetus from the socially exclusive world of English public school, but it swiftly shed this aura as working-class people created hundreds of local leagues and teams which drew large and partisan crowds. Rugby not only provided thrilling moments to treasure but also played a critical role in the formation of a modern Welsh identity. Members of the Welsh team which defeated the seemingly invincible New Zealand All Blacks in 1905 were celebrated as national heroes, and during its first golden age between 1900 and 1911 the national side captured six triple crowns. But, like every other sport, its fortunes were closely linked to the economic vicissitudes of the times. The depression brought gloom to the terraces and the dressing rooms alike, as adverse results and growing numbers of players were tempted to seek greater material rewards by playing rugby league in the north of England. Spirits were revived in the post-1945 era, though a second golden decade was delayed until 1969–79 when a fusion of affluence, brilliantly gifted talent and resurgent national pride produced a team which won six triple crowns and three grand slams. We judge our great sportsmen by their capacity to live long in the imagination, and by that yardstick the memory of the electrifying sidesteps of Gerald Davies, the unruffled poise of Barry John and the all-round excellence of Gareth Edwards – the finest rugby player to wear a Welsh jersey – will never fade. Such standards could not possibly be sustained, and from the 1980s the pattern of economic downturn and poor results on the field returned. Corinthian values (if ever they existed) disappeared as the power of money contaminated the game. 'Shamateurism' was replaced by professionalism, the Welsh Rugby Union took masochistic pleasure in provoking grassroots rebellions, defections to rugby league multiplied, and sweeping (even baffling) changes in the laws of the game consigned Welsh rugby to the doldrums. In desperation, taciturn coaches – hailed as redeemers – were summoned from the Antipodes to restore a modicum of self-respect, but the experience of the 2004–5 season confirmed that Welsh rugby prospers best when it marshals the enterprising running skills of its players.

From the outset, association football in Wales was an egalitarian sport. Rough, ready and rumbustious it might have been in the pre-1914 era, once it took root it was hard to contain. Spurred on by the Football Association of Wales, which was established as early as 1876, it had thrived in north-east Wales before venturing south to rival the handling code. But although, in terms of participation and support, it became an integral part of the social and recreational culture of the people, it was less widely used as an emblem of national pride. Like rugby, soccer's fortunes reflected the economic state of play, and the diaspora of players to the English Football League was a perennial problem. Yet, there were moments to savour. A fortuitous goal helped Cardiff to defeat mighty Arsenal in the FA cup final at Wembley in 1927, and there were raucous celebrations when Wales drubbed England before 58,000 ecstatic fans in Cardiff in 1938. But such swallows did not make a summer, and the exceptional home-grown talent bred in Swansea in the 1940s was spirited away to English Football League clubs. In 1957 the Cwmbwrla-born giant John Charles became the first Welsh superstar to move to Italy when he was transferred from Leeds to Juventus for a world record fee of £65,000. This handsome 'Gentle Giant', who never resorted to gamesmanship, sharp practice or cheating, was a fine role model for the young; those who were privileged to see him in his prime will never forget his soaring leaps, powerful headers and thunderous shots on goal. As Charles entered his footballing sunset in the late 1960s, there were fewer spectacles to thrill the crowds, though John Toshack's remarkable success in bringing Swansea City from the fourth division to the first within four seasons (1978–82) was a notable achievement. By contrast, the national side perfected the art of falling at critical hurdles in the qualifying stages of major championships.

A new political Wales was forged during the course of the twentieth century. The broad trends were as follows. Up to 1922 the Liberal Party dominated political life. By that stage, however, the Labour Party had established itself strongly in the valleys of south Wales and, as the years slipped by, its influence grew throughout Wales at the expense of Liberalism, which was edged out to the rural constituencies. From 1945 onwards Labour's hegemony remained largely unimpaired until the emergence of Plaid Cymru and, more especially, the resurgence of Conservatism from 1979. With these considerations in mind, political scientists at that time increasingly referred to a three-Wales model, based largely on a combination of linguistic patterns and perceptions of identity. In the Welsh-speaking heartland of north-west Wales, Plaid Cymru set the pace and the agenda. In the industrial valleys of south Wales, known as the Welsh Wales, Labour still reigned, though less powerfully. And finally, the coastal belts of north-east and south Wales comprised voters who saw themselves as part of a British Wales and for whom a Labour government or separatism were prospects too dreadful to contemplate. As the century drew to its close, something extraordinary happened. Buoyed by a new sense of optimism (and an abiding antipathy towards Conservative rule from Westminster), the Welsh endorsed a model of devolved governance in 1997. A National Assembly for Wales was established, an all-Wales representative body which arguably constituted the most significant milestone in the history of democratic government in Wales.

47. In 1957 John Charles became the first Welsh footballing superstar to be transferred to Italy. For such a powerful man, he had phenomenal balance, touch and control. Idolized as the 'Gentle Giant', his conduct on the field of play was exemplary. At a time when Italian defences, bolstered by the infamous *catenaccio* system, were almost impenetrable, he scored ninety-three goals and helped Juventus to win the Italian championship three times and the Italian Cup twice. (Glenda Charles)

These changes reflected a growing public demand for a more advanced and effective democratic process. It is worth recalling that, at the dawn of the twentieth century, all adult women and around 40 per cent of adult men in Britain were not entitled to vote. The pressure for female suffrage grew as militant suffragettes embarked on a campaign of 'physical' force which was blunted only by the intervention of total war. But in February 1918 the momentous Representation of the People Act ushered in universal manhood suffrage and voting rights to women above the age of thirty. War heroines, as well as former 'flappers', had good cause to feel aggrieved, but ten years elapsed before all women gained the same voting privileges as men. In 1969 the voting age was reduced to eighteen, and around the same time the devolution issue, promoted in fits and starts, opened up new possibilities of reducing the democratic deficit still further by freeing Wales from the shackles of Whitehall. By 2006 members of the National Assembly for Wales were housed in a handsome new building, designed by Lord Rogers, in Cardiff Bay. Presciently called *Senedd* (parliament), it offered another opportunity for the people of Wales to set themselves the goal of controlling their own destinies.

A hundred years earlier, the Welsh had pinned their faith on the cause of Liberalism. A stunning electoral landslide in 1906 provided them with all but one Welsh seat. Under a capacious umbrella, Liberalism assembled a striking coalition of farmers, industrial workers, petite bourgeoisie and coalowners who (briefly) flirted with home rule and campaigned strongly to liberate their Nonconformist supporters from an alien Anglican church. The dynamism of its cause, however, depended heavily on Lloyd George who, following the untimely death of Tom Ellis, another cottage-bred Liberal tribune, in 1899 had blossomed into a genuine celebrity. This incorrigible populist was a wonder to behold on the platform and, as he turned his wrath on aristocrats, peers and landowners, his conservative enemies looked increasingly edgy and vulnerable. Whenever he referred to the plight of the have-nots, he burned with indignation and shame, and his 'People's Budget' in 1909 proved to be a major fillip to the electoral fortunes of his party, which polled 48 per cent of the votes in Wales in 1910.

But the massive energy which had fuelled Liberalism in Victorian and Edwardian times was already waning when war broke out, and the old campaigns which had fired its leaders – land reform, temperance, home rule and disestablishment – had either been achieved or removed from the political agenda. As we shall see, the traditional

pieties of the Liberals meant little to members of the highly prole-
tarian society in south Wales, where the emerging Labour Party was
able to project itself as the standard-bearer of the will of the people
and a force for democratic renewal. From 1918 onwards Liberalism
seemed increasingly out of touch with the times. Even Lloyd
George's Midas touch deserted him. The vote of confidence he
gained in the 'coupon election' in 1918 simply delayed the inevitable. The price to be paid was a damaging split in Liberal ranks. Lloyd
George's personal image suffered badly in the wake of the bloody
atrocities perpetrated by the Black and Tans in strife-torn Ireland.
His presidential style and shady dealings with the honours system,
which prompted the catchy lines 'Lloyd George knew my father /
Father knew Lloyd George', as well as his highly publicized amor-
ality, brought about his downfall in October 1922. The Welsh
Wizard retreated from the political arena and, according to one
unkind historian, was obliged to experience 'the poignant satisfaction of attending his own protracted funeral'. Yet, the base of his
popularity remained strong in north Wales and he still believed that
his recall to public life was only a matter of time. The old lion roared
once more in 1929 when his radical programme, 'We Can Conquer
Unemployment', based on Keynesian principles, became a rallying
point for Liberal candidates throughout Wales. But the glory days
were over: only ten candidates were elected and the Liberal share of
the vote shrank to 24 per cent.

On 26 March 1945, Lloyd George, who had earlier been created
Earl Lloyd-George of Dwyfor, died. Labour had long wrested the
initiative by this stage, and by 1966 the sole Liberal seat was held by
Emlyn Hooson in the rural fastness of Montgomeryshire. Internal
schisms, brittle party organization and a palpable lack of electoral
ambition reduced the Welsh Liberals to pale shadows of themselves.
Drastic surgery was required, and in 1983 and 1987 the Liberal
Party campaigned with the Social Democratic Party as the Alliance,
before merging into the Liberal Democrats. It polled reasonably
well, especially in May 2005, when four MPs were returned, but
its share of the vote (18 per cent) revealed that it was still incapable
of fixing itself in the popular imagination. Only in the lifetime of
Lloyd George did Liberalism give politics in Wales its peculiar
flavour.

It might have been expected that the Conservative Party would have capitalized on the waning authority of Welsh Liberalism and played a prominent part in shaping policy, but the reverse proved to be the case. Before 1914 the opposition of the Anglican landowning class to disestablishment more or less sealed its fate, and at the time of the Liberal landslide in 1906 not one Conservative candidate was returned. Although Conservatism enjoyed better fortune in the inter-war years – nine MPs were elected in 1924 and six in 1935 – the overall percentage of the vote was as little as 21 per cent. The party's ramshackle organization, the lack of a popular figurehead and the crippling non-engagement with working-class people meant that its electoral appeal was confined to the affluent and the anglicized. The experiences of the 1930s meant that the Welsh associated Conservatism with unemployment, and during the 1945 election the cry 'Never again, never again the Tories' rang out loudly in working-class constituencies. In works such as *Why not Trust the Tories?* (1944), Aneurin Bevan reminded wavering voters (though there were not many) that no good ever came from espousing Conservatism, and although he later regretted his rashness in depicting the Tories as 'lower than vermin' the strength of anti-Tory feeling among the populace was unmistakable. In the 1945 election the Conservative Party, inextricably associated with unemployment, inertia and appeasement, was firmly rejected in Wales.

Although the Labour Party secured 60 per cent of the overall vote in Wales in the 1951 election, it lost the day in Britain to resurgent Toryism. The number of Welsh Conservative seats – five in 1951 and five in 1955 – were far too meagre to satisfy the party faithful, but even growing affluence could not persuade the Welsh to forfeit their loyalties to Labour. The mistaken policies of the past and the insensitive arrogance of their leaders meant that the Conservative Party never returned more than eight MPs in Wales between 1951 and 1974. Labour continued to prosper in Wales, especially after the Conservative government of 1970–4 ushered in a period of bitter industrial relations and the notorious 'three-day week'. From 1974 onwards the Callaghan government instituted severe public spending curbs which, having failed to stem inflation and unemployment, led to the so-called 'winter of discontent'. Alarmed by the threat to their affluence, growing numbers of Welsh voters came to believe

Map 11. From 1 April 1974 a bill reorganizing local government was implemented which swept away the shire system established in 1536. Wales became a land of eight counties and thirty-seven district councils. This system remained in place until 1 April 1996 when twenty-two unitary authorities were established (see map 12).

that a resurgent Conservative Party might after all possess the intelligence and the will to defend their interests in inflationary and turbulent times. Frustration with Labour opened the way in 1979 for the Thatcher era and eighteen years of Conservative rule from Westminster.

It is not hard to see why sectional and private interests in Wales found the robust monetary discipline imposed by Margaret

Thatcher from 1979 onwards an attractive alternative. There would be no more boom-and-bust, no compromise with trade unionists or devolutionists, and no concessions to Europe. This daughter of a Grantham shopkeeper was not for turning. In 1979 the Conservatives elected eleven MPs in Wales and captured 32 per cent of the vote. Three further members were added in 1983. Under the new neo-liberalism, the top rank of wealthy, powerful and influential people expanded appreciably, but the rest of society paid a heavy price. By deliberately shrinking the economy, Thatcher undermined manufacturing in Wales and drove up unemployment. Having dealt with General Galtieri in the Falklands War, Welsh coal miners were a much more accessible target for her. During the 1984–5 miners' strike thousands of policemen were drafted in to confront protesting and striking miners, and although women in particular resisted in a stout and courageous fashion on picket lines and by raising funds and food, the Iron Lady won the day. Much to the disapproval of Tory 'wets' in Wales, the privatization of public utilities proceeded apace and the number of quasi-autonomous non-elected government agencies (quangos), riddled with Tory appointees, increased alarmingly. Although Welsh voters shrank from further change by returning as few as eight Conservative MPs in 1987, another landslide gave Thatcher her third electoral success, at which point her stubbornness led to the introduction of the poll tax in 1990, a piece of folly which eventually brought about her downfall. By then Margaret Thatcher was as popular in Wales as a plague of locusts, and it was ironic that two Welshmen manqués, Michael Heseltine (b. Swansea) and Geoffrey Howe (b. Port Talbot), were prominent in the palace coup which deposed her with ruthless haste in November 1990. Her inexperienced successor, John Major, paid scant attention to Welsh affairs and the election of 1997, during which not a single Conservative MP was returned in Wales, proved to be as much an *annus horribilis* as 1906 had been. Welsh Conservatism ended the century as it had begun it: floundering badly and unable to meet the needs of the day.

It was in 1906, too, that the party which transformed the political landscape in Wales was born. Having begun life as the Labour Representation Committee in 1900, Labour became a fully fledged party in 1906. Although it did not set Wales ablaze in these early years, the social unrest which flared up in different parts of pre-war society worked to its advantage. This was a period of acute social antagonisms and disputes, as working people sought to improve conditions of work and rates of pay. Following years of seething activity, events came to a boil in Caernarfonshire where, in defiance of attempts by the Penrhyn family to browbeat them, 3,000 slate quarrymen embarked on a bitter strike in November 1900 which became the longest-lasting dispute in British history. Eventually the workforce submitted, but considerable bad feeling was stirred up and 'scabs' and 'traitors' were never forgiven. Such events were not exceptions or curiosities. A good deal was at stake. Violent insurgency broke out in the coalfields as the industrial workforce acquired a reputation for militancy. In 1910 riots at Tonypandy prompted Winston Churchill, the Home Secretary, to send troops to the district to assist the police. Violent clashes with the police led to one death and 500 injured. As a result, like Merthyr and Newport (as well as Peterloo and Tolpuddle), the name Tonypandy entered working-class mythology. In June 1911 the seamen of cosmopolitan Cardiff embarked on a spectacular strike, and during the rail strike in August there were fatalities in Llanelli. Militant firebrands stoked the flames of class conflict. Noah Ablett's celebrated *The Miners' Next Step* (1912) called on workers to embark on an escalating series of strikes in order to secure a minimum wage and the transfer of control over coal mines. Syndicalism, tinged with a strong millennial flavour, could not be ignored. Nor could the increasingly clamorous demands of suffragettes, who were determined to banish forever the Victorian image of women as demure inferior beings, be allowed to stir up further strife. All these developments gave the authorities ample food for thought.

As the valleys of south Wales echoed to the rhetoric of class conflict, greater numbers of working people became conscious of their rights, more vocal in expressing their grievances and more willing to pin their faith on trade union activity. Keir Hardie used to insist that the Welsh, like all Celts, were instinctive socialists, and even in the Liberal fortresses of north Wales, where the likes of R. Silyn Roberts and David Thomas were active, the Labour Party began to project itself as the authentic 'party of the people'. By doubling the size of the electorate, the Representation of the

People Act of 1918 boosted the prospects of the Labour Party, as did the heightened expectations of discharged servicemen. Unable to adapt to the shifting socio-economic realities of the time, Liberalism could make no headway in industrial regions where the South Wales Miners Federation (the 'Fed') invigorated the working man's sense of dignity and confidence. As the emollient voice of Lib–Lab leaders like Mabon became muted, the Fed took a more decisive leftward course, and by 1921 it boasted around 200,000 members. Following the non-implementation of the recommendations of the Sankey Commission of 1919 that miners' pay be increased and their working-day reduced to six hours, a wave of anger swept through the coalfields. The collapse of the national coal lockout in 1921 left a bitter taste, and the spectre of industrial decline, soaring unemployment and falling living standards played a critical part in the politicization of working people and in the emergence of Labour as the only alternative to capitalist governments.

The return to the gold standard in 1925 had extremely adverse effects for coalmining and it led indirectly to the general strike of 3–12 May 1926 which brought Britain to a standstill. A. J. Cook, the militant miners' leader, coined the pithy slogan – 'Not a penny off the pay; not a minute on the day' – but, as the glorious summer sunshine faded and wageless families faced destitution, even the miners were eventually forced to submit after a struggle of six months. The sense of bitterness cast a deep shadow over people's lives, and the poet Idris Davies's famous line 'And we shall remember 1926 until our blood is dry' would often be invoked thereafter by defiant miners and their descendants. Not surprisingly, the Tories won only one seat in Wales in 1929. By contrast, the Labour Party captured 25 seats and 37 per cent of the vote. The support given by the Labour movement to hunger marches, staydown stoppages and strikes, as well as the efforts it made to ameliorate the condition of the homeless, the unemployed and the sick, ensured its electoral dominance in the valleys of south Wales. Its only credible rival in the pocket 'Moscows' which sprouted in the South Wales Coalfield was the Communist Party, led by the self-styled 'incorrigible rebel', Arthur Horner. By the 1930s, however, consensual approaches were beginning to dominate. The labour movement was placed on a sure footing as representatives at union, local and national levels attended assiduously to the concern of their constituents. In the Rhondda, for instance, elected representatives in the most celebrated south Wales valley drew strength from 'deep collective and personal loyalties, and ... a rich associational culture' which enabled them to establish democratic structures and broaden the base of their appeal. The political hegemony of Labour also owed much to the way in which prominent trade unionists, local councillors and MPs had bettered themselves by attending workmen's institutes, WEA classes or adult education colleges like the Central Labour College in London or Coleg Harlech. The education they acquired not only enhanced their understanding of their heritage but also encouraged the growth of greater consensus and harmony. In many parts of Wales, therefore, Labour basked in its reputation as the champion of working-class rights and aspirations. Although its principal spokesman, Aneurin Bevan, provoked more than enough hatred in Conservative camps, by ensuring that his people became entitled to free medical, hospital and dental services from the cradle to the grave, he commanded greater popular esteem than any other twentieth-century Welsh politician. Inspired by him, Labour's star continued to rise: it polled a massive 58 per cent of the vote in 1950.

Thirteen years of so-called 'Tory misrule' enabled Labour to reach its zenith in 1966 when it gained 32 seats and 61 per cent of the vote. By that stage, Wales had become a land of safe Labour seats and seemingly impregnable majorities. As James Griffiths observed, the party's astonishing growth over three generations had provided 'a faithful mirror of the life and struggles of the Welsh people'. It had cemented its authority not simply by representing the needs of working people but also by appealing, from the days of Butskellism onwards, to a wider constituency of sentient, middle-class people and intellectuals throughout Wales. At a time when Conservatism attracted strong popular support elsewhere, it continued to poll well (45 per cent and 50 per cent in 1987 and 1992 respectively) in Wales. It was widely expected that the latter election would bring to 10 Downing Street the first Welsh-born Prime Minister, but a combination of eve-of-the poll hubris and the anti-Welsh vitriol of the London tabloid press – which depicted him as 'a weaselly Welsh windbag' – scuppered the hopes of the miner's son,

'I could not
vote Tory.
It is wrong'

48. Aneurin Bevan (1897–1960), the fieriest of Labour orators, could never bring himself either to respect or trust the Tories. He was widely vilified for his description of them as being 'lower than vermin'. His class-driven phrases still remain 'mint fresh in the mouths of others'. (The National Library of Wales)

Neil Kinnock. Five years went by before a Labour landslide occurred. The Labour Party in Wales triumphantly returned 34 MPs and the Conservatives were banished to the wilderness. As it turned out, Tony Blair's 'Third Way' was a combination of Thatcherism by other, more benign, means but, as the results of the 2005 election confirmed, even exasperated traditional Labour voters were reluctant to risk a return to another harsh dose of Conservatism administered from Westminster.

The political complexion of Wales also began to change from the mid-1920s onwards, following the emergence of a political party committed to the principle of national self-determination. At the National Eisteddfod in Pwllheli in August 1925, a small group of well-educated Welsh speakers, eager to protect the interests of their native tongue, established Plaid Genedlaethol Cymru (National Party of Wales). The party, which pledged itself to home rule in 1932, remained a weak plant for many years. Dominated by academics whose nationalism was defined and expressed in cultural terms and who did not relish the gritty and unappetizing work of canvassing, its constituency was small. Its president from 1926 to 1939 was Saunders Lewis. On the surface, he appeared to be the ideal figurehead. A champion of European civilization, a brilliant writer and a fervent patriot, he was one of the few Welshmen prepared to ask searching intellectual questions. But whereas Lloyd George was warm and affectionate, and Aneurin Bevan witty and engaging, Lewis was a cold fish. His reedy voice, bow tie, cerebral style and aristocratic contempt for the proletariat were hardly endearing qualities in a political leader, and his conversion to Catholicism lost him the sympathy of fervent Nonconformists. Heavily influenced by the discourse of right-wing French theorists, this profoundly authoritarian figure developed a grand strategy, such as it was, based on the deindustrialization of Wales. Such a scheme was both impractical and unpopular. It caused grave embarrassment to his socialist colleague, D. J. Davies, a progressive economist who, writing with force and passion, showed a much better grasp of the economic realities of the time and greater sensitivity towards the plight of working people. For all his intelligence and originality, Saunders Lewis was a major electoral handicap. Even when, in the company of two other respectable Welshmen, he set fire to an RAF bombing school at Penyberth, Llŷn, in September 1936 – a symbolic act against the subordination of Wales by England which earned the three arsonists a sentence of nine months in prison – his party's subsequent performance at the polls was inauspicious and often derisory. Only in future years did 'the fire in Llŷn' exert a powerful psychological influence on nationalist thinking. At the end of the Second World War, Plaid Cymru remained an underfunded, poorly organized pressure group, with no MPs and no prospect of derailing the Labour juggernaut. Forfeiting deposits had become almost a way of life for its weary and frustrated candidates.

From 1945, however, a new chapter opened in the chequered history of the nationalist cause. Gwynfor Evans, a native of Barry and a man dedicated to Christian values, pacifism and social justice, took up the reins as president of Plaid Cymru, a post which he held for thirty-six years. With Lloyd George and Aneurin Bevan, he formed a triumvirate of towering political figures in twentieth-century Wales. In many ways it is curious that such a mild-mannered and courteous man, who always exuded a sense of dignity and honour, was so bitterly hated by his political enemies. Part of the reason lies in the fact that, in the long run, he greatly improved the prospects of what Labour protagonists sardonically called 'the little party', but it is also true that under the benign, gentle face which Evans presented to the public lay an obstinate streak. He matured into a shrewd political operator who rebuilt his party. However, the corporatist agenda of the two main political parties in the post-war years meant that there was little room for manoeuvre. Parliamentary candidates travelled more in hope than expectation, and even as late as 1959 only 77,571 voters endorsed the vision of Plaid Cymru. But a sequence of events boosted its fortunes. From 1957 onwards an uproar followed parliament's decision to flood the village of Capel Celyn and the Tryweryn valley in order to provide water for the people of Liverpool. Together with Saunders Lewis's 'Fate of the Language' broadcast, this served to galvanize weary and dormant nationalists alike. It also fired the imagination of young protesters. Harold Wilson's Labour government of 1964 proved to be far less left-wing than had been anticipated, and its apparent lack of understanding of the growing appetite for self-government was a further stimulant. Disturbing tales of negligence and venality in local administration damaged Labour's reputation, and Plaid Cymru delighted in publicizing the strong whiffs of scandal which emerged. The growing swell of nationalist fervour by the mid-sixties meant that Plaid Cymru became a much more effective political force. The Labour seat at Carmarthen fell to Gwynfor Evans at a by-election in 1966, and the party came within a whisker of seizing Rhondda West (1967) and Caerphilly (1968) in Labour's major strongholds. In a desperate bid to spike nationalist guns, the investiture of Prince Charles was hastily organized at Caernarfon Castle in July 1969, and maximum publicity was given to the risible antics of the Free Wales Army, a gimcrack outfit with a reputation for flamboyant gestures rather than military prowess. By 1970, however, Plaid Cymru's total vote had increased to 175,000. Even so, it continued to fail to broaden its appeal in industrial and urban areas where Labour's hegemony was so powerful. In October 1974, when the nationalists captured three seats (none of which was in

49. 'Cofiwch Dryweryn' (Remember Tryweryn) is a slogan often to be seen or heard in Wales. In 1957 parliament passed the Tryweryn Bill, which allowed Liverpool County Council to purchase land and build a reservoir in Merioneth. Eight years later, 800 acres of land and the village of Capel Celyn were drowned in order to supply water for Liverpool. The protest of the above villagers was ignored and the scheme was implemented despite massive public opposition. (The National Library of Wales)

industrial constituencies), all but ten of the thirty-six candidates lost their deposits. Plaid Cymru's share of the vote rose only modestly, from 11 per cent in 1974 to 14 per cent in 2001. Had massive reserves of oil been discovered in Cardigan Bay similar to those of the North Sea, Plaid Cymru's cause could conceivably have been very different. But the devolution fiasco of 1979 fuelled a deep sense of disillusionment and, although by the twilight of the twentieth century a growing proportion of the population thought of themselves as 'Welsh' rather than 'British', this did not mean that they were willing to flock to Plaid Cymru's banner. Over a period of eighty years Welsh nationalism certainly breathed much-needed life into the body politic, but overall it failed to register strongly and consistently at the polls. Indeed, Plaid Cymru's share of the vote was dwarfed by that registered by the Conservative Party.

This brings us, finally, to the tangled story of the coming of devolved government to Wales. Despite its claims to the contrary, during the post-1918 period the Labour Party seldom took devolution seriously. Pro-unionist in its stance and centrist in its ethos, it continued to avert its eyes and stop up its ears whenever the subject was broached. Aneurin Bevan was an avowed anti-separatist, and there were many like him who believed that most of the failures and horrors of the modern era had sprung from nationalism. It amused Bevan to witness the false starts and stuttering steps which plagued the 'Parliament for Wales' campaign in the 1950s. Nevertheless, pro-devolutionists like James Griffiths, Cledwyn Hughes and Goronwy Roberts proved hard to resist and, as pressure mounted from nationalist quarters, Labour accelerated the process of institution-building by establishing the Welsh Office in 1964. Located in Cardiff, which had become the capital city since 1955, its first incumbent as Secretary of State was James Griffiths who, by his own admission, had committed his 'heart and soul' to this initiative. Some shocks and narrow escapes at the polls prompted the government to set up a royal commission on the constitution, headed by Lord Kilbrandon, whose report in 1974 called for a radical restructuring of political power. In response, there were signs that Labour was more willing to shed its centrist image and reputation for exercising top-down control. Faced by nationalist advances and weakened by its lack of an effective majority from 1974 onwards, the Labour government under James Callaghan brought matters to a head by putting the devolutionary case to a referendum.

This brought Labour's love–hate relationship with devolution into sharp relief and, not surprisingly, deep rifts emerged within its ranks. Absurdly, anti-devolutionists were given free rein to sabotage their own government's proposals. Led by Neil Kinnock and Leo Abse, the 'No' campaigners maintained that devolution would provide a slippery slope to the eventual extinction of the United Kingdom and also penalize non-Welsh-speakers. Equally, people living in north Wales feared that living under the 'tyranny' of a Labour-dominated assembly would be a joyless experience. The timidity of Labour devolutionists and the understandable reluctance of nationalists to campaign on behalf of an assembly without tax-raising powers put an end to hopes of an affirmative result. In the event, the outcome was entirely predictable. Devolution was emphatically rejected by four to one on (ironically) St David's Day 1979. The sense of shock and dismay was palpable. With Labour in disarray, this debacle paved the way for Margaret Thatcher, the fiercest of enemies to devolution, to become the first woman to enter 10 Downing Street. Trade union power was undermined, the miners were smitten hip and thigh, and the appointment of uncongenial right-wing ideologues to the Welsh Office provided a sharp reminder to anti-devolutionists of the folly of their ways.

Eighteen years of Conservative rule was a long time for devolutionists to lick their wounds. The lukewarm, trembling at the Prime Minister's name, abandoned the cause. But the ravages caused by monetarism prompted ardent devolutionists to stand by their principles. Sustained by the optimism which had carried them through so many trials, they were determined to complete unfinished business. When the Conservative vote collapsed in 1997, the new Labour Prime Minister, Tony Blair, admittedly with no great enthusiasm, honoured the promise of his predecessor John Smith to reactivate the devolution issue. This time, referenda held in Scotland and Wales in September 1997 produced dramatically different results. The Scots voted resoundingly in favour of devolution, while the Welsh followed suit, if only by a whisker. Subsequent writers have often commented on, or scoffed at, the tiny majority of 6,721 votes (0.6 per cent) which brought victory to the devolutionists on a night of high emotion, but the swing of 30 per cent in the 'Yes' vote between 1979 and 1997 was nothing short of remarkable. Much had changed in the intervening period. The most enthusiastic devolutionists were to be found in those regions – Gwynedd, Carmarthenshire, Neath-Port Talbot and the south Wales valleys – where the socio-economic repercussions of Conservatism had been most keenly felt. Moreover, young voters all over Wales, unscarred by the humiliations of 1979, were clearly determined to create a more democratic political culture in Wales. Crucially, too, on this occasion the Labour government punched its weight during the campaign.

The Government of Wales Act of July 1998 set up a National Assembly for Wales composed of 60 members (40 of whom were elected to represent constituencies and 20 by the additional member

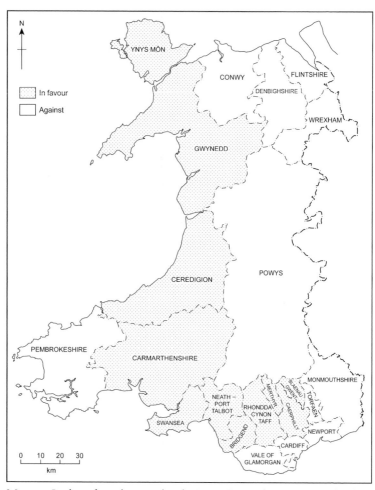

Map 12. In the referendum on devolution in September 1997 a wafer-thin majority of the voters (50.3 per cent) declared themselves in favour of a National Assembly for Wales. The voting configuration revealed a divided nation, uncertain about the devolution of power and its own identity.

system), whose powers were nowhere near as extensive as those granted to the Scottish Parliament. Yet, it was generally agreed that this was a pivotal moment in the history of Wales. It was widely expected that Ron Davies, Secretary of State for Wales, and the person who had driven the devolution programme forwards with

50. One of the success stories of post-devolution Wales was the exceptionally high level of representation achieved by women in the National Assembly. Following the elections of May 2003, women constituted 50 per cent of the membership of the Assembly, the highest proportion of women's representation in the world. Two Assembly members, Edwina Hart and Jane Davidson, were not present when this photograph was taken. (Western Mail & Echo Ltd)

all the zeal of a convert, would become First Minister. But following his self-confessed 'moment of madness' on Clapham Common, he withdrew from the public stage, and it took some time for Welsh politics to recover from this embarrassing stroke of misfortune. To lose a politician of his stature at this critical stage was a severe blow. Devolutionists were shaken to the core. A Blairite placeman, Alun Michael, filled the breach as Secretary of State (later First Minister), at the expense of the favoured candidate Rhodri Morgan who, on Michael's little lamented resignation in February 2000, eventually took office as First Minister. A garrulous figure given to sudden enthusiasms and with an endearing knack of flummoxing television presenters, Morgan projected a possibly spurious image of the unpretentious man-of-the-people. A hard-bitten professional politician, he set himself the aim of pursuing a peculiarly Welsh form of democratic socialism within the Labour-led administration which had gained the lion's share of the vote in the elections of May 1999.

But the new mood of optimism was soon blighted by divisions and animosities. The inclusive programme previously championed by Ron Davies was abandoned in favour of party loyalties. Ethnic minorities remained unrepresented and although women Assembly Members (AMs) constituted 50 per cent of the membership by 2003 (an admirable advance which made the Assembly an international leader in terms of women's representation), ideological and party rifts prevented politicians from working together for the common good. Preoccupied with messy feuds and petty bickering, the Assembly government was unable to reconcile antagonisms and appeared to lack the will to transform itself into a truly radical, creative institution. Its many critics, especially those who yearned for primary law-making and tax-raising powers, dubbed it a county council on stilts or an impotent talking shop. Rhodri Morgan resolutely maintained that the devolved settlement was 'a fragile flower' which required time to grow organically, but his own chronic indecisiveness was exposed by his response to the unanimous verdict of the independent Richard Commission, whose findings were published in 2004, that the Assembly should gain primary law-making powers. As this forward-looking report revealed, the prevailing system was riddled with so many jagged edges that it simply could not be expected to work effectively. But the First Minister and his colleagues displayed little enthusiasm for further and more radical constitutional change, and the report of the Richard Commission was left to gather dust. In a welter of muddled thinking, the UK government white paper, *Better Government for Wales*, published in June 2005, publicly rejected the Richard Commission's recommendations in favour of a half-way house between the status quo and greater legislative powers loosely akin to those acquired by the Scottish parliament. Meanwhile, Queen Elizabeth II was invited to open the handsome, environmentally friendly home to the Assembly in Cardiff on St David's Day 2006. It remains to be seen whether this critically important institution will embark on the constructive and serious decision-making required to win the support and affections of its people. As Ron Davies used to insist, devolution is a process rather than an event: 'Let no one think that now the devolution genie is out of his bottle he can be forced back in or that he won't want to stretch his muscles.'

8

Whither Wales?

Few twentieth-century poets who composed in Welsh were more widely admired than Waldo Williams. Although he did not produce a large corpus of work, as an imaginative interpreter of the Welsh sense of identity he had few equals. Poems such as *Cofio* (Remember) and *Cymru'n Un* (Wales Is One) resonate with historians as compelling expressions of the interdependence of geography, history, landscape, people and language. He referred to 'things that are long forgotten, / Now lost in dust of eras that have passed' and viewed the role of the remembrancer as 'keeping house amid a cloud of witnesses'. Thus, despite the title of this postscript, that which lies in the lap of the future is not part of a historian's remit. A nation is shaped by its history and by its people, and Wales, like every other nation, whether of long-standing or recent construction, requires a bank of cultural memory. History in all its forms, whether true or false, imagined or invented, spoken or written, told or retold, plays a critical role in a people's view of their identity. It is therefore worth considering how talismans of national identity have changed over the centuries and how historians have examined and fostered, according to the needs of their own times, an appreciation of the otherness of Wales. It bears repeating that Wales is an imagined community, a construct which, amoeba-like, changes its shape and character according to the desires of its people and the influence of external forces.

Scribes, chroniclers and poets in the Middle Ages thought of the Welsh as the original people of Britain. Their identity depended on the interplay between their lineal descent, their territory within the historic boundaries of Wales, the Welsh laws, the Christian religion and the native tongue. First as Britons, then as *Cymry*, they were proud of their inheritance, and they proved extraordinarily stubborn and resourceful in the face of Saxon, Irish, Viking and Norman incursions. In 1282 and, again in 1400, large numbers of them rose in rebellion, only to be bludgeoned by superior armies and fatally undermined by internal divisions. Past masters at brinkmanship, time and again they rescued defeat from the jaws of victory. Intractable internal divisions, both geographical and political, meant that this was a fragmented society in which the Welsh, as a conquered people, sought comfort in the many promises of the poets that a 'son of prophecy' would come and enable the first inhabitants of the island to recover their rightful inheritance.

When Henry Tudor became King of England in 1485, the stage was set on which a new phase of Welsh history could be enacted. No longer wallowing in self-pity over their stateless condition, the Welsh (or at least the landed elite who were the natural rulers of society) revelled in his victory as an act of liberation. The Acts of Union which followed referred to the 'amicable concord and unitie' which bound the English and the Welsh together. Tudor and Stuart historians loudly extolled the virtues of this gladsome marriage. The Elizabethan writer George Owen referred to Wales as a country within England and, in time, having already lost its native laws and with its native language relegated to a subaltern status, Wales was reckoned to have no independent history. 'Since the happy incorporation of the Welsh with the English', wrote William Wynne in 1697, 'the History of both Nations as well as the People is united.' The consensus among historians of the time was that England and Wales had been fused into a mutually beneficial entity. Insofar as the docile Welsh in the early modern period had a separate identity, it was based on their attachment to what satirists called their 'native gibberish', loyalty to the Protestant church and a love of genealogy. There was no real sense of Welsh national unity and, as a disadvantaged province of Britain whose loyalty for the most part was assured, Wales was not viewed as a meaningful political or economic unit. By Victorian times, it was simply seen as 'a geographical expression'.

When the United Kingdom of Great Britain and Ireland took root from 1800, there was a very real likelihood that Wales would be swallowed up by this Leviathan and would never again emerge in a recognizable form. Once more, however, the Welsh displayed considerable stubbornness and ingenuity in finding a niche within the notion of Britishness. From the mid-eighteenth century onwards, the Welsh literati (mostly middling sorts) established a rich variety of cultural institutions designed to highlight the distinctiveness of Wales and to inspire a renewed sense of nationality. In spite of its strength as a political and administrative construct, the new United Kingdom did not rule out the possibility of developing a modern Welsh identity based on language, culture and religion. Welsh historians in the nineteenth century thus seized new opportunities to fashion an image of Wales as a Protestant nation whose people – the *gwerin* (peasants) – were pious, temperate and cultured, and who, fired by the sacrifices of their forebears, had developed their own sense of identity despite the oppression of landlords, stewards, bishops and parsons. This romanticized view of the rural peasantry, sedulously fostered by the Oxford-trained historian O. M. Edwards, was constructed 'for the sake of Wales'. The Wales which had captured Edwards's affections claimed recognition for itself within the British state and within the British empire. The nation had pulled itself up by its bootstraps, its political life had been democratized, and industrial transformation and economic growth had given a new meaning to *Cymru Fydd* (the Wales to be).

In retrospect we can see that this perspective was deeply flawed but, until the foundation of the University of Wales in 1893, most remembrancers were enthusiastic amateurs. Legends, myths and rhetoric abounded, and there was little room for scholarly debate. The first to place the study of Welsh history on reputable academic foundations was J. E. Lloyd, whose magisterial two-volume *A History of Wales from the Earliest Times to the Edwardian Conquest* (1911) was a critical watershed in Welsh historiography. Serious historical writing in Wales thus began in 1911. Until then it had been for the most part anachronistic, partisan and teleological. Yet, in spite of the professionalization of the subject, it would be a mistake to believe that Wales now echoed to the sounds of lively historical discourse. Many complained bitterly that historical works were addressed to an exclusively academic audience and that the University of Wales had betrayed the *gwerin* who had founded it. Indeed, the historian J. F. Rees went so far as to claim that history had exercised a minimal influence in the formation of a sense of nationality in Wales. This alleged dereliction of duty was made all the more poignant by the sense of anger and cynicism engendered by the economic depression of the inter-war years, a malaise which deeply affected the poet Idris Davies: 'Who learns no lesson from history / Sleeps in the slough of slavery.' But the renewal of historical study in Europe was not reflected in Wales and only in the post-1945 period did the traditional mainstream narratives begin to change.

The upsurge of interest in Welsh historical studies proved to be one of the most heartening developments of the latter half of the twentieth century. The expansion of higher education, the archival revolution, growing affluence among the book-reading public and, most of all, the inspiring leadership of historians like David Williams and Glanmor Williams meant that greater numbers of people gained a genuine understanding of, and empathy with, their past. Historical journals like the *Welsh History Review* (1960–), *Llafur* (Labour) (1972–) and *Cof Cenedl* (A Nation's Memory) (1986–) offered different perspectives and alternative readings to the old Whiggish or Lib–Lab interpretations, so much so that by the early 1980s Eric Hobsbawm maintained that current historical writing in Wales was 'advanced, adventurous and unprovincial'. Several major developments – the decline of the traditional industries, the travails of a native tongue which had made such a distinctive contribution over the centuries, the ebbing fortunes of the Christian faith, the demise of the British empire, and the controversies over devolution and its aftermath – sharpened historians' awareness of issues regarding identity. The titles of history books – *Religion, Language and Nationality in Wales*, *When was Wales?*, *Wales! Wales?* and *The Welsh Question* – highlighted the way in which familiar markers of identity were being dismantled or deconstructed. Social scientists began identifying political splits within the 'three-Wales model' – *y fro Gymraeg* (the Welsh-speaking heartland), Welsh Wales and British Wales – and divisions over the language issue and devolution prompted Glanmor Williams to observe in 1979 that the Welsh were 'too small a people to indulge in the masochistic luxury of self-inflicted wounds'. His fellow Dowlais-born historian, Gwyn A. Williams, a marvellous communicator whose television performances dazzled the public, was equally sorely troubled in the post-1979 era by the manner in which Welsh communities were crumbling under the weight and contradictions of capitalism, and losing their markers of identity. No historian was more aware of the potential of the idea of a usable past, and he portrayed the history of Wales as a series of splits, ruptures and crises which the Welsh had survived by reinventing themselves. His chilling verdict in 1985 was that the Welsh had become no more than 'a naked people under an acid rain'. The Thatcherism which he loathed so heartily also coincided with the rise in popularity of 'British history', which helped to promote a new approach in medieval and early modern studies but which also, in other cases, turned out to be anglocentrism by another name. By the early 1990s the conflicting predictions of Welsh historians reflected the ambiguous and vulnerable mood of the times. Philip Jenkins insisted that 'Wales must be seen in a British context', while John Davies, in his masterly account of the entire history of Wales, asserted that his book had been written 'in the faith and confidence that the nation in its fullness is yet to be'. As it turned out, the odds swiftly stacked up behind the latter prediction as the Welsh, by the narrowest of margins, expressed in 1997 a desire to see their sense of nationhood and civic identity expressed through their own political institutions.

It is ironic, therefore, that whereas every recent poll or survey has revealed that growing proportions of the population think of themselves as being more Welsh than British, a constellation of forces in this post-modern world are making it more difficult, perhaps impossible, to sustain a coherent sense of identity. By the dawn of the third millennium, the fact that the Welsh were descended from the oldest and most authentic peoples of the island of Britain meant little in a Wales which had become a heterogeneous, multicultural society. The Welsh language which had produced one of the oldest and finest living literatures in Europe was the mother tongue of a dwindling number of people and, either as a result of choice or lack of opportunity, it was not spoken by four-fifths of the population. The Christian religion, which had been of fundamental importance to the Welsh since the Age of the Saints, could no longer be reckoned a bulwark of national identity. As Wales became a more diverse, eclectic society, and as new symbols of identity such as sport, music and the media provided renewed cultural assertiveness, it became harder to develop a sense of oneness. Indeed, in the changed circumstances of the early twenty-first century it may no longer be realistic to expect nations to be homogeneous entities. If the following trends continue and intensify – the relatively unfettered movement of peoples, a globalized economic system, technological advance, cultural amalgamation and especially the revolution in information technology – Wales will increasingly become a mutable and diverse community of peoples.

This brings us back to Waldo Williams, whose work was heavily influenced by the notion of the unity of the whole of humankind. In his intriguing sonnet 'Wales Is One' (*Cymru'n Un*), he memorably claimed: 'Within me, Wales is one. The manner I know not.' Although history shows that the Welsh have preferred to diverge than converge, poets like Williams have often been preoccupied with the need for unity and wholeness. Historians, on the other hand, are currently keener than ever before to explore Wales's diverse, fragmented and multi-faceted nature, and the time may come when constructing a common national identity will be judged to be neither feasible nor desirable. In the light of this, it would be reassuring to believe that, as the National Assembly for Wales sets about improving the quality of people's lives by providing them with effective democratic governance, it will assist the Welsh in every way to conserve the memory of the past as a means of strengthening their multi-layered identity or identities. Of one thing we can be sure: a nation without a memory has no future.

SOURCES OF QUOTATIONS

I. THE EARLIEST INHABITANTS

The negative portraits of Wales derive from Sir John Vanbrugh, *Aesop* (1697), quoted in Francis Jones, 'An Approach to Welsh Genealogy', *Transactions of the Honourable Society of Cymmrodorion* (1948), p. 429 and Ned Ward, *A Trip to North-Wales* (London, 1701), p. 6; the Welsh archaeologist was Glyn Daniel, *The National Museum as a Mirror of Ancient Wales* (Cardiff: National Museum of Wales, 1983), p. 14; Theophilus Evans dilated on the ancestry of the Welsh in *Drych y Prif Oesoedd* (Mwythig, 1740), p. 7; Iolo Morganwg on the origins of the universe is in The National Library of Wales 13093E, p. 167; the slur on Darwin is quoted in R. Tudur Jones, *Ffydd ac Argyfwng Cenedl: Cristionogaeth a Diwylliant yng Nghymru 1890–1914*, volume II: *Dryswch y Diwygiad* (Abertawe: Tŷ John Penry, 1982), p. 36; John Jones is quoted in Harri Williams, *Duw, Daeareg a Darwin* (Llandysul: Gomer Press, 1979), p. 18; the 'human story' of Paviland is told by Stephen Aldhouse-Green, *Paviland Cave and the 'Red Lady'* (Bristol: Western Academic and Specialist Press, 2000), p. xxiv; the 'snout of a glacier' is by Michael Reed, *The Landscape of Britain* (London: Routledge, 1990), p. 29; the 'first Golden Age' is by E. G. Bowen, *Britain and the Western Seaways* (London: Thames & Hudson, 1972), p. 25; Barry Cunliffe's comments on 'oceanic mentality' are in *Facing the Ocean: The Atlantic and its Peoples, 8000BC–AD1500* (paperback edn, Oxford: Oxford

University Press, 2004), p. 554; for stones that float to the sky, Vicki Cummings and Alasdair Whittle, *Places of Special Virtue: Megaliths in the Neolithic Landscapes of Wales* (Oxford: Oxbow Books, 2004), chapter 7; some of the 'schizophrenic signals' sent by proponents of 'Celtomania and Celtoscepticism' on this fraught battleground are decoded by Patrick Sims-Williams, 'Celtomania and Celtoscepticism', *Cambrian Medieval Celtic Studies*, 36 (1998), pp. 1–35; the glory of Celtic art is quoted in Miranda J. Green (ed.), *The Celtic World* (London: Routledge, 1995), p. 345; Caratacus's speech is quoted in Graham Webster, *Rome against Caratacus: The Roman Campaigns in Britain AD 48–58* (paperback edn, London: Routledge, 2003), p. 38; the alleged genocide in Anglesey is quoted in *The Annals of Tacitus*, XIV, p. 30; Domitilla's salutations are quoted in Christopher J. Arnold and Jeffrey L. Davies, *Roman and Early Medieval Wales* (Stroud: Sutton, 2000), pp. 41–2; the claims about Maximus were made by Gwyn A. Williams, *When was Wales? A History of the Welsh* (London: Black Raven, 1985), p. 20; for the words and score of 'Yma o Hyd', see *Yma o Hyd* (Pwllheli: Eisteddfod Genedlaethol Urdd Gobaith Cymru, 1998).

2. THE HEROIC AGE, 383–1063

The 'devouring of moths', uttered by Rhygyfarch, is quoted in A. W. Wade-Evans, 'Rhygyfarch's Life of Saint David', *Y Cymmrodor*, 24 (1913), p. 71; the 'croak of ravens' figures in Gwyn A. Williams, *Excalibur: The Search for Arthur* (London: BBC Books, 1994), p. 42; the Cynddylan *englynion* are quoted in A. O. H. Jarman, 'Saga Poetry – The Cycle of Llywarch Hen', in A. O. H. Jarman and Gwilym Rees Hughes (eds.), *A Guide to Welsh Literature*, volume I (revised edn, Cardiff: University of Wales Press, 1992), pp. 92–4; Hywel Dda as 'the Head and Glory' is quoted in Thomas Jones (ed.), *Brut y Tywysogyon or The Chronicle of the Princes* (Cardiff: University of Wales Press, 1952), p. 7; Gruffydd ap Llywelyn as 'the golden-torqued king' is quoted by Mike Davies, 'Gruffydd ap Llywelyn, King of Wales', *Welsh History Review*, 21, no. 2 (2002), p. 247; Gruffydd ap Llywelyn as the 'head and shield' appears in Jones (ed.), *Brut y Tywysogyon*, p. 15; Wendy Davies takes her colleagues to task in 'Looking Back to the Early Medieval Past: Wales and England, a Contrast in Approaches', *Welsh History Review*, 22, no. 2 (2004), p. 197; the 'Hywelian origin' point is made by Dafydd Jenkins in T. M. Charles-Edwards, Morfydd E. Owen and Paul Russell (eds.), *The Welsh King and his Court* (Cardiff: University of Wales Press, 2000), p. 17; the reference to the laws 'living in the mouths of lawyers' occurs in T. M. Charles-Edwards, *The Welsh Laws* (Cardiff: University of Wales Press, 1989), p. 6; on the openness of society, see Michael McCormick, *Origins of the European Economy: Communications and Commerce AD 300–900* (Cambridge: Cambridge University Press, 2002), p. 797; the saints as part of the 'package of Christianity' is by Wendy Davies, *Wales in the Early Middle Ages* (Leicester: Leicester University Press, 1982), p. 176; people's faith in God, revealed in the Juvencus *englynion*, is quoted in Ifor Williams, *The Beginnings of Welsh Poetry*, ed. Rachel Bromwich (Cardiff: University of Wales Press, 1972), p. 101; Gildas's animadversions on the 'rascally crew' are quoted in A. O. H. Jarman, *The Cynfeirdd: Early Welsh Poets and Poetry* (Cardiff: University of Wales Press, 1981), p. 2; Iolo Morganwg's hyperbole appears in The National Library of Wales 13144A, f. 389; the annihilation of 'golden-torqued' warriors is in Jarman, *The Cynfeirdd*, p. 54 and the whole text figures in John T. Koch, *The Gododdin of Aneirin* (Cardiff: University of Wales Press, 1997); the translation of the first extant piece of written Welsh is in Dafydd Jenkins and Morfydd E. Owen, 'The Welsh Marginalia in the Lichfield Gospels', *Cambrian Medieval Celtic Studies*, 5 (1983), p. 51; concepts of 'Wales' and 'Welsh' are discussed in Huw Pryce, 'British or Welsh? National Identity in Twelfth-Century Wales', *English Historical Review*, 116, no. 468 (2001), pp. 775–801.

3. THE ANGLO-NORMAN CONQUERORS, C. 1063–1282

Lloyd as the 'lantern-bearer' figures in Saunders Lewis's elegy to him: the poem is analysed by John Rowlands in R. Geraint Gruffydd (ed.), *Bardos: Penodau ar y Traddodiad Barddol Cymreig a Cheltaidd* (Caerdydd: Gwasg Prifysgol Cymru, 1982), pp. 111–27; the anecdote about King Henry figures in R. T. Jenkins, 'Syr John Edward Lloyd', *Y Llenor*, 26 (1947), p. 82; the depiction of the

Welsh as bestial is quoted in Alexander Grant and Keith J. Stringer (eds.), *Uniting the Kingdom? The Making of British History* (London: Routledge, 1995), p. 60; the compiler of *Brut y Tywysogyon* is quoted in Thomas Jones, 'Historical Writing in Medieval Welsh', *Scottish Studies*, 12, part 1 (1968), p. 24; gory Welsh poetry is translated by Joseph P. Clancy in *The Earliest Welsh Poetry* (London: Macmillan, 1970), pp. 145–6; the 1122 chronicler is in Jones (ed.), *Brut y Tywysogyon*, p. 49; the reference to cowering English settlers is by R. R. Davies in *Domination and Conquest: The Experience of Ireland, Scotland and Wales 1100–1300* (Cambridge: Cambridge University Press, 1990), p. 15; the Pembrokeshire divide is in George Owen, *The Description of Penbrokshire*, ed. Henry Owen (4 vols., London: Honourable Society of Cymmrodorion, 1892–1936), I, p. 47; William of Malmesbury is quoted in David C. Douglas and George W. Greenway (eds.), *English Historical Documents*, volume II: *1042–1189* (2nd edn, London: Eyre Methuen, 1981), p. 745; Rhygyfarch's lament is quoted in Michael Lapidge, 'The Welsh-Latin Poetry of Sulien's Family', *Studia Celtica*, 8/9 (1973–4), p. 91; the rheumy-eyed Old Man of Pencader is quoted in Gerald of Wales, *The Journey through Wales and The Description of Wales*, trans. Lewis Thorpe (London: Penguin Books, 2004), p. 274; defiant supporters of Llywelyn ap Gruffudd are quoted in Jones (ed.), *Brut y Tywysogyon*, p. 110; Gerald of Wales's thoughts on his grandfather are quoted in A. J. Roderick, 'Marriage and Politics in Wales, 1066–1282', *Welsh History Review*, 4, no. 1 (1968), p. 7; the ambivalence of Gerald of Wales is teased out in Pryce, 'British or Welsh? National Identity in Twelfth-Century Wales', pp. 775–801; the 'conqueror of the mighty' is quoted in Roger Turvey, *The Lord Rhys: Prince of Deheubarth* (Llandysul: Gomer Press, 1997), p. 109; Cynddelw Brydydd Mawr's command is quoted in Nerys Ann Jones and Ann Parry Owen (eds.), *Gwaith Cynddelw Brydydd Mawr* (2 vols., Cardiff: University of Wales Press, 1991), I, p. 5; Dafydd Benfras is quoted in N. G. Costigan et al. (eds.), *Gwaith Dafydd Benfras ac Eraill o Feirdd Hanner Cyntaf y Drydedd Ganrif ar Ddeg* (Caerdydd: Gwasg Prifysgol Cymru, 1995), p. 433; Llygad Gŵr is quoted by Peredur I. Lynch, 'Court Poetry, Power and Politics', in Charles-Edwards et al. (eds.), *The Welsh King*, p. 184; the transcriber of the Black Book is described by Daniel Huws in *Medieval Welsh Manuscripts* (Cardiff: University of Wales Press, 2000), pp. 71–2; the 'brave battle-lion' figures in Rhian M. Andrews et al. (eds.), *Gwaith Bleddyn Fardd a Beirdd Eraill Ail Hanner y Drydedd Ganrif ar Ddeg* (Caerdydd: Gwasg Prifysgol Cymru, 1996), p. 234; Llywelyn ap Gruffudd's stirring words are quoted by R. R. Davies in 'Edward I and Wales', in Trevor Herbert and Gareth E. Jones (eds.), *Edward I and Wales* (Cardiff: University of Wales Press, 1988), pp. 4–5; the subsequent 'irrelevance' of Llywelyn to nationhood is noted by Llinos Beverley Smith, 'Llywelyn ap Gruffudd and the Welsh Historical Consciousness', *Welsh History Review*, 12, no. 1 (1984), p. 27; the lament for Llywelyn is quoted in Joseph P. Clancy, *Medieval Welsh Poems* (Dublin: Four Courts Press, 2003), p. 173; Bleddyn Fardd's apocalyptic fears are quoted in Rhian Andrews et al. (eds.), *Gwaith Bleddyn Fardd*, p. 593.

4. PESTILENCE, REBELLION AND RENEWAL, C. 1283–1536

The prediction of Hwch Ddu is quoted in Wiliam Owen Roberts, *Pestilence* (Bridgend: Seren, 1991), p. 38; Llywelyn Fychan's poem is reproduced in Dafydd Johnston (ed.), *Galar y Beirdd. Poets' Grief* (Cardiff: Tafol, 1993), pp. 51–3; Clynn's words are quoted by Rosemary Horrox, *The Black Death* (Manchester: Manchester University Press, 1994), p. 84; the cry of disorientated Cardiganshire peasants is quoted in William Rees, 'The Black Death in Wales', *Transactions of the Royal Historical Society*, 4th series, 3 (1920), p. 244, n. 5; the 'hurricane' reference occurs in Glanmor Williams, *The Welsh Church from Conquest to Reformation* (revised edn, Cardiff: University of Wales Press, 1976), p. 153; the lugubrious annalist in 1282 figures in Thomas Jones (ed.), *Brenhinedd y Saesson or The Kings of the Saxons* (Cardiff: University of Wales Press, 1971), p. 259; the 'dragon's tooth' is by Tony Conran, *The Shape of My Country: Selected Poems and Extracts* (Llanrwst: Gwasg Carreg Gwalch, 2004), p. 44; the quotation from the Statute of Wales is in Ivor Bowen (ed.), *The Statutes of Wales* (London: T. Fisher Unwin, 1908), p. 2; the 'snake lying in the grass' is quoted in David Moore, *The Welsh*

Wars of Independence c. 410–c. 1415 (Stroud: Tempus, 2005), p. 268; giving effect to Merlin's prophecies is quoted in N. Denholm-Young, *The Life of Edward the Second* (London: Thomas Nelson & Sons Ltd, 1957), p. 69; the comment on the fecklessness of the Welsh is quoted in Rees Davies, 'Race Relations in Post-Conquest Wales: Confrontation and Compromise', *Transactions of the Honourable Society of Cymmrodorion* (1975), pp. 37–8; the reference to 'a nation of wretches' is by Gruffudd Llwyd and is reproduced in Rhiannon Ifans (ed.), *Gwaith Gruffudd Llwyd a'r Llygliwiaid Eraill* (Aberystwyth: University of Wales Centre for Advanced Welsh and Celtic Studies, 2000), p. 149; Shakespeare's portrayal is in *I Henry IV*, III. i; the 'alien in the land of his birth' is quoted by Brynley F. Roberts, 'Un o Lawysgrifau Hopcyn ap Tomas o Ynys Dawy', *Bulletin of the Board of Celtic Studies*, 22, part 3 (1967), p. 228; the 'sharp anguish' by R. S. Thomas is included in his *Collected Poems 1945–1990* (London: J. M. Dent, 1993), p. 32; Glyndŵr as a 'mighty lion' is quoted by Gruffydd Aled Williams, 'The Literary Tradition to c. 1560', in J. Beverley Smith and Llinos Beverley Smith (eds.), *Merioneth County History*, volume II (Cardiff: University of Wales Press, 2001), pp. 558–9; Adam of Usk is quoted in Ralph A. Griffiths, 'After Glyn Dŵr: An Age of Reconciliation?', *Proceedings of the British Academy*, 117 (2002), p. 142; 'deceit and guile' occurs in Keith Williams-Jones, 'The Taking of Conwy Castle, 1401', *Transactions of the Honourable Society of Cymmrodorion*, 39 (1978), p. 9; the point about a 'medieval think-tank' is made by David Walker, *Medieval Wales*, p. 175; 1410 as a climacteric was first advanced by Gwyn A. Williams in A. J. Roderick (ed.), *Wales through the Ages* (2 vols., Llandybïe: Christopher Davies, 1959–60), I, p. 183; the 'balm of the community' is quoted in Llinos Beverley Smith, 'Disputes and Settlements in Medieval Wales: The Role of Arbitration', *English Historical Review*, 421 (1991), p. 856; the 'blazing sensuousness' of Dafydd ap Gwilym is a depiction by Gwyn Thomas, *Dafydd ap Gwilym: His Poems* (Cardiff: University of Wales Press, 2001), p. xix; Siôn Cent's gloomy reminder is quoted in A. O. H. Jarman and Gwilym Rees Hughes (eds.), *A Guide to Welsh Literature 1282–c. 1550*, volume II, revised by Dafydd Johnston (Cardiff: University of Wales Press, 1997), p. 153;

'carpenters of praise' is quoted in Ifor Williams, *Lectures on Early Welsh Poetry* (Dublin: Dublin Institute for Advanced Studies, 1944), p. 7.

5. EARLY MODERN WALES, 1536–1776

Richard Price's notion of 'a separate community' is quoted in D. O. Thomas, *Richard Price 1723–1791* (Cardiff: University of Wales Press, 1976), p. 67; 'amicable Concord and Unity' figure among the sentiments proclaimed in the 1536 Act and reproduced in full in Bowen (ed.), *The Statutes of Wales*, pp. 75–93; disparagement from Grub Street is quoted in Geraint H. Jenkins, *Thomas Jones yr Almanaciwr 1648–1713* (Caerdydd: Gwasg Prifysgol Cymru, 1980), pp. 123–4; the *Landsker* is in Owen, *Description of Penbrokshire*, I, p. 47; Churchyard's assertion is quoted by A. H. Dodd, *Studies in Stuart Wales* (2nd edn, Cardiff: University of Wales Press, 1971), p. 75; coolness towards strangers is quoted in Rees L. Lloyd, 'Welsh Masters on the Bench of the Inner Temple', *Transactions of the Honourable Society of Cymmrodorion* (1937), p. 195; Elis Gruffydd is quoted in Prys Morgan, 'Elis Gruffudd of Gronant – Tudor Chronicler Extraordinary', *Flintshire Historical Society Publications*, 25 (1971–2), p. 11; Thomas Llewelyn on the monoglot Welsh is in *An Historical Account of the British or Welsh Versions and Editions of the Bible* (London: Richard Hett, 1768), p. 71; London as the centre of the world is by William Owen Pughe, *A Dictionary of the Welsh Language* (2 vols., London: Evan Williams, 1803), I, sig. clv; the 'swirl of enterprise', coined by Bernard Bailyn, is quoted in Nicholas Canny (ed.), *Europeans on the Move: Studies on European Migration 1500–1800* (Oxford: Clarendon Press, 1994), p. 2; the toiling serfs are described by Owen, *Description of Penbrokshire*, I, pp. 41–4; the tyrannical 'Copper King' is described in J. R. Harris, *The Copper King: A Biography of Thomas Williams of Llanidan* (new edn, Ashbourne: Landmark Publishing, 2003), p. xiv; Lewis Morris on untapped wealth is in *Plans of Harbours, Bars, Bays and Roads in St George's Channel* (London, 1748), p. 11; Bristol as the 'great Mart of south Wales' is in The National Library of Wales 1760 A, f. 12^r; extracts from the preamble to the 1536 Act of Union are from Bowen (ed.), *Statutes of Wales*, pp. 75–6; linguistic enclaves in England are described in David Powel, *The Historie of Cambria* (London: Rafe Newberie & Henrie Denham, 1584), p. 5; 'Magistrates of their own Nation' is from Owen, *Description of Penbrokshire*, III, p. 55; so is the advance of civility, Owen, *Description of Penbrokshire*, III, p. 91; Sir William Vaughan's words from *The Arraignment of Slander* (1630) are quoted by J. Gwynfor Jones, *The Welsh Gentry 1536–1640* (Cardiff: University of Wales Press, 1998), p. 244; references to 'king-killers' and 'monsters' may be found in Geraint H. Jenkins, *Protestant Dissenters in Wales 1639–1689* (Cardiff: University of Wales Press, 1992), pp. 39–40; the description of Philip Jones is by Austin Woolrych, *Britain in Revolution 1625–1660* (Oxford: Oxford University Press, 2002), p. 567; 'our Welsh Leviathans' is taken from The National Library of Wales 2532B, f. 377; Iolo Morganwg on 'pimps' is in The National Library of Wales 21319A, f. 38; the pugnacious cleric is quoted by Glanmor Williams, *Welsh Reformation Essays* (Cardiff: University of Wales Press, 1967), p. 40; for Welsh-language slander, see Richard Suggett, 'Slander in Early-Modern Wales', *Bulletin of the Board of Celtic Studies*, 39 (1992), pp. 119–53; for the 'Englishness' of parliament, see Mark Stoyle, *West Britons: Cornish Identities and the Early Modern State* (Exeter: University of Exeter Press, 2002), p. 5; Henry Vaughan's words are quoted in L. C. Martin (ed.), *The Works of Henry Vaughan* (2nd edn, Oxford: Clarendon Press, 1957), p. 166; Vavasor Powell's song on Roundheadism is in The National Library of Wales 366A, f. 9; the English proctor is quoted in Geraint H. Jenkins, ' "Horrid Unintelligible Jargon": The Case of Dr Thomas Bowles', *Welsh History Review*, 15, no. 4 (1991), p. 511; 'heap of Boys' occurs in Tom Beynon, 'Howell Harris's visits to Cardiganshire', *Historical Society of the Presbyterian Church of Wales*, 30, no. 1 (1945), p. 50; William Salesbury is quoted in Garfield H. Hughes (ed.), *Rhagymadroddion: 1547–1659* (Caerdydd: Gwasg Prifysgol Cymru, 2000), p. 11; the 'blotting out' of Wales is in Thomas Jones, *The British Language in its Lustre* (London, 1688), sig. A3^r; the Aborigines figure in 'Constitutions of the Honourable Society of Cymmrodorion', *Y Cymmrodor*, I (1877), p. 15; the 'proud hot Welshman' figures in J. H. Davies (ed.), *The Letters of Lewis, Richard, William and John Morris of Anglesey 1728–1765* (2 vols., Aberystwyth, 1907–9), I, p. 346.

6. A CRUCIBLE OF THE MODERN WORLD, 1776–1900

The report in the *Welshman* is quoted in H. Gethin Rhys, ' "Yr Haiarnfarch": Y Rheilffyrdd a'r Cymry yn ystod y Bedwaredd Ganrif ar Bymtheg', in Geraint H. Jenkins (ed.), *Cof Cenedl XX* (Llandysul: Gomer Press, 2005), pp. 112–13; the 'jagged peak' simile is by Williams, *When Was Wales?*, pp. 173–4; Iolo Morganwg and the 'man in the moon' is in The British Library Add. 15027, ff. 79–80; 'the Charon of the industrial century' is from D. Tecwyn Lloyd, *Safle'r Gerbydres ac Ysgrifau Eraill* (Llandysul: Gomer Press, 1970), p. 120; the 'vast black Klondyke' is a depiction by E. D. Lewis in K. S. Hopkins (ed.), *Rhondda Past and Future* (Rhondda: Rhondda Borough Council, [1975]), p. 23; the 'irresistible torrents' is used by Thomas Rees in *Miscellaneous Papers on Subjects relating to Wales* (London: John Snow & Co., 1867), p. 86; the monoglot Welsh-language rock is quoted in R. Merfyn Jones, *The North Wales Quarrymen, 1874–1922* (Cardiff: University of Wales Press, 1981), p. 78; the 'Irish in heart' is quoted by Paul O'Leary, *Immigration and Integration: The Irish in Wales 1798–1922* (Cardiff: University of Wales Press, 2000), p. 301; Edward Charles is quoted in E. G. Millward (ed.), *Cerddi Jac Glan-y-Gors* ([Abertawe]: Cyhoeddiadau Barddas, 2003), pp. 10–11; Joseph Jenkins's verdict on Australia is quoted in Bethan Phillips, *Pity the Swagman: The Australian Odyssey of a Victorian Diarist* (Aberystwyth: Cymdeithas Lyfrau Ceredigion, 2001), p. 261; conforming to 'Uncle Sam' is quoted in Aled Jones and Bill Jones, *Welsh Reflections: Y Drych and America 1851–2001* (Llandysul: Gomer Press, 2001), p. 65; Henry Richard on the law-abiding Welsh appears in Henry Richard, *Letters on the Social and Political Condition of the Principality of Wales* (London: Jackson, Walford & Hodder, [1867]), pp. 72–3; William Jones's anti-land-lord tirade is in The National Library of Wales 13221E, f. 387; Thomas Campbell Foster's fault-line is in the *Times*, 18 September 1843; the policeman in Rebecca country is quoted in David J. V. Jones, *Rebecca's Children: A Study of Rural Society, Crime and Protest* (Oxford: Clarendon Press, 1989), p. 41; the Liberal politician George Osborne Morgan on the Tithe War is quoted in J. P. D. Dunbabin, *Rural Discontent in Nineteenth Century Britain*

(London: Faber & Faber, 1974), p. 283; Lord Penrhyn's condem-
nation of the Welsh is quoted in *Cymru Fydd*, 3, no. 2 (1890),
p. 691; Junius is quoted in Ivor Wilks, *South Wales and the Rising
of 1839* (Llandysul: Gomer Press, 1989), p. 69; *Liberty's Address* is
quoted in ibid., pp. 87–8; the point about chapels as 'ornaments',
made by Thomas Rees, is quoted by Christopher Turner in 'The
Nonconformist Response', in Trevor Herbert and Gareth E. Jones
(eds.), *People and Protest: Wales 1815–1880* (Cardiff: University
of Wales Press, 1988), p. 103; the sparky Matthews Ewenni is
described in Sioned Davies, 'Performing from the Pulpit: An
Introduction to Preaching in Nineteenth-Century Wales', in Joseph
F. Nagy (ed.), *Identifying the Celtic: CSANA Yearbook 2* (Dublin:
Four Courts Press, 2002), p. 136 n. 88; David Rees's cry is quoted in
Thomas Rees, *History of Protestant Nonconformity in Wales* (2nd
edn, London: John Snow & Co, 1883), pp. 474–5; miners with a taste
for theology is quoted in David Evans, *The Sunday Schools of Wales*
(London: Sunday School Union, [1883]), p. 225; the 'Wellington of
choral singing' is quoted in Gareth Williams, *Valleys of Song: Music
and Society in Wales 1840–1914* (Cardiff: University of Wales Press,
1998), p. 91; the respectability of mid-Victorian Wales is a description by Ieuan Gwynedd Jones, *Explorations and Explanations:
Essays in the Social History of Victorian Wales* (Llandysul: Gomer
Press, 1981), p. 270; Welsh Methodism among the Khasi is quoted
by Aled Jones, 'The Other Internationalism? Missionary Activity
and Welsh Nonconformist Perceptions of the World in the
Nineteenth and Twentieth Centuries', in Charlotte Williams, Paul
O'Leary and Neil Evans (eds.), *A Tolerant Nation? Exploring
Ethnic Diversity in Wales* (Cardiff: University of Wales Press,
2003), p. 53; for birth control methods, see Russell Davies, *Secret
Sins: Sex, Violence and Society in Carmarthenshire, 1870–1920*
(Cardiff: University of Wales Press, 1996), p. 273 n. 69; Daniel
Owen on hypocrisy figures in Robert Rhys, 'Daniel Owen
(1836–1895)', in Hywel Teifi Edwards (ed.), *A Guide to Welsh
Literature c. 1800–1900* (Cardiff: University of Wales, 2000),
p. 149; the 'awful unwonted silence' is quoted in David Cooper
(ed.), *The Petrie Collection of the Ancient Music of Ireland* (Cork:
Cork University Press, 2002), p. 32; for the jaundiced 1847 commissioners, see *Reports of the Commissioners of Inquiry into the State*

of Education in Wales (London, 1847), PP 1847 (870), XXVII; the
'silent machinery' is quoted in *Y Punch Cymraeg*, 16 April 1864; the
Western Mail's bilious comment is in the *Western Mail*, 10 April
1891; 'the old happiness' is quoted in Ceri W. Lewis, *Iolo
Morganwg* (Caernarfon: Gwasg Pantycelyn, 1995), p. 158; the
'angel on the hearth' figures in R. Tudur Jones, 'Daearu'r
Angylion: Sylwadau ar Ferched mewn Llenyddiaeth, 1860–1900',
in J. E. Caerwyn Williams (ed.), *Ysgrifau Beirniadol XI* (Dinbych:
Gwasg Gee, 1979), pp. 191–226; Thomas Gibson aired his views on
the lot of women in the *Cambrian News*, 26 October 1885; 'We *will*
have the vote' is quoted in Kay Cook and Neil Evans, '"The Petty
Antics of the Bell-Ringing Boisterous Band": The Women's Suffrage
Movement in Wales, 1890–1918', in Angela V. John (ed.), *Our
Mother's Land* (Cardiff: University of Wales Press, 1991), p. 164;
the press as an 'engine under God' is quoted by Matthew Cragoe in
*An Anglican Aristocracy: The Moral Economy of the Landed Estate
in Carmarthenshire, 1832–1895* (Oxford: Clarendon Press, 1996),
p. 242; for the attempts to 'restore the Old Country', see Hywel Teifi
Edwards, *Codi'r Hen Wlad yn ei Hôl 1850–1914* (Llandysul:
Gomer Press, 1989), pp. 1–26; O. M. Edwards and the Union Jack
figures in Owen M. Edwards, *Llyfr Nest* (Gwrecsam: Hughes a'i
Fab, 1913), p. 53.

7. WALES AWAKENING? 1901–2006

Edward VIII's famous dictum is quoted in Ted Rowlands,
'Something Must be Done': South Wales v Whitehall 1921–1951
(Merthyr Tydfil: TTC Books, 2000), p. 97; Wales as a 'civilized
spot' is quoted in Colin Baber and L. J. Williams (eds.), *Modern
South Wales: Essays in Economic History* (Cardiff: University of
Wales Press, 1986), p. 203; 'King Coal' is quoted in David Lloyd
George, *Through Terror to Triumph* (London: Hodder &
Stoughton, 1915), pp. 178–9; Cardiff 'swimming on the tide' is by
R. T. Jenkins, *Edrych yn Ôl* (Llundain: Clwb Llyfrau Cymraeg,
1968), p. 231; Wales's exclusion from the 'industrial learning race'
is by John Elliott, *The Industrial Development of the Ebbw Valleys
1780–1914* (Cardiff: University of Wales Press, 2004), p. 178; the
backwardness of Cardiganshire is quoted by John Davies, 'The

Communal Conscience in Wales in the Inter-War Years',
Transactions of the Honourable Society of Cymmrodorion, new
series, 5 (1999), pp. 148–9; 'blood on the coal' is quoted in Bill
Jones and Chris Williams, *B. L. Coombes* (Cardiff: University of
Wales Press, 1999), p. 76; the 'Black Death on Wheels' is by the
novelist Gwyn Thomas in *The Subsidence Factor* (Cardiff:
University College Cardiff Press, 1979), p. 13; Bevan's 'empty
farce' jibe is quoted in Trevor Herbert and Gareth E. Jones (eds.),
Wales between the Wars (Cardiff: University of Wales Press, 1988),
p. 46; the 'simple, faithful folk', by the poet Idris Davies, figures in
Dafydd Johnston (ed.), *The Complete Poems of Idris Davies*
(Cardiff: University of Wales Press, 1994), p. 6; the tribute to
Dowlais families is in Glanmor Williams, *A Life* (Cardiff:
University of Wales Press, 2002), p. 1; James Griffiths's speech on
National Insurance is quoted in James Obelkevich and Peter
Catterall (eds.), *Understanding Post-War British Society* (London:
Routledge, 1994), p. 126; Aneurin Bevan and the consultants is
quoted in David Gladstone, *The Twentieth-Century Welfare State*
(Basingstoke: Macmillan, 1999), p. 127; Deirdre Beddoe bemoans
the missionary position in *Out of the Shadows: A History of Women
in Twentieth-Century Wales* (Cardiff: University of Wales Press,
2000), p. 178; for inflows and outflows of people, see Graham
Day, ' "A Million on the Move"?: Population Change and Rural
Wales', *Contemporary Wales*, 3 (1989), pp. 137–59; Lloyd George
as an 'anti-Briton' is quoted in Peter Warwick (ed.), *The South
African War: The Anglo-Boer War 1899–1902* (Harlow:
Longman, 1980), p. 220; Lord Salisbury on wars is quoted in John
Gooch (ed.), *The Boer War: Direction, Experience and Image*
(London: Frank Cass, 2000), p. 16; the Revd John Williams's call
to arms is quoted in Robert R. Hughes, *Y Parchedig John Williams,
D. D. Brynsiencyn* (Caernarfon: Gwasg y Cyfundeb, 1929), p. 228;
the 'wrench of losing the lads' figures in Alan Llwyd (ed.), *Cerddi
R. Williams Parry: Y Casgliad Cyflawn 1905–1950* (Dinbych:
Gwasg Gee, 1998), p. 66; for the 'wondrous Hercules', see Geraint
H. Jenkins (quoting Dr Thomas Richards) in Peter Stead and Huw
Richards (eds.), *For Club and Country: Welsh Football Greats*
(Cardiff: University of Wales Press, 2000), p. 23; the extract from
Hedd Wyn's poem is from Gerwyn Williams, 'The Literature of the

First World War', in Dafydd Johnston (ed.), *A Guide to Welsh Literature c. 1900–1998*, volume VI (Cardiff: University of Wales Press, 1998), pp. 26–7; David Ivon Jones's words are quoted in Baruch Hirson and Gwyn A. Williams, *The Delegate for Africa: David Ivon Jones 1883–1924* (London: Core Publications, 1995), p. 197; the watchword of the North Wales Women's Peace Council is quoted in Sydna A. Williams, ' "Love, not War – Hedd nid Cledd": Women and the Peace Movement in North Wales, 1926–1945', *Welsh History Review*, 18, no. 1 (1996), p. 79; for Mrs Jones, see Mari A. Williams, *Where is Mrs Jones Going?: Women and the Second World War in South Wales* (Aberystwyth: University of Wales Centre for Advanced Welsh and Celtic Studies, 1995); Waldo Williams's lines are quoted by Robert Rhys in 'Poetry 1939–1970', in Johnston (ed.), *A Guide to Welsh Literature*, 6, p. 98; the admonitions of the CWAECs are quoted by R. J. Moore-Colyer, 'The County War Agricultural Executive Committees: The Welsh Experience, 1939–1945', *Welsh History Review*, 22, no. 3 (2005), p. 573; 'a tough little race' figures in George Thomas, *Mr Speaker: The Memoirs of the Viscount Tonypandy* (London: Century Publishing, 1985), p. 211; the horrors of Bluff Cove are quoted in Simon Weston, *Walking Tall* (paperback edn, Rochester: 22 Books, 1995), p. 147; the Welsh philosopher's haunting words are those of J. R. Jones, *Gwaedd yng Nghymru* (Lerpwl: Cyhoeddiadau Modern Cymreig, 1970), pp. 81–2; for 'internal difference' and 'corresponding cultures', see M. Wynn Thomas, *Internal Difference: Twentieth-century Writing in Wales* (Cardiff: University of Wales Press, 1992) and *Corresponding Cultures: The Two Literatures of Wales* (Cardiff: University of Wales Press, 1999); 'a new and rainbow-like modernism' figures on the dust-jacket of Menna Elfyn and John Rowlands (eds.), *The Bloodaxe Book of Modern Welsh Poetry* (Tarset: Bloodaxe Books, 2003); 'the consumptive's flush of death' is quoted by D. Densil Morgan, 'Diwygiad Crefyddol 1904–5', in Jenkins (ed.), *Cof Cenedl XX*, p. 198; 'secret sins' may be found in The National Library of Wales 20033C, pp. 12–13; 'Big Bumptious Concern' is quoted in R. Alun Evans, *Stand By! Bywyd a Gwaith Sam Jones* (Llandysul: Gomer Press, 1998), p. 60; 'Thank God for the pictures' is quoted in Stephen Ridgwell, 'South Wales and the Cinema in the 1930s', *Welsh History Review*, 17, no. 4

(1995), p. 595; the sporting 'sense of "otherness" ' is expressed in Martin Johnes, *A History of Sport in Wales* (Cardiff: University of Wales Press, 2005), p. 112; Lloyd George's 'protracted funeral' is by Michael Bentley, 'The Liberal Party, 1900–1939: Summit and Descent', in Chris Wrigley (ed.), *A Companion to Early Twentieth-Century Britain* (Oxford: Blackwell, 2003), p. 35; for 'lower than vermin', see John Campbell, *Nye Bevan and the Mirage of British Socialism* (London: Weidenfeld & Nicolson, 1987), p. 204; Idris Davies on the 1926 strike is in Johnston (ed.), *The Complete Poems of Idris Davies*, p. 6; 'deep collective and personal loyalties' is a quote from Chris Williams, *Democratic Rhondda: Politics and Society 1885–1951* (Cardiff: University of Wales Press, 1996), pp. 207–8; James Griffiths is quoted in Duncan Tanner, Chris Williams and Deian Hopkin (eds.), *The Labour Party in Wales 1900–2000* (Cardiff: University of Wales Press, 2000), p. 117; Kinnock as a 'weaselly Welsh windbag' is quoted in James Thomas, '"Taffy was a Welshman, Taffy was a Thief": Anti-Welshness, the Press and Neil Kinnock', *Llafur*, 7, no. 2 (1997), p. 96; James Griffiths's 'heart and soul' commitment is quoted in Robert Griffiths, *Turning to London: Labour's Attitude to Wales 1898–1956* (Abertridwr: Y Faner Goch, 1978), p. 32; the Assembly government as 'a fragile flower' is quoted in Richard Rawlings, *Delineating Wales: Constitutional, Legal and Administrative Aspects of National Devolution* (Cardiff: University of Wales Press, 2003), p. 10; the 'devolution genie' is in Ron Davies, *Devolution: A Process not an Event* (Cardiff: Institute of Welsh Affairs, 1999), p. 9.

8. WHITHER WALES?

'Keeping house' is quoted in James Nicholas, *Waldo Williams* (Cardiff: University of Wales Press, 1975), p. 62; the 'happy incorporation' of the Welsh is by William Wynne, *The History of Wales* (London: M. Clark, 1697), p. 328; 'a geographical expression', used by Bishop Basil Jones, is quoted in Kenneth O. Morgan in *Rebirth of a Nation: Wales 1880–1980* (Oxford: Clarendon Press, 1981), p. 3; 'Who learns no lesson from history' is by Idris Davies, *The Angry Summer: A Poem of 1926* (Cardiff: University of Wales Press, 1993), p. 43; Hobsbawm's judgement was cited in a review in *Welsh History Review*, 2, no. 3 (1983), p. 425; the 'self-inflicted wounds' quotation is by Glanmor Williams in *Religion, Language and Nationality in Wales* (Cardiff: University of Wales Press, 1979), p. 33; the 'naked people' quotation is by Williams, *When was Wales?*, p. 305; seeing Wales in 'a British context' is by Philip Jenkins, *A History of Modern Wales 1536–1990* (London: Longman, 1992), p. 405; John Davies's comment on the 'nation in its fullness' is in *A History of Wales* (London: Allen Lane, 1993), p. 686; 'Wales Is One' figures in Nicholas, *Waldo Williams*, p. 4.

GUIDE TO FURTHER READING

REFERENCE WORKS

In the interests of space, the following list represents only a selection
of the works consulted in the writing of this volume. It does not
include publications in the Welsh language, works on British history, or articles.

Harold Carter (ed.), *The National Atlas of Wales* (Cardiff: University of
Wales Press, 1989).

Elwyn Davies, *A Gazetteer of Welsh Place-Names* (3rd edn, Cardiff:
University of Wales Press, 1975).

The Dictionary of Welsh Biography down to 1940 (London: The
Honourable Society of Cymmrodorion, 1959).

Philip Henry Jones, *A Bibliography of the History of Wales* (3rd edn,
Cardiff: University of Wales Press, 1989).

John T. Koch (ed.), *Celtic Culture: A Historical Encyclopedia* (5 vols., Santa
Barbara, CA: ABC-CLIO, 2006).

H. C. G. Matthew and Brian Harrison (eds.), *Oxford Dictionary of
National Biography* (Oxford: Oxford University Press, 2004).

Hywel Wyn Owen, *The Place-Names of Wales* (Cardiff: University of Wales
Press and The Western Mail, 1998).

Melville Richards, *Welsh Administrative and Territorial Units, Medieval
and Modern* (Cardiff: University of Wales Press, 1969).

Meic Stephens (ed.), *The New Companion to the Literature of Wales*
(Cardiff: University of Wales Press, 1998).

GENERAL

E. G. Bowen (ed.), *Wales: A Physical, Historical and Regional Geography*
(London: Methuen, 1957).

John Davies, *A History of Wales* (London: Allen Lane, 1993).

John Davies, *The Making of Wales* (Cardiff: Cadw. Welsh Historic Monuments, 1996).

R. R. Davies, Ralph A. Griffiths, Ieuan Gwynedd Jones and Kenneth O. Morgan (eds.), *Welsh Society and Nationhood* (Cardiff: University of Wales Press, 1984).

R. R. Davies and Geraint H. Jenkins (eds.), *From Medieval to Modern Wales* (Cardiff: University of Wales Press, 2004).

A. H. Dodd, *A Short History of Wales* (Ruthin: John Jones, 1998).

Frank V. Emery, *The World's Landscapes: Wales* (London: Longmans, 1969).

Gwynfor Evans, *Land of my Fathers* (6th edn, Talybont: Y Lolfa, 2000).

Trevor Fishlock, *Wales and the Welsh* (London: Cassell, 1972).

John B. Hilling, *The Historic Architecture of Wales* (Cardiff: University of Wales Press, 1976).

Emyr Humphreys, *The Taliesin Tradition* (new edn, Bridgend: Seren, 2000).

Philip Jenkins, *A History of Modern Wales 1536–1990* (London: Longman, 1992).

Martin Johnes, *A History of Sport in Wales* (Cardiff: University of Wales Press, 2005).

Dafydd Johnston, *The Literature of Wales* (Cardiff: University of Wales Press, 1994).

Gareth E. Jones, *Modern Wales: A Concise History c. 1485–1979* (2nd edn, Cambridge: Cambridge University Press, 1994).

Gareth E. Jones and Gordon W. Roderick, *A History of Education in Wales* (Cardiff: University of Wales Press, 2003).

Gareth E. Jones and Dai Smith (eds.), *The People of Wales* (Llandysul: BBC Radio Wales, 1999).

J. Graham Jones, *A Pocket Guide to the History of Wales* (Cardiff: University of Wales Press, 1990).

Philip Henry Jones and Eiluned Rees (eds.), *A Nation and its Books: A History of the Book in Wales* (Aberystwyth: The National Library of Wales, 1998).

Peter Lord, *The Visual Culture of Wales: Medieval Vision; Industrial Society; Imaging the Nation* (Cardiff: University of Wales Press, 1998–2003).

Prys Morgan (ed.), *Wales: An Illustrated History* (2nd edn, Stroud: Tempus, 2005).

Prys Morgan and David Thomas, *Wales: The Shaping of a Nation* (Newton Abbot: David & Charles, 1984).

Jan Morris, *The Matter of Wales: Epic Views of a Small Country* (Oxford: Oxford University Press, 1984).

D. Huw Owen (ed.), *Settlement and Society in Wales* (Cardiff: University of Wales Press, 1989).

Thomas Parry, *A History of Welsh Literature*, trans. H. Idris Bell (Oxford: Clarendon Press, 1970).

William Rees, *An Historical Atlas of Wales* (new edn, London: Faber &
    Faber, 1972).
A. J. Roderick (ed.), *Wales through the Ages* (2 vols., Llandybïe:
    Christopher Davies, 1972).
Dai Smith, *Wales: A Question for History* (Bridgend: Seren, 1999).
Dai Smith, *Wales! Wales?* (London: Allen & Unwin, 1984).
Peter Smith, *Houses of the Welsh Countryside* (2nd edn, London: HMSO,
    1988).
David Walker, *A History of the Church in Wales* (Penarth: Historical
    Society of the Church in Wales, 1976).
David Williams, *A History of Modern Wales* (2nd edn, London: John
    Murray, 1977).
Glanmor Williams, *Religion, Language and Nationality in Wales* (Cardiff:
    University of Wales Press, 1979).
Glanmor Williams, *The Welsh and their Religion* (Cardiff: University of
    Wales Press, 1991).
Gwyn A. Williams, *The Welsh in their History* (London: Croom Helm, 1982).
Gwyn A. Williams, *When Was Wales? A History of the Welsh* (London:
    Black Raven, 1985).
L. J. Williams, *Digest of Welsh Historical Statistics* (2 vols., Cardiff:
    Government Statistical Service, 1985–98).

1. THE EARLIEST INHABITANTS

Leslie Alcock, *Economy, Society and Warfare among the Britons and
    Saxons* (Cardiff: University of Wales Press, 1987).
Stephen Aldhouse-Green (ed.), *Paviland Cave and the 'Red Lady'* (Bristol:
    Western Academic and Specialist Press, 2000).
Christopher J. Arnold and Jeffrey L. Davies, *Roman and Early Medieval
    Wales* (Stroud: Sutton, 2000).
Martin J. Ball (ed.), *The Celtic Languages* (London: Routledge, 2002).
George C. Boon, *The Legionary Fortress of Caerleon-Isca* (Cardiff:
    National Museum of Wales, 1987).
E. G. Bowen, *Britain and the Western Seaways* (London: Thames &
    Hudson, 1972).
Richard J. Brewer, *Caerleon-Isca* (Cardiff: National Museum of Wales,
    1987).
Richard J. Brewer, *Caerleon and the Roman Army* (2nd edn, Cardiff:
    National Museums and Galleries of Wales, 2000).
Richard J. Brewer, *Caerwent Roman Town* (2nd edn, Cardiff: Cadw. Welsh
    Historic Monuments, 1997).
Steve Burrow, *Catalogue of the Mesolithic and Neolithic Collections in the
    National Museums and Galleries of Wales* (Cardiff: National
    Museums and Galleries of Wales, 2003).

Nora K. Chadwick, *The Druids* (2nd edn, Cardiff: University of Wales Press, 1997).

Vicki Cummings and Alasdair Whittle, *Places of Special Virtue: Megaliths in the Neolithic Landscapes of Wales* (Oxford: Oxbow Books, 2004).

Barry Cunliffe, *The Ancient Celts* (Oxford: Oxford University Press, 1997).

Barry Cunliffe, *Facing the Ocean: The Atlantic and its Peoples, 8000 BC–AD 1500* (paperback edn, Oxford: Oxford University Press, 2004).

Glyn E. Daniel and Idris Foster (eds.), *Prehistoric and Early Wales* (London: Routledge & Kegan Paul, 1965).

Jeffrey L. Davies and David P. Kirby (eds.), *Cardiganshire County History*, volume I: *From the Earliest Times to the Coming of the Normans* (Cardiff: University of Wales Press, 1994).

John Davies, *The Celts* (London: Cassell, 2000).

Miranda J. Green (ed.), *The Celtic World* (London: Routledge, 1995).

Miranda Green, *Exploring the World of the Druids* (London: Thames & Hudson, 1997).

Miranda Green and Ray Howell, *Celtic Wales* (Cardiff: University of Wales Press and The Western Mail, 2000).

Miranda Green and Ray Howell (eds.), *Gwent County History*, volume 1: *Gwent in Prehistory and Early History* (Cardiff: University of Wales Press, 2004).

Simon James, *The Atlantic Celts: Ancient People or Modern Invention?* (London: The British Museum, 1999).

Frances Lynch, *A Guide to Ancient and Prehistoric Wales: Gwynedd* (revised edn, Cardiff: Cadw. Welsh Historic Monuments, 2001).

Frances Lynch, *Prehistoric Anglesey* (revised 2nd edn, Llangefni: The Anglesey Antiquarian Society, 1991).

Frances Lynch, Stephen Aldhouse-Green and Jeffrey L. Davies, *Prehistoric Wales* (Stroud: Sutton, 2000).

William H. Manning, *Report on the Excavations at Usk 1965–1976* (2 vols., Cardiff: University of Wales Press, 1981, 1989).

William H. Manning, *Roman Wales* (Cardiff: University of Wales Press, 2001).

V. E. Nash-Williams, *The Roman Frontier in Wales*, ed. M. G. Jarrett (2nd edn, Cardiff: University of Wales Press, 1969).

Stuart Piggott, *The Druids* (Harmondsworth: Penguin, 1974).

Glanville Price (ed.), *The Celtic Connection* (Gerrards Cross: Colin Smythe, 1991).

Anne Ross, *Druids* (Stroud: Tempus, 1999).

H. N. Savory (ed.), *Glamorgan County History*, volume II: *Early Glamorgan* (Cardiff: Glamorgan County History, 1984).

Graham Webster, *Rome against Caratacus: The Roman Campaigns in Britain AD 48–58* (London: Routledge, 2003).

2. THE HEROIC AGE, 383–1063

E. G. Bowen, *Saints, Seaways and Settlements in the Celtic Lands* (Cardiff: University of Wales Press, 1969).

E. G. Bowen, *The Settlements of the Celtic Saints in Wales* (Cardiff: University of Wales Press, 1954).

Rachel Bromwich, A. O. H. Jarman and Brynley F. Roberts (eds.), *The Arthur of the Welsh* (Cardiff: University of Wales Press, 1991).

T. M. Charles-Edwards, *Early Irish and Welsh Kinship* (Oxford: Clarendon Press, 1993).

T. M. Charles-Edwards, *The Welsh Laws* (Cardiff: University of Wales Press, 1989).

T. M. Charles-Edwards, Morfydd E. Owen and Paul Russell (eds.), *The Welsh King and his Court* (Cardiff: University of Wales Press, 2000).

K. R. Dark, *Civitas to Kingdom: British Political Continuity 300–800* (Leicester: Leicester University Press, 1994).

Oliver Davies, *Celtic Christianity in Early Medieval Wales* (Cardiff: University of Wales Press, 1996).

Sean Davies, *Welsh Military Institutions, 633–1283* (Cardiff: University of Wales Press, 2004).

Wendy Davies, *Patterns of Power in Early Wales* (Oxford: Clarendon Press, 1990).

Wendy Davies, *Wales in the Early Middle Ages* (Leicester: Leicester University Press, 1982).

G. H. Doble, *Lives of the Welsh Saints*, ed. D. Simon Evans (Cardiff: University of Wales Press, 1971).

Nancy Edwards and Alan Lane, *Early Medieval Settlements in Wales AD 400–1100* (Cardiff: Early Medieval Wales Research Group, 1988).

Nancy Edwards and Alan Lane (eds.), *The Early Church in Wales and the West* (Oxford: Oxbow Books, 1992).

D. Simon Evans (ed.), *The Welsh Life of St David* (Cardiff: University of Wales Press, 1988).

Elissa R. Henken, *The Welsh Saints: A Study of Patterned Lives* (Cambridge: D. S. Brewer, 1991).

Daniel Huws, *The Medieval Codex* (Cardiff: University of Wales Press, 2000).

A. O. H. Jarman, *The Cynfeirdd: Early Welsh Poets and Poetry* (Cardiff: University of Wales Press, 1981).

Dafydd Jenkins, *The Law of Hywel Dda* (Llandysul: Gomer Press, 1986).

Dafydd Jenkins and Morfydd E. Owen, *The Welsh Law of Women* (Cardiff: University of Wales Press, 1980).

John T. Koch, *The Gododdin of Aneirin* (Cardiff: University of Wales Press, 1997).

John T. Koch (ed.), *The Celtic Heroic Age: Literary Sources for Ancient Celtic Europe and Early Ireland and Wales* (3rd edn, Aberystwyth: Celtic Studies Publications, 2000).
J. E. Lloyd, *A History of Wales from the Earliest Times to the Edwardian Conquest* (2 vols., 3rd edn, London: Longmans, 1939).
Henry R. Loyn, *The Vikings in Wales* (London: University College, 1976).
Kari L. Maund, *Ireland, Wales and England in the Eleventh Century* (Woodbridge: Brewers, 1991).
Kari L. Maund, *The Welsh Kings: The Medieval Rulers of Wales* (Stroud: Tempus, 2000).
David Moore, *The Welsh Wars of Independence c. 410–c. 1415* (Stroud: Tempus, 2005).
V. E. Nash-Williams, *The Early Christian Monuments of Wales* (Cardiff: University of Wales Press, 1950).
Mark Redknap, *The Christian Celts: Treasures of Late Celtic Wales* (Cardiff: National Museum of Wales, 1991).
Mark Redknap, *Vikings in Wales: An Archaeological Quest* (Cardiff: National Museums and Galleries of Wales, 2000).
Ifor Williams, *The Beginnings of Welsh Poetry* (2nd edn, Cardiff: University of Wales Press, 1990).

3. THE ANGLO-NORMAN CONQUERORS, c. 1063–1282

Richard Avent, *Cestyll Tywysogion Gwynedd. Castles of the Princes of Gwynedd* (Cardiff: HMSO, 1983).
Robert Bartlett, *Gerald of Wales 1146–1223* (Oxford: Clarendon Press, 1982).
A. D. Carr, *Llywelyn ap Gruffydd* (Cardiff: University of Wales Press, 1982).
A. D. Carr, *Medieval Wales* (Basingstoke: Macmillan Press, 1995).
F. G. Cowley, *The Monastic Order in South Wales, 1066–1349* (Cardiff: University of Wales Press, 1977).
R. R. Davies, *The Age of Conquest: Wales 1063–1415* (Oxford: Oxford University Press, 1990).
R. R. Davies, *The British Isles 1100–1500: Comparisons, Contrasts and Connections* (Edinburgh: John Donald, 1988).
R. R. Davies, *Domination and Conquest: The Experience of Ireland, Scotland and Wales 1100–1300* (Cambridge: Cambridge University Press, 1990).
R. R. Davies, *The First English Empire: Power and Identities in the British Isles 1093–1343* (Oxford: Oxford University Press, 2000).
Sioned Davies, *The Four Branches of The Mabinogi. Pedeir Keinc y Mabinogi* (Llandysul: Gomer Press, 1993).

Nancy Edwards (ed.), *Landscape and Settlement in Medieval Wales* (Oxford: Oxbow Books, 1997).

Trevor Herbert and Gareth Elwyn Jones (eds.), *Edward I and Wales* (Cardiff: University of Wales Press, 1988).

Daniel Huws, *Medieval Welsh Manuscripts* (Cardiff: University of Wales Press, 2000).

A. O. H. Jarman and Gwilym Rees Hughes (eds.), *A Guide to Welsh Literature*, volume I (revised edn, Cardiff: University of Wales Press, 1992).

Gwyn Jones and Thomas Jones (trans.), *The Mabinogion* (revised edn, London: J. M. Dent, 1993).

Huw Pryce (ed.), *The Acts of Welsh Rulers, 1120–1283* (Cardiff: University of Wales Press, 2005).

Huw Pryce (ed.), *Literacy in Medieval Celtic Societies* (Cambridge: Cambridge University Press, 1998).

Huw Pryce, *Native Law and the Church in Medieval Wales* (Oxford: Oxford University Press, 1993).

Brynley F. Roberts, *Gerald of Wales* (Cardiff: University of Wales Press, 1982).

Brynley F. Roberts, *Studies on Middle Welsh Literature* (Lampeter: The Edwin Mellen Press, 1992).

J. Beverley Smith, *Llywelyn ap Gruffudd Prince of Wales* (Cardiff: University of Wales Press, 1998).

J. Beverley Smith (ed.), *Medieval Welsh Society: Selected Essays by T. Jones Pierce* (Cardiff: University of Wales Press, 1972).

Ian Soulsby, *The Towns of Medieval Wales* (Chichester: Phillimore, 1983).

David Stephenson, *The Governance of Gwynedd* (Cardiff: University of Wales Press, 1984).

Arnold Taylor, *Studies in Castles and Castle-Building* (London and Ronceverte: Hambledon Press, 1985).

Arnold J. Taylor (ed.), *The Welsh Castles of Edward I* (London: Hambledon Press, 1986).

Roger Turvey, *The Lord Rhys: Prince of Deheubarth* (Llandysul: Gomer Press, 1997).

David Walker, *Medieval Wales* (Cambridge: Cambridge University Press, 1990).

David Walker, *The Norman Conquerors* (Swansea: Christopher Davies, 1977).

David H. Williams, *The Welsh Cistercians* (Leominster: Gracewing, 2001).

J. E. Caerwyn Williams, *The Court Poet in Medieval Wales* (Lampeter: The Edwin Mellen Press, 1997).

J. E. Caerwyn Williams, *The Poets of the Welsh Princes* (Cardiff: University of Wales Press, 1994).

4. PESTILENCE, REBELLION AND RENEWAL, *c.* 1283–1536

Rachel Bromwich, *Dafydd ap Gwilym* (Cardiff: University of Wales Press, 1974).

A. D. Carr, *Medieval Anglesey* (Llangefni: The Anglesey Antiquarian Society, 1982).

A. D. Carr, *Owen of Wales: The End of the House of Gwynedd* (Cardiff: University of Wales Press, 1991).

S. B. Chrimes, *Henry VII* (new edn, New Haven and London: Yale University Press, 1999).

R. R. Davies, *Lordship and Society in the March of Wales, 1282–1400* (Oxford: Clarendon Press, 1978).

R. R. Davies, *The Revolt of Owain Glyn Dŵr* (Oxford: Oxford University Press, 1995).

Huw M. Edwards, *Dafydd ap Gwilym: Influences and Analogues* (Oxford: Clarendon Press, 1996).

D. Simon Evans, *Medieval Religious Literature* (Cardiff: University of Wales Press, 1986).

H. T. Evans, *Wales and the Wars of the Roses* (new edn, Stroud: Alan Sutton Publishing, 1995).

Helen Fulton, *Dafydd ap Gwilym and the European Context* (Cardiff: University of Wales Press, 1989).

Ralph A. Griffiths (ed.), *The Boroughs of Medieval Wales* (Cardiff: University of Wales Press, 1978).

Ralph A. Griffiths, *Conquerors and Conquered in Medieval Wales* (Stroud: Alan Sutton Publishing, 1994).

Ralph A. Griffiths, *King and Country: England and Wales in the Fifteenth Century* (London: The Hambledon Press, 1991).

Ralph A. Griffiths, *The Principality of Wales in the Later Middle Ages*, volume II: *South Wales, 1277–1536* (Cardiff: University of Wales Press, 1971).

Ralph A. Griffiths, *Sir Rhys ap Thomas and his Family: A Study in the Wars of the Roses and Early Tudor Politics* (Cardiff: University of Wales Press, 1993).

Ralph A. Griffiths and Roger S. Thomas, *The Making of the Tudor Dynasty* (Stroud: Alan Sutton Publishing, 1985).

Elissa R. Henken, *National Redeemer: Owain Glyndŵr in Welsh Tradition* (Cardiff: University of Wales Press, 1996).

A. O. H. Jarman and Gwilym Rees Hughes (eds.), *A Guide to Welsh Literature 1282–c. 1550*, volume II, revised by Dafydd Johnston (Cardiff: University of Wales Press, 1992).

Francis Jones, *The Princes and Principality of Wales* (Cardiff: University of Wales Press, 1969).

J. E. Lloyd, *Owen Glendower* (Oxford: Clarendon Press, 1931).

Alan Palmer, *Princes of Wales* (London: Weidenfeld & Nicolson, 1979).

T. B. Pugh (ed.), *Glamorgan County History*, volume III: *The Middle Ages* (Cardiff: Glamorgan County History Committee, 1971).

William Rees, *South Wales and the March 1284–1415* (new edn, Bath: Cedric Chivers, 1974).

A. C. Reeves, *The Marcher Lords* (Llandybïe: Christopher Davies, 1983).

Glanmor Williams, *Harri Tudur a Chymru. Henry Tudor and Wales* (Cardiff: University of Wales Press, 1985).

Glanmor Williams, *Owain Glyndŵr* (revised edn, Cardiff: University of Wales Press, 2005).

Glanmor Williams, *Renewal and Reformation in Wales c. 1415–1642* (paperback edn, Oxford: Oxford University Press, 1993).

Glanmor Williams, *The Welsh Church from Conquest to Reformation* (revised edn, Cardiff: University of Wales Press, 1976).

Keith Williams-Jones (ed.), *The Merioneth Lay Subsidy Roll 1292–3* (Cardiff: University of Wales Press, 1976).

5. EARLY MODERN WALES, 1536–1776

T. M. Bassett, *The Welsh Baptists* (Swansea: Ilston House, 1977).

Lloyd Bowen, *The Politics of the Principality of Wales, c. 1603–1642* (Cardiff: University of Wales Press, 2006).

Ceri Davies (ed.), *Dr John Davies of Mallwyd: Welsh Renaissance Scholar* (Cardiff: University of Wales Press, 2004).

Ceri Davies, *Latin Writers of the Renaissance* (Cardiff: University of Wales Press, 1981).

A. H. Dodd, *Studies in Stuart Wales* (2nd edn, Cardiff: University of Wales Press, 1971).

E. D. Evans, *A History of Wales, 1660–1815* (Cardiff: University of Wales Press, 1976).

William P. Griffith, *Learning, Law and Religion: Higher Education and Welsh Society, c. 1540–1640* (Cardiff: University of Wales Press, 1996).

Trevor Herbert and Gareth Elwyn Jones (eds.), *The Remaking of Wales in the Eighteenth Century* (Cardiff: University of Wales Press, 1988).

Trevor Herbert and Gareth Elwyn Jones (eds.), *Tudor Wales* (Cardiff: University of Wales Press, 1988).

David W. Howell, *Patriarchs and Parasites: The Gentry of South-West Wales in the Eighteenth Century* (Cardiff: University of Wales Press, 1986).

David W. Howell, *The Rural Poor in Eighteenth-Century Wales* (Cardiff: University of Wales Press, 2000).

Melvin Humphreys, *The Crisis of Community: Montgomeryshire 1680–1815* (Cardiff: University of Wales Press, 1996).

Branwen Jarvis (ed.), *A Guide to Welsh Literature c. 1700–1800* (Cardiff: University of Wales Press, 2000).

Geraint H. Jenkins, *The Foundations of Modern Wales: Wales 1642–1780* (Oxford: Oxford University Press, 1993).

Geraint H. Jenkins, *Literature, Religion and Society in Wales, 1660–1730* (Cardiff: University of Wales Press, 1978).

Geraint H. Jenkins, *Protestant Dissenters in Wales, 1639–1689* (Cardiff: University of Wales Press, 1992).

Geraint H. Jenkins (ed.), *The Welsh Language before the Industrial Revolution* (Cardiff: University of Wales Press, 1997).

Philip Jenkins, *The Making of a Ruling Class: The Glamorgan Gentry 1640–1790* (Cambridge: Cambridge University Press, 1983).

David Ceri Jones, *'A Glorious Work in the World': Welsh Methodism and the International Evangelical Revival, 1735–1750* (Cardiff: University of Wales Press, 2004).

Gareth Elwyn Jones, *The Gentry and the Elizabethan State* (Swansea: Christopher Davies, 1977).

J. Gwynfor Jones (ed.), *Class, Community and Culture in Tudor Wales* (Cardiff: University of Wales Press, 1989).

J. Gwynfor Jones, *Concepts of Order and Gentility in Wales 1540–1640* (Llandysul: Gomer Press, 1992).

J. Gwynfor Jones, *Early Modern Wales, c. 1525–1640* (Basingstoke: Macmillan, 1994).

J. Gwynfor Jones, *Wales and the Tudor State* (Cardiff: University of Wales Press, 1989).

J. Gwynfor Jones, *The Welsh Gentry 1536–1640* (Cardiff: University of Wales Press, 1998).

M. G. Jones, *The Charity School Movement* (Cambridge: Cambridge University Press, 1938).

R. Tudur Jones, *Congregationalism in Wales*, ed. Robert Pope (Cardiff: University of Wales Press, 2004).

Derec Llwyd Morgan, *The Great Awakening in Wales* (London: Epworth, 1988).

Prys Morgan, *The Eighteenth Century Renaissance* (Llandybïe: Christopher Davies, 1981).

Geoffrey F. Nuttall, *The Welsh Saints, 1640–1660* (Cardiff: University of Wales Press, 1957).

Geraint Dyfnallt Owen, *Elizabethan Wales* (Cardiff: University of Wales Press, 1962).

William Rees, *Industry before the Industrial Revolution* (2 vols., Cardiff: University of Wales Press, 1968).

Thomas Richards, *The Puritan Movement in Wales, 1639–1654* (London: National Eisteddfod Association, 1920).

Michael Roberts and Simone Clarke (eds.), *Women and Gender in Early Modern Wales* (Cardiff: University of Wales Press, 2000).

Joan Thirsk (ed.), *The Agrarian History of England and Wales*, volume 5: *1640–1750* (2 vols., Cambridge: Cambridge University Press, 1985).

Hugh Thomas, *A History of Wales, 1485–1660* (Cardiff: University of Wales Press, 1972).

Peter D. G. Thomas, *Politics in Eighteenth-Century Wales* (Cardiff: University of Wales Press, 1998).

W. S. K. Thomas, *Stuart Wales* (Llandysul: Gomer Press, 1988).

W. S. K. Thomas, *Tudor Wales* (Llandysul: Gomer Press, 1983).

Geraint Tudur, *Howell Harris: From Conversion to Separation: 1735–1750* (Cardiff: University of Wales Press, 2000).

Glanmor Williams (ed.), *Early Modern Glamorgan: Glamorgan County History*, volume IV (Cardiff: Glamorgan County History Trust, 1974).

Glanmor Williams, *Renewal and Reformation: Wales c. 1415–1642* (paperback edn, Oxford: Oxford University Press, 1993).

Glanmor Williams, *Wales and the Reformation* (Cardiff: University of Wales Press, 1997).

Glanmor Williams, *Welsh Reformation Essays* (Cardiff: University of Wales Press, 1967).

Penry Williams, *The Council in the Marches of Wales under Elizabeth I* (Cardiff: University of Wales Press, 1958).

6. A CRUCIBLE OF THE MODERN WORLD, 1776–1900

Colin Baber and L. J. Williams (eds.), *Modern South Wales: Essays in Economic History* (Cardiff: University of Wales Press, 1986).

Dudley Baines, *Migration in a Mature Economy: Emigration and Internal Migration in England and Wales 1861–1900* (Cambridge: Cambridge University Press, 1985).

Matthew Cragoe, *An Anglican Aristocracy: The Moral Economy of the Landed Estate in Carmarthenshire, 1832–1895* (Oxford: Clarendon Press, 1996).

Matthew Cragoe, *Culture, Politics, and National Identity in Wales 1832–1886* (Oxford: Oxford University Press, 2004).

Andy Croll, *Civilizing the Urban: Popular Culture and Public Space in Merthyr, c. 1870–1914* (Cardiff: University of Wales Press, 2000).

Martin J. Daunton, *Coal Metropolis: Cardiff 1870–1914* (Leicester: Leicester University Press, 1977).

John Davies, *Cardiff and the Marquesses of Bute* (Cardiff: University of Wales Press, 1981).

Russell Davies, *Hope and Heartbreak: A Social History of Wales 1776–1871* (Cardiff: University of Wales Press, 2005).

Russell Davies, *Secret Sins: Sex, Violence and Society in Carmarthenshire, 1870–1920* (Cardiff: University of Wales Press, 1996).

A. H. Dodd, *The Industrial Revolution in North Wales* (3rd edn, Wrexham: Bridge Books, 1990).

Hywel Teifi Edwards (ed.), *A Guide to Welsh Literature c. 1800–1900* (Cardiff: University of Wales Press, 2000).

Chris Evans, '*The Labyrinth of Flames': Work and Social Conflict in Early Industrial Merthyr Tydfil* (Cardiff: University of Wales Press, 1993).

D. Gareth Evans, *A History of Wales 1815–1906* (Cardiff: University of Wales Press, 1989).

W. Gareth Evans, *Education and Female Emancipation: The Welsh Experience, 1847–1914* (Cardiff: University of Wales Press, 1990).

Trevor Herbert and Gareth E. Jones (eds.), *People and Protest: Wales 1815–1880* (Cardiff: University of Wales Press, 1988).

Trevor Herbert and Gareth E. Jones (eds.), *Wales 1880–1914* (Cardiff: University of Wales Press, 1988).

David W. Howell, *Land and People in Nineteenth Century Wales* (London: Routledge & Kegan Paul, 1977).

David Jenkins, *The Agricultural Community in South-West Wales at the Turn of the Twentieth Century* (Cardiff: University of Wales Press, 1971).

Geraint H. Jenkins (ed.), *Language and Community in the Nineteenth Century* (Cardiff: University of Wales Press, 1998).

Geraint H. Jenkins (ed.), *A Rattleskull Genius: The Many Faces of Iolo Morganwg* (Cardiff: University of Wales Press, 2005).

Geraint H. Jenkins (ed.), *The Welsh Language and its Social Domains 1801–1911* (Cardiff: University of Wales Press, 2000).

Geraint H. Jenkins and J. Beverley Smith (eds.), *Politics and Society in Wales 1840–1922* (Cardiff: University of Wales Press, 1988).

Angela V. John (ed.), *Our Mother's Land: Chapters in Welsh Women's History 1830–1939* (Cardiff: University of Wales Press, 1991).

Aled G. Jones, *Press, Politics and Society: A History of Journalism in Wales* (Cardiff: University of Wales Press, 1993).

David J. V. Jones, *Before Rebecca: Popular Protest in Wales, 1793–1835* (London: Allen Lane, 1973).

David J. V. Jones, *Crime in Nineteenth-Century Wales* (Cardiff: University of Wales Press, 1992).

David J. V. Jones, *The Last Rising: The Newport Chartist Insurrection of 1839* (Cardiff: University of Wales Press, 1999).

David J. V. Jones, *Rebecca's Children: A Study of Rural Society, Crime and Protest* (Oxford: Clarendon Press, 1989).

Dot Jones, *Statistical Evidence Relating to the Welsh Language 1801–1911* (Cardiff: University of Wales Press, 1998).

Ieuan Gwynedd Jones, *Communities: Essays in the Social History of Victorian Wales* (Llandysul: Gomer Press, 1987).

Ieuan Gwynedd Jones, *Explorations and Explanations: Essays in the Social History of Victorian Wales* (Llandysul: Gomer Press, 1981).

Ieuan Gwynedd Jones, *Mid-Victorian Wales: Observers and the Observed* (Cardiff: University of Wales Press, 1991).

R. Merfyn Jones, *The North Wales Quarrymen, 1874–1922* (Cardiff: University of Wales Press, 1981).

R. Tudur Jones, *Faith and the Crisis of a Nation: Wales 1890–1914*, ed. Robert Pope (Cardiff: University of Wales Press, 2004).

William D. Jones, *Scranton and the Welsh 1860–1920* (Cardiff: University of Wales Press, 1997).

W. R. Lambert, *Drink and Sobriety in Victorian Wales c. 1820–c. 1895* (Cardiff: University of Wales Press, 1983).

Louise Miskell, *'Intelligent Town': An Urban History of Swansea 1780–1855* (Cardiff: University of Wales Press, 2006).

Kenneth O. Morgan, *Wales in British Politics 1868–1923* (3rd edn, Cardiff: University of Wales Press, 1980).

J. H. Morris and L. J. Williams, *The South Wales Coal Industry, 1841–1875* (Cardiff: University of Wales Press, 1958).

Paul O'Leary, *Immigration and Integration: The Irish in Wales, 1798–1922* (Cardiff: University of Wales Press, 2002).

Paul O'Leary (ed.), *Irish Migrants in Modern Wales* (Liverpool: Liverpool University Press, 2004).

Gwenfair Parry and Mari A. Williams, *The Welsh Language and the 1891 Census* (Cardiff: University of Wales Press, 1999).

Gwyneth Tyson Roberts, *The Language of the Blue Books: The Perfect Instrument of Empire* (Cardiff: University of Wales Press, 1998).

David Smith (ed.), *A People and a Proletariat: Essays in the History of Wales 1780–1980* (London: Pluto/Llafur, 1980).

Robert Smith, *Schools, Politics and Society: Elementary Education in Wales, 1870–1902* (Cardiff: University of Wales Press, 1999).

Ryland Wallace, *Organise! Organise! Organise! A Study of Reform Agitations in Wales 1840–1886* (Cardiff: University of Wales Press, 1991).

Ivor Wilks, *South Wales and the Rising of 1839* (paperback edn, Llandysul: Gomer Press, 1989).

David Williams, *John Frost: A Study in Chartism* (Cardiff: University of Wales Press, 1939).

David Williams, *The Rebecca Riots* (Cardiff: University of Wales Press, 1955).

Gareth Williams, *Valleys of Song: Music and Society in Wales, 1840–1914* (Cardiff: University of Wales Press, 1998).

Glanmor Williams (ed.), *Merthyr Politics: The Making of a Working-Class Tradition* (Cardiff: University of Wales Press, 1966).

Gwyn A. Williams, *The Merthyr Rising* (2nd edn, Cardiff: University of Wales Press, 1988).

John Williams, *Was Wales Industrialized? Essays in Modern Welsh History* (Llandysul: Gomer Press, 1995).

J. Gwynn Williams, *The University Movement in Wales* (Cardiff: University of Wales Press, 1993).

7. WALES AWAKENING? 1901–2006

Jane Aaron (ed.), *Our Sisters' Land: The Changing Identities of Women in Wales* (Cardiff: University of Wales Press, 1994).

Martin Adeney and John Lloyd, *The Miners' Strike 1984–5: Loss Without Limit* (London: Routledge & Kegan Paul, 1986).

John Aitchison and Harold Carter, *Language, Economy and Society: The Changing Fortunes of the Welsh Language in the Twentieth Century* (Cardiff: University of Wales Press, 2000).

John Aitchison and Harold Carter, *Spreading the Word: The Welsh Language 2001* (Talybont: Y Lolfa, 2004).

Deirdre Beddoe, *Out of the Shadows: A History of Women in Twentieth-Century Wales* (Cardiff: University of Wales Press, 2000).

David Berry, *Wales and the Cinema* (revised edn, Cardiff: University of Wales Press, 1996).

John Campbell, *Nye Bevan and the Mirage of British Socialism* (London: Weidenfeld & Nicolson, 1987).

Paul Chambers, *Religion, Secularization and Social Change in Wales* (Cardiff: University of Wales Press, 2005).

D. Hywel Davies, *The Welsh Nationalist Party 1925–1945: A Call to Nationhood* (Cardiff: University of Wales Press, 1983).

John Davies, *Broadcasting and the BBC in Wales* (Cardiff: University of Wales Press, 1994).

Andrew Edwards, *The Decline of the Labour Party and the Rise of Plaid Cymru in North-West Wales, 1960–1975* (Cardiff: University of Wales Press, 2006).

D. Gareth Evans, *A History of Wales, 1906–2000* (Cardiff: University of Wales Press, 2000).

Hywel Francis, *Miners against Fascism: Wales and the Spanish Civil War* (new edn, Abersychan: Warren & Pell Publishing, 2004).

Hywel Francis and Dai Smith, *The Fed: A History of the South Wales Miners in the Twentieth Century* (Cardiff: University of Wales Press, 1998).

Angela Gaffney, *Aftermath: Remembering the Great War in Wales* (Cardiff: University of Wales Press, 1998).

K. D. George and Lyn Mainwaring (eds.), *The Welsh Economy* (Cardiff: University of Wales Press, 1988).

Keith Gildart, *North Wales Miners: A Fragile Unity 1945–1996* (Cardiff: University of Wales Press, 2001).

Trevor Herbert and Gareth E. Jones (eds.), *Post-War Wales* (Cardiff: University of Wales Press, 1995).

Trevor Herbert and Gareth Elwyn Jones (eds.), *Wales between the Wars* (Cardiff, University of Wales Press, 1988).

Trevor Herbert and Peter Stead (eds.), *Hymns and Arias: Great Welsh Voices* (Cardiff: University of Wales Press, 2001).

David W. Howell and Kenneth O. Morgan (eds.), *Crime, Protest and Police in Modern British Society* (Cardiff: University of Wales Press, 1999).

Colin Hughes, *Lime, Lemon and Sarsaparilla: The Italian Community in South Wales, 1881–1945* (Bridgend: Seren Books, 1991).

Trystan O. Hughes, *Winds of Change: The Roman Catholic Church and Society in Wales, 1916–1962* (Cardiff: University of Wales Press, 1999).

Graham Humphrys, *South Wales* (Newton Abbot: David & Charles, 1972).

Geraint H. Jenkins, *The University of Wales: An Illustrated History* (Cardiff: University of Wales Press, 1993).

Geraint H. Jenkins and Mari A. Williams (eds.), *'Let's Do Our Best for the Ancient Tongue': The Welsh Language in the Twentieth Century* (Cardiff: University of Wales Press, 2000).

Angela V. John (ed.), *Our Mothers' Land: Chapters in Welsh Women's History 1830–1939* (Cardiff: University of Wales Press, 1991).

Martin Johnes, *Soccer and Society: South Wales, 1900–1939* (Cardiff: University of Wales Press, 2002).

Dafydd Johnston (ed.), *A Guide to Welsh Literature c. 1900–1996*, volume VI (Cardiff: University of Wales Press, 1998).

Gareth Elwyn Jones, *Controls and Conflicts in Welsh Secondary Education 1889–1944* (Cardiff: University of Wales Press, 1982).

Glyn Jones, *The Dragon has Two Tongues*, ed. Tony Brown (revised edn, Cardiff: University of Wales Press, 2001).

Stephen Knight, *A Hundred Years of Fiction: Writing Wales in English* (Cardiff: University of Wales Press, 2004).

Richard Lewis, *Leaders and Teachers: Adult Education and the Challenge of Labour in South Wales, 1906–1940* (Cardiff: University of Wales Press, 1993).

Michael Lieven, *Senghennydd: The Universal Pit Village 1890–1930* (Llandysul: Gomer Press, 1994).

Laura McAllister, *Plaid Cymru: The Emergence of a Political Party* (Bridgend: Seren, 2001).

John McIlroy, Alan Campbell and Keith Gildart (eds.), *Industrial Politics and the 1926 Mining Lockout* (Cardiff: University of Wales Press, 2004).

Iain McLean and Martin Johnes, *Aberfan: Government and Disasters* (Cardiff: Welsh Academic Press, 2000).

Peter M. Miskell, *A Social History of the Cinema in Wales, 1918–1951* (Cardiff: University of Wales Press, 2006).

Densil Morgan, *The Span of the Cross: Christian Religion and Society in Wales 1914–2000* (Cardiff: University of Wales Press, 1999).

Kenneth O. Morgan, *Modern Wales: Politics, Places and People* (Cardiff: University of Wales Press, 1995).

Kenneth O. Morgan, *Rebirth of a Nation: A History of Modern Wales* (new edn, Oxford: Oxford University Press, 1998).

John Osmond (ed.), *The National Question Again: Welsh Political Identity in the 1980s* (Llandysul: Gomer Press, 1985).

Alan Butt Philip, *The Welsh Question: Nationalism in Welsh Politics 1945–1970* (Cardiff: University of Wales Press, 1985).

Robert Pope, *Building Jerusalem: Nonconformity, Labour and the Social Question in Wales, 1906–1939* (Cardiff: University of Wales Press, 1998).

David A. Pretty, *The Rural Revolt that Failed: Farm Workers' Trade Unions in Wales 1889–1950* (Cardiff: University of Wales Press, 1989).

Teresa Rees, *Women and Work* (Cardiff: University of Wales Press, 1999).

Ted Rowlands, *'Something Must be Done': South Wales v Whitehall 1921–1951* (Merthyr Tydfil: TTC Books, 2000).

Dai Smith, *Aneurin Bevan and the World of South Wales* (Cardiff: University of Wales Press, 1993).

David Smith and Gareth Williams, *Fields of Praise: The Official History of the Welsh Rugby Union* (Cardiff: University of Wales Press, 1980).

Peter Stead, *Acting Wales: Stars of Stage and Screen* (Cardiff: University of Wales, 2002).

Meic Stephens (ed.), *The Arts in Wales: 1950–1975* (Cardiff: Welsh Arts Council, 1979).

Robert Stradling, *Wales and the Spanish Civil War* (Cardiff: University of Wales Press, 2004).

Duncan Tanner, Chris Williams and Deian Hopkin (eds.), *The Labour Party in Wales 1900–2000* (Cardiff: University of Wales Press, 2000).

Brinley Thomas (ed.), *The Welsh Economy: Studies in Expansion* (Cardiff: University of Wales Press, 1962).

M. Wynn Thomas (ed.), *A Guide to Welsh Literature*, volume VII: *Welsh Writing in English* (Cardiff: University of Wales Press, 2003).

Steven Thompson, *Unemployment, Poverty and Health in Interwar South Wales* (Cardiff: University of Wales Press, 2006).

Chris Williams, *Capitalism, Community and Conflict: The South Wales Coalfield 1898–1947* (Cardiff: University of Wales Press, 1998).

Chris Williams, *Democratic Rhondda: Politics and Society, 1885–1951* (Cardiff: University of Wales Press, 1996).

Mari A. Williams, *A Forgotten Army: Female Munitions Workers of South Wales, 1939–1945* (Cardiff: University of Wales Press, 2002).

8. WHITHER WALES?

Jane Aaron and Chris Williams (eds.), *Postcolonial Wales* (Cardiff: University of Wales Press, 2005).

Paul Chaney, Tom Hall and Andrew Pithouse (eds.), *New Governance – New Democracy? Post-Devolution Wales* (Cardiff: University of Wales Press, 2001).

Graham Day, *Making Sense of Wales: A Sociological Perspective* (Cardiff: University of Wales Press, 2002).

David Dunkerley and Andrew Thompson (eds.), *Wales Today* (Cardiff: University of Wales Press, 1999).

Richard Rawlings, *Delineating Wales: Constitutional, Legal and Administrative Aspects of National Devolution* (Cardiff: University of Wales Press, 2003).

Bridget Taylor and Katarina Thomson (eds.), *Scotland and Wales: Nations Again?* (Cardiff: University of Wales Press, 1999).

M. Wynn Thomas, *Internal Difference: Twentieth-Century Writing in Wales* (Cardiff: University of Wales Press, 1992).

Charlotte Williams, Neil Evans and Paul O'Leary (eds.), *A Tolerant Nation? Exploring Ethnic Diversity in Wales* (Cardiff: University of Wales Press, 2003).

INDEX

CAMBRIDGE CONCISE
HISTORIES